Southern Living®
2024 Annual Recipes

MUSCADINE DUMPLINGS (PAGE 184)

CREAMY GARLIC SCAPE SOUP (PAGE 87)

SUMMER GARDEN TART (PAGE 144)

FALL SALAD WITH CANDIED BLACK WALNUTS (PAGE 198)

APPLE JAM
BABY BACK RIBS
(PAGE 240)

Recipes for Gathering

Dear Friends,

We live in a time of increasing complexity—all of the technologies that claim to bring us together don't always deliver the very human craving we have for community, for belonging, and for slowing down to spend time with loved ones.

There is no substitute for getting together in person with friends and family—whether that's around the dinner table every night to enjoy a good meal, outside the stadium of your favorite team before the big game, or at a holiday party. And when Southerners gather, good food follows. This 2024 edition of *Southern Living Annual Recipes* has a wealth of fresh ideas for every type of occasion and all the moments in between.

On a busy winter evening, stir up a pot of Weeknight Pasta Bolognese (page 28). In summer, stay cool with suppertime salads such as our BLT Seven-Layer Salad (page 163), Southern Niçoise Salad (page 163), or Shrimp-and-Feta Pasta Salad (page 167).

The Southern seasons endlessly inspire us. Winter greens shine in Kale Rigatoni with Crispy Sausage (page 15). In the spring, bake up a batch or two of buttery shortbread in lively flavors, such as Lemon-Thyme Shortbread (page 49), Pistachio Shortbread (page 49), or Strawberry Shortbread (page 49).

And in the fall, what's most in season in the South? Football, of course! This book features recipes and party ideas for watching the game—in your family room or fieldside—that will make you feel like a winner no matter the outcome of the matchup. Pair City Grocery Bloody Marys (page 180) with Cat-Head Biscuit Sandwiches (page 204). Or set up a Walking Tacos Bar (page 213) and let guests help themselves. For something sweet, stir up a batch of Knock-Ya-Naked Brownies (page 215). We even asked Southern chefs to weigh in on their favorite teams and game-day foods in "Super Fans" (pages 236-243).

Whatever the season or reason for gathering, the good food in this book will nourish you, comfort you, and bring some joy and spice to every day.

Lisa Cericola
Deputy Food Editor
Southern Living magazine

Contents

7	Recipes for Gathering
10	Top-Rated Recipes

13 January–February

14	Give 'Em Kale
16	All Fired Up
17	Pass the Potlikker
26	Double Dutch
32	Let's Jam
33	There's a New Queso in Town
35	Melt Someone's Heart
36	In Full Bloom
38	Here Comes the Sun
40	Cooking School

41 March

42	Pretty Peas
44	Memories by the Spoonful
46	A Taste of Spring
50	Let's Do Brunch
60	What a Ham
65	Pop Stars
66	Think Outside the Box
67	Green Eggs and...Prosciutto
68	Cooking School

69 April

70	Think Pink
71	Waffle Around
72	A Southern-Style Seder
76	Baby Cakes
82	Spring Treasures
90	Kick the Can
91	Worth the Wait
92	Spring Sizzle
95	A Culinary Guide to Jazz Fest

97	Batter Up
98	The Gift of Pudding
100	Cooking School

101 May

102	The Big Dill
104	Who Made the Potato Salad?
106	Strawberry Shortcake Forever
114	Spin the Bottle
119	Crunch Time
121	Hold the Pineapple
122	American Spirit
123	Million-Dollar Pancakes
124	I'll Bring the Bourbon
126	Cooking School

127 June–July

128	Use Your Melon
130	From Aleppo to Za'atar
137	When Life Gives You Lemons...
138	She's Got the Scoop
140	Not Your Mama's Meat 'n' Three
148	It's Peak Squash Season
149	Ready to Roll
150	Garden Party
152	Cooking School

153 August

154	Squash It
157	The Roots of Succotash
158	Pretty as a Peach Salad
162	Dress to Impress
169	Sundae Best

170	A Healthier Cobbler
171	The Morning Blend
172	Chicken Little
174	Cooking School

175 September

176	The Zing of Sumac
178	A Well-Designed Game Plan
181	Like Father, Like Son
184	The Mother of All Muscadines
186	Mushroom Magic
194	The Gift of Black Walnuts
200	Apple of Your Eye
203	A Winning Chicken Dinner
204	What Time Is Kickoff?
219	Notes From Home
220	Our Daily Cornbread
222	One & Done
227	A Sweet Slice of Fall
228	Good to the Core
230	Cooking School

231 October

233	Perfect Pears
235	Oktober Feast!
236	Super Fans
244	Super Bowls
246	Taking Root
253	French Twist
254	The Roast With the Most
255	Roll With It
256	Cooking School

257 November

258	Flower Power
261	Good Inside
262	Chess Moves
264	The Unsung Hero
266	Easier Than Pie
272	Let's Talk Turkey

277	More Peas, Please
278	Spiced-Up Sides
283	Go Big With Butternut
286	Sip and Savor
287	The Big Cheese
288	Cooking School

289 December

290	Precious Persimmons
292	The Gift of Fudge
293	Get In the Spirit
295	Party Like It's 1984
298	Elegant Made Easy
300	Festival of Bites
304	Just Heavenly
305	A Cake for Every Baker
312	Orange Crush
320	The Ultimate *Southern Living* Cookie Tin
330	Thumbs Up
332	Made With Love
334	The Delicious Mystery of Court Bouillon
336	The Legend of the Lasagna
338	Rosalynn Carter's Traveling Pimiento Cheese
339	Baking School
340	Cooking School

341 Bonus: Our Favorite Soups & Stews Recipes

355	Baking at High Altitudes
356	Metric Equivalents
357	Recipe Title Index
360	General Recipe Index

Top-Rated Recipes

We cook, we taste, we refine, we rate—and at the end of each year, our Test Kitchen shares the highest-rated recipes from each issue exclusively with *Southern Living Annual Recipes* readers

January–February

- **Spicy Kale Chips** (page 15) Kale chips make a great wintertime snack. They're simple to toss together and are packed with nutrients.
- **Roasted Lemon-Pepper Chicken** (page 26) Cooking a whole chicken takes a little bit of time, but this recipe is definitely worth the effort. Enjoy the roast chicken one night, then turn leftover shredded chicken into Sun-Dried Tomato Pasta with Chicken (page 31) on another.
- **Simple Strawberry Strudels** (page 32) Storebought puff pastry is the secret to these quick and tasty treats. Use strawberry preserves or your favorite fruit jam.
- **Sweet Potato Queso** (page 33) If you're looking for a healthier alternative to traditional queso, look no further. We've cut half the calories but kept the flavor and rich and creamy texture.
- **Orange-Roll Coffee Cake** (page 38) We combined two Southern staples into one perfect cake. It's sure to become a new favorite in your home.

March

- **Strawberry-Rhubarb Spritzes** (page 56) Skip the mimosas at your next brunch; and try this refreshing new cocktail. It's the perfect blend of spring flavors and will have all comers asking for the recipe.
- **Crispy-Ham Carbonara with Peas** (page 61) We created this recipe with leftover ham in mind, but you can easily pick up a few thick pieces of ham from your supermarket deli to make it anytime.
- **Easy Chicken Cordon Bleu** (page 64) You'll turn to this recipe again and again for Sunday suppers or special-occasion meals—it brings a sense of elegance and elevation to the table but is simple to make.
- **Macaroni and Cheese with Caramelized Onions** (page 66) We have perfected a healthier mac and cheese without skimping on flavor. It's even packed with bacon! So much flavor but half the fat.
- **Pesto Deviled Eggs** (page 67) Pesto, prosciutto, and Parmesan cheese add flavor (and fun color!) to this spin on a classic appetizer.

April

- **Waffle Iron Hash Browns with Fried Eggs** (page 71) If you love breakfast potatoes you must give this recipe a try! We like to top the crispy "waffles" with a fried egg and feta cheese, but you can swap in any savory ingredients you like—such as creamed chicken, sausage or mushroom gravy, or sautéed vegetables.
- **Sweet-and-Sour Braised Beef Brisket** (page 75) With only 45 minutes hands-on time, this brisket can't be beat. No smoker required—it cooks in your oven with minimal tending.
- **Tiny Caramel Cakes** (page 77) These bite-sized treats will make a big impression at your next event.
- **One-Pan Broccoli-Rice Casserole** (page 90) We swapped out the cans for fresh ingredients and cut the calories in this classic side dish. You'll never go back to your old recipe once you give this healthy version a try.
- **Cajun Shrimp Stir-Fry** (page 92) If you have 20 minutes, you can whip up this tasty stir-fry. It's a simple recipe that packs a ton of flavor.

MACARONI AND CHEESE WITH CARAMELIZED ONIONS

FROZEN LEMONADE PIE

May

- **Strawberry Shortcake Ice-Cream Cake** (page 109) Celebrate the arrival of summertime with this refreshing cream treat. You get cake and ice cream in every bite!
- **Savory Veggie Fajitas** (page 114) You won't miss the meat in this colorful weeknight staple. The trio of bright bell peppers, onions, and mushrooms is meaty and satisfying.
- **Secret Sauce Smashburgers** (page 118) The secret really is in the sauce! Once you give it a try, it'll be your new go-to condiment for burgers, chicken, and veggies.
- **Lemon-Ricotta Silver Dollar Pancakes** (page 123) Adding ricotta to the batter gives these pancakes an extra boost of protein, light texture, and rich flavor.

June–July

- **Corn Salad with Sumac and Feta** (page 134) Sumac—a spice made from the dried and ground berries of the sumac bush—is popular in Middle Eastern cuisine. It's the secret ingredient in this corn salad, balancing the sweetness of the corn with its distinctive lemony flavor.
- **Frozen Lemonade Pie** (page 137) Welcome summertime with this incredible (and easy!) no-bake pie. If you have any leftovers, freeze individual slices in the freezer for a quick anytime treat.
- **Fried-Okra Cornbread** (page 140) You just can't miss combining two old-school Southern favorites in this unexpected twist on tradition.
- **Summer Garden Tart** (page 144) Make the most of your bountiful summer harvest with this gorgeous veggie tart—it'll be your new summer potluck go-to.
- **Party Quesadillas** (page 149) Here's a whole new way to shape—and serve—quesadillas. (Hint: You'll never make flat quesadillas again.)

August

- **Peach-Mango Salad with Avocados** (page 158) There's nothing quite like a peach salad at the peak of the season. We love how serrano peppers perk up the sweetness of this summertime favorite with a hit of heat.
- **Chicken Taco Pasta Salad** (page 163) Mix up your taco Tuesday and give this one a try. You can leave out the pasta and serve the mixture over tortilla chips for a nacho-style appetizer.
- **Stone Fruit Cobbler** (page 170) Health food never tasted so good! This tasty mixed-fruit dessert is packed with nutrients and is surprisingly high in fiber.
- **Extra-Crispy Chicken Nuggets** (page 173) Whipped egg whites with a splash of pickle brine results in shatteringly crispy nuggets. You won't want to buy frozen again!

September

- **Pan-Seared Rib-Eye with Mushroom-Hunter's Sauce** (page 190) The secret to this juicy steak recipe is the rich, flavorful sauce—and it's not just for steak. Make a little extra to serve later on chicken or pork. It takes any protein to the next level.
- **Crispy Ranch Chicken Cutlets** (page 203) We developed this recipe with the kiddos in mind as a superior swap-out for the ever-faithful take-out nugget. But it's not just for the small fry! We added a couple of adult-approved recipes so everyone at the table gets exactly what they want to eat.
- **Sweet-and-Spicy Sausage Bites** (page 207) This quick and easy recipe makes a large batch—perfect as a saucy snack for a crowd.
- **Tailgate Margaritas** (page 210) The name says it all. We absolutely love these fresh-lime margaritas—and a pitcherful goes together in just 5 minutes.
- **Pimiento Cheese Cornbread** (page 215) What's better than really good cornbread? Really good, really cheesy cornbread with bits of smoky bacon, of course!

SWEET-AND-SPICY SAUSAGE BITES

CONECUH SAUSAGE CORN DOGS WITH BACK FORTY BEER MUSTARD

October

- **Pear, Bacon and Gorgonzola Flatbread** (page 233) The combination of sweet, smoky, and savory-umami flavors in this simple (and delicious!) flatbread make it special. Serve as an autumnal appetizer or with a green salad as a simple weeknight dinner.
- **Conecuh Sausage Corn Dogs with Back Forty Beer Mustard** (page 241) These are no ordinary corn dogs! Made with spicy smoked Cajun Conecuh sausage and served with a honey mustard spiked with brown ale, they're made for tailgating.
- **Vegetable-Beef Soup** (page 245) It's soup season! This hearty soup comes together in just 30 minutes, ready to warm your bowls and your souls!
- **Apple Cinnamon Rolls** (page 255) Everybody loves cinnamon rolls—especially in the fall. The addition of apples takes these pillowy, sweet, and fragrant favorites up a step.

November

- **Nashville Hot Fried Cauliflower Sandwiches** (page 258) You may love Nashville hot chicken, but if you're trying to eat less—or no—meat these days, give this gloriously crispy, spicy-hot plant-based take on this popular Southern sandwich a try.
- **Chocolate Chess Pie** (page 263) We love all of the flavors of this gooey, custardy, sweet, classically Southern pie—lemon, pumpkin, apple, orange-cranberry, and on and on—but this rich chocolate pie is one of our favorites.
- **French Onion Turkey** (page 276) We're fans of "French onion" anything, including soup, dip—and now turkey. Every year we try dozens of new turkey recipes, and this bird slathered with a rub of butter, onion dip mix, and crispy fried onions is outstanding.
- **Whipped Butternut Squash with Bacon Crumble** (page 284) Bacon makes everything better, including this creamy squash side dish.

December

- **Papaw's Peanut Butter Fudge** (page 292) This cherished family recipe is a labor of love that sparks sweet memories.
- **Party Cheese Ball** (page 297) This party favorite came from our archives—1984—and retains its appeal to this day.
- **Heavenly Angel Biscuits** (page 304) Yeast is the secret ingredient that makes these biscuits so light they almost fly off of your plate—and the dough can be made several days ahead of baking.
- **White Poinsettia Layer Cake with Cranberry-Orange Filling** (page 309) We're famous for the "Big White Cake" that graces our cover every December. This year's showstopper features a few fun variations so you can decide the cake's final form.
- **Orange Pavlova Wreath** (page 318) This gorgeous, light-as-air meringue dessert is bejeweled with candied blood oranges and kumquats. It's not hard to make, but is truly a showstopping end to a festive holiday meal.
- **Stained Glass Snowflakes** (page 321) We have so many cookies that are worthy of calling our "favorite," but these elegant and tasty treats came out on top this year. Fill tins with these beautiful snowflakes to share with friends and neighbors—and keep a few to leave out for Santa!

WHIPPED BUTTERNUT SQUASH WITH BACON CRUMBLE

January–February

14   **Give 'Em Kale**   Warm up with winter's hardiest leafy greens

16   **All Fired Up**   Pepper jelly adds a spicy-sweet kick to a classic game-day appetizer

17   **Pass the Potlikker**   Whether sipped by the spoonful or stirred into recipes, this Southern elixir soothes spirits and transcends generations

26   **Double Dutch**   Pull out your biggest pot, and cook two dinners at once

32   **Let's Jam**   Fill these flaky pastries with your favorite preserves

33   **There's a New Queso in Town**   A secret ingredient makes this dip healthier but still nice and cheesy

35   **Melt Someone's Heart**   Surprise your valentine with an ooey, gooey, supersize molten cake

36   **In Full Bloom**   Keyatta Mincey Parker, an award-winning mixologist and gardening enthusiast, understands that sipping spirits is an experience

38   **Here Comes the Sun**   Senior Test Kitchen Pro Ivy Odom whips up a citrusy coffee cake with a crunchy crumble topping

40   **Cooking School**   Our Test Kitchen professionals share tips for cooking with dried beans—and provide a simple recipe for making them

BOUNTY

Give 'Em Kale

Warm up with winter's hardiest leafy greens

CREAMY KALE SOUP

CRUNCH TIME
More than a pretty garnish, Spicy Kale Chips also make a great snack.

14   2024 JANUARY–FEBRUARY

KALE RIGATONI WITH CRISPY SAUSAGE

Kale Rigatoni with Crispy Sausage
ACTIVE 30 MIN. · TOTAL 35 MIN.
SERVES 4

Cook 1 lb. **rigatoni** in a large pot of boiling salted water until al dente, 8 to 10 minutes. Drain, reserving 2 cups cooking water. In same pot, melt 2 Tbsp. **unsalted butter** over medium-high. Add 12 oz. **mild Italian sausage** (casings removed); cook, stirring occasionally, until cooked through, about 10 minutes. Transfer to a plate; do not wipe pot clean. Melt 2 Tbsp. **butter** in same pot over medium. Add 2 cups thinly sliced **yellow onion** and 1 cup thinly sliced **fennel**; cook, scraping up any browned bits from bottom of pot, until vegetables are well browned, about 15 minutes. Add 16 cups torn **curly purple kale** (from 2 stemmed bunches), 2 tsp. minced **garlic**, and ½ tsp. **kosher salt**; cook, stirring occasionally, until kale is just tender, 3 to 4 minutes. Add pasta, sausage, 2 Tbsp. **butter**, and 1 cup **reserved cooking water** to pot. Cook over medium, gradually adding enough remaining cooking water to coat rigatoni, about 3 minutes. Season with more **kosher salt** to taste; garnish with crushed **Spicy Kale Chips** (recipe at right).

Creamy Kale Soup
ACTIVE 25 MIN. · TOTAL 35 MIN.
SERVES 6

Heat 2 Tbsp. **olive oil** in a large pot over medium-high. Add 2 cups chopped **yellow onion**, and cook, stirring often, until softened, about 5 minutes. Add 5 smashed **large garlic cloves**; cook and stir until toasted, 1 to 2 minutes. Add 16 packed cups chopped **curly kale leaves** (from 2 stemmed bunches); cook, stirring occasionally, until kale starts to wilt, 2 minutes. Stir in 5 cups **lower-sodium vegetable broth**; bring to a simmer over medium-high. Reduce heat to low. Cover and simmer until kale is tender, about 10 minutes. Remove from heat. Stir in 2½ cups torn **sourdough bread**, 1 Tbsp. **fresh lemon juice**, and 2 tsp. **kosher salt.** Working in batches, pour soup into a blender. Secure lid; remove center piece to let steam escape. Place a clean towel over the opening. Puree until smooth, about 1 minute per batch. Return soup to pot; bring to a simmer over medium-low. Stir in ¾ cup **half-and-half** and ½ cup grated **Parmesan cheese**. Add more **salt** to taste. Garnish with **Spicy Kale Chips** (recipe at right) and **crushed red pepper.**

Spicy Kale Chips
ACTIVE 10 MIN. · TOTAL 35 MIN.
SERVES 6

Toss together 8 cups **curly kale leaves** (from 1 stemmed and torn bunch) with 1 Tbsp. **extra-virgin olive oil** and ¼ tsp. each **kosher salt** and **crushed red pepper** in a large bowl. Divide between 2 large rimmed baking sheets. Bake at 300°F until just crisp, about 20 minutes. Remove from oven; sprinkle with ⅓ cup finely grated **Parmesan cheese** and 1 tsp. grated **lemon zest**. Return to oven, and bake at 300°F until crisp, 3 to 5 minutes.

SNACK TIME

All Fired Up

Pepper jelly adds a spicy-sweet kick to a classic game-day appetizer

Pepper Jelly–Glazed Chicken Wings

Chicken wings are sold whole, as drumettes, and as flats. If cutting them up yourself, trim off the wing tips and save them for making stock.

ACTIVE 30 MIN. · TOTAL 2 HOURS, 30 MIN.
SERVES 8

- 3 lb. chicken wings (flats and drumettes)
- 1 Tbsp. kosher salt
- 2 tsp. baking powder
- 1 tsp. onion powder
- 1 tsp. ground coriander
- ½ tsp. black pepper
- 1 cup hot red pepper jelly
- 2 Tbsp., plus 2 tsp. apple cider vinegar, divided
- 2 Tbsp. unsalted butter, cubed
- ¼ tsp. crushed red pepper
- ½ cup bottled buttermilk ranch dressing
- Chopped fresh cilantro

1. Pat chicken dry with paper towels; place in a large bowl. Stir together kosher salt, baking powder, onion powder, ground coriander, and black pepper in a small bowl. Sprinkle salt mixture over chicken; toss well to coat. Arrange chicken skin side down on a wire rack fitted over a rimmed baking sheet. Refrigerate chicken uncovered for 1 hour. Remove pan from refrigerator 15 minutes before baking. Preheat oven to 450°F.

2. Pat chicken dry again, and arrange skin side down in a single layer on a large rimmed baking sheet lined with parchment paper. Bake in preheated oven for 25 minutes.

3. While chicken cooks, stir together pepper jelly and 2 tablespoons of the apple cider vinegar in a medium saucepan; bring to a boil over medium high. Cook, stirring often, until jelly is melted, 1 to 2 minutes. Stir in butter and red pepper; remove from heat. Reserve ¼ cup pepper jelly mixture for brushing.

4. Remove chicken from oven. Using tongs, carefully turn chicken, and brush with reserved ¼ cup pepper jelly mixture. Return to oven; bake until well browned and crispy and a thermometer inserted into thickest portion of chicken registers at least 165°F, 18 to 20 minutes. Cool 5 minutes.

5. Stir together ranch and remaining 2 teaspoons cider vinegar. Transfer chicken wings to a large bowl. Add ½ cup pepper jelly mixture; toss well to coat. Arrange wings on a serving platter; drizzle with remaining pepper jelly mixture, and sprinkle with cilantro. Serve with ranch dip.

Pass the Potlikker

Whether sipped by the spoonful or stirred into recipes, this Southern elixir soothes spirits and transcends generations

ANYTHING CHICKEN SOUP CAN DO, POTLIKKER CAN DO BETTER. The rich, dense broth that results from the classically long, low, and slow cooking of a mess of greens with a seasoning piece of smoked meat is traditionally thought to be a cure-all reputed to alleviate ailments, cut short colds, and do darn near everything but heal broken hearts.

Potlikker is also considered a birthright by proud Southerners of all stripes. Recall the great potlikker-and-corn pone debate that went on in 1931 between Julian Harris (no relation to me), an editor of the *Atlanta Constitution*, and Huey Long, governor of Louisiana and Senator-elect from that state, which kept readers of the paper riveted for weeks.

The discussion centered on whether the correct way to consume the two was by crumbling the corn pone in the potlikker or—the "heresy" proposed by Long—dunking the pone in the liquid. A tireless potlikker advocate, Long later went on to present a detailed description of how to prepare it during a 1935 filibuster on the Senate floor, resulting in his recipe becoming a permanent part of the Congressional Record.

John T. Edge's 2017 book, *The Potlikker Papers*, discusses both events and reveals how the beloved liquid runs in the veins of some Southerners. Many, however, don't realize that potlikker is a culinary legacy from enslaved Africans. It was those people and their descendants who initially understood the importance of consuming the vitamin-rich broth that came from the slow-cooking of greens. They had been doing just that for centuries in many different corners of the African continent.

Even the way this term is written can be controversial. Spell-check reminds me of that every time I type "potlikker." It's so contested that in 1982, Zell Miller, who was then the lieutenant governor of Georgia, spoke for many when he weighed in on the orthography for *The New York Times*: "Only a culinarily-illiterate damnyankee (one word) who can't tell the difference between beans and greens would call the liquid left in the pot after cooking greens 'pot liquor' (two words) instead of 'potlikker' (one word) as yours did. And don't cite Webster as a defense because he didn't know any better either."

I am a potlikker aficionada and have long been a lover of greens. I'm especially fond of collards but won't turn up my nose at a mess of mustard or turnip greens or even a long-cooked batch of kale. I'll add chopped onions and a splash of hot sauce. But I don't tread into the debate about dunking or crumbling cornbread, because I'm a purist. However, I was delighted to discover the following new uses for the South's miraculous healing tonic. When potlikker is added to recipes, it adds depth and complexity in ways that few other ingredients can. —Jessica B. Harris

Double Potlikker Greens

(Photo, page 18)

ACTIVE 25 MIN. - TOTAL 1 HOUR, 45 MIN.

SERVES 8

- 2 hickory-smoked thick-cut bacon slices, chopped (about ½ cup)
- 1 large yellow onion, sliced (about 3 cups)
- 5 medium garlic cloves, smashed
- 1 tsp. kosher salt, plus more to taste
- ½ tsp. black pepper
- ¼ tsp. crushed red pepper (optional)
- ⅓ cup bourbon
- 1 Tbsp. dark brown sugar
- 1 large bunch fresh collard greens (about 1 lb.), stemmed and chopped (about 8 cups)
- 8 cups unsalted chicken stock
- 2 lb. smoked ham hocks (2 to 3 large hocks)
- 2 fresh bay leaves
- 2 tsp. apple cider vinegar, plus more to taste

1. Heat a large Dutch oven over medium. Add bacon, and cook, stirring occasionally, until browned and crisp, 5 to 7 minutes. Transfer bacon to a paper towel–lined plate to drain. Do not wipe Dutch oven clean.

2. Add onion to drippings in Dutch oven, and cook over medium-high, stirring occasionally, until onion is softened and lightly browned, about 10 minutes. Stir in garlic, salt, black pepper, and, if desired, crushed red pepper. Cook, stirring often, until garlic is lightly toasted, 1 to 2 minutes. Add bourbon and sugar, stirring to release any browned bits from bottom of Dutch oven. Add collard greens, stirring to coat. Stir in chicken stock, ham hocks, and bay leaves. Bring to a simmer over medium-high; reduce heat to low. Cover and simmer, undisturbed, until collard greens are tender and liquid has concentrated in flavor, about 1 hour, 15 minutes. Remove from heat, and stir in vinegar.

Continued on page 20

HOT POTLIKKER CORNBREAD (PAGE 22)

DOUBLE POTLIKKER GREENS (PAGE 17)

THINK OUTSIDE THE POT
Want a hands-off option? For the greens on page 17, omit the bacon, and combine the other ingredients (except the vinegar) in an 8-quart slow cooker. Cover; cook on low for nine hours. Stir in the vinegar before serving.

POTLIKKER BOILED PEANUTS (PAGE 20)

POTLIKKER BLOODY MARYS (PAGE 20)

Continued from page 17

3. Remove and discard bay leaves. Transfer ham hocks to a cutting board, and let cool slightly, about 10 minutes. Use a fork to shred meat from ham hocks. Discard bones and skin. Return shredded ham hocks to Dutch oven with collard greens, or reserve for another use. Season potlikker with additional salt and vinegar to taste. Top with cooked bacon, and serve. (Note: If preparing collard greens and potlikker for later use, let cool to room temperature, about 1 hour. Pour cooled greens through a fine mesh strainer set over a large bowl. Transfer greens to an airtight container. Skim and discard as much fat as possible from strained potlikker, and transfer liquid to another airtight container. Store greens, potlikker, and reserved shredded ham hocks in refrigerator up to 5 days or in freezer up to 3 months.)

Potlikker Boiled Peanuts

(Photo, page 19)
ACTIVE 15 MIN. - TOTAL 7 HOURS, 15 MIN.
SERVES 8

- 1 medium garlic head
- 1 lb. raw peanuts in shell, rinsed and drained
- 4 cups potlikker (reserved from Double Potlikker Greens; recipe, page 17)
- 1½ cups cooked collard greens (reserved from Double Potlikker Greens)
- ⅓ cup kosher salt, plus more to taste
- 2 tsp. smoked paprika
- 1 tsp. crushed red pepper
- 2 fresh bay leaves
- 3 Tbsp. apple cider vinegar

1. Cut top off garlic head just enough to expose the cloves; discard top. Add trimmed garlic head to a large Dutch oven along with peanuts, 6 cups water, potlikker, collard greens, salt, smoked paprika, crushed red pepper, and bay leaves; stir to combine. Bring to a boil over high. Reduce heat to low, and simmer, covered, for 3 hours.
2. Taste peanuts to check for salinity and texture; add salt, 1 tablespoon at a time, as desired. Cover and continue simmering, tasting and adjusting seasoning every hour until peanuts

are tender and broth has darkened in color, 3 to 5 more hours, adding water as needed to keep peanuts just covered throughout the cooking process.
3. Once peanuts are tender, remove from heat. Stir in vinegar. Cover and let peanuts marinate 1 hour. Remove and discard bay leaves. Store peanuts in shells in an airtight container in refrigerator up to 1 week.

Potlikker Bloody Marys

(Photo, page 19)
ACTIVE 10 MIN. - TOTAL 25 MIN.,
PLUS 45 MIN. COOLING
SERVES 2

- 2 cups cold potlikker (reserved from Double Potlikker Greens; recipe, page 17)
- 1 cup vegetable juice (such as V8)
- 2 Tbsp. fresh lemon juice
- 1 Tbsp. fresh lime juice
- 2 tsp. whole-grain mustard
- 1 tsp. liquid from peppers in vinegar, plus peppers for garnish
- ¾ tsp. garlic salt
- ½ tsp. black pepper
- ¾ cup (6 oz.) vodka
  Ice
  Cocktail onions
  Collard greens (reserved from Double Potlikker Greens)

1. Remove and discard any fat that has risen to the top of cold potlikker. Bring potlikker to a boil in a medium saucepan over high. Cook, undisturbed, until reduced by half and concentrated in flavor, about 15 minutes. Remove from heat, and let cool to room temperature, about 45 minutes. Cover and refrigerate until ready to use.
2. Place concentrated potlikker, vegetable juice, lemon juice, lime juice, mustard, liquid from peppers in vinegar, garlic salt, and black pepper in a small pitcher; stir until well combined. Stir in vodka.
3. Fill 2 (16-oz.) glasses with ice, and pour vodka mixture evenly into each glass. Garnish each glass with a pick threaded with pickled peppers in vinegar, cocktail onions, and collard greens.

Brothy Clams with Potlikker

ACTIVE 25 MIN. - TOTAL 45 MIN.
SERVES 4

- 24 littleneck clams (about 2 lb., 6 oz. total)
- 1 Tbsp. olive oil
- 1 cup thinly sliced fennel bulb (from 1 small fennel bulb), fronds reserved for garnish
- 2 large garlic cloves, thinly sliced
- 2 Tbsp. tomato paste
- ¼ tsp. crushed red pepper
- ¾ cup dry white wine
- 1 cup potlikker (reserved from Double Potlikker Greens; recipe, page 17)
- ⅓ cup shredded ham hock (reserved from Double Potlikker Greens)
- 2 Tbsp. cold unsalted butter, cut into pieces
  Lemon wedges

1. Place clams in a large bowl, and cover with cold water. Let clams soak 20 minutes. Drain and rinse under cold running water; scrub clams clean, discarding any that are open and won't close when lightly tapped on a firm surface. Set scrubbed clams aside.
2. Heat oil in a large high-sided skillet over medium. Add fennel and garlic; cook, stirring often, until just softened, about 2 minutes. Add tomato paste and crushed red pepper; cook, stirring often, until paste darkens slightly, about 1 minute. Add wine, and cook, stirring occasionally, until liquid is reduced by half, 1 to 2 minutes.
3. Stir in potlikker and ½ cup water. Add scrubbed clams and shredded ham hock. Bring to a boil over medium-high. Cover; reduce heat to medium; and cook, shaking the skillet occasionally, until the clams open, 6 to 8 minutes.
4. Using tongs, transfer clams to a shallow serving bowl, discarding any that have not opened. Return liquid to a boil over medium-high. Cook, stirring occasionally, until liquid is slightly reduced and reaches desired saltiness, about 4 minutes. Remove from heat, and add butter; swirl and stir in butter until melted and combined, about 1 minute. Pour hot broth over clams. Sprinkle with fennel fronds, and serve with lemon wedges.

BROTHY CLAMS
WITH POTLIKKER

Know Your Greens

While any Southern green will work in these recipes, each variety brings its own character to the dish. Here's a rundown of what to expect:

Collard Greens
By far the "meatiest" of the bunch, collards hold their texture the best and can stand up to hours of simmering. Even though the stems will soften, remove them just below the leaves before cooking.

Turnip Greens
Depending on when they are harvested, these greens can have slightly sweet or bitter notes, which are tamed during braising. They are softer than collards, so they don't take as long to cook. Trim and discard long stems.

Mustard Greens
These frilly leaves get their name from their peppery bite, which is reminiscent of tangy Dijon mustard. They are tender like turnip greens, so cook them less or (if you're using them along with collards) stir them in during the last 20 minutes of cooking.

Hot Potlikker Cornbread

(Photo, page 18)
ACTIVE 20 MIN. - TOTAL 20 MIN.
SERVES 8

- ¾ cup plus 2 Tbsp. fine yellow cornmeal
- ½ cup all-purpose flour
- 1 Tbsp. baking powder
- ¾ tsp. kosher salt
- 1 cup potlikker (reserved from Double Potlikker Greens; recipe, page 17)
- ½ cup cooked collard greens (reserved from Double Potlikker Greens), chopped
- 1 Tbsp. unsalted butter, melted
- 6 Tbsp. vegetable oil, divided

1. Whisk together cornmeal, flour, baking powder, and salt in a large bowl until well combined. Place the potlikker in a microwavable measuring cup; microwave on HIGH until very hot, about 2 minutes. Pour ¾ cup of the hot potlikker over cornmeal mixture; discard remaining potlikker, or reserve for another use. Add chopped collard greens and melted butter to cornmeal mixture; stir until just combined (batter will be very thick).
2. Heat 4 tablespoons of the oil in a 12-inch cast-iron skillet over medium. Using a 2-tablespoon scoop, carefully drop 6 balls of batter (1 inch apart) into skillet. Lightly coat the bottom of a heatproof measuring cup with cooking spray; gently flatten each ball into a 2-inch circle. Cook until an even, golden brown crust forms on bottoms and batter puffs up slightly, about 2 minutes per side. Transfer to a paper towel–lined plate. Repeat procedure twice, adding 1 more tablespoon oil per batch. Serve warm.

One-Pot Chicken Thighs and Potlikker Rice

(Photo, page 24)
ACTIVE 20 MIN. - TOTAL 40 MIN.
SERVES 4

- 3 large fresh whole collard green leaves (4½ oz. total), stemmed and quartered
- 2 Tbsp. olive oil, divided
- 2 tsp. kosher salt, divided
- 4 (7-oz.) bone-in, skin-on chicken thighs
- ¾ tsp. black pepper
- 1 Tbsp. minced garlic (from 3 large cloves)
- 1½ cups potlikker (reserved from Double Potlikker Greens; recipe, page 17)
- 1 cup cooked collard greens (reserved from Double Potlikker Greens), roughly chopped
- 1 cup uncooked Carolina Gold or jasmine rice, well rinsed
- 4 tsp. benne seeds or sesame seeds, lightly toasted
- 1 tsp. dried garlic flakes
- ¼ tsp. crushed red pepper

1. Preheat oven to 350°F with racks in middle and top third positions. Divide collard green pieces evenly among 2 baking sheets. Brush both sides of collard green pieces with 1 tablespoon of the oil, and sprinkle with ¼ teaspoon of the salt. Bake on middle rack until crispy, 10 to 12 minutes, flipping collard green pieces halfway through. Remove baking sheets from oven; set collard green chips aside to cool, about 15 minutes. Do not turn oven off.
2. Meanwhile, heat remaining 1 tablespoon oil in a large high-sided ovenproof skillet (cast iron preferred) over medium until shimmering. Sprinkle chicken with black pepper and 1 teaspoon of the salt. Place chicken, skin side down, in hot oil. Cook, undisturbed, until skin is golden brown and easily releases from the pan, 8 to 10 minutes. Flip chicken, and continue to cook until bottom is lightly browned, 1 to 2 minutes. Transfer chicken to a plate.

3. Add garlic to drippings in skillet; cook, stirring constantly, until fragrant and lightly browned, about 30 seconds. Stir in potlikker, cooked collard greens, rice, and remaining ¾ teaspoon salt. Nestle browned chicken, skin side up, in rice mixture; bring to a boil over high. Cover and transfer the skillet to top oven rack. Bake at 350°F until rice is just tender and a thermometer inserted into thickest portion of chicken registers 165°F, about 20 minutes.

4. Remove lid from skillet, and increase oven temperature to broil. Broil until the chicken skin is crispy, about 5 minutes. Remove from oven.

5. Meanwhile, combine baked collard green chips, benne seeds, dried garlic flakes, and crushed red pepper in a mortar; crush with a pestle until the mixture reaches a flaky consistency. (Alternatively, pulse the mixture in a food processor until greens are finely chopped.)

6. To serve, fluff rice with a fork, and sprinkle ¼ cup of the crushed collard green mixture over chicken and rice in skillet. Divide chicken and rice among plates, and top with additional crushed collard green mixture, if desired. Serve warm.

Potlikker Pappardelle

(Photo, page 25)
ACTIVE 30 MIN. · TOTAL 30 MIN.
SERVES 4

- 6 Tbsp. cold unsalted butter, cubed, divided
- 1 (8-oz.) pkg. sliced fresh cremini mushrooms
- ¼ cup finely chopped shallot (from 1 large shallot)
- 3 large garlic cloves, thinly sliced
- 1 medium bunch fresh collard greens (about ¾ lb.), stemmed and cut crosswise into ¾-inch-thick strips (about 6 cups)
- 2½ cups potlikker (reserved from Double Potlikker Greens; recipe, page 17), divided
- ⅓ cup shredded ham hock (reserved from Double Potlikker Greens)
- 1 tsp. kosher salt, plus more to taste
- ½ tsp. cracked black pepper
- 12 oz. uncooked pappardelle or fettuccine pasta
- 1 oz. Parmesan cheese, grated (about ¼ cup), plus shaved Parmesan for serving
- 1 Tbsp. aged sherry vinegar
- 1 tsp. grated lemon zest (from 1 lemon)

1. Bring a large pot of water to a boil over high. Meanwhile, melt 2 tablespoons of the butter in a large high-sided skillet over medium. Add mushrooms, and increase heat to medium-high; cook, stirring occasionally, until mushrooms begin to soften, about 4 minutes. Add shallot and garlic; cook, stirring occasionally, until mushrooms are browned, about 4 minutes. Stir in collard greens; cook, stirring occasionally, until collards begin to wilt and turn bright green, about 1 minute.

2. Add 2 cups of the potlikker, stirring to loosen any browned bits from the bottom of the skillet. Stir in shredded ham hock, salt, and pepper. Bring to a simmer over medium. Cover and cook until collard greens are just tender, 5 to 6 minutes.

3. Meanwhile, add a generous amount of salt to the boiling water. Add pasta to boiling water, and cook until al dente according to package instructions, 6 to 8 minutes; drain.

4. Add cooked pasta, Parmesan, vinegar, and remaining 4 tablespoons butter to collard green mixture; cook over medium, stirring constantly, until a creamy sauce forms and coats pasta, 2 to 3 minutes. Stir in remaining ½ cup potlikker, as needed, until sauce reaches desired consistency. Remove from heat; season with additional salt to taste.

5. Divide pasta evenly among 4 bowls, and sprinkle with lemon zest and shaved Parmesan. Serve immediately.

Add Hock

There's only one hard-and-fast rule when it comes to greens and potlikker: Use what you have, and make it work. Most recipes include pork of some kind; here are a few of our favorite options.

Smoked Ham Hocks

These cuts from the back legs of the pig are packed with collagen that enriches the broth. They're inexpensive and widely available.

Pork Neck Bones

A little harder to find, these are meatier than ham hocks, so they're ideal for dishes like the easy Potlikker Pappardelle on this page.

Smoked Sausage

Sold in most grocery stores, it provides a bold punch of flavor, but you won't get the richness that comes from bone-in pork.

Bacon

Opt for thick-cut slices when cooking greens. They will add extra fat, which you can skim from the surface of the potlikker if you wish.

Pork-Free Potlikker?

You can use smoked turkey wings to add a light yet meaty richness to the potlikker, thanks to their bones. The wings are available in many grocery stores year-round; look for them with the ham and other smoked meats. If you want to stray from tradition a step further, Tabitha Brown, author of *Cooking from the Spirit*, proves that adding pork isn't the only path to good potlikker. Her vegan recipe for Stewed Collard Greens uses meatless ingredients such as coconut aminos (a vegan, gluten-free substitute for soy sauce) and a dash of liquid smoke to mirror the rich umami of pork.

ONE-POT
CHICKEN THIGHS
AND POTLIKKER RICE
(PAGE 22)

POTLIKKER
PAPPARDELLE
(PAGE 23)

SUPPERTIME

Double Dutch

Pull out your biggest pot, and cook two dinners at once

Roasted Lemon-Pepper Chicken
ACTIVE 20 MIN. · TOTAL 1 HOUR, 45 MIN.
SERVES 4

- 4 tsp. kosher salt, plus more for serving
- 2 garlic cloves, minced (about 2 tsp.)
- 2 tsp. black pepper
- 1 lemon, zested and halved, divided
- 1 (4½-lb.) whole chicken, giblets removed, patted dry
- 2 garlic heads, cut in half crosswise
- 4 Tbsp. unsalted butter, melted
- Fresh thyme leaves
- Lemon wedges

1. Preheat oven to 400°F. Place salt, minced garlic, pepper, and lemon zest in a small bowl, and rub together with fingertips until well combined.
2. Place chicken in a large Dutch oven. Sprinkle salt mixture evenly over outside and in cavity of chicken. Tie legs together with kitchen twine. Nestle garlic head halves and lemon halves around chicken. Drizzle melted butter over chicken.
3. Bake in preheated oven, uncovered, until golden brown and a thermometer inserted into thickest portion of chicken registers 165°F, about 1 hour, 10 minutes to 1 hour, 20 minutes. Remove pan from oven, and let rest 15 minutes. Sprinkle chicken with fresh thyme leaves.
4. Cut chicken into pieces as desired. Squeeze lemon halves over pieces, and sprinkle with more salt, if desired. Shred meat from 1 thigh and 1 drumstick to yield 2 cups; squeeze roasted garlic from garlic halves. Reserve shredded chicken and roasted garlic for **Sun-Dried Tomato Pasta with Chicken** (recipe, page 31). Serve remaining chicken with lemon wedges.

Low-and-Slow Beef Pot Roast
ACTIVE 25 MIN. · TOTAL 3 HOURS, 55 MIN.
SERVES 6

- 1 Tbsp. kosher salt
- 1½ tsp. black pepper, divided
- 1 (4-lb.) boneless chuck roast
- 2 Tbsp. canola oil
- 2 medium-size yellow onions, sliced ½ inch thick (about 4 cups)
- 4 large carrots, cut into 3-inch pieces (about 3 cups)
- 1 (12-oz.) bottle chili sauce
- 1 (1-oz.) envelope onion soup and dip mix
- 2 (3-inch) rosemary sprigs, plus leaves for garnish
- 1 lb. Yukon Gold potatoes, peeled and cut into 2-inch pieces

1. Preheat oven to 325°F. Sprinkle salt and 1 teaspoon of the black pepper over roast. Heat oil in a large Dutch oven over medium-high. Add roast to pan, and cook, turning occasionally, until browned on all sides, 12 to 15 minutes. Transfer to a plate; set aside. Reduce heat to medium. Add onions and remaining ½ teaspoon pepper; cook, stirring often and scraping bottom of Dutch oven to loosen browned bits, until onions begin to soften, about 5 minutes. Stir in carrots, chili sauce, soup mix, 1½ cups water, and rosemary sprigs; return roast to pan. Bring to a simmer over medium.

2. Cover and transfer to oven. Bake in preheated oven 1 hour, 30 minutes. Add Yukon Gold potatoes; cook, covered, until roast and potatoes are fork-tender, about 2 more hours. Transfer roast to a cutting board; use a fork to shred into bite-size pieces. Reserve 2 cups roast and 1 cup gravy for **Po'Boys with Debris** (recipe, page 31). Toss remaining beef with gravy and vegetables. Garnish with rosemary leaves.

Weeknight Pasta Bolognese

ACTIVE 45 MIN. - TOTAL 45 MIN.
SERVES 10

- 2 Tbsp. olive oil
- 2 lb. 85/15 lean ground beef
- 1 lb. sweet Italian sausage, casings removed
- 10 large cloves garlic, minced (about ¼ cup)
- 2 Tbsp. dried oregano
- 2 Tbsp. kosher salt
- 1½ Tbsp. fennel seeds
- ½ tsp. crushed red pepper
- 2 cups dry red wine, such as Cabernet Sauvignon
- 2 (28-oz.) cans crushed tomatoes
- ½ cup heavy whipping cream
- 4 oz. Parmesan cheese, grated (about 1 cup), plus more for serving
- 8 cups hot cooked pappardelle or fettuccine (from 1 lb. uncooked pasta)
- Fresh basil leaves

1. Heat oil in a large Dutch oven over medium-high. Add beef and sausage; cook, stirring and breaking up meat with a wooden spoon, until browned and beginning to stick to edges of pan, 15 to 20 minutes. Stir in garlic, oregano, salt, fennel seeds, and red pepper. Cook, stirring often, until fragrant, about 2 minutes. Stir in wine, scraping bottom of pan to loosen browned bits. Cook, stirring occasionally, until reduced by three-quarters, 6 to 8 minutes. Stir in crushed tomatoes.

2. Bring to a boil; reduce heat to medium-low; and simmer, stirring occasionally, about 15 minutes. Stir in cream; cook, stirring occasionally, about 5 minutes. Remove from heat, and stir in Parmesan until melted and combined. Reserve 2 cups meat sauce for **Italian Sloppy Joes** (recipe, page 31). Serve remaining meat sauce over hot cooked pasta. Top with additional Parmesan cheese, and garnish with basil leaves.

Smoky Black Bean Soup

ACTIVE 25 MIN. - TOTAL 1 HOUR, 55 MIN.
SERVES 6

- 2 Tbsp. olive oil
- 2 medium-size green bell peppers, chopped (about 2 cups)
- 4 garlic cloves, smashed
- 1 large red onion, chopped (about 2 cups), divided
- 1 (14-oz.) can fire-roasted diced tomatoes
- 1 Tbsp. finely chopped chipotle chile plus 1 Tbsp. adobo sauce (from 1 [7-oz.] can)
- 1 lb. dried black beans
- 1 Tbsp. kosher salt, plus more to taste
- 2 tsp. dried oregano
- 1½ tsp. ground cumin

Sour cream, fresh cilantro leaves, chopped avocado, lime wedges

1. Heat oil in a large Dutch oven over medium-high. Add bell peppers, garlic, and 1½ cups of the onion. Cook, stirring often, until onion is just tender, about 5 minutes. Stir in tomatoes, chipotle chile, and adobo sauce; cook, stirring often, about 3 minutes. Add black beans, 8 cups water, salt, oregano, and cumin. Bring to a boil. Reduce heat to medium-low, and simmer, stirring every 30 minutes, until beans are tender and creamy, 1 hour, 30 minutes to 2 hours. (Add water as needed during cooking to keep beans covered.)

2. Pour 3 cups of the bean mixture into a blender. Secure lid on blender; remove center piece to allow steam to escape. Place a towel over opening. Process until smooth, about 1 minute. Pour pureed bean mixture into Dutch oven. Add more salt, if desired. Add more water, as needed, to reach desired consistency. Reserve 3 cups soup for **Cheesy Black Bean Tostadas** (recipe, page 31). Serve remaining soup with sour cream, cilantro, avocado, lime wedges, and remaining ½ cup onion.

Ginger-Citrus Pork Roast
ACTIVE 10 MIN. - TOTAL 3 HOURS, 10 MIN.
SERVES 6

- ¾ cup lower-sodium soy sauce
- ¾ cup fresh orange juice (from 2 large oranges)
- 6 Tbsp. honey
- 6 Tbsp. fresh lime juice (from 2 limes)
- 10 cloves garlic, smashed
- 1 (3-inch) piece fresh ginger, peeled and minced (about 3 Tbsp.)
- 1½ Tbsp. toasted sesame oil
- 1 tsp. black pepper
- 1 (4-lb.) boneless pork shoulder, cut into 4 pieces
- Cooked white rice and steamed broccoli, for serving
- Chopped scallions
- Toasted sesame seeds

1. Preheat oven to 325°F. Stir together soy sauce, orange juice, honey, lime juice, garlic, ginger, sesame oil, and pepper in a large Dutch oven. Add pork pieces, turning to coat in sauce mixture.
2. Bake, covered, in preheated oven, turning pork pieces halfway through cook time, until pork is tender and shreds easily, about 3 hours, removing lid during last 20 minutes of cook time.
3. Remove pork from Dutch oven; shred with a fork. Remove and discard fat from surface of sauce. Return shredded pork to Dutch oven, and toss gently to evenly coat with sauce. Reserve 2 cups pork and ¼ cup sauce for **Spicy Pork Lettuce Wraps** (recipe, opposite). Serve remaining pork and sauce with rice and broccoli; garnish with scallions and sesame seeds.

Entrée Encore

Leftovers are far from boring when they're used in these easy next-day meals.

Sun-Dried Tomato Pasta with Chicken
ACTIVE 20 MIN. - TOTAL 20 MIN.
SERVES 6 TO 8

Place 5 cups chopped **fresh spinach** in a colander in sink. Cook 1 lb. **penne pasta** in boiling salted water according to package directions for al dente. Reserve 1 cup cooking water; drain pasta over spinach. Set aside. Heat 1 Tbsp. **sun-dried tomato oil** (from jar) in a stockpot over medium-high. Add 1 cup sliced **sun-dried tomatoes** and 1 cup chopped **yellow onion**; cook, stirring often, until tender, about 4 minutes. Add 2 tsp. sliced **garlic**, 2 Tbsp. leftover **roasted garlic** from Roasted Lemon-Pepper Chicken (page 26), 1 tsp. **kosher salt**, and ¼ tsp. **crushed red pepper**; cook 1 minute. Add 1½ cups **heavy whipping cream**; cook until reduced slightly, about 3 minutes. Stir in pasta, spinach, ½ cup grated **Parmesan cheese**, and 2 cups leftover shredded **Roasted Lemon-Pepper Chicken**. Stir to combine; add reserved pasta water gradually until pasta is saucy. Season to taste with **kosher salt**; serve with additional **Parmesan**.

Italian Sloppy Joes
ACTIVE 15 MIN. - TOTAL 20 MIN.
SERVES 4

Preheat oven to 450°F. Line a large rimmed baking sheet with aluminum foil. Place 4 (3-oz.) **ciabatta rolls**, cut sides up, on prepared baking sheet. Stir together 2 Tbsp. melted **butter** and 1 grated **garlic clove** in a small bowl; brush over cut sides of rolls. Bake until toasted, 4 to 6 minutes. Remove from oven; set top halves of rolls aside, leaving bottom halves on baking sheet. Spoon ½ cup warmed leftover meat sauce from **Weeknight Pasta Bolognese** (page 28) over each roll bottom; top each with 3 Tbsp. shredded **mozzarella cheese**. Return to oven; bake until cheese is melted, 3 to 4 minutes. Remove from oven; top evenly with ¼ cup **banana pepper rings**, 2 cups **arugula**, and reserved roll halves.

Po'Boys with Debris
ACTIVE 10 MIN. - TOTAL 10 MIN.
SERVES 4

Split 1 (8-oz.) **loaf French bread** in half lengthwise; spread cut sides with ¼ cup **mayonnaise** and 2 tsp. **whole-grain mustard**. Top bottom bread half with 2 cups leftover **Low-and-Slow Beef Pot Roast** (page 27), shredded **lettuce**, sliced **tomatoes**, and top bread half. Cut into quarters. Serve with **pickles** and 1 cup leftover **Low-and-Slow Beef Pot Roast gravy** for dipping.

Cheesy Black Bean Tostadas
ACTIVE 20 MIN. - TOTAL 20 MIN.
SERVES 6

Preheat oven to 350°F. Strain 3 cups leftover **Smoky Black Bean Soup** (page 29) with a fine mesh strainer, and discard liquid. Heat 1 Tbsp. **olive oil** in a nonstick skillet over medium-high. Add bean mixture, and cook, stirring constantly, until thickened, 4 to 5 minutes. Remove from heat. Place 6 **corn tostada shells** on a foil-lined baking sheet. Spread ¼ cup mashed bean mixture over each tostada. Sprinkle evenly with 1½ cups **Monterey Jack cheese**. Bake until cheese is melted, 4 to 6 minutes. Remove from oven; top tostadas evenly with 1 sliced **avocado**, ¼ cup sliced **radishes**, and ½ cup **pico de gallo**. Top with **cilantro** and **hot sauce**.

Spicy Pork Lettuce Wraps
ACTIVE 10 MIN. - TOTAL 10 MIN.
SERVES 4

Divide 2 cups leftover **Ginger-Citrus Pork Roast** (opposite) evenly among 12 **Bibb lettuce leaves**. Top with **fresh cilantro leaves**, shredded **carrot**, chopped **scallions**, **Sriracha chile sauce**, and sliced **serrano chile**. Serve with warmed leftover sauce from Ginger-Citrus Pork Roast for dipping.

OVER EASY

Let's Jam

Fill these flaky pastries with your favorite preserves

SMART SHORTCUT
Store-bought puff pastry is the secret to these strudels. For best results, let it thaw in the fridge overnight before using.

Simple Strawberry Strudels
ACTIVE 25 MIN. - TOTAL 1 HOUR, 15 MIN.
MAKES 6

- 1 (17.3-oz.) pkg. frozen puff pastry sheets, thawed (such as Pepperidge Farm)
- ½ cup strawberry preserves (from 1 [16-oz.] jar)
- 2 tsp. cornstarch
- ¾ tsp. grated lemon zest (from 1 lemon)
- 1 large egg
- ¼ cup, plus 1 Tbsp. heavy whipping cream, divided
- 1 cup powdered sugar, sifted
- ¼ tsp. vanilla extract
- ⅛ tsp. kosher salt

1. Preheat oven to 400°F. Unroll 1 puff pastry sheet on a clean surface; cut into 6 rectangles (about 4½ x 3¼ inches each). Place on a parchment paper–lined large rimmed baking sheet at least ½ inch apart. Repeat process with a second puff pastry sheet; set aside.
2. In a small bowl, stir together preserves, cornstarch, and lemon zest. Place 1 heaping tablespoon of the preserves mixture in the center of each of 6 pastry rectangles, leaving a ½-inch border around edges.
3. Whisk together egg and 1 tablespoon of the cream in a small bowl; lightly brush edges of preserves-topped pastry rectangles with egg mixture. Prick 6 reserved rectangles all over using a fork; place on top of preserves-topped rectangles, pressing edges to seal. Crimp edges using a fork. Brush tops lightly with egg mixture.
4. Bake in preheated oven until golden brown, 18 to 20 minutes, rotating baking sheet halfway through bake time. Remove from oven. While strudels are still warm, use a spatula to gently press them to flatten slightly, if desired. Let cool completely on baking sheet, about 30 minutes.
5. Whisk together powdered sugar, vanilla, salt, and remaining ¼ cup cream in a bowl until smooth. Drizzle evenly over strudels. Serve immediately, or store in an airtight container in refrigerator for up to 3 days.

LIGHTEN UP

There's a New Queso in Town

A secret ingredient makes this dip healthier but still nice and cheesy

Sweet Potato Queso
ACTIVE 20 MIN. - TOTAL 20 MIN.
SERVES 8

- 2 bacon slices, chopped
- ¼ cup finely chopped yellow onion (from 1 small onion)
- 1 Tbsp. finely chopped garlic (from 3 garlic cloves)
- 1 tsp. ground cumin
- 1 tsp. kosher salt
- ½ tsp. smoked paprika
- 1½ cups whole milk
- 2 tsp. cornstarch
- 1 cup pureed or mashed cooked sweet potato (from 1 small sweet potato)
- 1 (7-oz.) can chopped green chiles
- 6 oz. American cheese, shredded (about 1½ cups)
- Thinly sliced jalapeño
- Fresh cilantro leaves
- Homemade Tortilla Chips (recipe below right)

1. Cook bacon in a 10-inch cast-iron skillet over medium, stirring often, until crisp, about 5 minutes. Transfer to a paper towel–lined plate, reserving drippings in skillet.
2. Add onion to drippings in skillet; cook over medium, stirring often, until softened, 3 to 5 minutes. Stir in garlic, cumin, salt, and smoked paprika; cook, stirring often, until mixture is fragrant, about 30 seconds.
3. Whisk together milk and cornstarch in a bowl. Add milk mixture to onion mixture in skillet; cook, stirring often, until bubbly and slightly thickened, about 4 minutes. Add sweet potato and green chiles; whisk until smooth, about 1 minute. Add cheese, and whisk until melted, about 1 minute. Remove from heat, and sprinkle with reserved bacon, jalapeño slices, and cilantro. Serve warm with Homemade Tortilla Chips.

Homemade Tortilla Chips
Preheat oven to 375°F. Brush both sides of 12 (6-inch) corn tortillas with 1 Tbsp. canola oil. Stack tortillas, and cut into quarters; arrange in a single layer on 2 large rimmed baking sheets. Sprinkle evenly with ½ tsp. each kosher salt and chili powder. Bake until crisp and lightly golden, about 13 minutes, rotating baking sheets between top and bottom racks halfway through bake time.

Before Recipe Makeover:
CALORIES: **270** – FAT: **21 G** – SODIUM: **1,259 MG**

After Recipe Makeover:
CALORIES: **157** – FAT: **9 G** – SODIUM: **731 MG**

RASPBERRY MOLTEN CHOCOLATE CAKE

PIECE OF CAKE

Melt Someone's Heart

Surprise your valentine with an ooey, gooey, supersize molten cake

PEANUT BUTTER MOLTEN CHOCOLATE CAKE

Raspberry Molten Chocolate Cake
ACTIVE 15 MIN. - TOTAL 50 MIN.
SERVES 9

- Baking spray
- ¼ cup all-purpose flour
- 2 Tbsp. Dutch-process cocoa
- ½ tsp. kosher salt
- ½ tsp. instant espresso granules
- 1¼ cups bittersweet chocolate chips
- 1 cup unsalted butter, cut into small pieces
- 4 large eggs, at room temperature
- ¾ cup granulated sugar
- 1 cup fresh raspberries
- Vanilla ice cream (optional)

1. Preheat oven to 350°F. Coat an 8-inch square baking dish with baking spray. Sift together flour, cocoa, salt, and espresso granules into a small mixing bowl. Set aside.
2. Place chocolate chips and butter in a medium microwave-safe bowl, and microwave on HIGH for 1 minute; stir. Microwave in 30-second intervals, stirring after each interval, until fully melted, about 2 minutes total; set aside.
3. Beat eggs and sugar in a large bowl with an electric mixer on medium-high speed until pale and doubled in volume, about 2 minutes. Beat in flour mixture on low speed until just combined, about 30 seconds. Gradually beat in melted chocolate mixture just until no streaks of chocolate remain, 30 seconds to 1 minute.
4. Pour batter into prepared baking dish; top evenly with raspberries. Bake in preheated oven until edges of cake start to pull away from sides of baking dish and center still jiggles slightly, 30 to 35 minutes. (If using a dark metal baking pan, begin checking at 25 minutes.) Serve immediately with vanilla ice cream, if desired.

Peanut Butter Molten Chocolate Cake
Prepare recipe as directed through Step 3. In Step 4, pour half of batter into prepared baking dish. Dollop 9 Tbsp. creamy peanut butter (not the all-natural kind) evenly over batter. Top with remaining batter. Omit berries; sprinkle with 3 Tbsp. chopped roasted salted peanuts. Bake and serve as directed.

2024 JANUARY–FEBRUARY

MIX MASTER

In Full Bloom

Keyatta Mincey Parker, an award-winning mixologist and gardening enthusiast, understands that sipping spirits is an experience

"I'VE ALWAYS BEEN the kind of person who will present a vibrantly colored cocktail with beautiful garnishes, because I feel like you drink with your eyes first," explains Keyatta Mincey Parker, an Atlanta-based entrepreneur.

The daughter of a Liberian father and an American mother, Mincey Parker emigrated from Liberia in 1990 and dove headfirst into the U.S. hospitality industry. For over two decades now, she has built a reputation for serving creative and innovative drinks.

Inspired by a passion for growing her own produce, Mincey Parker proposed a community-garden concept for mixologists, which landed her in the top three finalists for Bombay Sapphire's Most Imaginative Bartender competition in 2020. Here, Mincey Parker shares her fresh ways to toast the New Year.

Bless My Heart
ACTIVE 5 MIN. - TOTAL 5 MIN.
SERVES 1

Fill a cocktail shaker with **crushed ice**; add 3 Tbsp. **vodka** (such as Old Fourth Distillery), 1½ Tbsp. **fresh lemon juice**, 1 Tbsp. **simple syrup**, ½ Tbsp. **allspice liqueur** (such as St. Elizabeth), ½ Tbsp. **spiced-pear liqueur** (such as St. George), and 4 dashes **Angostura bitters**. Shake hard; double strain over **ice** in a rocks glass. Garnish with a strip of **orange peel**.

Ms. Ruby Mae
ACTIVE 5 MIN. - TOTAL 5 MIN.
SERVES 1

Fill a cocktail shaker with **crushed ice**; add 4 Tbsp. **rhum agricole**, 2 Tbsp. **Cherry Syrup** (recipe follows), 1½ Tbsp. **fresh lime juice**, and ½ Tbsp. **elderflower liqueur** (such as St-Germain). Shake hard; strain into a coupe glass. Garnish with an **edible flower**, like a pansy.

Cherry Syrup
ACTIVE 5 MIN. - TOTAL 25 MIN.
MAKES ABOUT ¾ CUP

Heat ½ cup each **brown sugar** and **tart cherry juice** in a small saucepan over medium, stirring often, until sugar dissolves, about 3 minutes. Remove from heat; let cool completely, about 20 minutes. Store, covered, in refrigerator up to 1 week.

Hibiscus Nectar
ACTIVE 5 MIN. - TOTAL 5 MIN.
SERVES 1

Fill a cocktail shaker with **crushed ice**. Add ½ cup brewed **hibiscus tea**, 4 Tbsp. **rye whiskey**, 2 Tbsp. **Sage-Honey Syrup** (recipe follows), 2 Tbsp. **cranberry juice**, and 1½ Tbsp. **fresh lemon juice**. Shake hard; strain into a tall collins glass over **ice**. Garnish with a **fresh sage leaf**.

Sage-Honey Syrup
ACTIVE 5 MIN. - TOTAL 1 HOUR, 5 MIN.
MAKES ABOUT 1 CUP

Chop 4 **fresh sage leaves**; combine with ½ cup **honey** and ¼ cup **boiling water**. Stir until honey is thin but not watery. Let stand 30 minutes; strain into a container with a lid. Chill completely before using, about 30 minutes. Store, covered, in refrigerator up to 1 week.

The Southern Sling
ACTIVE 5 MIN. - TOTAL 5 MIN.
SERVES 1

Fill a cocktail shaker with **ice**; add 2 Tbsp. **muscadine cider**, 1½ Tbsp. **simple syrup**, 1½ Tbsp. **pineapple juice**, 1½ Tbsp. **fresh lime juice**, 1 Tbsp. **vodka**, 1 Tbsp. **gin**, and 4 dashes **Angostura bitters**. Shake hard; double strain over a **large ice cube** in a rocks glass. Garnish with a **dehydrated lime wheel**.

BLESS MY HEART

36 2024 JANUARY–FEBRUARY

IVY'S KITCHEN

Here Comes the Sun

Senior Test Kitchen Pro Ivy Odom whips up a citrusy coffee cake with a crunchy crumble topping

I HAD NEVER HEARD of orange rolls until I moved to Birmingham to work for *Southern Living*. A distant cousin of cinnamon buns, the zesty glazed pastries make an appearance at nearly every gathering the same way coffee cakes do in my hometown in South Georgia. Both are sweet enough to be served for dessert but not so sugary that they're banned from breakfast. My Orange-Roll Coffee Cake combines the two—it's a hug from my past and a celebration of my present in a way that's comforting yet new. That's what I love about being a Southerner: Certain foods ground us and make us feel at home, no matter where we are.

Orange-Roll Coffee Cake

When making this recipe, I usually go for an old-school tube pan, but a Bundt will also do the trick.

ACTIVE 25 MIN. - TOTAL 1 HOUR, 30 MIN., PLUS 2 HOURS COOLING

SERVES 12

- 3¾ cups bleached cake flour, divided, plus more for pan
- 1½ cups packed light brown sugar, divided
- 2⅛ tsp. grated orange zest, plus 1 to 2 Tbsp. fresh juice (from 2 navel oranges), divided
- 1½ tsp. kosher salt, divided
- ¼ tsp. ground nutmeg, divided
- 1 cup unsalted butter, softened and divided, plus more for pan
- 1 cup granulated sugar
- 10 oz. cream cheese, softened and divided
- 4 large eggs
- 1 tsp. vanilla extract
- 2 tsp. baking powder
- ¼ tsp. baking soda
- ¼ cup powdered sugar

1. Combine 1¼ cups of the flour, 1 cup of the brown sugar, 1 teaspoon of the zest, 1 teaspoon of the salt, and ⅛ teaspoon of the nutmeg in a bowl. Place ¼ cup of the butter in a microwavable dish; microwave on HIGH until melted, about 30 seconds. Add to flour mixture; stir until crumbles form. Chill, covered, until ready to use.

2. Preheat oven to 350°F. Lightly grease a 10-inch tube pan with butter, and dust with flour; set aside. Stir together granulated sugar, 1 teaspoon of the zest, and remaining ½ cup brown sugar in a medium bowl, rubbing zest and sugars between your fingers; set aside. Beat 8 ounces of the cream cheese and remaining ¾ cup butter in bowl of a stand mixer fitted with a paddle attachment on medium speed until smooth, about 1 minute. Add sugar mixture to cream cheese mixture, and beat on medium speed until light and fluffy, about 4 minutes. Add eggs, 1 at a time, beating well after each addition, scraping down sides of bowl as needed. Beat in vanilla until combined.

3. Stir together baking powder, baking soda, and remaining 2½ cups flour, ½ teaspoon salt, and ⅛ teaspoon nutmeg in a bowl. Gradually add flour mixture to cream cheese mixture, beating on low speed until combined, about 2 minutes. Spoon half of batter into prepared pan, spreading in an even layer. Top with half of reserved crumble mixture. Repeat layers once with remaining batter and crumble mixture.

4. Bake in preheated oven until a wooden pick inserted in center comes out clean, 50 to 55 minutes, tenting with aluminum foil after 35 minutes. Cool cake in tube pan on a wire rack for 15 minutes. Invert onto a plate; invert again onto wire rack, crumble side up. Let cool completely, about 2 hours.

5. Beat powdered sugar, 1 tablespoon of the orange juice, and remaining ⅛ teaspoon zest and 2 ounces cream cheese with an electric mixer on medium speed until smooth, about 1 minute. Add up to remaining 1 tablespoon orange juice, 1 teaspoon at a time, until desired consistency is reached. Drizzle glaze over cooled cake as desired.

Make Ahead You can freeze this coffee cake (unglazed is best) for up to a month. Cover it tightly in plastic wrap followed by a layer of heavy-duty foil. Let it thaw on the counter for 24 hours before serving. Prepare the glaze on the day you're planning to enjoy the cake.

COOKING SCHOOL
TIPS AND TRICKS FROM THE SOUTH'S MOST TRUSTED KITCHEN

The Scoop on Dried Beans
Learn the basics on how to prepare this pantry staple like a pro

UPGRADE YOUR AROMATICS

DRIED CHILES
Bring the heat with guajillo, ancho, or other dried peppers.

LEMON PEELS
Add bright notes with these common kitchen scraps.

PARMESAN RINDS
Infuse the cooking liquid with the savory richness of our favorite hard Italian cheese.

FENNEL
Swap out your go-to onions for the sweet anise taste of this crunchy vegetable.

Easy Southern-Style Beans
ACTIVE 20 MIN. - TOTAL 1 HOUR, 30 MIN.
SERVES 12

Place 1 lb. **dried beans** (picked over and rinsed), 4 cups **lower-sodium chicken broth**, 4 cups **water**, 1 (14-oz.) **smoked ham hock**, 1 **Vidalia onion** (cut into eighths), 4 **garlic cloves**, 2 **thyme sprigs**, 2 **bay leaves**, and 1 Tbsp. **baking soda** in a large Dutch oven. Bring to a boil; stir in 1 Tbsp. **salt**, and reduce heat to medium-low. Cover and simmer, stirring occasionally, until beans are tender, 1 to 3 hours (refer to package instructions for suggested cook time), adding water as needed to ensure beans remain covered. Remove from heat. Remove and discard ham hock, thyme sprigs, and bay leaves. Stir in 1 Tbsp. **pepper sauce**. Season with additional **salt** and **pepper sauce** to taste. Garnish with **fresh thyme leaves**.

SORT: Comb through dried beans before adding them to the pot to make sure they don't contain any debris.
COVER: Keep the liquid above the beans as they cook so they soften and don't start to dry out.
SAVE: Don't toss the cooking liquid—freeze it to add to soups or stews for richness and depth.

March

42   **Pretty Peas**   As the weather begins to warm, crisp, sweet sugar snaps start popping up at the market. Enjoy some by the handful, or add them to a fresh salad

44   **Memories by the Spoonful**   This French-style vegetable soup is as unfussy as it is elegant

46   **A Taste of Spring**   Bake a batch (or two!) of buttery shortbread sprinkled with colorful garnishes

50   **Let's Do Brunch**   Celebrate springtime with best friends, bubbles, and a festive menu

60   **What a Ham**   Slice after slice, this showstopper makes dinners easier all week long

65   **Pop Stars**   Ditch the mix, and make these lemony treats from scratch

66   **Think Outside the Box**   Mac and cheese with about half the fat—and did we mention it has bacon?

67   **Green Eggs and...Prosciutto**   Amp up the flavor (and fun) of this go-to appetizer

68   **Cooking School**   Our Test Kitchen professionals demonstrate a handy trick for making parchment circles for cake baking, and highlight the best tool for checking the doneness of baked goods

BOUNTY

Pretty Peas

As the weather begins to warm, crisp, sweet sugar snaps start popping up at the market. Enjoy some by the handful, or add them to a fresh salad

PULLING STRINGS
Removing the fibrous "threads" that run along the top seams of the pods is entirely optional.

Speedy Grain Salad with Sugar Snap Peas

ACTIVE 30 MIN. - TOTAL 30 MIN.
SERVES 6

Fill a large bowl with **ice water**, and add 2 Tbsp. **kosher salt**; set aside. Bring a large pot of **salted water** to a boil over high. Add 1 lb. **fresh sugar snap peas** to boiling water; cook, undisturbed, until tender-crisp, about 5 minutes. Transfer sugar snap peas to ice water; let cool 5 minutes. Drain well. Whisk together 1½ Tbsp. **red wine vinegar**, 4 tsp. **Dijon mustard**, 2 tsp. **light brown sugar**, ¾ tsp. **garlic powder**, and ½ tsp. **kosher salt** in a large bowl; gradually whisk in 6 Tbsp. **extra-virgin olive oil** until smooth and combined. Set aside ¼ cup dressing in a small bowl for serving. Add 4 cups **cooked farro or quinoa**, 3 cups **shredded cooked chicken**, cooled sugar snap peas (halved if desired), 6 oz. crumbled **feta cheese**, ½ cup chopped **pitted kalamata olives**, ½ cup chopped **salted roasted pistachios**, 2 Tbsp. chopped **fresh flat-leaf parsley**, and 1 Tbsp. chopped **fresh mint** to dressing in large bowl; toss to coat. Garnish with additional chopped **pistachios** and **mint**, if desired. Serve with reserved dressing.

SPEEDY GRAIN SALAD WITH SUGAR SNAP PEAS

SUGAR SNAP SALAD WITH LEMON-PARMESAN BREADCRUMBS

Sugar Snap Salad with Lemon-Parmesan Breadcrumbs

ACTIVE 20 MIN. - TOTAL 25 MIN.
SERVES 4

Heat 1 Tbsp. **extra-virgin olive oil** in a medium skillet over medium. Add ⅓ cup **panko breadcrumbs**; cook, stirring often, until oil is absorbed and panko begins to toast, 2 minutes. Add 1 grated **garlic clove**; cook, stirring constantly, until panko is golden brown and garlic is fragrant, 2 minutes. Transfer to a small bowl; let cool 5 minutes. Stir in ¼ cup finely shredded **Parmesan**, 1½ tsp. **lemon zest**, and ¼ tsp. **kosher salt**; set aside. Whisk together 2 Tbsp. **lemon juice**, 1½ tsp. **honey**, 1 tsp. **Dijon mustard**, and ½ tsp. **kosher salt** in a large bowl; gradually whisk in ¼ cup **olive oil** until combined. Add 1 lb. halved **fresh sugar snap peas**, 2 cups **baby arugula**, ½ cup shaved **Parmesan**, and ⅓ cup thinly sliced **shallot**; toss to coat. Top with panko mixture and **edible flowers**, if desired.

2024 MARCH 43

THE WELCOME TABLE

Memories by the Spoonful

This French-style vegetable soup is as unfussy as it is elegant

THERE ARE SEVERAL Souths in my life: South Jamaica, New York, where I was born; the American South, where I write and research; and the South of France. Whenever the latter comes to mind, I always think of writer and civil rights activist James Baldwin and my first meal at his house in Saint-Paul-de-Vence, an ancient village that became a haven for artists.

When I spent a week at his home in the 1970s, I was in my twenties, a terribly naive young guest of a friend and way out of my depth in the stellar crowd that I met there. I recall dropping my suitcase in my appointed bedroom and heading out for lunch at a place under tall cypress trees. Baldwin called this alfresco dining spot his "Welcome Table" in reference to the traditional spiritual that also inspired the name of this column.

The first meal I had at Baldwin's house was simple: loaves of crusty French bread, a wine from the region, and a tureen filled with a hearty soupe au pistou. Baldwin ate, chatted, and then vanished. I was too nervous to properly appreciate the light yet filling vegetable soup that seemed like a French garden in a bowl, but it has remained in my memory all these years.

I would later learn that soupe au pistou is a true Provençal specialty that is thought to date back to the 18th century. It may have originated in Italy and is clearly a close cousin of that country's minestrone. Prepared with pasta and a potager's worth of fresh vegetables, it's an ideal dish for springtime and late summer in the American South, when carrots, potatoes, and fava beans make their appearance at farmers' markets. It is finished with a slurry of garlic, basil, and olive oil that is called a Provençal pistou—a simpler take on Italy's pesto. As it doesn't have the pine nuts (or other nuts) found in the Italian kind, it's the perfect sauce for those with nut allergies. Some versions, like this one, also include a grated hard cheese such as Parmesan—I always save some to sprinkle over each bowl at the table.

When served with a crusty baguette and a chilled Provençal rosé, it is a delicious introduction to the simple, hearty food of this region. You'll have to sample it without the incandescence of Baldwin himself, but you, too, will become a fan of the satisfying, uncomplicated dish that he appreciated.

Soupe au Pistou
ACTIVE 30 MIN. - TOTAL 45 MIN.
SERVES 6

PISTOU
- 1 small tomato, cored, seeded, and chopped (about ¾ cup)
- 1 cup packed fresh basil leaves
- 1 cup packed fresh flat-leaf parsley leaves
- 2 garlic cloves, smashed
- ½ cup olive oil
- 1 oz. Parmesan cheese or Gruyère cheese, grated (about ¼ cup), plus more for garnish
- ¾ tsp. kosher salt

SOUP
- 2 Tbsp. olive oil
- 1 large leek, white and light green parts only, thinly sliced (1½ cups)
- 1 medium celery stalk, chopped (⅓ cup)
- 1 medium carrot, peeled and chopped (⅔ cup)
- 1 (5-inch) thyme sprig
- ¼ tsp. black pepper
- 2¼ tsp. kosher salt, divided
- 1 large Yukon Gold potato, unpeeled and cut into bite-size pieces (1½ cups)
- 2 large bunches Lacinato kale, stemmed and coarsely chopped (8 cups)
- 1 medium zucchini or yellow squash, cut into bite-size pieces (1⅔ cups)
- ½ lb. fresh fava beans, shelled (about 1 cup, from 2 lb. pods)
- ¾ cup uncooked small pasta shells

1. Prepare the Pistou: Pulse tomato, basil, parsley, and garlic in a food processor until chopped, about 5 pulses, stopping to scrape down sides as needed. With processor running, gradually pour oil through food chute until tomato mixture is finely chopped and creamy, about 30 seconds. Transfer to a small bowl; stir in cheese and salt. Set aside until ready to use.

2. Prepare the Soup: Heat oil in a large heavy-bottomed pot or large Dutch oven over medium. Add leek, celery, carrot, thyme, pepper, and ½ teaspoon of the salt. Cook, stirring occasionally, until leek starts to turn golden brown, about 10 minutes.

3. Add 8 cups water and potato, scraping up any browned bits stuck to bottom of pot. Bring to a boil over high. Reduce heat to medium-low, and simmer, undisturbed, until potato is tender, about 10 minutes. Add kale, zucchini, fava beans, and pasta. Bring to a boil over medium-high. Boil, stirring occasionally, until pasta and vegetables are tender, about 10 minutes.

4. Remove pot from heat. Stir in ½ cup of the Pistou and remaining 1¾ teaspoons salt. Garnish Soup with grated cheese, and serve with remaining Pistou for topping.

MAKE IT YOUR WAY
This soup may come from France, but feel free to put a Southern spin on it. The vegetables should be selected based on their freshness, not on the recipe's ingredient list. If string beans or sweet peas look good, then use them. Consider adding pistachios or walnuts to the pistou, or vary the herbs by tossing in a hint of mint. Your version may not be the classic soupe au pistou, but it will be a nice mixture of produce at its peak.

PIECE OF CAKE

A Taste of Spring

Bake a batch (or two!) of buttery shortbread sprinkled with colorful garnishes

PISTACHIO SHORTBREAD (PAGE 49)

LEMON-THYME
SHORTBREAD
(PAGE 49)

Strawberry Shortbread

ACTIVE 45 MIN. - TOTAL 1 HOUR, 15 MIN., PLUS 1 HOUR CHILLING AND 1 HOUR COOLING AND STANDING

MAKES ABOUT 20 COOKIES

- 1 cup freeze-dried strawberries (from 1 [1-oz.] pkg.), plus more for garnish
- ¾ cup unsalted butter, softened
- 1½ cups powdered sugar, divided
- ½ tsp. vanilla bean paste or extract
- 1½ cups all-purpose flour, plus more for work surface and cutters
- ½ tsp. kosher salt
- 2 Tbsp. fresh lemon juice (from 1 lemon)

1. In a food processor, process freeze-dried strawberries until finely ground (the consistency of granulated sugar), about 30 seconds. Set aside.
2. Beat butter and ½ cup of the powdered sugar in a stand mixer fitted with a paddle attachment on medium speed until smooth, about 1 minute. Beat in vanilla and ground dried strawberries until combined, about 30 seconds.
3. Whisk together flour and salt in a medium bowl until combined. With mixer on low speed, gradually add flour mixture to butter mixture, beating just until dough comes together, about 1 minute, stopping to scrape down sides of bowl as needed. Shape dough into a 6-inch disk, and wrap in plastic wrap. Let chill until firm, at least 1 hour or up to 24 hours.
4. Preheat oven to 350°F. Line a large rimmed baking sheet with parchment paper. Roll out dough on a lightly floured work surface to ¼-inch thickness. Cut desired shapes using lightly floured 2-inch cookie cutters. Chill, reroll, and cut dough scraps as needed. Transfer shapes to prepared baking sheet, spacing 1 inch apart. Freeze until firm, about 10 minutes.
5. Bake in preheated oven until the edges are set, 14 to 16 minutes. Let cool on baking sheet for 5 minutes. Transfer cookies to a wire rack; let cool completely, about 30 minutes.
6. In a medium bowl, whisk together lemon juice and remaining 1 cup powdered sugar until smooth. Dip, drizzle, or spread glaze over cooled cookies as desired. Crush additional freeze-dried strawberries; sprinkle over cookies. Let stand until glaze is set, about 30 minutes.

Pistachio Shortbread

(Photo, page 46)

Omit Step 1. In Step 2, omit strawberries; beat in ½ cup finely chopped **pistachios** with the vanilla. Continue with recipe as directed; in Step 6, replace crushed strawberries with additional chopped **pistachios** for garnish.

Lemon-Thyme Shortbread

(Photo, page 47)

Omit Step 1. In Step 2, omit strawberries; beat in 2 Tbsp. **lemon zest** and 1½ tsp. chopped **fresh thyme** with the vanilla. Continue with recipe as directed; in Step 6, replace crushed strawberries with additional **lemon zest** and **thyme leaves** for garnish.

> **PRO TIP**
> Elevate the cookies with edible flowers, or mix and match the garnishes to create your own unique flavors.

Let's Do Brunch

Celebrate springtime with best friends, bubbles, and a festive menu

HERE'S TO THE FOLKS who love to brunch–those who gleefully clink mimosa glasses, generously butter their biscuits, and soak in the laughter that flows so freely when good friends share delicious food. Breakfast, lunch, and dinner are utilitarian meals, intended to keep us fed, productive, and sustained. Not brunch. It's designed purely for fun. When else can you sip champagne in the middle of the day, eat bacon and dessert in one sitting, and be as leisurely as you like? "Brunch... is cheerful, sociable, and inciting," wrote Guy Beringer in an 1895 edition of *Harper's Weekly* (the first printed mention of our favorite hybrid meal). "It puts you in a good temper; it makes you satisfied with yourself and your fellow-beings." Well said. As spring rushes upon the South in all its glory, gather your crew around a welcoming table filled with the following extra-special yet easy-to-prepare dishes. Then sit back, and raise a toast to the good times that keep us going.

SHAVED SPRING VEGETABLE SALAD WITH PARMESAN CRUNCH (PAGE 56)

CHEESE-TOAST PALMIERS
(PAGE 57)

CINNAMON-TOAST PALMIERS
(PAGE 57)

CREAM CHEESE BISCUITS WITH SHARP CHEDDAR BUTTER AND QUICK STRAWBERRY-GINGER JAM (PAGE 59)

UPGRADE YOUR BISCUIT BOARD
For some sweet heat, simmer 1 cup honey, 2 seeded and sliced fresh Fresno chiles, and 2 dried guajillo chiles in a saucepan over medium-high for 5 minutes; strain and serve.

Strawberry-Rhubarb Spritzes

(Photo, page 51)

Move over, mimosas—there's a brand-new beverage in town. The ideal balance of sweet, tart, and herbaceous, this blushing, sparkly cocktail is a fresh and fun way to kick your next brunch up a notch.

ACTIVE 1 HOUR, 10 MIN. · TOTAL 1 HOUR, 10 MIN., PLUS 1 HOUR COOLING

SERVES 8

STRAWBERRY-RHUBARB SIMPLE SYRUP
- 1 lb. fresh strawberries, hulled
- 1 lb. fresh or frozen rhubarb, chopped
- 1 cup granulated sugar
- 1/3 cup thinly sliced peeled fresh ginger (from 1 [2-inch] piece ginger)
- 1/2 tsp. grated lemon zest, plus 4 Tbsp. fresh juice (from 2 large lemons), divided

SPRITZES
- Ice
- 2 cups (16 oz.) gin
- 2 cups sparkling water, plus more to taste
- Fresh strawberry halves, lemon slices, and mint sprigs

1. Prepare the Strawberry-Rhubarb Simple Syrup: Place strawberries, rhubarb, sugar, 1 cup water, ginger, and lemon zest in a saucepan. Bring to a boil over medium-high, stirring occasionally. Reduce heat to medium-low, and simmer, stirring occasionally, until fruit is very soft, about 20 minutes.

2. Remove from heat, and pour strawberry mixture through a fine mesh strainer into a medium bowl; discard solids. Stir lemon juice into strained syrup. Let syrup cool to room temperature, 1 to 2 hours. Store in an airtight container in the refrigerator for up to 3 weeks.

3. Prepare the Spritzes: Fill a cocktail shaker with ice; add 1/2 cup Strawberry-Rhubarb Simple Syrup and 1/2 cup gin. Cover shaker with lid; shake until mixture is chilled, 15 to 30 seconds. Strain into 2 ice-filled wineglasses. Top each with 1/4 cup sparkling water, plus more to taste. Repeat process with remaining Strawberry-Rhubarb Simple Syrup, gin, and sparkling water to make remaining drinks. Garnish with strawberries, lemon slices, and mint sprigs.

Swiss Chard-and-Bacon Grits Quiche

(Photo, page 51)

A Gruyère-enriched grits crust is a gourmet upgrade to this staple. Be sure to wrap your springform pan tightly with aluminum foil to help prevent any leaks.

ACTIVE 45 MIN. · TOTAL 3 HOURS, 15 MIN.

SERVES 8

- 6 thick-cut bacon slices, cut crosswise into 3/4-inch pieces
- 2 1/4 cups whole milk
- 2 Tbsp. unsalted butter
- 1/2 cup uncooked stone-ground grits
- 2 tsp. kosher salt, divided
- 1 tsp. black pepper, divided
- 8 oz. Gruyère cheese, shredded (about 2 cups), divided
- 6 large eggs
- 2 oz. Parmesan cheese, grated (1/2 cup)
- 1 (7 1/2-oz.) bunch Swiss chard, stemmed and chopped (about 3 cups)
- 1 cup thinly sliced spring onions (from about 3 medium onions)
- 2 1/2 cups half-and-half
- Fresh dill

1. Grease a 9-inch springform pan with cooking spray, and wrap exterior tightly with heavy-duty aluminum foil. Set aside.

2. Cook bacon in a large skillet over medium, stirring often, until crisp, 10 to 15 minutes. Remove bacon using a slotted spoon; let drain on a paper towel–lined plate. Transfer 2 teaspoons bacon drippings to a medium saucepan. Reserve 2 teaspoons bacon drippings in skillet; reserve remaining drippings for another use.

3. Preheat oven to 350°F. Add milk and butter to drippings in saucepan; bring to a boil over medium, stirring occasionally. Gradually whisk in grits, 1 teaspoon of the salt, and 1/2 teaspoon of the pepper; cook, whisking constantly, until very thick, 6 to 10 minutes. Remove from heat; let stand in pan 10 minutes. Stir 1 cup of the Gruyère into grits mixture; let stand 5 minutes. Stir 1 egg into grits mixture until well combined. Transfer mixture to prepared springform pan; spread in an even layer.

4. Bake in preheated oven until set, 20 to 25 minutes. Remove from oven;

leave oven on. Sprinkle Parmesan and remaining 1 cup Gruyère cheese over grits to edges of pan in an even layer. Let stand 10 minutes. Place pan on a foil-lined rimmed baking sheet.

5. Add chard to reserved drippings in skillet; cook over medium-high, stirring often, until just wilted, 1 to 2 minutes. Transfer chard to a paper towel–lined plate, gently patting and squeezing to drain excess moisture.

6. Layer cooked bacon, chard, and spring onions evenly on grits. Whisk remaining 5 eggs in a large bowl until smooth. Whisk in half-and-half and remaining 1 teaspoon salt and 1/2 teaspoon pepper until well combined. Pour egg mixture over grits.

7. Bake at 350°F for 20 minutes. Reduce temperature to 325°F (leave quiche in oven), and bake until just set, 50 to 55 minutes. Transfer pan to a wire rack; gently loosen quiche sides from pan using a butter knife. Let cool in pan 30 minutes. Discard foil; gently remove sides of pan. Garnish with dill just before slicing and serving.

Shaved Spring Vegetable Salad with Parmesan Crunch

(Photo, page 52)

Wafer-thin slices of radishes and beets plus delicate ribbons of multicolored carrots team up to make a bright and colorful dish that's almost too pretty to eat. Dog-ear this page, because you'll want to sprinkle the Parmesan Crunch on every salad you eat from here on out.

ACTIVE 30 MIN. · TOTAL 30 MIN.

SERVES 6

VINAIGRETTE
- 1/2 cup white balsamic vinegar
- 1/2 cup extra-virgin olive oil
- 1 Tbsp. whole-grain Dijon mustard
- 1 tsp. honey
- 1 1/2 tsp. kosher salt
- 1/4 tsp. black pepper

SALAD
- 3 medium radishes, thinly sliced (about 1/2 cup)
- 3 medium multicolored carrots, scrubbed and shaved (about 2 1/3 cups)
- 2 small golden beets, peeled and thinly sliced (about 2/3 cup)
- 1 small fennel bulb, shaved (about 2 cups)

3 packed cups spring mix salad greens (about 3 oz. total)

4 oz. goat cheese, crumbled (about ½ cup)

Parmesan Crunch (recipe follows)

1. Prepare the Vinaigrette: Whisk together vinegar, oil, mustard, honey, salt, and pepper in a small bowl until combined.

2. Prepare the Salad: Toss together radishes, carrots, beets, fennel, and 3 tablespoons Vinaigrette in a medium bowl until combined. Divide salad greens evenly among 6 plates. Top evenly with shaved vegetables and crumbled goat cheese. Sprinkle each with ¼ cup Parmesan Crunch. Drizzle with remaining Vinaigrette just before serving.

Parmesan Crunch

(Photo, page 52)

Bound into savory clusters with Parmesan cheese, this crispy topping is hard to resist eating by the handful. Make a double batch so you don't have to limit yourself.

ACTIVE 10 MIN. · TOTAL 1 HOUR, 10 MIN.

MAKES 2 CUPS

¾ cup uncooked old-fashioned regular rolled oats

½ cup blanched whole almonds

⅓ cup roasted salted pumpkin seed kernels (pepitas)

⅓ cup pre-shredded Parmesan cheese

2 Tbsp. sesame seeds

2 Tbsp. extra-virgin olive oil

1 large egg white, beaten

1 Tbsp. honey

1 tsp. kosher salt

½ tsp. garlic powder

⅛ tsp. cayenne pepper

1 Tbsp. fresh rosemary leaves, finely chopped

1 Tbsp. fresh thyme leaves, finely chopped

1. Preheat oven to 300°F. Line a large rimmed baking sheet with parchment paper.

2. Stir together oats, almonds, pepitas, cheese, sesame seeds, olive oil, egg white, honey, salt, garlic powder, and cayenne in a large bowl until combined. Transfer oat mixture to prepared pan, spreading evenly.

3. Bake in preheated oven 15 minutes. Gently stir in rosemary and thyme, preserving as many clusters as possible. Bake at 300°F until lightly toasted, 5 to 8 minutes. Cool completely, about 30 minutes. Store in an airtight container for 2 to 3 days.

Cheese-Toast Palmiers

(Photo, page 53)

These crispy, savory appetizers are just like your childhood favorite—only fancier! Here's a make-ahead hint: Freeze unbaked palmiers on baking sheets, transfer to an airtight container, and keep in the freezer for up to a month. Bake from frozen, increasing the time by a few minutes.

ACTIVE 15 MIN. · TOTAL 1 HOUR

SERVES 10

All-purpose flour, for rolling

1 (17.3-oz.) pkg. frozen puff pastry, thawed overnight in the refrigerator

1 large egg

2 tsp. smoked paprika

½ tsp. kosher salt

½ tsp. garlic powder

½ tsp. cayenne pepper

½ tsp. black pepper

4 oz. extra-sharp cheddar cheese, shredded (1 cup), divided

1½ oz. Parmesan cheese, grated (about ½ cup), divided

1. Line 2 large rimmed baking sheets with parchment paper.

2. On a lightly floured surface, unfold 1 puff pastry sheet. Whisk egg in a small bowl until frothy. Stir together paprika, salt, garlic powder, cayenne, and black pepper in a separate small bowl until combined. Brush pastry sheet with some of the egg; sprinkle with half of the cheddar and Parmesan cheeses and half of the paprika mixture. Unfold remaining pastry sheet, and place on top. Brush top with egg; sprinkle with remaining cheeses and remaining paprika mixture.

3. Using a floured rolling pin, roll stacked pastry sheets into a 14- x 10½-inch rectangle. Starting on 1 long side, roll the pastry into a tight spiral, stopping at the middle of the pastry. Starting on the other long side, roll the pastry into a tight spiral, stopping at the middle of the pastry. Brush with egg where the two spirals meet, and gently press together. Using a serrated knife, cut into ½-inch-thick slices. Place 2 inches apart on prepared baking sheets. Refrigerate, uncovered, until chilled, about 15 minutes. Preheat oven to 400°F.

4. Bake in preheated oven, 1 baking sheet at a time, until golden brown and puffed, 15 to 18 minutes per batch. Cool completely, about 15 minutes. Serve.

Cinnamon-Toast Palmiers

(Photo, page 53)

Since you can't have savory without a little sweet, serve these sugary twists alongside their cheesy counterparts.

ACTIVE 15 MIN. · TOTAL 1 HOUR

SERVES 10

All-purpose flour, for rolling

1 (17.3-oz.) pkg. frozen puff pastry, thawed overnight in the refrigerator

1 large egg

¾ cup granulated sugar

1 Tbsp. ground cinnamon

1. Line 2 large rimmed baking sheets with parchment paper.

2. On a lightly floured surface, unfold 1 puff pastry sheet. Whisk egg in a small bowl until frothy. Stir together sugar and cinnamon in a separate small bowl until combined. Brush pastry sheet with some of the egg, and sprinkle with half of the sugar mixture. Unfold remaining pastry sheet, and place on top. Brush top with egg, and sprinkle with remaining sugar mixture.

3. Using a floured rolling pin, roll stacked pastry sheets into a 14- x 10½-inch rectangle. Starting on 1 long side, roll the pastry into a tight spiral, stopping at the middle of the pastry. Starting on the other long side, roll the pastry into a tight spiral, stopping at the middle of the pastry. Brush with egg where the two spirals meet, and gently press together. Using a serrated knife, cut into ½-inch-thick slices. Place 2 inches apart on prepared baking sheets. Refrigerate, uncovered, until chilled, about 15 minutes. Preheat oven to 400°F.

4. Bake in preheated oven, 1 baking sheet at a time, until golden brown and puffed, 15 to 18 minutes per batch. Let cool completely, about 15 minutes. Serve.

STRAWBERRY-ORANGE FOOLS

Strawberry-Orange Fools

Delightfully simple to make, these British-born "fools" are culinary cousins to parfaits. Use fresh orange juice in place of liqueur to make these alcohol free, if preferred.

ACTIVE 40 MIN. - TOTAL 50 MIN.

SERVES 8

- 4 large navel oranges
- 1 lb. fresh strawberries, hulled and thinly sliced (about 3 cups)
- 2 Tbsp. (1 oz.) orange liqueur, optional
- 6 Tbsp. granulated sugar, divided
- 2 cups heavy whipping cream
- 1 (6-inch) vanilla bean, halved lengthwise
- 1 (8-oz.) pkg. crème fraîche or sour cream
- 4 store-bought waffle cones, roughly crushed
  Honey, for topping

1. Cut top and bottom ends off oranges using a serrated knife. Cut off rinds, following the curve of each orange, removing all of outer white pith. Using orange membranes as guides, cut out segments, removing and discarding any seeds. Squeeze juice out of membranes into a small bowl; reserve juice for another use, and discard membranes.
2. Stir together orange segments, strawberries, orange liqueur (if desired), and 4 tablespoons of the sugar in a large bowl until combined. Let mixture stand, undisturbed, until strawberries begin to release their juices, about 10 minutes.
3. Beat cream in a large bowl with an electric mixer on high speed until soft peaks form, 1 to 2 minutes. Scrape seeds from both halves of vanilla bean with the edge of a knife; add seeds to cream mixture, and discard bean. Add crème fraîche or sour cream and remaining 2 tablespoons sugar to cream mixture with vanilla seeds; stir using a spatula until just combined. Beat mixture on high speed with an electric mixer until soft peaks form and mixture thickens slightly, 15 to 30 seconds.
4. Divide about one-third of the strawberry mixture among 8 (8-ounce) glasses; divide about one-third of the whipped cream mixture among glasses, spreading in an even layer over strawberry mixture. Reserve 8 larger pieces of waffle cone for garnish; sprinkle about half of remaining waffle cone pieces into each glass. Repeat layers with one-third of the strawberry mixture, one-third of the whipped cream mixture, and remaining half of the waffle cone pieces. Top with remaining strawberry mixture and whipped cream mixture. Top with 8 reserved large waffle cone pieces and a drizzle of honey. Serve immediately.

Cream Cheese Biscuits

(Photo, page 54)

Along with the butter, cream cheese makes these layered biscuits extra tender. To prepare them ahead, follow the recipe through Step 3 (waiting to use the egg wash and flaky sea salt just before baking). Freeze up to a month. Bake from frozen as directed, adding a few minutes to the time.

ACTIVE 45 MIN. - TOTAL 1 HOUR, 10 MIN.

SERVES 8

- 3½ cups soft wheat all-purpose flour, plus more for work surface
- 2 Tbsp. granulated sugar
- 1 Tbsp. baking powder
- 2 tsp. kosher salt
- ½ tsp. baking soda
- 1 cup cold unsalted butter, cubed
- 4 oz. cold cream cheese (about ½ cup), cut into ¾-inch pieces
- 1 cup cold whole buttermilk
- 1 large egg, beaten
  Flaky sea salt
  Sharp Cheddar Butter (recipe right)
  Quick Strawberry-Ginger Jam (recipe right)

1. Preheat oven to 425°F. Line a large rimmed baking sheet with parchment paper.
2. Whisk together flour, sugar, baking powder, kosher salt, and baking soda in a large bowl. Using a pastry blender or 2 forks, cut in cold butter until pieces are the size of peas. Add cream cheese; use your fingers to gently rub it and the butter into flour mixture in flattened flakes. Stir in cold buttermilk until a crumbly dough forms.
3. Turn out dough onto a lightly floured surface. Pat into a rough square; cut into 4 even portions. Stack dough portions on top of each other; pat down into a square again. Repeat process 3 more times. Pat or roll dough into a 9½-inch square (about ½ inch thick), trimming edges as needed. Cut into 16 squares. Place at least ½ inch apart on prepared baking sheet. Freeze, uncovered, 10 minutes. Brush tops evenly with egg; sprinkle with sea salt.
4. Bake in preheated oven until golden brown, 13 to 15 minutes. Cool on baking sheet on a wire rack 5 minutes. Serve with Sharp Cheddar Butter and Quick Strawberry-Ginger Jam.

Sharp Cheddar Butter

(Photo, page 54)

ACTIVE 5 MIN. - TOTAL 5 MIN.

MAKES ABOUT 1 CUP

- 4 oz. extra-sharp cheddar cheese, grated (about 1 cup)
- ½ cup unsalted butter, at room temperature
- ½ tsp. kosher salt
- ¼ tsp. black pepper

Stir cheese, butter, salt, and pepper in a small bowl until combined. Serve at room temperature. Store in an airtight container in refrigerator for up to 1 week. Let come to room temperature before serving.

Quick Strawberry-Ginger Jam

(Photo, page 55)

Whipping up your own jam from scratch is quite easy, and the flavor is hard to beat.

ACTIVE 45 MIN. - TOTAL 45 MIN., PLUS 2 HOURS COOLING

MAKES ABOUT 1½ CUPS

- 16 oz. fresh strawberries, hulled and quartered (about 2¾ cups)
- 1 cup granulated sugar
- ¼ cup thinly sliced peeled fresh ginger (from 1 [2-inch] piece)
- 2 Tbsp. fresh lime juice (from 1 large lime)

1. Add strawberries, sugar, and ginger to a medium saucepan. Mash mixture with a potato masher to break up strawberries.
2. Bring mixture to a boil over medium-high. Boil, stirring often, for 10 minutes. Stir in lime juice, and cook, stirring constantly, until mixture returns to a boil and is thickened enough to coat the back of the spoon, about 10 minutes.
3. Remove jam from heat, and transfer to a heatproof jar or bowl. Let cool to room temperature, about 2 hours. Store, covered, in refrigerator for up to 10 days.

SUPPERTIME

What a Ham

Slice after slice, this showstopper makes dinners easier all week long

HONEY-GLAZED HAM

Honey-Glazed Ham
ACTIVE 25 MIN. - TOTAL 2 HOURS, 55 MIN.
SERVES 10

- 1 (9- to 10-lb.) fully cooked bone-in spiral-cut half ham
- 1 cup orange marmalade
- ⅔ cup orange blossom honey
- ¼ cup rice vinegar
- 1 Tbsp. chopped fresh thyme, plus sprigs for garnish
- 2 tsp. grated fresh ginger
- 1 tsp. kosher salt
- ½ tsp. black pepper
- Oranges, tangerines, and kumquats (optional)

1. Preheat oven to 350°F. Let ham stand at room temperature 30 minutes. Line a roasting pan with aluminum foil; top with an ovenproof rack. For glaze, stir together marmalade, honey, vinegar, thyme, ginger, salt, and pepper in a small bowl.

2. Place ham on rack in prepared pan; brush ⅔ cup of the glaze over ham and in between slices. Turn ham fat side down, with bone running parallel to bottom of pan, and pour 3 cups water into pan. Cover tightly with foil. Bake in preheated oven 1½ hours.

3. Remove from oven; remove and discard foil. Baste with pan drippings; brush ⅓ cup of the glaze over ham and in between slices. Return to oven, and bake at 350°F until a thermometer inserted in thickest portion of ham registers 140°F, 30 to 40 minutes, basting ham with pan drippings and brushing with ⅓ cup of the glaze about every 10 minutes. Remove from oven; reserve drippings for **Bourbon-Glazed Ham Steaks** (page 63). Carefully transfer ham to a serving platter. Garnish with fresh thyme sprigs, sliced oranges, halved tangerines, and kumquats, if desired. Store leftover ham in an airtight container in refrigerator up to 10 days.

Crispy-Ham Carbonara with Peas

ACTIVE 25 MIN. - TOTAL 25 MIN.
SERVES 4

- 3 oz. Parmigiano-Reggiano cheese, grated (about ¾ cup), plus more for garnish
- 3 oz. Pecorino Romano cheese, grated (about ¾ cup)
- 7 large egg yolks
- ½ tsp. black pepper
- 1 (16-oz.) pkg. spaghetti
- 2 Tbsp. olive oil
- 8 oz. leftover Honey-Glazed Ham (opposite), diced (about 1½ cups)
- 1 cup fresh or frozen sweet peas
- 1 medium shallot, thinly sliced (about ⅓ cup)
- 2 tsp. finely chopped garlic (from 2 cloves)
- ½ cup chopped fresh mixed tender herbs (such as basil, tarragon, and/or chives), plus leaves for garnish

1. Bring a medium pot of salted water to a boil over high. Whisk together cheeses, egg yolks, and pepper in a medium bowl until combined; set aside.

2. Add pasta to boiling water; cook, stirring occasionally, until pasta is cooked according to package directions for al dente, 7 to 8 minutes. Drain pasta in a colander over a bowl, reserving 1 cup of the cooking water. Return drained pasta to pot, and let cool 3 minutes.

3. While pasta cooks, heat oil in a large nonstick skillet over medium-high. Add ham; cook, stirring every 2 minutes, until browned, about 6 minutes. Add peas, shallot, and garlic; cook, stirring occasionally, until peas are just tender, about 2 minutes. Remove from heat.

4. Ladle ⅓ cup of the reserved cooking water into egg mixture; whisk until blended. Whisk in another ⅓ cup cooking water to loosen the egg mixture. Quickly and gently toss egg mixture into cooked pasta so eggs don't scramble. Continue tossing gently until cheeses are melted and a creamy sauce forms and coats pasta, about 1 minute. Add chopped fresh herbs and ham mixture; toss gently to combine.

5. Divide pasta mixture among 4 plates. Garnish with additional herb leaves and grated cheese.

HOT TIP
Residual heat from the pasta and its salty, starchy water gently cooks the eggs, creating a creamy sauce.

Ham-and-Cabbage Gratin

ACTIVE 30 MIN. · TOTAL 1 HOUR, 10 MIN.
SERVES 4

- 12 oz. multicolored fingerling potatoes, halved lengthwise (about 8 small potatoes)
- 1 tsp. kosher salt, divided
- 1 medium head green cabbage, tough outer leaves removed
- 2 Tbsp. olive oil
- 1½ cups heavy whipping cream
- 1½ Tbsp. Dijon mustard
- 2 tsp. fresh thyme leaves, plus more for garnish
- ½ tsp. grated garlic (1 clove)
- ¼ tsp. cayenne pepper
- 1 oz. Parmesan cheese, grated (about ¼ cup)
- 1 cup chopped leftover Honey-Glazed Ham (page 60)

1. Preheat oven to 400°F. Place potatoes, 2 tablespoons water, and ¼ teaspoon of the salt in a medium-size microwave-safe bowl; cover with plastic wrap. Microwave on HIGH until potatoes are partially cooked, about 4 minutes. Carefully remove plastic wrap; drain potatoes, and set aside.
2. Meanwhile, stand the cabbage stem side down, and cut it in half through the core. Cut 1 cabbage half into 4 wedges, keeping core intact. Reserve remaining half for another use.
3. Heat oil in a large, deep cast-iron skillet over medium-high until shimmering. Sprinkle cabbage wedges with ½ teaspoon of the salt. Add cabbage wedges to skillet, and cook, turning once, until charred, 8 to 10 minutes per side. Remove from heat.
4. While cabbage cooks, whisk together cream, Dijon, thyme, garlic, cayenne pepper, and remaining ¼ teaspoon salt. Nestle potatoes around cabbage wedges; re-whisk cream mixture, and pour over cabbage and potatoes. Sprinkle with Parmesan.
5. Bake in preheated oven until cabbage is tender and cream mixture has thickened, about 25 minutes, sprinkling with chopped ham halfway through bake time. Remove from oven, and let cool slightly, about 10 minutes. Sprinkle with more thyme before serving.

HEADS UP
Don't let leftover cabbage go to waste. Shred it to use as a topping for tacos, or chop it up and simmer with chicken stock, garlic, white beans, and diced tomatoes for a hearty soup.

Bourbon-Glazed Ham Steaks

ACTIVE 25 MIN. - TOTAL 25 MIN.
SERVES 4

- 2 Tbsp. olive oil
- 8 (3-oz.) leftover Honey-Glazed Ham slices (page 60)
- 3 Tbsp. cold unsalted butter, cut into pieces, divided
- 1 small shallot, finely chopped (about 2 Tbsp.)
- 2 garlic cloves, finely chopped (about 1 tsp.)
- ½ tsp. black pepper
- ⅓ cup bourbon
- 1 cup reserved Honey-Glazed Ham drippings or lower-sodium chicken stock
- 1 Tbsp. whole-grain mustard

1. Heat oil in a large cast-iron skillet over medium-high. Add 4 of the ham slices to skillet; cook until browned, 1½ to 2 minutes per side. Remove from skillet, and transfer to a small rimmed baking sheet. Cover with aluminum foil to keep warm. Repeat with remaining 4 ham slices. Wipe skillet clean.

2. Melt 1 tablespoon of the butter in skillet over medium-high. Add shallot, garlic, and pepper; cook, stirring constantly, until softened and fragrant, about 30 seconds. Remove skillet from heat; add bourbon. Return skillet to heat; cook, stirring constantly, until reduced by half, about 15 seconds. Add Honey-Glazed Ham drippings and mustard; bring to a simmer over medium-high. Continue simmering, stirring occasionally, until reduced by half, 5 to 6 minutes. Swirl in the remaining 2 tablespoons butter until melted, about 1 minute.

3. Divide warm ham slices among 4 plates. Spoon bourbon glaze evenly over ham, and serve with **Spring Vegetable Sauté** (recipe right).

Spring Vegetable Sauté

ACTIVE 20 MIN. - TOTAL 20 MIN.
SERVES 4

Melt 2 Tbsp. **butter** in a large skillet over medium-high. Add 2½ cups peeled, trimmed, and halved **multicolored carrots** cut into 2-inch pieces; 1½ cups halved or quartered **radishes**; 2 tsp. **granulated sugar**; ¾ tsp. **kosher salt**; and ¼ tsp. **black pepper**. Stir to combine. Cover; cook, stirring occasionally, until carrots are tender-crisp, about 8 minutes. Uncover; add 1 cup trimmed and halved **snow peas**. Cook over medium-high, stirring often, 1 minute. Add 1 cup **fresh** or **frozen sweet peas** and 1 Tbsp. **butter**; cook, stirring often, until peas are warmed through and butter is melted, about 1 minute. Remove from heat; stir in 2 tsp. **fresh lemon juice** and 2 Tbsp. chopped **fresh chives**. Garnish with additional **chives** before serving.

Easy Chicken Cordon Bleu
ACTIVE 45 MIN. - TOTAL 45 MIN.
SERVES 4

- 4 (7-oz.) boneless, skinless chicken breasts
- 1½ tsp. kosher salt, divided, plus more for sprinkling
- ½ tsp. black pepper, divided
- 4 (1-oz.) Swiss cheese slices, each cut into 3 strips
- 4 (1-oz.) leftover Honey-Glazed Ham slices (page 60), halved lengthwise
- ¼ cup all-purpose flour
- 1 large egg, beaten
- 1½ cups panko breadcrumbs
- Canola oil, for frying
- Herby Dijonnaise (recipe right)

1. Preheat oven to 350°F. Place an oven-safe wire rack inside a rimmed baking sheet, and set aside. Place chicken between 2 pieces of parchment paper; use a rolling pin to flatten to about ¼-inch thickness.
2. Place chicken breasts, smooth sides down, on a plate. Sprinkle evenly with ½ teaspoon of the salt and ¼ teaspoon of the pepper. Place 3 Swiss cheese strips crosswise in the center of each chicken breast; place ham slices on top of cheese. Fold each chicken breast in thirds, like an envelope, over ham and cheese to seal; secure with wooden picks.
3. Place flour, egg, and panko in 3 separate wide, shallow bowls. Stir remaining 1 teaspoon salt and ¼ teaspoon pepper into panko. Working with 1 chicken breast at a time, dredge in flour, and shake off excess. Dip in egg, letting excess drip off. Dredge in panko to coat, pressing to adhere. Place on prepared wire rack.
4. Pour oil to a depth of ¼ inch in a large skillet, and heat over medium. Working in 2 batches, place breaded chicken in hot oil; fry until golden brown, 2 to 4 minutes per side. Return chicken to prepared rack.
5. Bake in preheated oven until chicken is cooked through, 5 to 7 minutes. Remove from oven; lightly sprinkle with additional salt. Remove and discard wooden picks. Serve chicken with Herby Dijonnaise.

Herby Dijonnaise
ACTIVE 5 MIN. - TOTAL 5 MIN.
MAKES ABOUT 1 CUP

Whisk together ⅓ cup each **mayonnaise** and **sour cream**, ¼ cup chopped **fresh tender herbs** (such as chives, tarragon, and flat-leaf parsley), ¼ cup **buttermilk**, 3 Tbsp. **Dijon mustard**, and ¼ tsp. each **kosher salt** and **black pepper** in a bowl. Cover and refrigerate until ready to serve.

64 2024 MARCH

OVER EASY

Pop Stars

Ditch the mix, and make these lemony treats from scratch

Lemon-Poppy Seed Muffins
ACTIVE 20 MIN. - TOTAL 1 HOUR
MAKES 12

- 2½ cups all-purpose flour
- 2 Tbsp. poppy seeds
- 2 tsp. baking powder
- ½ tsp. baking soda
- ½ tsp. kosher salt
- 1 cup granulated sugar
- 1 cup canola oil
- ½ cup sour cream
- ½ cup whole buttermilk
- 1 tsp. vanilla extract
- 2 large eggs
- 2 Tbsp. grated lemon zest, plus 3 Tbsp. fresh juice (from 2 lemons), divided
- 2 Tbsp. sliced almonds
- 1¼ cups powdered sugar, divided

1. Preheat oven to 400°F. Line a 12-cup muffin tray with paper liners; set aside.
2. Whisk together flour, poppy seeds, baking powder, baking soda, and salt in a large bowl until smooth. In a medium bowl, whisk granulated sugar, oil, sour cream, buttermilk, vanilla, eggs, lemon zest, and 1 tablespoon of the lemon juice until well combined. Gently fold sugar mixture into flour mixture until just combined, being careful not to overmix. Spoon batter into prepared wells, about ⅓ cup per well. Sprinkle batter evenly with sliced almonds.
3. Bake in preheated oven until tops are light golden and a wooden pick inserted in centers comes out clean, 18 to 20 minutes. Remove from oven, and let cool in muffin tray for 5 minutes. Remove muffins from tray, and let cool on a wire rack 15 minutes.
4. Meanwhile, whisk together 1 cup of the powdered sugar and remaining 2 tablespoons lemon juice in a medium bowl until smooth, about 45 seconds. For a slightly thicker glaze, whisk in remaining ¼ cup powdered sugar, 1 tablespoon at a time, until mixture reaches desired consistency. Drizzle over cooled muffins.

LIGHTEN UP

Think Outside the Box

Mac and cheese with about half the fat—and did we mention it has bacon?

Macaroni and Cheese with Caramelized Onions
ACTIVE 55 MIN. · TOTAL 1 HOUR, 30 MIN.
SERVES 10

- 3 center-cut bacon slices, chopped
- ¼ cup unsalted butter
- 4 cups chopped yellow onions (about 3 medium onions)
- 4 cups whole milk
- 2½ tsp. kosher salt
- 2 tsp. Dijon mustard
- 2 tsp. Worcestershire sauce
- 1 tsp. garlic powder
- ¼ tsp. black pepper
- ¼ tsp. ground turmeric
- 2 Tbsp. cornstarch
- 2 Tbsp. cold water
- 6 oz. extra-sharp yellow cheddar cheese, shredded (about 1½ cups), divided
- 6 oz. Gruyère cheese, shredded (about 1½ cups), divided
- 1 lb. chickpea pasta (such as Banza), cooked according to package directions for al dente
- 2 Tbsp. chopped fresh chives

1. Preheat oven to 350°F with oven rack about 8 inches from heat source. Lightly coat a broiler-safe 13- x 9-inch baking dish with cooking spray; set aside. Cook bacon in a large Dutch oven over medium, stirring occasionally, until crisp, about 6 minutes. Using a slotted spoon, transfer bacon to a paper towel–lined plate, reserving drippings in Dutch oven.
2. Add butter to reserved bacon drippings, stirring over medium heat until melted. Add onions; cook, stirring occasionally, until onions are soft, 5 to 7 minutes. Reduce heat to medium-low; cook, stirring occasionally, until onions turn golden brown, 30 to 35 minutes (stir in a splash of water if onions begin to stick).
3. Add milk, salt, Dijon mustard, Worcestershire sauce, garlic powder, black pepper, and ground turmeric to onions in Dutch oven. Bring to a simmer over medium; cook, stirring occasionally, about 5 minutes. Whisk together cornstarch and cold water in a small bowl. Drizzle cornstarch mixture into onion mixture; cook, whisking constantly, until thickened, about 2 minutes. Remove from heat, and gradually add 1¼ cups each of the cheddar and Gruyère cheeses, whisking constantly until melted and smooth, about 2 minutes. Stir in cooked pasta; pour mixture into prepared baking dish.
4. Bake in preheated oven until bubbly and golden, 20 to 25 minutes. Remove from oven; increase oven temperature to broil. Sprinkle evenly with remaining ¼ cup each cheddar and Gruyère cheeses; broil until cheeses are melted and golden, 3 to 4 minutes. Remove from oven; cool slightly on a wire rack, about 10 minutes. Sprinkle with chives and bacon just before serving.

Before Recipe Makeover:
CALORIES: **636** – FAT: **42 G** – FIBER: **2 G**

After Recipe Makeover:
CALORIES: **425** – FAT: **22 G** – FIBER: **7 G**

SNACK TIME

Green Eggs and...Prosciutto

Amp up the flavor (and fun) of this go-to appetizer

Pesto Deviled Eggs
ACTIVE 20 MIN. - TOTAL 20 MIN.
SERVES 6

- 1 (½-oz.) prosciutto slice
- 1 Tbsp. toasted pecans
- 1 garlic clove, coarsely chopped (about ½ tsp.)
- 1 cup firmly packed fresh basil leaves, plus more for garnish
- 1 oz. Parmesan cheese, finely shredded (about ⅓ cup)
- 1½ Tbsp. extra-virgin olive oil
- ¼ tsp. grated lemon zest, plus 1½ tsp. fresh juice (from 1 lemon), divided
- 6 hard-cooked large eggs, peeled
- 1 Tbsp. mayonnaise
- ¼ tsp. kosher salt
- Crushed red pepper

1. Preheat oven to 350°F. Place prosciutto on a parchment paper–lined baking sheet. Bake until just crispy, about 10 minutes. Set aside to cool slightly, about 5 minutes. Break into 12 pieces; set aside.
2. While prosciutto bakes, combine pecans and garlic in a food processor; pulse until finely chopped, about 5 seconds. Add basil, Parmesan, oil, and zest. Process until mostly smooth, about 20 seconds, stopping to scrape down sides as needed.
3. Cut eggs in half lengthwise, and remove yolks; set egg whites aside. Using a fork, mash together yolks and mayonnaise in a small bowl. Add pesto, lemon juice, and salt; stir well to combine.
4. Spoon or pipe egg yolk mixture into egg white halves. Top with prosciutto pieces; garnish with crushed red pepper and additional basil, if desired. Serve immediately, or store, covered, in refrigerator up to 1 day.

COOKING SCHOOL

TIPS AND TRICKS FROM THE SOUTH'S MOST TRUSTED KITCHEN

Sticky Cake Layers No More!
Stop tracing circles. Break out the parchment paper, and try this clever technique

1

Start with a piece of parchment paper slightly larger than the cake pan. Fold it in half and then in half again to make a rectangle.

2

Fold the rectangle in half to make a triangle. Then repeat to create an even narrower triangle (one end may be uneven).

3

Place the narrow end of triangle in the center of an upside-down cake pan. Trim outer edge of triangle where edge of pan meets parchment.

4

Unfold to reveal a circle. Nestle the parchment into the bottom of a greased pan; coat with baking spray, and proceed with your recipe.

THE BEST WAY TO TEST BAKED GOODS

Hint: It's not a toothpick

A thermometer is a quick and accurate tool to tell if a cake (or brownies or muffins) is fully baked—no guesswork involved. Simply insert the probe halfway through its center, making sure not to touch the bottom of the pan. The middle should register around 200°F, with the exception of denser pound cakes, which should reach 210°F to ensure doneness. And if there are a few moist crumbs stuck to your thermometer, there's no need to worry—that's exactly what you want to see.

ThermoPop 2 thermometers, from $35 each; *thermoworks.com*

April

70 Think Pink Watermelon radishes brighten dishes with their color and peppery flavor. Enjoy them while they're peaking

71 Waffle Around Try this simple technique for the crispiest breakfast potatoes ever

72 A Southern-Style Seder Laurence Faber and Emily Williams set the table for Knoxville's Jewish community

76 Baby Cakes Make a big impression at your next party with these adorably petite desserts

82 Spring Treasures The joys of this season are as fleeting as cherry blossoms. This is especially true at the farmers' market, where you'll find the assortment of fresh produce changing from week to week

90 Kick the Can A homemade filling gives this classic side a wholesome boost

91 Worth the Wait For Lisa van der Reijden, it wouldn't be Easter without her mother's late-night soup

92 Spring Sizzle Break out your trusty skillet to whip up something tasty

95 A Culinary Guide to Jazz Fest Come for the music, and stay for the foods you won't find anywhere else

97 Batter Up A layer of creamy cheesecake takes brownies to a delicious new level

98 The Gift of Pudding A secret ingredient makes this banana dessert celebration worthy

100 Cooking School Our Test Kitchen professionals show you how to organize your fridge for maximum efficiency and freshness

BOUNTY

Think Pink

Watermelon radishes brighten dishes with their color and peppery flavor.
Enjoy them while they're peaking

Watermelon Radish Salad with Brown Butter Vinaigrette
ACTIVE 20 MIN. - TOTAL 25 MIN.
SERVES 4

Melt 5 Tbsp. **unsalted butter** in a medium stainless-steel skillet over medium, stirring constantly, until golden brown, 4 to 6 minutes. Pour 3 Tbsp. brown butter into a large bowl; reserve remaining butter in skillet. Return skillet to medium-low heat; add 6 **watermelon radishes** (peeled, trimmed, and cut into wedges) and 1 tsp. **kosher salt.** Cook, stirring often, until radishes are lightly browned and just tender, 3 to 4 minutes. Let cool 5 minutes. Add 3 Tbsp. each **olive oil** and **champagne vinegar,** 1 Tbsp. **honey,** 1 tsp. **Dijon mustard,** and ½ tsp. **kosher salt** to reserved brown butter in bowl; whisk until smooth and combined. Divide 2 (5-oz.) pkg. **Little Gem lettuce** evenly among 4 plates. Top evenly with ½ cup chopped **toasted pecans,** ½ cup shaved **Pecorino Romano cheese,** and cooked radishes. Serve with dressing.

WATERMELON RADISH SALAD WITH BROWN BUTTER VINAIGRETTE

Avocado Toasts with Watermelon Radishes and Herbs
ACTIVE 10 MIN. - TOTAL 10 MIN.
SERVES 4

Stir together ¼ cup each **extra-virgin olive oil,** chopped **fresh mint,** and chopped **fresh parsley;** 1 Tbsp. **lemon juice;** ½ tsp. minced **garlic;** and ¼ tsp. each **crushed red pepper** and **kosher salt** in a small bowl until combined. Gently mash together 2 **medium avocados,** 1½ Tbsp. **lemon juice,** and ½ tsp. **kosher salt** in a medium bowl. Brush 1 side of 4 toasted **sourdough bread** slices with some of the herb oil. Top evenly with mashed avocado mixture and 1 cup thin **watermelon radish** slices (from 4 peeled radishes). Drizzle with more herb oil, and garnish with fresh mint leaves, if desired.

AVOCADO TOASTS WITH WATERMELON RADISHES AND HERBS

OVER EASY

Waffle Around

Try this simple technique for the crispiest breakfast potatoes ever

Waffle Iron Hash Browns with Fried Eggs
ACTIVE 20 MIN. - TOTAL 50 MIN.
SERVES 8

- 1 (30-oz.) pkg. frozen shredded hash browns, thawed
- 1½ cups matchstick carrots (from 1 [10-oz.] pkg.)
- ¾ cup thinly sliced large scallions (about 3 large)
- 2 Tbsp. cornstarch
- 1½ tsp. garlic powder
- ½ tsp. black pepper
- ½ cup, plus 2 Tbsp. canola or peanut oil, divided, plus more for waffle iron
- 2½ tsp. kosher salt, divided
- 8 large eggs
- 4 oz. feta cheese, crumbled (about 1 cup)
- ¼ cup finely chopped fresh herbs (such as dill, chives, and mint)

1. Preheat a 4-square Belgian waffle iron to medium and an oven to 200°F. Squeeze out any excess moisture from thawed hash browns, and place in a large bowl. Add carrots, scallions, cornstarch, garlic powder, black pepper, ½ cup of the oil, and 2 teaspoons of the salt; toss to coat.
2. Lightly brush preheated waffle iron with oil. Scoop about ⅔ cup hash brown mixture into each well, spreading in an even layer.
3. Close appliance tightly, and cook until golden and crispy, 15 to 17 minutes. Gently transfer cooked hash browns to a baking sheet; keep warm in preheated oven. Brush waffle iron with oil; repeat procedure with remaining hash brown mixture.
4. While second batch of hash browns cooks, heat 1 tablespoon of the oil in a medium nonstick skillet over medium. Crack 4 of the eggs into skillet, and sprinkle with ¼ teaspoon of the salt. Cover and cook until desired degree of doneness (2 to 3 minutes for over easy). Repeat with remaining 1 tablespoon oil, 4 eggs, and ¼ teaspoon salt.
5. Top each hash brown waffle with a cooked egg; sprinkle evenly with crumbled feta and fresh herbs. Serve immediately.

PASSOVER TRADITIONS

A Southern-Style Seder

Laurence Faber and Emily Williams set the table for Knoxville's Jewish community

"**I WAS OBSESSED** with food as a kid but grew up thinking most Jewish dishes were gross," says Laurence Faber, chef at Knoxville's Potchke deli, which he co-owns with his wife, Emily Williams. Back then, he was more interested in things like hummus and falafel than the traditional Ashkenazi recipes like strudel, vareniki (dumplings), eggplant salad, and matzo ball soup that were handed down by his great-grandmother, who came to America from the border of Moldova and Ukraine in 1921. "She passed away when I was a couple years old, so I never got to actually taste her cooking," Faber says. Nevertheless, the dishes that she made were cherished by his family and ultimately guided him on his culinary journey.

A Memphis native, Faber grew up immersed in the Jewish community, but when it came to customs like keeping kosher, his family wasn't strict—except for on holidays. "I've always loved Passover because it is the most food oriented," Faber says. The eight-day celebration starts with cleansing the home of all hametz (foods or drinks containing leavening agents) and bringing in the matzo, followed by the Seder, a special meal typically held on the first and second nights. "My family would always go to my uncle Richard's house for the Seder, set up a giant table in the living room, and gather around to read the Haggadah [which includes the retelling of the Jewish people's exodus from Egypt]," he says. "The meal would end with all the kids running around the house searching for the afikomen (hidden piece of matzo)."

Faber found his place in the kitchen at a young age and was self-taught from hours spent watching the Food Network and poring over cookbooks. "I started cooking more when my mom went to night school to finish college," he recalls. "I'd print out a recipe, she'd buy the ingredients, and my brother and I would make a meal." After moving to Knoxville for college, Faber lost touch with some Jewish traditions. A string of restaurant jobs meant he had to work weekend nights and often couldn't join in celebrations.

Eventually, he landed a position as a pastry chef at Blackberry Farm, where he honed his skills, explored new ingredients, and met influential Jewish guest chefs like Alon Shaya, Zachary Engel, and Michael Solomonov. "I became super interested in cooking Jewish food, because it was my heritage, and started teaching myself more about other areas of the cuisine," he says.

In 2022, he and Williams opened Potchke (he says the Yiddish name loosely translates "to mess around" or "to make a fuss" in the kitchen), and they look forward to Passover each year. They even celebrated Williams' first Seder with customers who have become friends. "It's been rewarding to see people use our restaurant as a Jewish community space," says Williams.

Here, Faber shares an approachable Seder menu that combines old and new ingredients and techniques, with brisket as the star of the show. "Every Jewish family has a secret recipe for that," he says. "Each Passover, there's going to be a brisket, but it's always a little bit different."

Leafy Green Salad with Sunflower Seed Dressing

ACTIVE 20 MIN. - TOTAL 20 MIN.
SERVES 8

SUNFLOWER SEED DRESSING
- 1 cup loosely packed mixed tender herbs (such as flat-leaf parsley, cilantro, and dill)
- ⅔ cup unrefined sunflower oil* or extra-virgin olive oil
- ¼ cup salted roasted sunflower seeds*
- ¼ cup apple cider vinegar
- 1 Tbsp. fresh lemon juice
- 2 tsp. honey
- 1 tsp. kosher salt
- 1 tsp. whole-grain mustard*

SALAD
- 10 cups mixed salad greens
- 1 tsp. kosher salt, divided
- 1½ cups loosely packed mixed tender herbs (such as tarragon, flat-leaf parsley, cilantro, and dill), chopped
- 6 radishes, sliced into wedges (about 1½ cups)
- ¾ cup thinly sliced spring onions or baby Vidalia onions
- 2 Tbsp. fresh lemon juice

1. Prepare the Sunflower Seed Dressing: Process herbs, oil, sunflower seeds, vinegar, lemon juice, honey, salt, and mustard in a blender until smooth, about 45 seconds.
2. Prepare the Salad: Toss greens with ½ teaspoon of the salt and about ⅓ cup Sunflower Seed Dressing in a large bowl until coated. In a medium mixing bowl, stir together herbs, radishes, onions, lemon juice, and remaining ½ teaspoon salt. Add one-third of dressed greens to a large bowl, and top with one-third of herb mixture; repeat layers 2 times. Serve immediately.
*Sunflower seeds and mustard aren't kosher for Passover for those who strictly observe (per the Orthodox Union).

Sweet-and-Sour Braised Beef Brisket

ACTIVE 45 MIN. - TOTAL 7 HOURS, 45 MIN., PLUS 8 HOURS CHILLING
SERVES 8

- 1 (6- to 7-lb.) flat-cut beef brisket, trimmed
- 2 Tbsp. olive oil
- 1 Tbsp. Hungarian paprika
- 1 tsp. black pepper
- 2 Tbsp. kosher salt, divided, plus more to taste
- 1 large yellow onion, roughly chopped (about 2½ cups)
- 3 medium carrots, peeled and cut into 1-inch pieces (about 1½ cups)
- 3 large celery stalks, cut into 1-inch pieces (about 2 cups)
- 3 garlic cloves, cut in half
- 2 cups beef stock
- 1 (15-oz.) can crushed tomatoes
- 1 cup kosher grape juice
- ¼ cup apple cider vinegar, plus more to taste
- 2 Tbsp. golden raisins
- 2 fresh bay leaves
- 2 Tbsp., plus ½ cup raisins, divided

1. Preheat oven to 400°F. Pat brisket dry with paper towels; rub evenly with oil. Generously coat brisket with paprika, pepper, and 1 tablespoon of the salt; place in a large roasting pan. Roast until browned on both sides, about 30 minutes, turning once halfway through cook time.
2. Remove from oven; add onion, carrots, celery, and garlic to pan. Top with stock, tomatoes, grape juice, vinegar, golden raisins, bay leaves, remaining 1 tablespoon kosher salt, and 2 tablespoons of the raisins. Reduce oven to 325°F, and cover roasting pan tightly with foil. Bake, covered, 3 hours. Remove foil, and bake, uncovered, until brisket is very tender, about 1 hour. (The meat should give very little resistance when poked with a fork.) Remove from oven, uncover, and let cool slightly, about 1 hour. Chill, loosely covered, until cooled completely, at least 8 hours or up to 24 hours.
3. Preheat oven to 250°F. Remove and discard layer of fat on the surface and any vegetables clinging to fat. Process vegetables and liquid from pan in a blender until very smooth, 1 to 2 minutes. Place mixture in a saucepan; bring to a simmer over medium, stirring occasionally. Stir in remaining ½ cup raisins. Taste sauce, and add salt and/or vinegar, as desired.
4. Place brisket on a cutting board, and slice down the middle lengthwise. Cut each half into ½- to ¾-inch-thick slices. Pour a layer of the sauce (about 3 cups) into a roasting pan. Top with brisket slices, and ladle remaining sauce over brisket. Cover tightly with aluminum foil. Reheat in preheated oven until warmed through, about 1 hour. Uncover, and cook until top caramelizes slightly, about 30 minutes. Serve with sauce.

Charoset

ACTIVE 10 MIN. - TOTAL 40 MIN.
SERVES 8

- 3 medium Honeycrisp apples
- 3 medium Granny Smith apples
- 1 Tbsp. fresh lemon juice
- 2 cups kosher grape juice
- 1¾ cups toasted pecans, chopped
- 1½ Tbsp. honey
- 1 tsp. ground cinnamon
- ½ tsp. kosher salt

1. Grate apples on large holes of a box grater or a food processor fitted with a large shredding disk. Transfer grated apples to a large bowl, and immediately stir in lemon juice, tossing to coat.
2. Stir in grape juice, pecans, honey, cinnamon, and salt. Let stand 30 minutes. Serve, or store in an airtight container in refrigerator up to 2 days.

Potato Kugel with Schmaltzy Onions

ACTIVE 45 MIN. - TOTAL 2 HOURS
SERVES 8

- 4 Tbsp. schmaltz (rendered chicken fat) or olive oil, divided
- 3 large Vidalia onions, thinly sliced (about 9 cups)
- 3 fresh bay leaves
- 1 tsp., plus 1 Tbsp. kosher salt, divided
- 3 large Yukon Gold potatoes
- 3 medium russet potatoes
- 3 Tbsp. unsalted matzo meal or potato flour
- 4 large eggs
- 1 tsp. black pepper

POTATO KUGEL WITH SCHMALTZY ONIONS

1. Heat 2 tablespoons of the schmaltz in a large skillet over medium. Add onions, bay leaves, and 1 teaspoon of the salt. Cook, stirring occasionally, until onions soften and are starting to brown, 15 to 20 minutes. Reduce heat to medium-low; cook, stirring occasionally, until onions begin to turn golden brown, about 15 minutes. Remove from heat, and set aside. Let cool slightly, about 5 minutes. Remove and reserve bay leaves; set aside. Preheat oven to 400°F.
2. While onions cook, peel potatoes. Using large holes of a box grater or a food processor fitted with a grating disk, grate potatoes; immediately transfer potatoes to a large bowl of cold water to keep them from turning brown. Transfer potatoes to a colander, and let drain 5 minutes. Transfer drained potatoes to a baking sheet lined with several layers of paper towels, and press dry with additional paper towels.
3. Stir together potatoes, caramelized onions, matzo meal, eggs, pepper, remaining 2 tablespoons schmaltz, and remaining 1 tablespoon salt until well combined. Coat an 11- x 7-inch or 2½-quart baking dish with cooking spray. Transfer potato mixture to prepared dish, pressing gently into an even layer. Arrange reserved bay leaves on top.
4. Place dish on a rimmed baking sheet, and transfer to preheated oven; reduce oven temperature to 375°F. Bake, uncovered, until lightly browned on top and potatoes are tender, 50 minutes to 1 hour. Let stand 15 minutes before serving.

Baby Cakes
Make a big impression at your next party with these adorably petite desserts

ITTY-BITTY LEMON CAKES WITH LAVENDER GLAZE (PAGE 81)

Tiny Caramel Cakes
ACTIVE 35 MIN. - TOTAL 1 HOUR, PLUS 1 HOUR, 10 MIN. COOLING
MAKES 6

CAKES
- Baking spray
- 1⅓ cups all-purpose flour
- 1 tsp. baking powder
- ½ tsp. kosher salt
- ⅔ cup unsalted butter, at room temperature
- 1 cup granulated sugar
- 1 large egg, at room temperature
- 1 large egg yolk, at room temperature
- 2 tsp. vanilla extract
- ⅓ cup whole milk, at room temperature

TOPPING
- ¾ cup packed dark brown sugar
- ¼ cup heavy whipping cream
- 3 Tbsp. unsalted butter, softened
- ½ tsp. kosher salt
- Flaky sea salt (such as Maldon)

1. Prepare the Cakes: Preheat oven to 350°F. Coat a 6-cup mini Bundt tray with baking spray; set aside.
2. Whisk together flour, baking powder, and kosher salt in a medium bowl; set aside. Beat butter and granulated sugar with a hand mixer in a large bowl on medium-high speed until light and fluffy, about 3 minutes. Add egg and egg yolk, 1 at a time, beating until combined after each addition. Beat in vanilla until combined, about 30 seconds. Gradually add flour mixture in thirds, alternating with milk, beating just until combined after each addition and stopping to scrape down sides as needed.
3. Divide batter evenly among prepared wells in Bundt tray (about ½ cup each); smooth tops using the back of a spoon. Firmly tap tray on counter several times to release any large air bubbles.
4. Bake in preheated oven until a wooden pick inserted in center comes out clean, 15 to 20 minutes. Let Cakes cool in tray on a wire rack 10 minutes. Remove from tray; let cool completely on wire rack, 1 to 2 hours.
5. Prepare the Topping: When Cakes are cool, add brown sugar, cream, butter, and kosher salt to a small saucepan. Bring to a boil over medium-high, stirring often. Reduce heat to medium-low, and cook, stirring often, 1 minute. Remove from heat; transfer Topping to a small heatproof bowl, and let cool slightly, uncovered, at room temperature 10 minutes. Spoon Topping over cooled Cakes as desired. Garnish each Cake with sea salt.

Double Up: To make a dozen cakes, line a 12-cup muffin tray with paper liners. Fill each well with 3 tablespoons batter. Reduce bake time to 12 to 15 minutes.

How To Assemble Mini Layer Cakes

1. After sheet cake has cooled completely, cut into 24 rounds using a 2½-inch cookie cutter. Transfer rounds to a plate or other clean work surface. Reserve cake scraps for a sundae topping, or use in a parfait.

2. Place buttercream in a piping bag fitted with the tip of your choice. (We used a ½-inch fluted open star tip.) Pipe an even layer of buttercream on the tops of half of the cake rounds.

3. Cover each buttercream-topped round with an unfrosted cake round; pipe buttercream on top of each stack as desired. Garnish frosted cakes with toasted coconut.

Little Carrot Layer Cakes with Coconut Buttercream

ACTIVE 40 MIN. - TOTAL 55 MIN., PLUS 1 HOUR COOLING
MAKES 12

CAKE
- 2¼ cups all-purpose flour
- 1 cup packed light brown sugar
- ½ cup sweetened shredded coconut
- ¼ cup granulated sugar
- 2 tsp. baking soda
- 2 tsp. ground cinnamon
- ¾ tsp. kosher salt
- ½ tsp. ground ginger
- ¼ tsp. ground nutmeg
- 3 large eggs, at room temperature
- 1 cup canola oil
- ½ cup whole milk
- 1½ cups shredded carrots (from 2 large peeled carrots)
- ⅓ cup finely chopped toasted walnuts
- ⅓ cup golden raisins, finely chopped

COCONUT BUTTERCREAM
- 1½ cups unsalted butter, softened
- 2½ tsp. vanilla extract
- ½ tsp. kosher salt
- ½ tsp. coconut extract (optional)
- 6 cups powdered sugar
- 3-4 Tbsp. well-shaken and stirred coconut milk (from 1 [13½-oz.] can)
- Toasted sweetened shredded coconut

1. **Prepare the Cake:** Preheat oven to 350°F. Line a rimmed 17½- x 12½-inch baking sheet with parchment paper; set aside. Stir together flour, brown sugar, coconut, granulated sugar, baking soda, cinnamon, salt, ginger, and nutmeg in a large bowl until combined; set aside.

2. Whisk together eggs, oil, and milk in a medium bowl. Add egg mixture to flour mixture; stir until smooth. Fold in carrots, walnuts, and raisins until combined.

3. Spread batter evenly into prepared baking sheet using a spoon or an offset spatula. Bake in preheated oven until a wooden pick inserted in center of Cake comes out clean, 15 to 20 minutes, rotating pan 180 degrees halfway through bake time. Let cool completely in pan on a wire rack, about 1 hour.

4. **Prepare the Coconut Buttercream:** When Cake is cool, beat butter, vanilla, salt, and coconut extract (if desired) in a large bowl with a hand mixer on medium-high speed until light and fluffy, 1 to 2 minutes. Reduce mixer speed to low; gradually add powdered sugar, 2 cups at a time, alternating with 1 tablespoon of the coconut milk after each addition, beating until combined. Beat in remaining 1 tablespoon coconut milk, 1 teaspoon at a time, as needed to achieve a smooth and thick consistency. Place Coconut Buttercream in a piping bag fitted with a ½-inch French (fluted) open star tip.

5. Use a 2½-inch round cookie cutter to cut Cake into 24 rounds. (Reserve scraps for another use.) Place 1 cut Cake round on a plate or platter; pipe an even layer of the Coconut Buttercream over top, and cover with another Cake round. Pipe buttercream on top of stacked rounds as desired. Repeat with remaining Cake rounds and buttercream. Garnish with toasted coconut. Store in refrigerator until ready to serve.

BABY BOURBON-
CHOCOLATE BOMBES

Baby Bourbon-Chocolate Bombes

ACTIVE 35 MIN. - TOTAL 1 HOUR, PLUS 1 HOUR COOLING AND CHILLING

MAKES 12

CAKES

- Baking spray
- 1 cup all-purpose flour
- ¾ cup granulated sugar
- ¼ cup packed light brown sugar
- ¼ cup unsweetened cocoa, sifted
- 1 tsp. baking soda
- ½ tsp. baking powder
- ½ tsp. kosher salt
- 1 large egg, at room temperature
- ¼ cup sour cream, at room temperature
- ¼ cup vegetable oil
- ¼ cup bottled cold-brew coffee concentrate, at room temperature
- ½ tsp. vanilla extract
- ½ tsp. bourbon
- ½ cup hot water

BOURBON GANACHE

- 2 (4-oz.) 60% cacao bittersweet chocolate bars, finely chopped
- ½ cup heavy whipping cream
- 1 Tbsp. light corn syrup
- 2 Tbsp. bourbon
- Chopped toasted pecans

1. Prepare the Cakes: Preheat oven to 350°F. Coat a 12-cup muffin tray with baking spray. Line bottom of each well with a round of parchment paper; set aside.
2. Whisk together flour, granulated sugar, brown sugar, cocoa, baking soda, baking powder, and salt in a large bowl. Whisk together egg, sour cream, oil, coffee concentrate, vanilla, and bourbon in a medium bowl. Add egg mixture to flour mixture; whisk just until combined. Add hot water, whisking until combined and mostly smooth.
3. Divide batter evenly among prepared wells. Bake in preheated oven until a wooden pick inserted in center comes out clean, 12 to 15 minutes. Let cool in tray on a wire rack 5 minutes; invert Cakes onto wire rack. Remove and discard parchment paper. Let cool completely, 30 to 45 minutes.

4. Prepare the Bourbon Ganache: When Cakes are cool, add water to a medium saucepan, filling to a depth of 1 inch. Bring to a boil over medium-high; reduce heat to medium-low, and simmer. Place chocolate, cream, and corn syrup in a medium-size heatproof bowl; place over simmering water in pan. (Make sure bottom of bowl does not touch water.) Cook over medium-low, stirring occasionally and adjusting heat as needed to maintain a simmer, until chocolate mixture is melted and smooth, 4 to 5 minutes. Remove from heat; whisk in bourbon until smooth and combined.
5. Place Cakes on wire rack over a parchment paper–lined baking sheet. Spoon enough Bourbon Ganache over 1 cooled Cake to coat as desired; repeat with remaining Cakes and Bourbon Ganache. Garnish tops with pecans. Chill until ganache is set, about 30 minutes.

Itty-Bitty Lemon Cakes with Lavender Glaze

(Photo, page 76)

ACTIVE 30 MIN. - TOTAL 1 HOUR, PLUS 55 MIN. COOLING

MAKES 12

CAKES

- Baking spray
- 1⅓ cups all-purpose flour
- ½ tsp. kosher salt
- ⅛ tsp. baking soda
- ½ cup unsalted butter, softened
- ⅔ cup granulated sugar
- ⅓ cup packed light brown sugar
- 1 Tbsp. grated lemon zest (from 2 lemons), plus more for garnish
- 2 large eggs, at room temperature
- ¼ cup sour cream, at room temperature
- ¼ cup whole milk, at room temperature
- 1 tsp. vanilla extract

LAVENDER GLAZE

- ¼ cup whole milk
- ½ tsp. dried culinary lavender
- 1½ cups powdered sugar
- ¼ tsp. kosher salt
- ⅛ tsp. vanilla extract

1. Prepare the Cakes: Preheat oven to 325°F; coat 2 (6-cup) mini cake trays with baking spray.
2. Whisk together flour, salt, and baking soda in a medium bowl. Beat butter, granulated sugar, brown sugar, and lemon zest with a stand mixer fitted with a paddle attachment on medium speed until light and fluffy, about 3 minutes. Add eggs, 1 at a time, beating until combined after each addition.
3. Whisk together sour cream, milk, and vanilla in a small bowl until well combined. With mixer on low speed, gradually add flour mixture to butter mixture, alternating with sour cream mixture, beating just until combined, 1 to 2 minutes.
4. Divide batter evenly among wells of prepared trays (about 3 tablespoons each), smoothing tops with back of a spoon. Firmly tap trays on counter several times to release large air bubbles.
5. Bake in preheated oven until a wooden pick inserted in center comes out clean, 18 to 20 minutes. Let cool in trays on wire racks 10 minutes. Remove from trays, and let cool completely on wire racks, 45 minutes to 1 hour.
6. Prepare the Lavender Glaze: When Cakes are cool, place milk in a small microwavable bowl; microwave on HIGH for 1 minute. Add lavender; let steep 10 minutes. Strain milk mixture through a fine mesh strainer into a small bowl; discard lavender. Stir together powdered sugar, salt, and vanilla in a medium bowl just until combined. Gradually stir in steeped milk, 1 teaspoon at a time, to achieve a pourable consistency. Drizzle cooled Cakes with Lavender Glaze. Garnish with additional lemon zest and edible flowers, if desired.

Spring Treasures

The joys of this season are as fleeting as cherry blossoms. This is especially true at the farmers' market, where you'll find the assortment of fresh produce changing from week to week. Now if you're lucky enough to come across special ingredients like garlic scapes, fava beans, and morel mushrooms, you'll know exactly what to do with them

Morel Mushrooms

Hollow with honeycomb-like pitted caps, these mushrooms are different from the ones you're likely used to eating. When buying morels, seek out firm, plump specimens. Store them, unwashed, in a paper bag in the refrigerator for no more than a couple of days. Clean them right before using: Swish quickly in water, or wipe gently with a damp paper towel.

Pasta with Morel-and-Pea Cream Sauce

Morel mushrooms seem almost otherworldly; they have porous, spongy caps that generously soak up any surrounding flavors. Here, they absorb the creamy sauce with shallot-infused butter, fortified wine, and the soft anise notes of tarragon. If you can't find morels at the farmers' market, feel free to substitute a mix of wild or cremini mushrooms from the grocery store; regular chives can stand in for garlic chives. Casarecce noodles are about an inch long; you can swap them out for any short, tubular pasta, such as penne or cavatappi.

ACTIVE 30 MIN. - TOTAL 30 MIN.
SERVES 4

- 12 oz. uncooked casarecce pasta
- 2 Tbsp. olive oil
- 8 oz. fresh morel mushrooms, halved lengthwise (about 5 cups)
- 2 Tbsp. unsalted butter
- ¼ cup minced shallot (from 1 large shallot)
- 1 cup shelled green peas (or thawed frozen peas)
- ¼ cup Madeira wine (or Marsala wine or sherry)
- ¾ cup heavy whipping cream
- 1 oz. Pecorino Romano cheese, grated (about ¼ cup)
- Kosher salt, to taste, plus more for salting water
- Black pepper, to taste
- 2 Tbsp. finely chopped fresh garlic chives
- 2 Tbsp. fresh tarragon leaves

1. Bring a large saucepan of salted water to a boil over high. Add pasta, and cook according to package directions for al dente. Drain, reserving ¾ cup cooking water.

2. While pasta cooks, heat a large skillet over medium-high. Add olive oil to skillet, swirling to coat. Add mushrooms; cook, stirring occasionally, until mushrooms start to brown and soften, about 4 minutes. Add butter, shallot, and peas. Cook, stirring often, until shallot softens and mushrooms are brown in spots, about 3 minutes. Stir in wine; cook, stirring occasionally, until wine evaporates, about 1 minute. Stir in cream, cooked pasta, and ⅓ cup of the reserved cooking water. Cook, stirring often, until sauce clings to pasta, 3 to 4 minutes. Remove from heat, and gradually stir in cheese. Season to taste with salt and pepper; add remaining cooking water, 2 tablespoons at a time, as needed to keep sauce creamy. Sprinkle with garlic chives and tarragon. Serve immediately.

FIDDLEHEAD-
AND-BACON TART
(PAGE 86)

RAMP-AND-RYE FOCACCIA (PAGE 87)

Fiddlehead Ferns

Think of these as curled-up baby fern leaves with a flavor similar to asparagus. Look for bright green, tightly wound coils. If you see some papery brown skin, simply rub to remove. Raw fiddleheads aren't safe to eat, so be sure to cook them thoroughly. Store rinsed and dried fiddleheads in your refrigerator's crisper drawer for up to a week.

Ramps

Similar in appearance to scallions but with broad, flat leaves, ramps taste great raw, cooked, or pickled. They have a strong garlicky flavor, which is most pronounced in the stems and bulbs. Wrap unwashed ramps in a damp paper towel, and store in a plastic bag in the refrigerator up to three days. Wash well and pat dry before using.

Fiddlehead-and-Bacon Tart

(Photo, page 84)

If you're a cook who loves to taste raw ingredients, resist the urge when it comes to fiddlehead ferns—you'll likely get a stomachache. Wait until they're boiled and then baked in this cheesy tart to enjoy their fresh, asparagus-like flavor. Not all varieties are edible, so source ostrich fern fiddleheads from a reputable provider at your local farmers' market or online to ensure you get the right kind.

ACTIVE 45 MIN. - TOTAL 2 HOURS, 5 MIN., PLUS 1 HOUR, 15 MIN. CHILLING

SERVES 6

- 4 thick-cut applewood-smoked bacon slices, chopped
- ¼ cup cold unsalted butter, cut into small pieces, plus melted butter for drippings, if needed
- 1½ cups all-purpose flour, plus more for dusting
- 1 tsp. kosher salt, divided, plus more for salting water
- 3-4 Tbsp. ice water, plus more for ferns
- 1½ cups trimmed fresh edible fiddlehead ferns
- 2 large eggs
- 1 large egg yolk
- 1 cup half-and-half
- 1½ oz. Parmesan cheese, grated (about ⅓ cup)
- ¼ tsp. ground white pepper

1. Heat a small skillet over medium. Add bacon; cook, stirring occasionally, until fat has rendered and bacon is crisp, 8 to 10 minutes. Using a slotted spoon, remove bacon from skillet to a paper towel–lined plate. Scrape bacon drippings into a heatproof glass measuring cup to equal ¼ cup. (Stir melted butter into drippings as needed to equal ¼ cup.) Freeze drippings, uncovered, until firm, about 45 minutes.

2. Place flour and ½ teaspoon of the salt in a food processor; pulse to combine, 2 to 3 pulses. Add cold butter; pulse until mixture resembles coarse meal, about 8 pulses. Remove bacon drippings from freezer, and remove from measuring cup. Cut drippings into small pieces, and add to flour mixture. Pulse until mixture resembles coarse meal, about 5 pulses. Drizzle 3 tablespoons of the ice water over top of flour mixture; pulse just until dough starts to come together and is crumbly, 10 to 12 pulses. Add additional 1 tablespoon ice water, 1 teaspoon at a time, if needed. Turn dough mixture out onto a large piece of plastic wrap; gently bring dough together using edges of plastic wrap, and pat into a 1-inch-thick disk. Wrap in plastic wrap, and chill for 30 minutes.

3. Preheat oven to 350°F. Unwrap dough, and roll into a 12-inch circle on a floured work surface. Gently fit dough into a 9-inch tart pan with a removable bottom, pressing dough into bottom and up sides of pan. Trim and discard excess dough. Line dough with parchment paper, and top with pie weights or dried beans. Bake for 20 minutes. Carefully remove parchment paper and pie weights. Bake at 350°F until just light golden, 25 to 30 minutes. Remove pan from oven; cool tart shell to room temperature, about 15 minutes. Do not turn oven off.

4. Meanwhile, bring a small saucepan of lightly salted water to a boil over high. While water comes to a boil, fill a medium bowl with ice water; set aside. Add ferns to boiling water; boil until tender-crisp, 5 to 7 minutes. Drain and plunge ferns into ice water; let stand 5 minutes. Drain ferns, and thoroughly pat dry.

5. Whisk together eggs and egg yolk in a medium bowl until well combined. Add half-and-half, Parmesan, pepper, and remaining ½ teaspoon salt; whisk until well blended. Place tart pan on an aluminum foil–lined baking sheet. Sprinkle bacon inside baked tart shell. Pour egg mixture over bacon, and top with ferns. Bake at 350°F until eggs are set, 30 to 35 minutes. Remove from oven. Serve warm or at room temperature.

Ramp-and-Rye Focaccia

(Photo, page 85)

Layered with ramps inside and out, this easy no-knead dough comes together in the food processor. Rye flour adds depth to the fluffy focaccia.

ACTIVE 25 MIN. - TOTAL 45 MIN., PLUS 3 HOURS STANDING
SERVES 12

- 1⅓ cups warm water (about 110°F)
- 1¼ tsp. active dry yeast (from 1 [¼-oz.] envelope)
- 1 tsp. granulated sugar
- 5 Tbsp. extra-virgin olive oil, divided
- 3 cups all-purpose flour
- ⅔ cup medium rye flour
- 2 tsp. kosher salt
- ⅓ cup chopped fresh ramp leaves
  Flaky sea salt (optional)
- 6-8 whole ramps, bulbs removed
- 3 Tbsp. unsalted butter, melted

1. Stir together water, yeast, and sugar in the bowl of a food processor. Let stand until yeast just starts to bubble and foam, 5 to 10 minutes. Drizzle 2 tablespoons of the oil over yeast mixture. Whisk together all-purpose flour, rye flour, and kosher salt in a medium bowl. Add flour mixture to yeast mixture in food processor. Pulse until dough comes together in a single mass, about 5 pulses. Scrape down sides of food processor bowl. Add chopped ramp leaves; process until dough is smooth and sticky, allowing dough to spin around bowl, about 30 seconds.
2. Lightly coat a 13- x 9-inch metal baking pan with cooking spray. Drizzle 2 tablespoons of the oil over pan, tilting to completely coat bottom of pan. Scrape dough into prepared pan, and turn to coat completely in oil; pat dough out to fill pan. Loosely cover with plastic wrap coated with cooking spray, and let stand in a warm place until at least doubled in size, 3 to 4 hours.
3. Preheat oven to 450°F. Uncover dough, and drizzle with remaining 1 tablespoon oil. Dimple dough all over with your fingertips, pressing all the way down to bottom of pan. Sprinkle dough with flaky sea salt, if desired. Top with ramps, gently pressing into dough, being careful not to collapse air pockets. Coat ramps with cooking spray. Bake until browned on top and very crisp on bottom, 20 to 25 minutes. Brush focaccia with melted butter, and serve.

Creamy Garlic Scape Soup

Loaded with handfuls of baby spinach and chunks of tender Yukon Gold potatoes, this verdant soup is blended until it's velvety smooth. A generous dollop of sour cream adds a tangy finish. If you have trouble finding garlic scapes, substitute an equal amount of chives and one finely minced garlic clove.

ACTIVE 35 MIN. - TOTAL 50 MIN.
SERVES 4

- ¼ cup unsalted butter, divided
- 2 cups cubed baguette
- 1¼ tsp. kosher salt, divided
- 1 cup chopped garlic scapes, plus 2 Tbsp. thinly sliced garlic scapes, divided
- 1 lb. Yukon Gold potatoes, peeled and coarsely chopped (about 3 cups)
- 3 cups unsalted chicken stock
- 2 fresh bay leaves
- 2 cups loosely packed fresh baby spinach
- ½ cup sour cream

1. Preheat oven to 350°F. Melt 2 tablespoons of the butter in a large saucepan over medium. Remove from heat. Arrange bread cubes on an aluminum foil–lined baking sheet. Drizzle with melted butter, and sprinkle with ¼ teaspoon of the salt; toss well to coat. Reserve saucepan; do not wipe clean. Bake bread cubes until toasted, about 12 minutes, stirring once after 8 minutes. Remove croutons from oven, and set aside.
2. Melt remaining 2 tablespoons butter in reserved saucepan over medium. Add chopped garlic scapes; cook, stirring occasionally, until slightly softened, about 3 minutes. Add potatoes, stock, bay leaves, and remaining 1 teaspoon salt. Bring to a boil over high. Partially cover, reduce heat to low, and simmer until potatoes are tender, 12 to 14 minutes. Uncover and stir in spinach. Remove from heat.
3. Pour potato mixture into a blender. Secure lid on blender, and remove center piece to allow steam to escape. Place a clean towel over opening. Process until smooth, about 45 seconds. Add sour cream, and process until well combined, about 20 seconds. Ladle soup into bowls; top evenly with croutons and sliced garlic scapes.

Garlic Scapes

These curly stems grow up from bulbs that are buried in the soil. They taste similar to chives with a faint, sweet whiff of garlic. If stored in a plastic bag in the refrigerator, they will stay good for several weeks. Raw garlic scapes add a punch to dips or pestos; when they're cooked, their flavor mellows a little.

2024 APRIL 87

RADISHES WITH MISO-SESAME BUTTER

FAVA-AND-WHIPPED FETA BRUSCHETTA

Radishes with Miso-Sesame Butter

Complement fresh, peppery radishes with good butter and crunchy sea salt for a low-effort yet elegant appetizer that's been perfected by the French. Here, soy-based miso and sesame oil add extra layers of savory, toasty richness.

ACTIVE 10 MIN. - TOTAL 10 MIN.

MAKES 2/3 CUP BUTTER

- 1/2 cup unsalted butter, softened
- 2 Tbsp. white miso
- 1 tsp. toasted sesame oil
- Flaky sea salt
- 2 bunches mixed radishes, for serving
- Baguette slices, for serving

Place butter and miso in a small bowl. Beat with an electric mixer on medium speed until well blended, about 1 minute. Add oil; beat until creamy and blended, about 20 seconds. Transfer butter mixture to a small serving bowl, and sprinkle with salt. Serve butter with radishes and baguette slices.

Fava–and–Whipped Feta Bruschetta

Fava beans require a little extra work, but they are absolutely worth it. Thankfully the favas can be shelled, blanched, and peeled in advance. The prepped beans can be refrigerated for up to three days, making this recipe a breeze to throw together for guests. Creamy ricotta and briny feta make the ideal blank canvas for these sautéed favas, which are accented with lemon, mint, and parsley.

ACTIVE 1 HOUR - TOTAL 1 HOUR, 10 MIN.

MAKES 16

- Ice water
- 2 lb. unshelled fresh fava beans
- 16 (1/2-inch-thick) diagonal baguette slices
- 1/2 cup extra-virgin olive oil, divided
- 1/4 cup whole-milk ricotta cheese
- 4 oz. sheep's milk feta cheese, crumbled (about 1 cup)
- 2 Tbsp. finely chopped shallot (from 1 large shallot)
- 1/2 tsp. kosher salt, plus more for salting water
- 1/2 tsp. black pepper
- 1/4 cup finely chopped fresh flat-leaf parsley
- 1 Tbsp. finely chopped fresh mint
- 2 tsp. grated lemon zest (from 1 lemon)

1. Preheat oven to 350°F. Bring a medium saucepan of lightly salted water to a boil over high. While water comes to a boil, fill a medium bowl with ice water; set aside. Shell fava beans, discarding pods. Add shelled fava beans to boiling water; boil 30 seconds. Drain beans, and plunge beans into ice water; let stand 5 minutes. Drain beans. Peel off and discard outer skins; set peeled beans aside.
2. Arrange baguette slices on an aluminum foil–lined baking sheet; brush both sides of slices with 3 tablespoons of the oil. Bake in preheated oven until crisp and light golden, 10 to 12 minutes. Let toasted baguette slices cool 5 minutes.
3. Meanwhile, place ricotta cheese and crumbled feta in a mini food processor; process until well combined, about 30 seconds, stopping to scrape down sides as needed. Add 2 tablespoons of the oil; process until completely smooth and creamy, about 1 minute.
4. Heat remaining 3 tablespoons oil in a medium skillet over medium. Add shallot, and cook, stirring often, until slightly softened, about 1 minute. Add reserved peeled fava beans, salt, and pepper; cook, stirring often, until beans are tender-crisp, about 3 minutes. Remove from heat, and stir in parsley, mint, and lemon zest.
5. Spread about 2½ teaspoons feta mixture onto each toasted baguette slice; top each with about 2 tablespoons fava bean mixture. Transfer to a serving platter.

Radishes

The heirloom French breakfast radish is sweeter and more delicate in flavor than "hotter" varieties. Select bunches with fresh-looking leaves. Remove the tops, and store them (unwashed) in a damp paper towel in a plastic bag for up to a week. Sauté the greens with pasta or grains, roast them for an easy side, or use them raw in salads.

Fava Beans

Fresh favas are nestled in big, fat pods, so you'll need to shell them. Each bean is also covered in a tough outer layer; simply blanch them for a few seconds, cool in ice water, and peel away the skins. You'll be left with bright green gems that have a sweet, buttery, nutty taste. Store unshelled beans in the fridge for about a week.

LIGHTEN UP

Kick the Can

A homemade filling gives this classic side a wholesome boost

One-Pan Broccoli-Rice Casserole
ACTIVE 25 MIN. - TOTAL 35 MIN.
SERVES 8

- 3 Tbsp. olive oil, divided
- 1 cup chopped yellow onion (about 1 medium onion)
- 1 (8-oz.) pkg. sliced fresh cremini mushrooms
- 1½ cups uncooked instant long-grain brown rice (such as Minute)
- 1 tsp. kosher salt
- 1 tsp. garlic powder
- 1 tsp. dry mustard
- ½ tsp. paprika
- ½ tsp. black pepper
- 2½ cups chicken broth
- ¾ cup panko breadcrumbs
- 4 cups fresh broccoli florets, cut into 1-inch pieces
- 4 oz. Colby Jack cheese, shredded (about 1 cup)
- 3 oz. extra-sharp cheddar cheese, shredded (about ¾ cup)

1. Heat 2 tablespoons of the oil in a large (11-inch) broiler-safe high-sided skillet over medium-high. Add onion and mushrooms, and cook, stirring occasionally, until mushrooms are lightly browned and their liquid has evaporated, 7 to 8 minutes. Stir in rice, salt, garlic powder, dry mustard, paprika, and black pepper; cook, stirring constantly, until mixture is fragrant and rice is coated in oil and spices, about 1 minute. Stir in broth, and bring to a boil. Reduce heat to medium to maintain a simmer; cover and cook for about 8 minutes. (There will still be liquid remaining in the skillet, and the rice will not be tender.)
2. Meanwhile, stir together panko and remaining 1 tablespoon oil until panko is well coated. Set aside.
3. Uncover rice mixture, and stir in broccoli; cover and cook until broccoli is tender and bright green and rice is tender, 5 to 7 minutes. Remove skillet from heat, and uncover; stir in Colby Jack cheese until melted and creamy, about 1 minute. Sprinkle top evenly with extra-sharp cheddar cheese and panko mixture.
4. Preheat broiler with oven rack about 5 inches from heat source. Broil until cheddar is melted and panko is golden, about 2 minutes.

Before Recipe Makeover:
CALORIES: **584** – CARB: **51 G** – FAT: **35 G**

After Recipe Makeover:
CALORIES: **263** – CARB: **25 G** – FAT: **14 G**

HOSPITALITY

Worth the Wait

For Lisa van der Reijden, it wouldn't be Easter without her mother's late-night soup

"**THE GREEKS DO THINGS** a little differently," says Auburn, Alabama, restaurant owner Lisa van der Reijden. As opposed to having lunch after church, which is typical for many Americans who celebrate Easter, her family's meal was enjoyed much later. After the midnight Greek Orthodox service, they would gather to break their fast. "Everyone was tired, but there was always excitement when we walked through the door, well past 2 a.m., knowing that my mother would have this soup waiting for us," she says. "We'd all sit down together, sleep-deprived and hungry yet filled with joy from the service. The stories and laughter flowed as she somehow kept bringing us bowl after bowl of soup—a miracle in itself."

Avgolemono Soup

Symbolizing Jesus' sacrifice, red-dyed eggs are an Eastern Orthodox tradition.
ACTIVE 20 MIN. - TOTAL 35 MIN.
SERVES 6

- 2 Tbsp. olive oil
- 1 cup chopped yellow onion (from 1 onion)
- 1 cup chopped carrots (from 2 peeled carrots)
- 1 cup chopped celery (from 2 stalks)
- ½ tsp. kosher salt, divided
- 6 cups chicken broth
- ½ cup uncooked long-grain white rice, rinsed
- 2 large eggs
- 5 Tbsp. fresh lemon juice (from 2 lemons)
- 2½ cups shredded rotisserie chicken (from 1 chicken)
- 2 Tbsp. fresh dill fronds
- ½ tsp. black pepper
- Lemon wedges (optional)

1. Heat olive oil in a Dutch oven or heavy-bottomed pot over medium. Add onion, carrots, celery, and ¼ teaspoon of the salt; cover and cook, stirring occasionally, until softened, 8 to 10 minutes.
2. Stir in chicken broth and rice; bring mixture to a boil over medium-high. Reduce heat to medium; simmer, uncovered and undisturbed, until rice is almost tender, about 10 minutes.
3. Whisk together eggs and lemon juice in a bowl until frothy. Gradually stir 1 cup of hot broth from Dutch oven into egg mixture. Whisking vigorously, gradually add 1 cup additional hot broth to egg mixture, taking care not to add it too quickly to avoid scrambling the eggs.
4. Whisk egg mixture into Dutch oven; stir in chicken and remaining ¼ teaspoon salt. Remove from heat, and stir until warmed through, about 2 minutes.
5. Ladle soup into bowls. Top evenly with fresh dill and black pepper, and serve with lemon wedges, if desired.

SUPPERTIME

Spring Sizzle

Break out your trusty skillet to whip up something tasty

STIR-FRY SUCCESS
For restaurant-quality results, prep and measure the ingredients before you start cooking and make sure the pan is nice and hot.

Cajun Shrimp Stir-Fry
ACTIVE 20 MIN. - TOTAL 20 MIN.
SERVES 4

- 1 lb. large peeled, deveined raw shrimp
- 1 Tbsp. Cajun seasoning
- 3 Tbsp. canola oil, divided
- 6 oz. fresh snow peas, trimmed (about 1 cup)
- 2 Tbsp. finely chopped garlic (about 6 cloves)
- 1 Tbsp. finely chopped fresh ginger
- 3 medium scallions, thinly sliced (white, light green, and dark green parts separated), divided
- 3 Tbsp. rice vinegar
- ¼ cup unsalted butter, cut into 4 even pieces
- 1½ Tbsp. fish sauce
- 2 tsp. fresh lime juice (from 1 lime)
- 2 tsp. hot sauce
- ¼ cup roasted, salted peanuts, chopped
- 2 Tbsp. fresh cilantro leaves
- Cooked white rice, for serving

1. Place shrimp in a large bowl. Add Cajun seasoning and 1 tablespoon of the oil; toss to coat. Heat 1 tablespoon of the oil in a large skillet over medium-high. Add shrimp in an even layer; cook until browned on both sides but not fully cooked through, about 2 minutes total. Transfer shrimp to a large plate, and set aside.

2. Return skillet to medium; add remaining 1 tablespoon oil. Add snow peas, garlic, ginger, and white and light green parts of scallions; cook, stirring occasionally, until garlic and ginger are fragrant and snow peas are just tender-crisp, about 2 minutes. Add vinegar, and cook, stirring constantly, until almost fully reduced, about 1 minute. Reduce heat to low, and add butter, fish sauce, lime juice, and hot sauce, stirring until butter melts. Add shrimp; stir until coated in sauce and cooked through, about 2 minutes. Remove from heat; top with peanuts, cilantro, and dark green parts of scallions. Serve over rice.

FLIP THE SCALES
Did you buy skin-on fillets? No problem. Start salmon skin side down to get it crispy, then turn it to finish cooking.

Bourbon-Glazed Salmon
ACTIVE 20 MIN. - TOTAL 20 MIN.
SERVES 4

- 2 Tbsp. olive oil
- 4 (6-oz.) skinless salmon fillets
- ½ tsp. black pepper
- ¼ tsp. kosher salt
- 1 medium orange
- ½ cup bourbon
- 2 Tbsp. honey
- 1 Tbsp. light brown sugar
- 1 Tbsp. soy sauce
- 2 Tbsp. unsalted butter
- 1 Tbsp. thinly sliced fresh chives
- Flaky sea salt

1. Heat oil in a large nonstick skillet over medium-high until shimmering. Season salmon fillets evenly with pepper and kosher salt, and place in skillet. Cook until golden brown on both sides and almost cooked through (an instant-read thermometer inserted into thickest portion of salmon should register 130°F), about 7 minutes total. Remove skillet from heat; transfer salmon to a plate. Let skillet cool slightly, about 2 minutes.
2. While salmon cooks, zest orange to yield 1 teaspoon grated zest; set aside. Cut orange in half; slice 1 portion into half-moons. Reserve remaining orange half for another use.
3. After skillet cools slightly, wipe clean and add bourbon, honey, brown sugar, soy sauce, and orange slices. Bring to a simmer over medium. Cook, stirring often, until slightly thickened, about 2 minutes. Return salmon to skillet; spoon bourbon mixture over salmon until fillets are coated and sauce is thickened, about 1 minute. Remove from heat; add butter to sauce in skillet. Gently swirl until butter is melted and combines with the sauce. Serve salmon with sauce, and top with chives and reserved orange zest. Garnish with flaky sea salt.

2024 APRIL 93

Skillet Pasta Primavera

ACTIVE 30 MIN. - TOTAL 30 MIN.
SERVES 4

- 1 lb. uncooked bow tie pasta
- ½ cup extra-virgin olive oil, divided
- 2 medium leeks, well cleaned, white and light green parts thinly sliced (about 2 cups)
- 1½ tsp. kosher salt, divided, plus more for cooking water
- 2 Tbsp. thinly sliced garlic (from 4 cloves)
- 1 lb. trimmed asparagus spears, cut into 2-inch pieces (about 3½ cups)
- 1 cup fresh or frozen green peas
- ½ tsp. crushed red pepper
- 4 oz. Parmigiano-Reggiano cheese, grated (about 1 cup), divided
- 1 tsp. grated lemon zest (from 1 lemon), divided
- 1 cup cherry tomatoes, halved
- ¼ cup packed fresh basil leaves

1. Bring a large pot of salted water to a boil over high. Add pasta to boiling water; cook until al dente, about 10 minutes. Drain pasta, reserving 1 cup cooking water.

2. While pasta cooks, heat 6 tablespoons of the oil in a large high-sided skillet or saucepan over medium-low. Add leeks and 1 teaspoon of the salt; cook, stirring often, until leeks have softened and are starting to caramelize, about 10 minutes. Reduce heat to low, and add garlic. Continue to cook, stirring occasionally, until the leeks are caramelized, about 3 minutes.

3. Add asparagus pieces and remaining ½ teaspoon salt to skillet; increase heat to medium-high. Cook, stirring occasionally, until asparagus is bright green, about 2 minutes. Add peas and crushed red pepper; cook, stirring constantly, until peas are bright green, about 1 minute.

4. Add drained pasta and ½ cup of the reserved cooking water to skillet; cook, stirring constantly, until liquid has mostly absorbed, about 2 minutes. Add remaining ½ cup cooking water; continue cooking, stirring constantly, until liquid has mostly absorbed and mixture has thickened slightly. Remove skillet from heat, and stir in ¾ cup of the Parmigiano-Reggiano, ½ teaspoon of the lemon zest, and remaining 2 tablespoons oil. Stir constantly until sauce is creamy, about 30 seconds. Stir in tomatoes until coated and combined. Top pasta mixture with basil leaves, remaining ¼ cup Parmigiano-Reggiano, and remaining ½ teaspoon lemon zest. Serve immediately.

> **IS IT AL DENTE?**
> To make sure the pasta isn't over- or undercooked, cut or bite one noodle in half; you should see a bit of white in the center.

SOUTHERN FESTIVALS

A Culinary Guide to Jazz Fest

Come for the music, and stay for the foods you won't find anywhere else

LONG BEFORE Dr. John sang about "crawfish, jambalaya, red beans, and fine pralines" in "Goin' Back to New Orleans," food and music were always intertwined in this city. There is no better time to experience both than during the New Orleans Jazz & Heritage Festival, which is held every spring. The legendary event, now in its 54th year, draws people from around the world. But the name can be a bit misleading.

Although there are dozens of jazz performances (plus blues, folk, zydeco, rap, country, bluegrass, and more), the week-and-a-half-long celebration is just as much about eating.

Forget the usual hot dogs and fries—many Jazz Fest dishes are restaurant worthy. Dine on crawfish strudel, duck and shrimp pasta, and catfish almondine, but save room for desserts like praline-stuffed beignets and strawberry shortcake. You'll also find all the regional specialties like jambalaya, gumbo, étouffée, and muffulettas plus po'boys aplenty—including alligator sausage, fried soft-shell crab, Vietnamese meatball, and turducken. Many of these are available only at the festival, so grabbing a bite is as big a priority as catching your favorite musicians.

If that seems like an overwhelming feat, Alon Shaya, chef at local restaurants Saba and Miss River, can help. An admitted Jazz Fest fanatic, he has called the city home for 20 years and has been to the event at least that many times. Among his favorites are strawberry lemonade, gumbo, Crawfish Monica, fried pork chop sandwiches, and crawfish salad rolls.

Miss River's Louisiana Crawfish Rolls

If you can't make it to Jazz Fest, try Shaya's recipe, an homage to the crawfish-salad roll by Smitty's Restaurant & Oyster Bar.
ACTIVE 10 MIN. · TOTAL 10 MIN.
MAKES 4

Stir together ½ cup **mayonnaise,** 2 tsp. prepared **horseradish,** 2 tsp. **Creole mustard,** ½ tsp. grated **lemon zest,** 4 tsp. fresh **lemon juice,** ½ tsp. **kosher salt,** ½ tsp. **Cajun seasoning,** and ¼ tsp. **hot sauce** in a medium bowl until smooth. Add 1 lb. cooked and peeled **crawfish tails;** stir to coat. Melt 4 Tbsp. unsalted **butter** in a large skillet over medium; add 4 **top-split hot dog buns,** and toast until golden on both sides, 1 to 2 minutes per side. Fill toasted buns with crawfish mixture; sprinkle evenly with 4 tsp. minced **fresh chives.** Serve with **lemon wedges,** if desired.

2024 APRIL 95

CHERRY-CHEESECAKE BROWNIES

PIECE OF CAKE

Batter Up

A layer of creamy cheesecake takes brownies to a delicious new level

DULCE DE LECHE BROWNIES

COOKIES-AND-CREAM CHEESECAKE BROWNIES

Cherry-Cheesecake Brownies
ACTIVE 15 MIN. · TOTAL 1 HOUR, PLUS 2 HOURS COOLING AND CHILLING
SERVES 9

- 1 (8-oz.) pkg. cream cheese, softened
- ¼ cup powdered sugar
- 4 large eggs, at room temperature
- ¾ tsp. kosher salt, divided
- ½ cup all-purpose flour
- ⅓ cup Dutch-process cocoa
- ½ cup unsalted butter
- ½ cup 60% cacao bittersweet chocolate chips
- 1 cup granulated sugar
- ¼ cup packed dark brown sugar
- 1 tsp. vanilla extract
- ¾ cup cherry pie filling

1. Preheat oven to 350°F. Coat an 8-inch square metal baking pan with cooking spray; line with parchment paper or aluminum foil, leaving a 2-inch overhang on all sides. Set aside.
2. In a medium bowl, beat cream cheese and powdered sugar with an electric mixer on low speed until light and fluffy, about 1 minute. Add 1 of the eggs and ¼ teaspoon of the salt; beat until just combined, and set aside. Whisk together flour, cocoa, and remaining ½ teaspoon salt in a small bowl until no lumps remain; set aside.
3. Add butter and chocolate chips to a large microwavable bowl. Microwave on HIGH in 30-second intervals, whisking after each interval, until chocolate is melted, about 1 minute. Whisk in granulated sugar and brown sugar until combined. Add vanilla and remaining 3 eggs; whisk until combined. Add flour mixture, whisking until no dry streaks remain.
4. Add batter to prepared baking pan, spreading in an even layer. Gently spread cream cheese mixture over batter; dollop cherry pie filling over cream cheese mixture. Using the tip of a butter knife, swirl cherry pie filling into cream cheese mixture as desired. Bake in preheated oven until cream cheese mixture is lightly browned around edges, 45 to 50 minutes. Let cool to room temperature in pan on a wire rack, about 1 hour. Chill at least 1 hour before slicing.

Cookies-and-Cream Cheesecake Brownies
Prepare recipe as directed through Step 3. In Step 4, omit pie filling. Sprinkle 8 roughly chopped **cream-filled chocolate sandwich cookies** over cream cheese mixture. Proceed with recipe as directed.

Dulce de Leche Brownies
Prepare recipe as directed through Step 3. In Step 4, omit pie filling; bake as directed. Microwave ½ cup **dulce de leche** until warmed, about 30 seconds. Spread over hot brownies. Cool and chill as directed; sprinkle with **flaky sea salt.**

IVY'S KITCHEN

The Gift of Pudding

A secret ingredient makes this banana dessert celebration worthy

WHEN I WAS A KID, I was a strict rule follower—and I still am. But on my birthday in mid-April, there was one rule I looked forward to breaking. Before supper, I would sneak into the refrigerator when no one was watching and eat a heaping scoop of my present—Aunt Brenda's famous banana pudding (my parents graciously pretended not to notice the missing spoonful when it was time to serve). You see, instead of a gift, my aunt gave me a big bowl of this dessert each year. Although I had secretly hoped for a golf cart, I happily accepted the pudding instead. This version is my standard for every other recipe. Her secret? Sour cream. The added tang and creaminess balance out the typically overly sweet treat, making it perhaps a little too easy to eat, especially when no one is looking.

Aunt Brenda's Sour Cream Banana Pudding

Although brown bananas are great for quick breads, you'll want them to be a little prettier for this pudding. Shop for yellow ones with peels speckled with tiny brown spots; they will yield neat slices that are soft and full of flavor but not mushy or discolored.

ACTIVE 25 MIN. - TOTAL 25 MIN., PLUS 4 HOURS CHILLING

SERVES 12

- 2 cups cold whole milk
- 1 (5.1-oz.) pkg. vanilla instant pudding and pie filling
- 3 cups heavy whipping cream
- ½ cup powdered sugar
- 1 tsp. vanilla extract
- 1 (8-oz.) container sour cream
- 1 (14-oz.) can sweetened condensed milk
- 8 cups vanilla wafers (from 2 [11-oz.] pkg.)
- 2¾ lb. ripe bananas (about 9 bananas), cut into ¼-inch-thick slices

1. Whisk together milk with instant pudding and pie filling in a large bowl until smooth. Let stand until very thick, 5 to 7 minutes. Meanwhile, beat cream with an electric mixer on high speed until soft peaks form, 1 to 2 minutes. Gradually add powdered sugar; beat until stiff peaks form, 30 seconds to 1 minute. Stir in vanilla. Reserve 1½ cups of the whipped cream in a small bowl; set aside.

2. Whisk sour cream and sweetened condensed milk into thickened pudding mixture until smooth. Fold in remaining 5¾ cups whipped cream until smooth and fluffy.

3. Cover the bottom of a 3-quart trifle dish or straight-sided serving bowl with a single layer of vanilla wafers. Top wafers with a single layer of banana slices (about ¾ cup); gently spread about 1 cup of the pudding mixture to cover banana slices.

4. Stand up wafers around inside of dish to create a ring, tucking them into the pudding mixture slightly for support. Lay down additional wafers on pudding mixture inside ring in a single layer. Top wafers with a single layer of banana slices; gently spread about 1 cup of the pudding mixture to cover banana slices. For the next layer, stand up banana slices around inside of dish to create a ring, tucking them into the pudding mixture. Lay down wafers on pudding mixture inside ring in a single layer; top with a single layer of banana slices. Gently spread about 1 cup of the pudding mixture to cover banana slices.

5. Reserve 4 vanilla wafers for garnish; repeat Step 4 with remaining wafers, banana slices, and pudding mixture. Top with reserved 1½ cups whipped cream, spreading as desired. Lightly crush reserved wafers; sprinkle over whipped cream. Chill, covered, in refrigerator at least 4 hours or up to 24 hours.

COOKING SCHOOL
TIPS AND TRICKS FROM THE SOUTH'S MOST TRUSTED KITCHEN

Five Smart Ways to Organize Your Fridge

1. Stack Like the Pros
Chefs often arrange their refrigerators based on whether foods are ready to eat. Items like salads or dips are kept on top, and raw meats go on the bottom, where it's usually coldest.

2. Invest in Bins
Clear containers are great for corralling things and keeping your fridge tidy. We love using them to hold packaged raw proteins; this helps prevent leaks and avoid cross contamination.

3. Learn to Label
Use masking tape and a permanent marker to easily and inexpensively note when items are opened or purchased so you'll know how long you have to consume them.

4. Ditch the Door
Milk and eggs stay fresh longer on the middle shelves, which are consistently cooler than the door. Place your condiments there instead.

5. Stock Like a Grocer
If you have multiples of the same product (who can resist a BOGO sale?), place the ones that expire sooner toward the front so you grab those first.

How Often Should You Wash Kitchen Towels?

More frequently than you think—though it does depend on how they are used. If you're cleaning up messes involving raw meat, they should be washed immediately. When you're drying dishes, they should be changed out regularly—daily, if possible. It's also more sanitary to have a separate cloth reserved for hand drying that you replace every week.

SOUTHERN STAPLE: BAR KEEPERS FRIEND

Like many things, this all-purpose cleanser was discovered by accident. In 1882, chemist George William Hoffman was cooking rhubarb and realized that the spring favorite left his pan shinier. He set out to explain the reaction and found that the natural oxalic acid in the vegetable helped break down tarnish, rust, and lime stains. He developed a product using his findings and sold it as a polish for brass rails. Appreciative tavern owners called it "Bar Keepers Friend." Here are four unexpected ways to use it:

- Buff scratches off dishes.
- Clean gunked-up grill grates.
- Remove sticky label residue.
- Erase scuff marks on sneakers.

100 2024 APRIL

May

102 The Big Dill Brighten up spring appetizers with this frilly member of the parsley family

104 Who Made the Potato Salad? An Alabama writer tries to discover the magic behind her mom's signature dish

106 Strawberry Shortcake Forever Try a playful new take on berries and cake

114 Spin the Bottle Reach for your favorite condiments to liven up weeknight dinners

119 Crunch Time Southern-style okra, no deep-frying required

121 Hold the Pineapple Flip the script on upside-down cake

122 American Spirit Chef Edward Lee's new book explores Kentucky's beloved drink

123 Million-Dollar Pancakes A sweet and simple breakfast to celebrate Mother's Day

124 I'll Bring the Bourbon Senior Lifestyle Editor Ivy Odom makes a strong case for this Southern spirit

126 Cooking School Our Test Kitchen professionals cover great gear and clever hacks to take your summer grilling skills to the next level

BOUNTY

The Big Dill

Brighten up spring appetizers with this frilly member of the parsley family

FRESH DILL DIP

Fresh Dill Dip
ACTIVE 15 MIN. - TOTAL 15 MIN.
SERVES 6

Heat 2 Tbsp. **olive oil** in a small saucepan over medium-low. Add 3 thinly sliced **garlic cloves**; cook, stirring often, until just golden brown, about 3 minutes. Transfer garlic and oil to a small bowl; set aside. Grate 3 additional **garlic cloves** over a medium bowl. Add 1 cup each **mayonnaise** and **sour cream or crème fraîche**, ⅓ cup chopped **fresh dill**, 1 tsp. grated **lemon zest**, 1 Tbsp. **fresh lemon juice**, and ½ tsp. each **kosher salt** and **black pepper**, stirring until combined. Transfer mixture to a bowl. Stir in reserved garlic oil, and top with reserved fried garlic slices; garnish with **fresh dill**. Serve with **crudités** and **potato chips**.

Double-Dill Deviled Eggs
To dress up deviled eggs for company, pipe the filling using a pastry bag fitted with a star tip.
ACTIVE 15 MIN. - TOTAL 15 MIN.
SERVES 6

Peel 6 hard-cooked **large eggs**; cut each in half lengthwise. Transfer egg yolks to a medium bowl. Stir in 3 Tbsp. chopped **dill pickles**, 2 ½ Tbsp. **mayonnaise**, 1 Tbsp. chopped **fresh dill**, 2 tsp. **Dijon mustard**, ¼ tsp. **kosher salt**, and ¼ tsp. **black pepper** until mostly smooth. Pipe or spoon yolk mixture evenly into egg halves; garnish with **fresh dill fronds**.

FLAVOR FOR LATER
Wrap fresh dill sprigs in a damp paper towel; place in a ziplock bag in the crisper drawer of the refrigerator. To dry it, hang a tightly bound bundle in the pantry for two weeks; store in a lidded jar.

DOUBLE-DILL
DEVILED EGGS

HOSPITALITY

Who Made the Potato Salad?

An Alabama writer tries to discover the magic behind her mom's signature dish

THE QUESTION MIGHT be asked in a dramatic stage whisper. Or it might be said loudly—because it's a very serious matter, one that divides palates and has the ability to make or break your meal. "Who made the potato salad?" Depending on how it's spoken, it can be a withering insult or a high compliment. If my mother was the cook, the answer is always met with a sigh of relief.

When potato salad is not on the table, it's missed. It may be composed of humble ingredients, but there's nothing simple about it. Get it wrong, and every skill you possess or decision you've made may come into question. When done right, it creates memories that remain long after the dishes have been washed and the leftovers are packed away.

Mama prepares hers from memory—meaning there's no written recipe. But it always has precisely the same ingredients added to the bowl in the same order.

In our family, everyone has at least one signature dish, and when they're all put together, they form a complete meal. How my mom was assigned potato salad is something of a mystery. "I don't know why I got it," she tells me. "I think my sister Meriel's was always the version to have. But somehow someone tasted mine, and I just started doing it. I fixed it for a party one time, and everybody really liked it and asked where it came from."

My mother, like many Southern mamas, is a saint. If she is guilty of any potato salad sin, it's making too much. In her defense, she learned by preparing it for a large family—six brothers, six sisters, and her parents. It was also her working-mom hack to ensure we always had leftovers. "We cooked in large quantities, so I was used to that," she says. "If someone showed up unexpectedly (and people often did), you wanted to have enough for them to join the meal. Nobody ever refused a plate or left hungry."

I thought writing this story would be a sneaky way to finally learn my mother's recipe. But while I sit at the kitchen table grading undergraduates' papers one afternoon, she graciously begins without me. "I'll just put the potatoes on to boil. That will save us time," she says. That's my mother: always thinking ahead, trying to make everyone's life easier.

Before I know it, she's swiftly moved on to mashing, scooping, mixing, and seasoning—with no laptop, tablet, or cookbook in sight to guide her. She's just doing what she's always done: selflessly stepping up to whip things into shape.

I don't mind only being needed in my childhood roles of chief taste tester, dishwasher, and sous-chef. I dip a spoon into the bowl and savor the still-warm salad. It's perfect—flavorful and fluffy, substantial without being heavy, moist but not runny.

All that's left is the garnish. My mother never dumps food on a plate or serves from aluminum pans. "How you do one thing is how you do everything," she taught me. So this dish is done with a flourish: She delicately slices a boiled egg, dusts it with paprika and parsley, and layers the slices on the surface.

Once, my brother sneaked a taste of a batch that had been set aside for Mama's grandfather's repast—enough for hundreds of guests. In his haste to grab a bite, it fell to the kitchen floor. Hours of work all went to waste. What happened next? "I think I went blank," my mother demurs. But I remember: She pulled out a pot and began to prepare more.

"You've just got to have some potato salad with a Sunday supper or a soul food dinner. A good barbecue has to have it too," Mama insists. "Collard greens, macaroni and cheese, sliced tomatoes, stewed okra, cornbread, baked or candied sweet potatoes, and potato salad—to me, that's a soul-satisfying meal that makes me feel... home." –Alexis E. Barton

Maude Crawford Barton's Potato Salad

ACTIVE 30 MIN. · TOTAL 1 HOUR, 30 MIN.

SERVES 8

- 3 medium russet potatoes, peeled and cut into 1-inch chunks (about 4 cups)
- 9 large eggs
- 3/4 cup sweet pickle relish (from 1 [16-oz.] jar, such as Mt. Olive)
- 1/2 cup mayonnaise
- 1/3 cup drained diced pimientos (from 1 [4-oz.] jar)
- 1/4 cup yellow mustard
- 1 1/2 Tbsp. dried parsley flakes, plus more for garnish
- 1 Tbsp. white vinegar
- 1/2 tsp. kosher salt
  Paprika

1. Place potatoes and eggs in a large pot, and cover with cold water. Bring to a boil over high; reduce heat to medium-high, and cook, uncovered, until eggs are hard-cooked, about 12 minutes. Immediately transfer eggs to a bowl of ice water; let cool. Continue cooking potatoes until fork-tender, about 3 minutes more.

2. Drain potatoes, and place in a large bowl. Add pickle relish to warm potatoes, and mash mixture using a potato masher, removing all lumps. Fold in mayonnaise, pimientos, mustard, parsley, vinegar, and kosher salt until combined.

3. Remove eggs from ice water. Peel eggs; set aside 1 egg for garnish, if desired. Coarsely chop remaining 8 eggs, and gently fold into potato mixture. Cover and refrigerate until chilled, about 1 hour.

4. Transfer mixture to a serving bowl. Thinly slice remaining egg; garnish potato salad with paprika, additional parsley flakes, and sliced egg, if desired.

104 2024 MAY

Strawberry Shortcake Forever

Try a playful new take on berries and cake

Strawberry-Ginger Poke Cake with Toasted Vanilla Meringue

Many recipes for poke cakes call for boxed ingredients, but this made-from-scratch version is worth every minute. Fresh strawberries and ginger simmer down into a warm syrup that soaks right into the fluffy vanilla sheet cake.

ACTIVE 50 MIN. - TOTAL 1 HOUR, 30 MIN.
SERVES 18

CAKE
- 2½ cups cake flour
- 2 tsp. baking powder
- ½ tsp. baking soda
- ½ tsp. kosher salt
- 1¼ cups granulated sugar
- ¾ cup unsalted butter, softened
- 2 large eggs, at room temperature
- 1 tsp. vanilla extract
- 1¼ cups plain whole-milk strained (Greek-style) yogurt

STRAWBERRY SYRUP
- ¾ lb. fresh strawberries, stemmed and quartered
- ⅔ cup packed dark brown sugar
- 1 (2-inch) piece fresh ginger, peeled and sliced

MERINGUE
- ½ cup granulated sugar
- 3 large egg whites
- 1 tsp. vanilla extract
- ¼ tsp. cream of tartar
- Halved strawberries, for garnish

1. Prepare the Cake: Preheat oven to 350°F. Coat a 13- x 9-inch broiler-safe baking dish with cooking spray, and line with parchment paper, leaving a 1-inch overhang on 2 long sides. Set aside. Whisk together flour, baking powder, baking soda, and salt in a medium bowl. Set aside.
2. Beat granulated sugar and butter with a stand mixer fitted with a paddle attachment on medium speed until light and fluffy, 3 to 4 minutes. Add eggs 1 at a time, beating until just combined after each addition. Beat in vanilla and yogurt until combined. Add the flour mixture in thirds, beating until smooth after each addition, about 2 minutes total.
3. Spread batter evenly in prepared baking dish. Bake in preheated oven until Cake is golden around the edges and a wooden pick inserted in center comes out clean, 25 to 30 minutes. Let cool about 30 minutes.
4. Meanwhile, prepare the Strawberry Syrup: Place strawberries, brown sugar, ⅔ cup water, and ginger in a saucepan. Bring to a simmer over medium; cook, stirring occasionally, until berries release their juices and liquid becomes syrupy, about 8 minutes. Let cool 30 minutes. Pour mixture through a fine mesh strainer into a bowl; discard solids.
5. Remove Cake from baking dish, and transfer to a platter. Using the wide end of a chopstick, poke holes 1 inch apart all over Cake. Pour Strawberry Syrup over Cake and into holes. Set aside.
6. Prepare the Meringue: Fill a saucepan with water to a depth of 1 inch. Set a heatproof bowl on top of pan, making sure bottom of bowl doesn't touch water. Whisk together granulated sugar and egg whites in bowl; cook over medium, stirring occasionally, until sugar is dissolved, 2 to 3 minutes. Carefully remove bowl from heat, and add vanilla and cream of tartar. Beat with a hand mixer on medium-high speed until stiff peaks form, about 5 minutes.
7. Spoon Meringue onto Cake; spread Meringue using the back of a spoon to create decorative peaks and swirls. Using a kitchen torch, brown Meringue, holding torch 1 to 2 inches away and moving torch back and forth. Alternatively, broil topped Cake, watching closely, until topping is toasted, 2 to 3 minutes. Garnish with halved strawberries.

Strawberry Shortcake Ice-Cream Cake

Cornmeal shortcake, berry sorbet, and strawberry ripple ice cream add up to one tasty dessert. The key to preparing this just right is to use two loaf pans that are the same size—one for baking the cake and the other for layering and freezing the ice cream and sorbet.

ACTIVE 25 MIN. - TOTAL 25 MIN., PLUS 7 HOURS FREEZING

SERVES 8

CAKE LAYER
- 1 cup all-purpose flour
- ¾ cup granulated sugar
- ⅓ cup plain yellow cornmeal
- 1½ tsp. baking powder
- ½ tsp. kosher salt
- ½ cup whole buttermilk
- ⅓ cup vegetable oil
- 1 large egg, at room temperature

ICE-CREAM LAYER
- 1 cup heavy whipping cream
- 3 large fresh strawberries, hulled and roughly chopped (⅔ cup)
- ¼ cup strawberry preserves
- ¼ cup sweetened condensed milk (from 1 [14-oz.] can)
- ½ tsp. vanilla extract
- 1 pt. strawberry sorbet, softened

TOPPING
- 1 lb. fresh strawberries, hulled and sliced (optional)
- 3 Tbsp. granulated sugar (optional)

1. Prepare the Cake Layer: Preheat oven to 375°F. Coat an 8½- x 4½-inch loaf pan with cooking spray; line with parchment paper, leaving a 1-inch overhang on 2 long sides. Whisk together flour, sugar, cornmeal, baking powder, and salt in a medium bowl. Add buttermilk, oil, and egg; whisk to combine. Pour batter into prepared pan. Bake until edges are golden and a wooden pick inserted into center comes out clean, about 30 minutes. Transfer loaf pan to a wire rack. Let Cake Layer cool completely, about 1 hour.

2. Meanwhile, prepare the Ice-Cream Layer: Line another 8½- x 4½-inch loaf pan with parchment paper. Beat whipping cream in a large bowl with a hand mixer on high speed until stiff peaks form, 2 to 3 minutes. Gently fold in chopped strawberries, preserves, condensed milk, and vanilla (for a rippled appearance, stop stirring before berries and preserves are fully combined). Spread mixture evenly in pan. Freeze, uncovered, until firm, about 1 hour. Remove from freezer; spread sorbet evenly over ice cream. Return to freezer.

3. Remove cooled Cake Layer from loaf pan. Using a serrated knife, trim the domed top of Cake Layer to make it flat and even. Remove Ice-Cream Layer from freezer. Place Cake Layer, cut side down, on top of sorbet. Cover and freeze until Ice-Cream Layer is solid, about 6 hours.

4. If desired, prepare the Topping: Stir together strawberries and sugar in a medium bowl until combined. Let stand, stirring occasionally, until strawberries begin to release their juices, about 10 minutes. (If making the cake ahead of time, wait until just before serving to stir together the Topping.)

5. Remove ice-cream cake from freezer. Run a butter knife along the edges to loosen from pan. Invert onto a platter; top with strawberry mixture, if desired. Serve immediately, or cover tightly with plastic wrap and freeze up to 1 month.

STRAWBERRY TRIFLE WITH COCONUT-LIME WHIPPED CREAM (PAGE 112)

STRAWBERRY SHORTCAKE BISCUIT "PUDDING" (PAGE 112)

Strawberry Ladyfinger Cake

This is a whimsical way to enjoy the best berries of the season without a lot of fuss. Store-bought ladyfinger cookies are layered with light and airy mascarpone whipped cream and lemony strawberries for an easy icebox cake that you can whip up in advance.

ACTIVE 20 MIN. - TOTAL 35 MIN., PLUS 8 HOURS CHILLING

SERVES 8

- 1¼ lb. fresh strawberries, hulled and sliced (about 2½ cups)
- ¼ cup granulated sugar
- ½ tsp. grated lemon zest, plus 2 Tbsp. fresh juice (from 1 lemon), divided
- 1 cup mascarpone or cream cheese
- ½ cup powdered sugar
- 2½ cups heavy whipping cream
- 1 tsp. vanilla extract
- 2 (7-oz.) pkg. crunchy ladyfingers, as needed, divided
- Mint leaves for garnish

1. Stir together strawberries, granulated sugar, and lemon juice in a medium bowl. Let stand, stirring occasionally, until berries have released their juices, about 15 minutes. Using a slotted spoon, transfer macerated berries to a separate medium bowl; reserve juices in original bowl.
2. Beat mascarpone and powdered sugar in a large bowl with a hand mixer on medium speed until light and airy, about 15 seconds. Add whipping cream, vanilla, and lemon zest. Beat on high speed until stiff peaks form, 2 to 3 minutes.
3. Trim away an inch from 1 end of about 25 ladyfingers; reserve cookie trimmings. Spread ½ cup mascarpone whipped cream in the bottom of a 9-inch springform pan. Stand the trimmed cookies, cut sides down, around the pan edges. Dip leftover cookie trimmings into reserved strawberry juices, and cover mascarpone layer in pan with a single layer of cookie trimmings. Spread half of the remaining mascarpone whipped cream over trimmings, and top evenly with half of the berries.
4. For the next layer, top strawberries with dipped cookie trimmings (using additional cookies from second package as needed) and then remaining mascarpone; finish by topping with remaining berries. Drizzle cake with any remaining strawberry juices in bowl. Loosely cover cake with plastic wrap. Chill until firm, at least 8 hours or up to 12 hours. Cake may be covered and stored in refrigerator up to 2 days. Garnish with mint leaves just before serving.

Strawberry Trifle with Coconut-Lime Whipped Cream

(Photo, page 110)

Inspired by the classic British dessert Eton mess, this layered trifle wows with macerated berries and crisp meringue cookies combined with lime-flecked whipped cream. It's best to serve it right after assembling so guests can enjoy the mix of crunchy and creamy textures before the delicate cookies soften.

ACTIVE 20 MIN. - TOTAL 30 MIN.

SERVES 10

- 2 lb. fresh strawberries, hulled and halved lengthwise
- ¼ cup packed dark brown sugar
- 2¼ cups heavy whipping cream
- ⅓ cup cream of coconut (from 1 [13.66-oz.] can)
- 1½ tsp. grated lime zest (from 2 limes)
- 4 cups meringue cookies, broken into about ½-inch pieces
- ½ cup toasted sweetened flaked coconut

1. Stir together strawberries and brown sugar in a medium bowl; let stand 10 minutes. Using a fork, crush about half of the strawberries in bowl. Stir; set aside.
2. Beat whipping cream, cream of coconut, and lime zest in a stand mixer fitted with a whisk attachment on high speed until stiff peaks form, 2 to 3 minutes. Gently fold in meringue cookies.
3. Spoon one-third of the strawberry mixture (about 1 cup) into a 3-quart trifle dish. Top with half of the meringue mixture (about 3 cups). Repeat layers once. Top with remaining strawberry mixture. Sprinkle with toasted coconut. Serve immediately.

Strawberry Shortcake Biscuit "Pudding"

(Photo, page 111)

Buttery biscuits serve as an irresistible substitute for sliced bread in this berry-filled delight brightened with a hint of orange. Store-bought biscuits (frozen or from the bakery) make this recipe a cinch to prepare for cooks of all skill levels.

ACTIVE 20 MIN. - TOTAL 2 HOURS

SERVES 8

- Unsalted butter, for greasing dish
- 5 large egg yolks
- 2¼ cups heavy whipping cream
- ¾ cup granulated sugar
- 1 tsp. grated orange zest (from 1 orange)
- 1 tsp. vanilla bean paste
- ½ tsp. kosher salt
- 8 cups cubed (1-inch pieces) day-old biscuits (about 6 extra large)
- ¾ lb. fresh strawberries, hulled and diced (about 2 cups), plus halved strawberries for garnish
- ¼ cup strawberry preserves
- Powdered sugar

1. Preheat oven to 350°F. Grease an 8-inch baking dish with butter, and set aside. Whisk together egg yolks, whipping cream, granulated sugar, orange zest, vanilla bean paste, and salt in a large bowl. Add biscuit cubes; gently toss to coat.
2. Cover bottom of prepared baking dish with half of the soaked biscuit cubes. Sprinkle with half of the diced strawberries, and dot with half of the preserves. Repeat layers once. Pour remaining egg yolk mixture over contents in baking dish; let stand 10 minutes.
3. Bake in preheated oven until set in center, about 1 hour, 10 minutes, rotating baking dish from front to back halfway through bake time and loosely covering with aluminum foil after 45 minutes. Remove from oven; let cool slightly, about 15 minutes. Dust with powdered sugar, and garnish with halved strawberries just before serving.

STRAWBERRY
LADYFINGER CAKE

SUPPERTIME

Spin the Bottle

Reach for your favorite condiments to liven up weeknight dinners

Savory Veggie Fajitas
ACTIVE 30 MIN. - TOTAL 30 MIN.
SERVES 4

- 3 Tbsp. vegetable oil, divided
- 4 large (about 1 lb. total) portobello mushrooms, stemmed, gills removed, and sliced ½ inch thick (8 cups)
- 3 small assorted bell peppers, sliced ¼ inch thick (about 2½ cups)
- 1 small red onion, sliced ¼ inch thick (about 1 cup)
- 1 tsp. kosher salt, divided
- 1 tsp. finely chopped garlic (about 2 garlic cloves)
- 1 tsp. ground cumin
- 1 tsp. smoked paprika
- ½ tsp. chipotle chile powder (optional)
- 5 Tbsp. Worcestershire sauce
- 2 Tbsp. ketchup
- 8 (6-inch) flour tortillas, warmed
- Toppings: fresh cilantro leaves, lime wedges, salsa, and sour cream

1. Heat 2 tablespoons of the oil in a large cast-iron skillet over high until shimmering, about 3 minutes. Add mushrooms in a single layer, and cook, turning once halfway through, until browned and softened, about 6 minutes. Transfer to a plate; set aside.
2. Without wiping skillet clean, add remaining 1 tablespoon oil to skillet; heat over high until shimmering, about 30 seconds. Add bell peppers, onion, and ½ teaspoon of the salt; cook, stirring occasionally, until softened and charred in spots, 6 to 8 minutes.
3. Reduce heat to medium. Return mushrooms to skillet with garlic, cumin, smoked paprika, chipotle chile powder (if using), and remaining ½ teaspoon salt. Cook, stirring often, until fragrant, about 30 seconds. Stir in Worcestershire sauce and ketchup; cook, stirring occasionally, until vegetables are evenly coated, about 1 minute. Serve immediately with warm tortillas and desired toppings.

DYNAMIC DUO
Umami-packed Worcestershire sauce and ketchup join forces to amp up these veggie fajitas.

114   2024 MAY

Mustardy Glazed Barbecue Ribs

ACTIVE 35 MIN. - TOTAL 3 HOURS, 30 MIN.
SERVES 4

- 1 (3-lb.) rack St. Louis-style pork spareribs
- 4 tsp. kosher salt
- 4 tsp. smoked paprika
- 4 tsp. chili powder
- 4 tsp. light brown sugar
- 2 tsp. black pepper, plus more for garnish
- 1½ tsp. garlic powder
- ¾ cup yellow mustard
- 6 Tbsp. honey
- ¼ cup bottled barbecue sauce
- 2 Tbsp. apple cider vinegar
- ½ tsp. hot sauce

1. Preheat oven to 300°F with rack about 8 inches from heat source. Line a large rimmed baking sheet with aluminum foil; set an oven-safe wire rack inside lined baking sheet, and set aside. Remove thin outer membrane on back of ribs by loosening with a sharp knife and pulling it off; discard membrane. Set ribs aside.

2. Stir together salt, paprika, chili powder, brown sugar, pepper, and garlic powder in a small bowl. Transfer 1 teaspoon spice mixture to a small bowl, and set aside. Sprinkle remaining spice mixture on both sides of ribs, gently patting to coat. Wrap ribs in heavy-duty aluminum foil; place on prepared wire rack.

3. Bake in preheated oven until ribs are fork-tender, 2 hours, 45 minutes to 3 hours. Meanwhile, whisk together mustard, honey, barbecue sauce, vinegar, hot sauce, and reserved 1 teaspoon spice mixture in a small bowl until well combined; cover and chill until ready to use.

4. Remove ribs from oven. Unwrap and discard aluminum foil. Brush top of rib rack evenly with ⅓ cup of the mustard sauce. Increase oven temperature to broil; return ribs to oven. Broil until sauce starts to caramelize, 5 to 8 minutes. Remove from oven; brush with ⅓ cup of the sauce. Let rest 5 minutes. Slice ribs in between bones; transfer to a platter. Serve with remaining mustard sauce, and garnish with pepper.

GO FOR THE GOLD
South Carolina is known for its tangy, mustard-spiked barbecue sauce. Don't use Dijon—the plain yellow kind works best here.

Crispy Ranch Shrimp

ACTIVE 30 MIN. - TOTAL 35 MIN.
SERVES 4

- Vegetable oil, for frying
- 1 cup plain yellow cornmeal
- ¼ cup self-rising flour
- 1 tsp. kosher salt
- ½ tsp. black pepper, plus more for garnish
- 1 (1-oz.) envelope ranch dressing mix, divided
- ½ cup bottled ranch dressing (such as Hidden Valley), plus more for serving
- ½ cup whole milk
- 1 large egg
- 1 lb. jumbo peeled, deveined raw shrimp, tail-on
- Chopped fresh dill

1. Pour oil to a depth of 2 inches in a large Dutch oven; heat over medium-high until a deep-fry thermometer registers 325°F.

2. Meanwhile, whisk together cornmeal, flour, salt, pepper, and 2 tablespoons of the ranch dressing mix in a shallow bowl until well combined; set aside. Whisk together bottled ranch dressing, milk, egg, and remaining 2 teaspoons ranch mix in a medium bowl until well combined. Working in batches, dip shrimp in milk mixture, allowing excess liquid to drip off. Press shrimp into cornmeal mixture, turning to coat all sides. Transfer to a baking sheet; repeat with remaining shrimp.

3. Working in batches, add about 6 breaded shrimp to hot oil; fry, turning occasionally, until golden brown and cooked through, about 2 minutes. Remove from oil using a slotted spoon; transfer to a wire rack set over a rimmed baking sheet. Repeat process with remaining shrimp, adjusting heat as needed to maintain temperature. Serve with additional ranch dressing, and garnish with dill and pepper.

DOUBLE-DIP
These fried shrimp are packed with tangy ranch flavor from two sources—bottled dressing and seasoning mix.

Hot-Honey Grilled Chicken

ACTIVE 40 MIN. · TOTAL 1 HOUR
SERVES 4

- 4 (8- to 9-oz. each) boneless, skinless chicken breasts
- 1 Tbsp. olive oil
- 2 tsp. finely chopped garlic (about 4 garlic cloves)
- 1¼ tsp. kosher salt
- ½ tsp. black pepper
- 3 Tbsp. unsalted butter
- ¾ cup honey
- ¼ cup hot sauce
- 1 Tbsp. apple cider vinegar
- 2 tsp. paprika
- Sliced scallions
- Flaky sea salt (optional)

1. Add chicken breasts, olive oil, garlic, salt, and pepper to a large bowl; toss until chicken is fully coated. Let stand at room temperature, uncovered, 20 minutes.

2. Meanwhile, preheat a gas grill to high (450°F to 500°F) on one side. While grill preheats, melt butter in a saucepan over medium-high. Whisk in honey and hot sauce. Bring to a boil over medium-high, stirring occasionally. Reduce heat to medium-low; simmer, stirring occasionally, until thickened and syrupy, 10 to 12 minutes. Remove from heat; stir in vinegar and paprika. Transfer 3 tablespoons hot-honey glaze to a small bowl, and set aside for serving.

3. Place chicken on oiled grates over lit side of grill. Grill, covered, until grill marks form, about 3 minutes. Turn chicken, transferring to unlit side of grill. Brush top of each chicken breast with about 1½ teaspoons of the hot-honey glaze. Close lid; grill until a thermometer inserted into the thickest portion of chicken registers 165°F, 10 to 12 minutes, brushing each chicken breast with about 1½ teaspoons hot-honey glaze every 2 minutes.

4. Remove chicken from grill, and place on a platter. Let stand 5 minutes. Brush with reserved 3 tablespoons hot-honey glaze. Garnish with sliced scallions, and sprinkle with flaky sea salt, if desired.

DON'T GET TOO FIRED UP

While honey tames the heat in this recipe, not all hot sauces are created equal. Choose one that's on the milder side, like Frank's RedHot or Tabasco.

Secret Sauce Smashburgers

ACTIVE 35 MIN. - TOTAL 35 MIN.
SERVES 4

- 1 Tbsp. hot sauce
- 1 Tbsp. spicy brown mustard
- 1 Tbsp. Worcestershire sauce
- 1 tsp. finely grated fresh garlic (from 2 garlic cloves)
- ¾ cup Thousand Island dressing
- 1 tsp. black pepper, divided
- 1 lb. ground chuck
- 2 tsp. kosher salt
- 4 (¾-oz.) American cheese slices
- 4 sesame seed hamburger buns, toasted
- Toppings: shredded lettuce, thinly sliced red onions, sliced tomatoes, and dill pickle chips

1. Stir together hot sauce, mustard, Worcestershire sauce, grated garlic, Thousand Island dressing, and ½ teaspoon of the pepper in a medium bowl until well combined. Transfer ¼ cup sauce to a small bowl; set aside for basting. Cover and reserve remaining sauce until ready to assemble burgers.

2. Portion ground chuck into 8 (2-oz.) loosely packed meatballs; season with salt and remaining ½ teaspoon pepper. Heat a large cast-iron skillet or griddle over high until smoking, about 4 minutes. Working in batches, add 2 meatballs to skillet; flatten each to ¼-inch thickness using a wide, sturdy spatula. Cook until bottoms are crisp and deeply browned, about 45 seconds. Baste tops of patties with about ¾ teaspoon of sauce from small bowl. Flip patties, and brush each with about ¾ teaspoon sauce from small bowl. Place a slice of cheese on 1 of the patties; cook until bottoms are well browned and cheese is melted, about 30 seconds. Stack plain patty on cheese-topped patty. Transfer stack to a plate; cover tightly with aluminum foil. Quickly wipe skillet clean, and repeat process with the remaining 6 meatballs, sauce from small bowl, and 3 cheese slices.

3. Spread 1 tablespoon of reserved sauce from medium bowl on the bottom half of each bun. Add stacked burger patties; layer desired toppings. Spread 1 tablespoon reserved sauce on the top half of each bun, and cover burgers with bun tops. Serve with potato chips and remaining reserved sauce on the side.

EXTRA-SPECIAL SAUCE
Every burger joint has its own unique condiment. Customize this recipe to suit your taste by adding a splash of Sriracha or a pinch of smoked paprika.

LIGHTEN UP

Crunch Time

Southern-style okra, no deep-frying required

Smashed Oven-Fried Okra
ACTIVE 25 MIN. - TOTAL 45 MIN.
SERVES 4

- ½ cup low-fat buttermilk
- 1 large egg
- ⅔ cup plain yellow cornmeal
- 1 tsp. Creole seasoning
- ¾ tsp. kosher salt, divided
- 1 lb. fresh okra pods
- 2 Tbsp. canola oil
- Lemon wedges (optional)
- Speedy Creole Comeback Sauce (recipe below right)

1. Preheat oven to 450°F. Whisk together buttermilk, ⅓ cup water, and egg in a medium bowl. Stir together cornmeal, Creole seasoning, and ½ teaspoon of the kosher salt in a shallow dish.
2. Line two baking sheets with parchment paper. Working with 1 pod at a time, place okra on a clean work surface and crush with a rolling pin until split in places (the pod should remain intact). Repeat with remaining okra.
3. Dip each smashed okra pod in buttermilk mixture; add to cornmeal mixture. Turn pods, pressing lightly to coat. Place coated okra on prepared baking sheets; drizzle with oil. Bake in preheated oven until golden brown and crispy on both sides, about 20 minutes, carefully turning halfway through baking. Remove from oven, and immediately sprinkle with remaining ¼ teaspoon salt. Transfer to a platter. Serve with lemon wedges, if desired, and Speedy Creole Comeback Sauce for dipping.

Speedy Creole Comeback Sauce
ACTIVE 5 MIN. - TOTAL 5 MIN.
MAKES ABOUT ½ CUP

Stir together ¼ cup each **mayonnaise** and **plain whole-milk yogurt**, 1 Tbsp. **ketchup**, 1 tsp. **Worcestershire sauce**, and ½ tsp. **Creole seasoning** in a small bowl. Cover and chill until ready to serve.

GOOD FOR YOU!
Fried okra is a classic, but it can be very greasy. Roasting this breaded veggie in the oven cuts down on the fat without sacrificing the super-crispy crust.

Before Recipe Makeover:
CALORIES: 300 – CARB: 47 G – SODIUM: 823 MG

After Recipe Makeover:
CALORIES: 227 – CARB: 31 G – SODIUM: 594 MG

BERRY BASKET UPSIDE-DOWN CAKE

PIECE OF CAKE

Hold the Pineapple

Flip the script on upside-down cake

SPICED PLUM UPSIDE-DOWN CAKE

PEANUT BUTTER–BANANA UPSIDE-DOWN CAKE

Berry Basket Upside-Down Cake
ACTIVE 15 MIN. - TOTAL 1 HOUR, 15 MIN.
SERVES 8

- ⅓ cup light brown sugar
- 4 Tbsp. unsalted butter
- 1 tsp. kosher salt, divided
- 3 cups mixed fresh berries (such as blueberries, blackberries, and raspberries)
- 2 large eggs, at room temperature
- 1 cup granulated sugar
- ½ cup sour cream, at room temperature
- ½ cup vegetable oil
- 1 tsp. vanilla extract
- 1½ cups all-purpose flour
- 2 tsp. baking powder
- 1 tsp. ground cinnamon

1. Preheat oven to 350°F. Coat a 9-inch round cake pan with cooking spray. Stir together brown sugar, butter, 1 tablespoon water, and ¼ teaspoon of the salt in a small saucepan; cook over medium until sugar is dissolved, 1 to 2 minutes. Transfer mixture to prepared pan; spread in an even layer. Top evenly with berries. Set aside.

2. Whisk together eggs, granulated sugar, sour cream, oil, vanilla, and remaining ¾ teaspoon salt in a large bowl. Sift in the flour, baking powder, and cinnamon. Gently fold flour mixture into sour cream mixture using a spatula until just combined. Spread batter over berries in an even layer.

3. Bake in preheated oven until top is golden brown and a wooden pick inserted into center of cake comes out mostly clean, 45 to 50 minutes. Let cool in pan on a wire rack for 15 minutes. Place a cake plate on top of pan; invert cake onto plate. Serve warm or at room temperature.

Two Tasty Variations

Peanut Butter–Banana Upside-Down Cake
Prepare the recipe as directed, substituting **dark brown sugar** for the light brown sugar and 3 **medium bananas** (sliced lengthwise) for the mixed berries in Step 1. Place bananas in pan cut sides down; sprinkle with ¼ cup chopped **salted roasted peanuts**. In Step 2, whisk ⅓ cup **smooth peanut butter** into egg mixture. Proceed with recipe as directed. Top with additional **peanuts**.

Spiced Plum Upside-Down Cake
Prepare the recipe as directed, substituting 2 cups sliced **plums** (from 3 to 4 whole plums, cut ½ inch thick) for the mixed berries in Step 1. In Step 2, substitute ½ tsp. **ground cardamom** for the cinnamon. Proceed with recipe as directed.

DINING IN

American Spirit

Chef Edward Lee's new book explores Kentucky's beloved drink

BOURBON HAS TAKEN on many different cultural identities throughout the United States. In chef and writer Edward Lee's latest book, *Bourbon Land: A Spirited Love Letter to My Old Kentucky Whiskey*, he focuses on the quintessential liquor of his home state from its earliest iterations to today—or as he puts it, "from the temperance movement, when it was blamed for every evil, to now, when it's the trendiest, coolest thing on the planet."

Lee characterizes the amber spirit as "time trapped in a bottle." It's an apt description for a drink that distinctly captures a specific place and tradition. It was once forsaken in favor of clear alcohols such as gin and vodka, but the resurgence in classic cocktails like the old-fashioned, coupled with factors like a post-9/11 desire to buy American-made products, led to a mid-2000s bourbon boom. His new book contextualizes its ever-growing popularity and extensive production process.

"I don't think people understand how much time goes into bourbon. They see an age statement (like four, five, or six years) and think that's the total amount of time it took. But it's actually far more than that. Think about how long it takes for the corn to grow—plus the 70 or so years required for the tree to mature," he says, referencing the oak needed for the barrels.

The liquor's flavor is often as misunderstood as its production. "It has been misrepresented as something sweet, but to me, the really interesting notes of bourbon start with the savory," Lee says. He appreciates its earthy hints of leather or hay and the smoky aroma that comes from aging it in charred casks.

Not only will this tome convince you to take a sip, but it will also make you want to cook with bourbon. Lee even recommends using the spirit in tandem with delicate ingredients like fish or in a refreshing watermelon salad (recipe at right) despite its robust flavor.

Lee also collected cocktail recipes from notable mixologists—exemplifying how far bourbon has come since the early days of his career when it was relegated to being a cook's postshift drink. "The bartender wasn't going to give you the high-end vodka that was selling, so he poured you a shot of Wild Turkey because it sat in the back of the bar. No one drank it," he says. Thankfully, times have changed.

Watermelon, Mint, Feta, and Fried-Peanut Salad
ACTIVE 10 MIN. - TOTAL 20 MIN.
SERVES 8

Place 8 cups seeded and cubed **watermelon** in a large bowl. Add 1 cup loosely packed **fresh mint leaves** (chopped), ⅔ cup crumbled **feta cheese**, 2 Tbsp. **toasted sesame seeds**, 1 Tbsp. **olive oil**, and 1 tsp. **fresh lemon juice**. Toss gently until just combined; set aside. Cook 1 cup **unsalted dry-roasted peanuts** in a skillet over medium heat, stirring occasionally, until just lightly toasted, about 2 minutes. Add 1 Tbsp. **bourbon**, 2 tsp. **soy sauce**, and 1½ tsp. **granulated sugar**; cook, shaking skillet vigorously, until skillet is almost dry, 15 to 30 seconds. Transfer peanuts to a plate; let cool 10 minutes. Assemble salad on a platter; top with fried peanuts, and sprinkle with **Bourbon Salt** (recipe follows) to taste.

Bourbon Salt
ACTIVE 5 MIN. - TOTAL 1 HOUR, 40 MIN.
MAKES 1 CUP

Line a rimmed baking sheet with parchment. Bring 2½ cups **bourbon** to a simmer in a pan over medium. Cook, undisturbed, until reduced by half, about 10 minutes. Add 1 cup **coarse sea salt**; bring to a simmer. Cook, undisturbed, until most of bourbon has evaporated, about 8 minutes. Spread salt on baking sheet in an even layer. Bake at 200°F until dry, about 1 hour. Let cool 15 minutes. Break up large pieces; store in an airtight container at room temperature up to 1 month.

OVER EASY

Million-Dollar Pancakes

A sweet and simple breakfast to celebrate Mother's Day

GO BIG
Dollop the batter on the pan in ¼-cup portions for regular-size pancakes.

Lemon-Ricotta Silver Dollar Pancakes
ACTIVE 25 MIN. - TOTAL 25 MIN.
SERVES 6

- 2 cups all-purpose flour
- 3 Tbsp. granulated sugar
- 2 tsp. baking powder
- 1 tsp. baking soda
- ½ tsp. kosher salt
- 2 cups whole-milk ricotta cheese
- ¾ cup whole milk
- 3 Tbsp. melted unsalted butter, plus more for brushing griddle
- 2 large eggs
- 2 tsp. grated lemon zest, plus ¼ cup fresh juice (from 2 lemons), plus more zest and wedges for garnish
- Powdered sugar
- Butter
- Maple syrup

1. Whisk together all-purpose flour, granulated sugar, baking powder, baking soda, and salt in a large bowl until combined.
2. Whisk together ricotta, milk, melted butter, eggs, lemon zest, and lemon juice in a separate bowl. Form a well in flour mixture; add ricotta mixture, stirring until just combined (batter will be lumpy). Let batter stand at room temperature while griddle heats.
3. Heat a griddle or large skillet over medium-high, and brush with melted butter. Working in batches, dollop 2-tablespoon scoops of batter onto pan 2 inches apart. Cook until browned on each side, about 2 minutes per side, adjusting heat as needed.
4. Garnish with powdered sugar and lemon zest and wedges. Serve with butter and syrup.

IVY'S KITCHEN

I'll Bring the Bourbon

Senior Lifestyle Editor Ivy Odom makes a strong case for this Southern spirit

EXACTLY ONE MONTH before my wedding, my then fiancé, Luis, and I dug a hole in my parents' yard, but we weren't landscaping. We were burying a bottle of W.L. Weller Special Reserve in the spot where we'd get married. I insisted on this wedding tradition, as it was said to guarantee good weather for our big day. I also wanted to use bourbon in a signature drink at the reception. The cocktail—which we affectionately named the Basil Smash after our dog, Basil—combined my beloved Kentucky whiskey with the fragrant herb and bright lemon. Our guests, both bourbon aficionados and novices alike, still rave about it years later.

While I adore this spirit, it has a reputation of being for the boys. But why should they have all the fun? The easy cocktails below, including the famous Basil Smash, are my favorite ways to use it. I created them for the women in my life, because bourbon is for everyone. And don't worry—we dug up that bottle of Weller (I was in my white dress, no less) to enjoy after the ceremony.

Basil Smash
ACTIVE 10 MIN. - TOTAL 45 MIN.
SERVES 2

Bring ½ cup each **granulated sugar, water,** and packed **fresh basil leaves** to a boil over medium; boil until sugar dissolves, about 2 minutes. Remove from heat; let cool completely, about 30 minutes. Pour basil simple syrup through a fine mesh strainer into a small heatproof container, discarding leaves. Muddle 8 **fresh basil leaves** in bottom of a cocktail shaker using a muddler or the handle of a wooden spoon. Add ½ cup **ice,** ½ cup **bourbon,** ¼ cup **fresh lemon juice,** and 3 Tbsp. basil simple syrup to shaker. Shake vigorously until chilled, about 30 seconds. Fill 2 rocks glasses with **ice.** Pour cocktail through fine mesh strainer into glasses, and garnish with **basil sprigs** and **lemon slices.**

Bourbon Mule
Hold with tradition by serving this cocktail in a metal cup.
ACTIVE 5 MIN. - TOTAL 5 MIN.
SERVES 1

Fill a silver julep cup or copper mule mug with 1 cup **ice.** Add ¼ cup **bourbon** and 1 Tbsp. **fresh lime juice,** and stir to combine. Top with ½ cup **nonalcoholic ginger beer,** and garnish with **fresh mint.**

Bourbon-Pineapple Slush
Orgeat syrup is sweet and slightly creamy. It's made from almonds, sugar, and orange flower water. If you can't find it, substitute amaretto.
ACTIVE 5 MIN. - TOTAL 5 MIN., PLUS 2 HOURS FREEZING
SERVES 4

Process 2 cups **pineapple juice,** 1 cup **bourbon,** 1 cup **cream of coconut,** ½ cup **fresh orange juice,** ¼ cup **orgeat syrup,** 2 Tbsp. **honey,** and ¼ tsp. **ground cinnamon** in a blender on low speed until smooth, about 10 seconds. Cover blender container tightly with plastic wrap, and place in freezer until very cold, at least 2 hours. Add 4 cups **ice** to mixture in blender, and process until smooth, about 1 minute. Divide among 4 glasses, and garnish with **fresh pineapple wedges, pineapple leaves,** and grated **nutmeg.**

Stock Your Bar
Two must-try bottles

Woodford Reserve Kentucky Straight Bourbon Whiskey
Woodford is easy to find, no matter where you live. Even better, it's crafted by a female master distiller, Elizabeth McCall. It's complex but approachable and great for sipping, mixing, cooking, and everything in between.

Eagle Rare 10 Year Kentucky Straight Bourbon Whiskey
This one may require a hunt but is well worth it. While it's not the most expensive on the shelf, the scarcity makes it a little more special than your average bottle. Whether served neat or on the rocks, Eagle Rare will impress even your serious whiskey-drinking friends.

COOKING SCHOOL
TIPS AND TRICKS FROM THE SOUTH'S MOST TRUSTED KITCHEN

Upgrade Your Cookout
Great gear and clever hacks for top-notch summer grilling

DITCH THAT OLD, RUSTY BRUSH

An onion will remove stuck-on food with ease

It's never fun cleaning grill grates, but there's a surprising solution that tackles the mess without harsh chemicals or wire brushes: half of a raw onion. Use tongs or a long grill fork to rub the onion, cut side down, over the hot grates. The heat will release steam from the vegetable, which will help loosen cooked-on bits. For extra cleaning power, spray the grates with a little lemon juice or vinegar first.

Say Goodbye to Wooden Skewers
Try this sustainable option instead

Choose stainless steel skewers for your kebabs. Sturdier than wood or bamboo, they don't require soaking and are reusable. We like the OXO 6-Piece Grilling Skewer Set, which features a flat design to keep ingredients from spinning. Their long handles are ideal for grabbing with tongs, and the sharp tips easily pierce meat, veggies, and more for effortless threading. Bonus: They're dishwasher-safe; $15/set of six; *oxo.com*

Three Kebab Commandments

1
Don't combine other proteins with chicken on the same skewer; it takes longer to cook.

2
Use dry rubs and spice mixes instead of brushing on sauces that can burn.

3
Keep all ingredients roughly the same size for even heating and easy eating.

TAKE IT INSIDE

Pick the right pan to bring the fun indoors

If it's raining or you're not in the mood for open-fire cooking, one work-around for indoor barbecues is a grill pan. Cast-iron ones tend to be more durable than nonstick versions, and they retain heat better too. Be sure to preheat your pan on medium-high before adding food to achieve good charring. To test whether it's hot enough, flick a little water across the pan's surface; it should sizzle. To make up for the lack of flame-kissed flavor, season your food with smoky ingredients like paprika, bacon, and chipotle peppers. Minimize cleanup by avoiding sugary sauces.

126 2024 MAY

June–July

128   **Use Your Melon** Refreshing recipes to showcase the versatile and sweet cantaloupe

130   **From Aleppo to Za'atar** A fresh take on summer sides inspired by the flavors of the Middle East

137   **When Life Gives You Lemons...** Chill out with this nostalgic no-bake dessert

138   **She's Got the Scoop** In Richmond, Virginia, Rabia Kamara creates ice cream that celebrates Black culture and her heritage

140   **Not Your Mama's Meat 'n' Three** Old-school Southern dishes learn a few new tricks

148   **It's Peak Squash Season** This roasted riff on a classic side reduces the fat but keeps the crunchy topping

149   **Ready to Roll** Forget those flat quesadillas–this pull-apart version is party perfect

150   **Garden Party** Simple tricks for preserving produce–no canning required

152   **Cooking School** Our Test Kitchen professionals tell the truth about tomatoes–specifically, how to store and keep them fresh and juicy

BOUNTY

Use Your Melon

Refreshing recipes to showcase the versatile and sweet cantaloupe

Cantaloupe Salad with Chile-Lime Dressing
ACTIVE 20 MIN. - TOTAL 20 MIN.
SERVES 8

Peel 1 (2¾-lb.) **cantaloupe,** and cut in half lengthwise; reserve 1 half for another use. Remove and discard seeds from remaining half; thinly slice melon lengthwise into ⅛-inch-thick slices using a knife or mandoline. Peel 1 (1-lb.) **jicama,** and cut in half lengthwise. Reserve 1 half for another use. Thinly slice remaining half lengthwise into ¹⁄₁₆-inch-thick slices. Arrange cantaloupe, jicama, 1 cup thinly shaved **cucumber** (from 1 cucumber), and ¼ cup thinly sliced **red onion** (from 1 onion) on a platter. Whisk together ¼ cup plus ½ Tbsp. **bottled chamoy sauce** (such as Tajín), ¼ cup **canola oil,** 2 Tbsp. each **lime juice** and **honey,** and 1 tsp. **kosher salt** in a small bowl. Drizzle half of dressing over salad on platter. Sprinkle with ½ cup **fresh cilantro leaves,** ¼ cup crumbled **Cotija cheese,** and 1 tsp. **chili-lime seasoning** (such as Tajín). Serve with additional **Cotija, lime wedges,** and remaining dressing.

No-Churn Cantaloupe–White Balsamic Sorbet
ACTIVE 20 MIN. - TOTAL 20 MIN., PLUS 4 HOURS, 30 MIN. FREEZING
SERVES 6

Place 3 cups chopped **cantaloupe** (from 1 [2-lb.] cantaloupe) on a baking sheet lined with parchment paper. Freeze, uncovered, until firm, at least 1 hour, 30 minutes or up to 8 hours. Heat ¼ cup **water** and 3 Tbsp. each **granulated sugar** and **honey** in a saucepan over medium, stirring constantly, until sugar dissolves, 2 to 4 minutes. Let cool 10 minutes. Process frozen cantaloupe, sugar mixture, ½ cup **water,** 3 Tbsp. **white balsamic vinegar,** and ⅛ tsp. **kosher salt** in a food processor until smooth, 3 to 5 minutes. Pour into a freezer-safe airtight container. Freeze until firm, 3 to 4 hours. Store in freezer up to 7 days.

CANTALOUPE SALAD WITH CHILE-LIME DRESSING

NO-CHURN CANTALOUPE–WHITE BALSAMIC SORBET

SHOP SMART
When looking for the best melon, pick one that is tan in color; feels heavy for its size; sounds solid when tapped; and has a sweet, floral scent. The skin should be firm with a little give, like a pineapple.

From Aleppo to Za'atar

A fresh take on summer sides inspired by the flavors of the Middle East

CHARRED ZUCCHINI-AND-HALLOUMI KEBABS WITH LEMON-TAHINI SAUCE (PAGE 134)

CORN SALAD WITH SUMAC AND FETA (PAGE 134)

ARABIC SALAD

POMEGRANATE MOLASSES–GLAZED EGGPLANT WITH TOUM-YOGURT SAUCE

THE BOLD SPICES, sauces, and condiments in Middle Eastern kitchens are popping up at grocery stores all over the South. Lucky for us, they pair wonderfully with summer produce from our backyard gardens and farmers' markets. Ingredients like creamy, nutty tahini; tangy pomegranate molasses; and salty preserved lemons are just what you need to fall in love with your favorite vegetables all over again.

Pomegranate Molasses–Glazed Eggplant with Toum-Yogurt Sauce

Classic Southern molasses is sweet and bitter; the pomegranate kind has a deep, tangy flavor and a rich garnet color. Combined with spicy harissa, it's a punchy way to amp up mild eggplant.

ACTIVE 45 MIN. - TOTAL 45 MIN.

SERVES 6

- 2 small eggplants
- 2¾ tsp. kosher salt, divided
- 3 Tbsp. pomegranate molasses
- 1½ Tbsp. harissa paste
- 1½ Tbsp. olive oil
- 1½ Tbsp. fresh lime juice (from 1 lime)
- 1½ tsp. Aleppo pepper
- ¾ cup plain whole-milk strained (Greek-style) yogurt
- ½ cup Toum (recipe, right)
- 2 Tbsp. vegetable oil
  Crumbled feta cheese, for serving
  Torn fresh mint leaves, for serving

1. Cut each eggplant in half lengthwise, and then cut each half into 1½-inch-thick wedges. Rub eggplant wedges with 2 teaspoons of the salt. Place on a paper towel–lined baking sheet, and let stand 30 minutes.
2. Preheat grill to medium-high (400°F to 450°F). While grill preheats, whisk together pomegranate molasses, harissa, olive oil, lime juice, Aleppo pepper, and remaining ¾ teaspoon salt in a small bowl until smooth. Transfer 3 tablespoons of the mixture to a small bowl for serving, and set aside. Reserve remaining mixture for basting. Stir together yogurt and Toum in a medium bowl until well combined. Spread mixture onto a serving platter; set aside.

3. Pat eggplant pieces dry with a paper towel, and rub all over with vegetable oil. Place eggplant pieces, cut sides down, on oiled grates, and grill, uncovered, basting often with pomegranate molasses mixture and flipping once, until tender, 4 to 5 minutes per side. Place grilled eggplant pieces on top of Toum mixture on serving platter. Drizzle with reserved 3 tablespoons pomegranate molasses mixture. Garnish with feta and mint. Serve hot.

Toum

Toum (pronounced "toom") translates to "garlic" in Arabic. It's a pungent whipped sauce that comes together similarly to a mayonnaise by emulsifying oil into garlic paste. To tame its raw intensity, soak the cloves in ice water for 30 minutes before preparing. Swirled into yogurt and served under the grilled eggplant, toum adds a bold, sharp flavor.

ACTIVE 30 MIN. - TOTAL 30 MIN.

MAKES 2 CUPS

- 2 small garlic heads, broken into cloves and peeled
- 1 tsp. kosher salt
- 2 Tbsp., plus 1½ cups vegetable oil, divided
- 5 Tbsp. fresh lemon juice (from 2 large lemons)

1. Slice each garlic clove in half lengthwise using a paring knife. With the tip of the knife, remove and discard the germs (the center sprouts of the garlic cloves that can be very bitter).
2. Combine garlic, salt, and 2 tablespoons of the oil in the bowl of a food processor. Process until mixture becomes a mostly smooth, thick paste, about 2 minutes, stopping to scrape down the sides of the bowl as needed.
3. With processor running, gradually drizzle in ¼ cup of the oil in a thin stream, followed by 1 tablespoon of lemon juice. Continue alternating additions of ¼ cup oil and 1 tablespoon lemon juice until all oil and lemon juice are added. Process mixture until very fluffy, about 30 more seconds. Transfer to an airtight container, and store in refrigerator up to 2 weeks.

Arabic Salad

This chopped cucumber-and-tomato salad can be found across the Middle East. It goes by many names and comes in multiple variations. Some recipes might use a different kind of onion, opt to peel the cucumber, or incorporate cabbage or lettuce. This version uses plenty of za'atar, a Levantine spice mix, for extra savory and lemony notes. It's just one style of the versatile dish that can be served alongside practically anything.

ACTIVE 15 MIN. - TOTAL 15 MIN.

SERVES 6

- 1 medium English cucumber, chopped (about 2¼ cups)
- 3 medium plum tomatoes, chopped (about 2 cups)
- 1 medium-size red bell pepper, chopped (about 1 cup)
- 4 scallions, thinly sliced (about 1 cup)
- 1 cup chopped fresh flat-leaf parsley (from 1 [4-oz.] bunch)
- 1 small jalapeño, stemmed, seeded, and finely chopped (about 2 Tbsp.)
- 3 Tbsp. olive oil
- 2 Tbsp. fresh lemon juice (from 1 lemon)
- 1 Tbsp. za'atar, plus more for garnish
- 3 garlic cloves, grated (2 tsp.)
- ¾ tsp. kosher salt, plus more to taste

1. Stir together cucumber, tomatoes, bell pepper, scallions, parsley, and jalapeño in a large bowl; set aside.
2. Whisk together olive oil, lemon juice, za'atar, garlic, and salt in a small bowl until well combined. Pour over cucumber mixture in large bowl, and toss until evenly coated. Season with additional salt to taste. Transfer to a serving bowl, and garnish with additional za'atar. Serve immediately.

2024 JUNE–JULY 133

Charred Zucchini-and-Halloumi Kebabs with Lemon-Tahini Sauce

(Photo, page 130)

Halloumi, a firm goat cheese from Cyprus, was traditionally made by the Bedouins and is best served cooked, usually over a grill or fire, where it develops a crisp, charred crust without melting. The inspiration for this recipe comes from Lebanon, where it's commonly referred to as kebab cheese and is threaded onto skewers to be grilled. Here, it's paired with Lemon-Tahini Sauce, made from sesame paste that's thinned with lemon juice and water so it can be drizzled.

ACTIVE 30 MIN. · TOTAL 1 HOUR

SERVES 6

- ½ cup olive oil
- ¼ cup chopped fresh cilantro (from 1 bunch), plus more for garnish
- 2 Tbsp. preserved lemon paste (such as New York Shuk)
- 4 garlic cloves, grated (about 2 tsp.)
- 1 tsp. Aleppo pepper, plus more for garnish
- ½ tsp. black pepper
- 2 (8.8-oz.) blocks Halloumi cheese, each cut into 6 (1½-inch) cubes
- 3 medium zucchini or yellow squash, very thinly sliced lengthwise on a mandoline
- Toasted sesame seeds, for garnish
- Lemon-Tahini Sauce (recipe right), for serving

1. Whisk together olive oil, cilantro, preserved lemon paste, garlic, Aleppo pepper, and black pepper until well combined. Gently stir in Halloumi cubes until evenly coated; cover and set aside to marinate at room temperature at least 30 minutes or up to 24 hours. (If marinating any longer than 1 hour, mixture should be placed in refrigerator.)
2. Preheat grill to medium-high (400°F to 450°F). Stack 2 zucchini slices together; fold into a loose accordion-like shape, and thread onto a (12-inch) skewer. Add 1 Halloumi cube, followed by 2 zucchini stacks, 1 Halloumi cube, and 1 zucchini stack. Place prepared skewer on a plate. Repeat procedure with remaining zucchini slices and Halloumi cubes to make a total of 6 skewers. Brush skewers evenly with any remaining marinade in bowl.
3. Place prepared skewers on oiled grates. Grill, uncovered, turning occasionally, until Halloumi is hot and lightly charred and zucchini is tender, 4 to 6 minutes.
4. Transfer skewers to a serving platter. Garnish with additional cilantro, sesame seeds, and Aleppo pepper. Serve warm with Lemon-Tahini Sauce.

Lemon-Tahini Sauce

ACTIVE 5 MIN. · TOTAL 5 MIN.
MAKES ABOUT ⅔ CUP

Whisk together ⅓ cup **tahini**, ¼ cup **water**, 3 Tbsp. **fresh lemon juice**, 1 Tbsp. **olive oil**, and ½ tsp. **salt** in a small bowl until smooth. If sauce is too thick, add additional **water**, 1 Tbsp. at a time, to loosen to the desired consistency.

Corn Salad with Sumac and Feta

(Photo, page 131)

Mediterranean sumac (which is different from varieties native to North America) is a staple in many Middle Eastern cuisines. The name of the spice comes from the Arabic word "summaq," meaning "dark red," a nod to its vibrant color. Aside from its brightness, it can be slightly sweet, which plays well off the grilled corn in this summery side.

ACTIVE 30 MIN. · TOTAL 40 MIN.

SERVES 6

SALAD

- 4 medium ears fresh yellow corn, husks removed
- 2 Tbsp. vegetable oil
- ½ tsp. kosher salt
- ½ cup finely chopped red onion (from 1 small onion)
- 2 oz. feta cheese, crumbled (about ½ cup), plus more for garnish
- ¼ cup chopped fresh flat-leaf parsley (from 1 bunch)
- ¼ cup chopped pistachios
- 3 Tbsp. chopped fresh mint leaves (from 1 bunch)
- 1 Tbsp. finely chopped jalapeño (from 1 medium jalapeño)

DRESSING

- ⅓ cup olive oil
- 2 tsp. grated lemon zest plus ¼ cup fresh lemon juice (from 1 large lemon)
- 1 Tbsp. honey
- 2 tsp. ground sumac, plus more for garnish
- ½ tsp. kosher salt
- ½ tsp. black pepper

1. Prepare the Salad: Preheat grill to medium-high (400°F to 450°F). Rub corn with vegetable oil; season evenly with salt. Place corn on oiled grates. Grill, covered, turning occasionally, until lightly charred and tender, 10 to 15 minutes. Set aside until cool enough to handle, about 10 minutes.
2. Cut kernels from corn into a large bowl. Add onion, feta, parsley, pistachios, mint, and jalapeño; mix to combine.
3. Prepare the Dressing: Whisk together olive oil, lemon zest and juice, honey, ground sumac, salt, and pepper until well combined.
4. Pour ⅓ cup of the Dressing over corn mixture; stir until evenly coated. Transfer mixture to serving bowl, and top with additional crumbled feta and a sprinkle of additional sumac. Serve warm or chilled with remaining Dressing on the side.

Muhammara

This roasted red pepper–and–walnut spread is beloved in many countries across the Middle East. If you don't want to char your own peppers, feel free to use jarred brands that have already done that work for you. While delicious scooped up with warm pita triangles and crudités, this dip also pairs well with your favorite crackers or as a sauce for grilled chicken.

ACTIVE 30 MIN. · TOTAL 50 MIN.
SERVES 8

- 3 large red bell peppers
- 2 Tbsp. vegetable oil
- ⅓ cup olive oil
- 1 tsp. Aleppo pepper
- 1 tsp. smoked paprika
- ½ tsp. ground cumin
- 1½ cups cubed white bread
- 1 cup toasted walnuts
- 2 Tbsp. fresh lemon juice (from 1 lemon)
- 2 Tbsp. pomegranate molasses
- 1 tsp. kosher salt
- 3 garlic cloves
- Pomegranate arils, for garnish

MUHAMMARA

Chopped fresh flat-leaf parsley, for garnish

Pita triangles, for serving

Crudités (such as carrot sticks, celery sticks, mini bell peppers, and sliced cucumbers), for serving

1. Preheat grill to medium-high (400°F to 450°F). Rub bell peppers with vegetable oil, and place on oiled grates. Grill peppers, covered, turning every few minutes, until skin is completely blackened, 20 to 25 minutes. Transfer peppers to a bowl, and cover with plastic wrap. Let stand until skins are loosened, about 15 minutes.

2. Heat olive oil in a small saucepan over medium. Stir in Aleppo pepper, paprika, and cumin. Cook, stirring constantly, until fragrant, about 30 seconds. Pour mixture into a heatproof liquid measuring cup, and set aside.

3. Using your hands, remove and discard bell pepper skins, stems, and seeds. Set peeled peppers aside.

4. Process bread cubes in a food processor until they become fine crumbs, 45 to 60 seconds. Add toasted walnuts, lemon juice, pomegranate molasses, salt, garlic, and reserved peeled peppers to food processor bowl with breadcrumbs. Process until well combined, about 30 seconds, scraping down sides of bowl as needed. With processor running, gradually drizzle in oil mixture until combined, about 20 seconds. Mixture should be creamy but not completely smooth.

5. Transfer mixture to a serving bowl; top with pomegranate arils and chopped parsley. Serve with pita and crudités.

Spice Up Your Pantry
Make room for these flavorful staples of Middle Eastern cuisine

Sumac
Made from the dried and ground red berries of the sumac plant, this spice is prized for its lemonlike tartness that instantly brightens rich foods like lamb. When ground, it can be clumpy, so some brands add salt to keep the granules separate. The spice is naturally reddish purple but varies in color depending on season and origin.

HOW TO USE: Sprinkle it on grilled meat, or incorporate it into lemon desserts.

Aleppo Pepper
A mild and fruity chile, Aleppo has far more complexity than your average crushed red pepper flakes. Although native to Syria, this spice is frequently sourced from Turkey today. When purchasing, look for small, bright red flakes that are not stuck together and are slightly shiny from natural oils. It's often added as a garnish to provide color and subtle heat.

HOW TO USE: Stir it into a pasta sauce, mix it into dry rubs, or rim cocktail glasses.

Preserved Lemons
Tangy and a little funky (in a good way), this North African ingredient is made from fresh lemons that are split and then heavily salted. Over time, the entire fruit softens, including the rind. Preserved lemon can be intense, so dice it finely to distribute it evenly throughout a dish. A great shortcut is to go with New York Shuk's preserved lemon paste.

HOW TO USE: Mince and stir it into a salsa, or rub it on a chicken before roasting.

Pomegranate Molasses
When pomegranate juice is reduced down, you get this dark, sticky, tangy syrup. Molasses may be in the name, but it is quite tart and often used in savory recipes or as a finishing touch instead of a squeeze of lemon. Look for brands that list pomegranate juice as the only ingredient.

HOW TO USE: Swap it in for balsamic vinegar in dressings; drizzle it over roasted vegetables like Brussels sprouts.

Tahini
More than just a component in hummus, tahini is a paste made from ground sesame seeds that's used in many Middle Eastern dishes, including sweets such as halvah. Store it at room temperature, and don't worry if it separates—just give it a good shake or stir before using.

HOW TO USE: Treat it like peanut butter in baking (it's great with chocolate). You can also substitute it for other fats in dressings and dips.

Harissa
This fiery Tunisian condiment's name is derived from the Arabic word "harasa," which translates to "crush" or "pound." It's fitting, as harissa is a paste made from dried chiles ground with oil; salt; spices like coriander, caraway, or cumin; and garlic. Depending on the brand, heat levels can vary widely.

HOW TO USE: Fold it into meatballs, mix it into yogurt for a creamy dipping sauce, or stir it into any soup for an extra-flavorful broth.

Za'atar
An essential, it is both a green herb indigenous to the Levant and a spice blend that features it prominently. Mixes can also include salt, sesame seeds, and sumac but vary regionally and can contain other spices like cumin. This is a versatile seasoning that packs a tart, herbaceous punch and adds a subtle nuttiness to dishes.

HOW TO USE: Mix it into biscuit dough, add it to the breading for chicken, or sprinkle it on a sunny-side up egg.

PIECE OF CAKE

When Life Gives You Lemons...

Chill out with this nostalgic no-bake dessert

Frozen Lemonade Pie
ACTIVE 30 MIN. - TOTAL 30 MIN., PLUS 4 HOURS FREEZING
SERVES 8

- 2 cups graham cracker crumbs (from about 15 graham cracker sheets)
- ½ cup butter, melted
- ⅓ cup packed light brown sugar
- 1 (8-oz.) pkg. cream cheese, softened
- 1 (14-oz.) can sweetened condensed milk
- 1 (12-oz.) can frozen lemonade concentrate, thawed
- 1 Tbsp. grated lemon zest (from 2 large lemons), plus more for garnish
- ¼ tsp. kosher salt
- 1½ cups heavy whipping cream, divided
- 2 Tbsp. powdered sugar

1. Coat a 9-inch deep-dish pie plate with cooking spray. Stir together graham cracker crumbs, melted butter, and brown sugar in a medium bowl. Press mixture into bottom and up sides of prepared pie plate. Freeze until firm, about 15 minutes.

2. Meanwhile, beat cream cheese in a large bowl with an electric mixer on medium speed until light and fluffy, about 1 minute, stopping to scrape down sides of bowl as needed. Add condensed milk, and beat on medium speed until smooth, about 1 minute. Add lemonade concentrate, lemon zest, and salt; beat on low speed until incorporated, about 1 minute. Set aside.

3. Beat ½ cup of the heavy cream in a medium bowl with electric mixer on medium speed until medium peaks form, about 2 minutes. Gently fold whipped cream into cream cheese mixture. Spoon mixture into prepared crust, spreading evenly. Freeze, uncovered, until firm, about 4 hours or up to 12 hours. Remove from freezer about 10 minutes before serving.

4. Beat powdered sugar and remaining 1 cup heavy cream in a medium bowl with electric mixer on medium speed until stiff peaks form, 2 to 3 minutes. Top pie with whipped cream; garnish with additional lemon zest. Serve immediately. Store leftovers, covered, in freezer up to 1 week.

JUNETEENTH

She's Got the Scoop

In Richmond, Virginia, Rabia Kamara creates ice cream that celebrates Black culture and her heritage

RABIA KAMARA got a first glimpse of her future career at the age of 8 when her mom bought her a Mrs. Fields dessert cookbook and told her to note any recipes she'd like to make. "I basically marked all of them," she says. "I told my parents I wanted to be the next Mrs. Fields, and I didn't even know what that meant when I said it." Now as the owner of Ruby Scoops, an ice-cream shop in Richmond, Virginia, she is closer to realizing her childhood dream than she ever imagined.

After Kamara graduated from Virginia Commonwealth University, she was all set to attend law school when she decided that if she was going to spend the rest of her life working, it should be doing something she loved. She enrolled in L'Academie de Cuisine Culinary School in Gaithersburg, Maryland, where she reignited her passion for sweets and also discovered an obsession with making confections.

"Something in my brain just kind of clicked," she remembers. "I like to create, and it's easy with ice cream because it's such a blank canvas. As long as it freezes and scoops, it can be any flavor."

Kamara began experimenting with less common ingredients like rhubarb, red bean, persimmon, and black sesame during all of her free hours in culinary school. She continued the practice during her first job as a pastry chef and eventually decided to turn her hobby into a pop-up business in the Maryland/D.C. metro area in 2015. Kamara found a permanent home for Ruby Scoops in 2020 in her former college town of Richmond.

Kamara, whose father is from Sierra Leone and whose mother is Egyptian as well as Mauritian by way of India, says global cuisine was a big part of her upbringing as a first-generation American. "I grew up in Montgomery County, Maryland, which has some of the most diverse cities in the country. All my neighbors were immigrants

or children of immigrants," she says. She recalls going to friends' houses for Ethiopian food one night and Vietnamese the next. "I try to take things that seem foreign or out of the ordinary to people and present them as ice cream because that's one thing that everyone knows."

Flavors at Ruby Scoops are super seasonal, with summer options like Calamansi, Ube Cookies 'n Cream, and Raspberry-Peach Balsamic Sorbet. Kamara also rolls out specialty menus throughout the year, including one for Juneteenth with choices such as Banana Pudding, Candied Yam, Hot Honey Cornbread, and Jubilee Punch Sorbet. The latter features watermelon and Kool-Aid fruit punch, two ingredients that she says people have negatively attributed to Black people though they are actually meaningful to their culture and history.

"Black people started selling watermelons because it was the only thing they could do to be financially free," she says. "There isn't always a history lesson [associated with a flavor], but if there is, we're going to share it." Kamara's Blacker the Berry ice cream combines fresh blackberries with dark fudge brownies for an unexpected combo and a tongue-in-cheek play on the familiar adage, "The blacker the berry, the sweeter the juice."

For Kamara, who grew up in an African household where Juneteenth was a distant concept, her themed menu is a way for her to celebrate with the Black American community in the shop's neighborhood of Northside as well as to contribute to the nationwide observance.

"We can teach the kids about Juneteenth and remind the older folks why it's so important to them," she says. "This kind of plays up who I am, what's meaningful to me, and also what's important to the Richmond community."

Blackberry-Brownie Ice-Cream Sundaes

ACTIVE 30 MIN. - TOTAL 30 MIN., PLUS 8 HOURS FREEZING

SERVES 6

- 1½ cups fresh or thawed frozen blackberries (6 oz.), plus more for garnish
- 1 Tbsp. granulated sugar
- ¼ tsp. vanilla extract
- ½ cup semisweet chocolate chips (from 1 [12-oz.] pkg.)
- ½ cup dark chocolate chips (from 1 [12-oz.] pkg.)
- 1½ Tbsp. coconut oil
  Pinch of salt
- 1 (14-oz.) can sweetened condensed milk
- 2 cups heavy whipping cream, chilled
- 1 (18-oz.) pkg. brownie mix, prepared according to pkg. directions and cooled, divided
  Whipped cream

1. Process blackberries, sugar, and vanilla in a blender until smooth, about 30 seconds. Pour mixture through a fine mesh strainer into a bowl; discard solids.
2. Stir together semisweet chocolate chips, dark chocolate chips, coconut oil, and salt in a small microwavable bowl. Microwave on HIGH in 30-second intervals, stirring between each interval until completely melted, 1 minute to 1 minute, 30 seconds.
3. In a large bowl, whisk together sweetened condensed milk and reserved blackberry puree until well combined. Beat heavy cream in a cold bowl with an electric mixer on high speed until stiff peaks form, about 2 minutes.
4. Gently fold whipped cream into condensed milk mixture until combined, being careful not to overmix. Cut half of brownies into ¾-inch chunks, and fold into condensed milk mixture. Drizzle with some melted chocolate mixture.
5. Transfer to a freezer-safe container; drizzle additional chocolate mixture over top, if desired. Cover and freeze at least 8 hours or up to 1 week. Serve over warmed leftover brownies or with whipped cream and fresh blackberries.

138 2024 JUNE–JULY

BROWNIE BONANZA
To make a sundae, serve the ice cream over warmed leftover brownies. You can also skip the brownies and just enjoy the ice cream with whipped cream and fresh blackberries.

SUPPERTIME

Not Your Mama's Meat 'n' Three

Old-school Southern dishes learn a few new tricks

Pepper Jelly–Glazed Pork Chops

ACTIVE 20 MIN. - TOTAL 30 MIN., PLUS 24 HOURS CHILLING

SERVES 4

- 1 tsp. light brown sugar
- ½ tsp. smoked paprika
- ½ tsp. black pepper
- 2½ tsp. kosher salt, divided
- 4 (12-oz., 1-inch-thick) bone-in pork chops
- 1 cup red pepper jelly
- 2 Tbsp. apple cider vinegar
- ¼ tsp. cayenne pepper (optional)

1. Stir together brown sugar, paprika, black pepper, and 2 teaspoons of the salt in a small bowl; sprinkle evenly over both sides of pork chops. Chill, uncovered, 24 hours, or grill immediately, if desired.
2. Preheat grill to high (450˚F to 500˚F). Heat pepper jelly, apple cider vinegar, cayenne pepper (if desired), and remaining ½ teaspoon salt in a small saucepan over medium, stirring until smooth, about 3 minutes. Remove from heat, and reserve ¼ cup of the pepper jelly mixture in a small bowl; set aside. (Do not discard remaining pepper jelly mixture in saucepan; set aside.)
3. Spray seasoned pork chops with cooking spray; place pork chops on oiled grates. Grill, covered, until grill marks form, about 6 minutes. Turn pork chops; brush evenly with reserved ¼ cup pepper jelly mixture. Reduce heat to medium (350˚F to 400˚F); grill, covered, until a thermometer inserted into thickest portion of pork chop registers 140˚F, about 6 minutes. (Let rest 5 minutes to complete cooking.) Transfer pork chops to a platter; brush evenly with ¼ cup of the pepper jelly mixture in saucepan. Serve with the remaining pepper jelly mixture.

Easy Peas and Greens

ACTIVE 20 MIN. - TOTAL 40 MIN.

SERVES 6 TO 8

- 2 Tbsp. olive oil
- 1 small yellow onion, chopped (about 1 cup)
- 3 garlic cloves, smashed
- ¼ cup bourbon (optional)
- 6 cups lower-sodium chicken broth
- 6 cups mixed chopped fresh greens (from 1 [16-oz.] bag chopped fresh turnip greens and 1 [16-oz.] bag chopped fresh collard greens)
- 4 cups fresh lady peas or black-eyed peas (about 1 lb., 4 oz.)
- 1 smoked ham hock or smoked turkey wing (optional)
- 2 (3-inch) thyme sprigs, plus leaves for garnish
- 1 dried bay leaf
- 1 tsp. kosher salt, plus more to taste
- ½ tsp. black pepper
- ¼ tsp. crushed red pepper
- 2 Tbsp. apple cider vinegar

1. Heat olive oil in a large Dutch oven over medium. Add onion and garlic; cook, stirring occasionally, until softened, about 5 minutes. Add bourbon, if desired, and cook, scraping bottom of Dutch oven to loosen browned bits, until reduced slightly, about 1 minute. Add chicken broth, chopped greens, lady peas, ham hock (if desired), thyme sprigs, bay leaf, salt, black pepper, and crushed red pepper; bring to a boil over medium-high.
2. Reduce heat to low; simmer, uncovered, stirring occasionally, until peas are just tender, about 35 minutes. Remove from heat, and stir in vinegar. Taste and add more salt, if desired. If using ham hock, remove and pick meat from bone; return meat to Dutch oven, and discard bone. Garnish with thyme leaves.

Fried-Okra Cornbread

ACTIVE 30 MIN. - TOTAL 1 HOUR

SERVES 8

- 2 cups sliced fresh okra
- 1¾ cups whole buttermilk, divided
- 2½ cups self-rising white or yellow cornmeal mix, divided
- 2 large eggs
- ½ tsp. kosher salt
- ½ tsp. black pepper
- ¼ cup, plus 3 Tbsp. peanut oil, divided
- Unsalted butter

1. Preheat oven to 425˚F. Add okra and ¼ cup of the buttermilk to a medium bowl; toss to combine. Sprinkle with ½ cup of the cornmeal mix; toss with fingers to coat. Transfer okra to a plate, and set aside. In same bowl, add eggs, salt, pepper, remaining 2 cups cornmeal mix, and remaining 1½ cups buttermilk; whisk together until combined. Set aside.
2. Heat ¼ cup of the oil in a 10-inch cast-iron skillet over medium-high until shimmering, about 1 minute. Add coated okra to skillet; fry, turning often, until golden brown, about 4 minutes. Remove okra from skillet using a slotted spoon; transfer fried okra to a paper towel–lined plate to absorb excess oil. Add remaining 3 tablespoons oil to skillet, and heat over medium-high until shimmering, about 1 minute. Pour hot oil into cornmeal batter; whisk until combined. Add cornmeal batter to hot skillet (batter should sizzle); do not stir. Sprinkle fried okra evenly over top of batter.
3. Bake in preheated oven until top is golden brown, about 25 minutes. Immediately invert onto a wire rack, and remove skillet. Invert cornbread again, placing okra side up; let cool on wire rack 10 minutes. Serve with butter.

140   2024 JUNE–JULY

PEPPER JELLY–GLAZED PORK CHOPS, SLICED TOMATOES, EASY PEAS AND GREENS, AND FRIED-OKRA CORNBREAD

MIX & MATCH
Combine these meats and sides any way you like, or fill up on nothing but veggies.

FRIED-PICKLE CHICKEN TENDERS, PEPPERED MELON SALAD, FRENCHED GREEN BEAN SALAD, AND CREAMED CORN MAC AND CHEESE

Fried-Pickle Chicken Tenders

ACTIVE 30 MIN. - TOTAL 30 MIN., PLUS 30 MIN. CHILLING

SERVES 4 TO 6

- ½ cup spicy dill pickle juice (from 1 [24-oz.] jar)
- 1 large egg
- 1½ cups whole buttermilk, divided
- 2 lb. chicken breast tenders
  Peanut or vegetable oil
- 2 cups self-rising flour
- 1 Tbsp. seasoned salt
- 2 tsp. black pepper, plus more for serving
- ½ tsp. cayenne pepper (optional)
- 1 cup spicy dill pickle chips, plus more for serving
  Honey

1. Whisk together pickle juice, egg, and 1 cup of the buttermilk in a medium bowl until smooth. Add chicken tenders to the buttermilk mixture; cover and chill at least 30 minutes or up to 4 hours.
2. Remove chicken tenders from marinade (do not discard marinade). Add oil to a large cast-iron skillet or Dutch oven, filling to a depth of 1½ inches. Heat over medium-high until oil reaches 350°F, about 10 minutes.
3. Meanwhile, stir together flour, seasoned salt, black pepper, cayenne pepper (if desired), and 3 tablespoons of the marinade in a shallow bowl until well combined. Working with 2 or 3 chicken tenders at a time, dredge in flour mixture, patting to coat. Shake off excess flour mixture, and transfer to a plate. Repeat with remaining chicken tenders and flour mixture.
4. Working in batches, fry breaded chicken tenders, turning occasionally, until golden brown and an instant-read thermometer inserted into thickest portion of chicken registers 165°F, 4 to 6 minutes per batch. Transfer to a paper towel–lined plate to absorb excess oil. (Allow oil to return to 350°F between batches.)
5. Combine pickle chips and remaining ½ cup buttermilk in a small bowl. Use a slotted spoon to transfer pickle chips to remaining flour mixture; toss to coat. Add pickles to hot oil; fry until golden brown, about 2 minutes. Transfer to a paper towel–lined plate to absorb excess oil. (Discard any remaining oil.)
6. Transfer fried chicken tenders and fried pickle chips to a platter. Sprinkle with black pepper, and drizzle with honey. Serve with additional pickle chips, if desired.

Creamed Corn Mac and Cheese

ACTIVE 30 MIN. - TOTAL 35 MIN.

SERVES 4 TO 6

- ¼ cup unsalted butter
- ½ cup chopped sweet onion (from 1 small onion)
- 1½ tsp. kosher salt
- ½ tsp. black pepper
- 5 cups fresh corn kernels (from 10 ears), divided
- 1½ Tbsp. all-purpose flour
- 2 cups whole milk
- 12 oz. sharp cheddar cheese, shredded (about 3 cups), divided
- 8 oz. cavatappi pasta or elbow macaroni, cooked according to pkg. directions
  Finely chopped fresh chives

1. Melt butter in a 10-inch cast-iron skillet over medium. Add onion, salt, pepper, and 4½ cups of the corn; cook, stirring occasionally, until tender-crisp, about 8 minutes. Stir in flour, and cook, stirring constantly, 1 minute. Stir in milk; bring to a simmer over medium. Stir in 2½ cups of the cheddar until melted, about 1 minute. Remove from heat; add cooked pasta, stirring to combine.
2. Preheat oven to broil with rack about 6 inches away from heat source. Sprinkle remaining ½ cup corn kernels and ½ cup cheddar evenly over pasta mixture, and broil until top is golden brown, 6 to 9 minutes. Remove from oven, and let cool 5 minutes. Garnish with chives.

Frenched Green Bean Salad

ACTIVE 15 MIN. - TOTAL 15 MIN., PLUS 1 HOUR COOLING

SERVES 6 TO 8

- 1½ lb. fresh green beans, trimmed and cut crosswise into 3-inch pieces (about 8 cups)
- 1 pt. heirloom cherry tomatoes, halved (about 2 cups)
- 2 (6-inch) dill sprigs, plus fronds for garnish
- 1 cup white wine vinegar
- 3 Tbsp. granulated sugar
- 3½ tsp. kosher salt
- ½ tsp. black pepper
- ¼ tsp. crushed red pepper

1. Fit a food processor with a 2-mm thin slicing disk. Working in batches, stack trimmed green beans in food chute horizontally; process green beans, cutting them into thin slices. Transfer sliced green beans to a 13- x 9-inch baking dish; add tomatoes and dill sprigs, spreading in an even layer. Set aside.
2. Add 1½ cups water, vinegar, sugar, kosher salt, black pepper, and crushed red pepper to a medium saucepan; bring to a boil over medium-high, stirring occasionally. Remove from heat; pour over green bean mixture in baking dish. Let cool to room temperature, about 1 hour, before serving. If desired, transfer green bean mixture to an airtight container, and chill up to 3 days. Garnish with fresh dill fronds just before serving.

Peppered Melon Salad

ACTIVE 5 MIN. - TOTAL 5 MIN.

SERVES 4 TO 6

Toss together 2 cups seeded and cubed **watermelon** (from 1 small watermelon) and 2 cups cubed **cantaloupe** (from 1 medium cantaloupe) in a medium bowl. Sprinkle with ½ tsp. each **black pepper** and **Aleppo pepper**; drizzle with 1 Tbsp. each **sherry vinegar** and **honey**. Toss gently to combine. Garnish with **flaky sea salt** and **fresh mint leaves.**

Greek Diner Meatballs
ACTIVE 35 MIN. · TOTAL 50 MIN.
SERVES 4 TO 6

- ½ cup panko breadcrumbs
- ¼ cup whole milk
- 1 lb. ground chuck
- ½ lb. mild Italian sausage
- 3 garlic cloves, grated (about 1½ tsp.)
- 1½ tsp. kosher salt, divided
- 2 tsp. grated lemon zest, divided (from 1 lemon)
- ¾ tsp. ground cumin, divided
- ¾ tsp. black pepper, divided
- ¾ tsp. ground cinnamon, divided
- 1 large egg, lightly beaten
- 1 (24-oz.) jar marinara sauce
- ¼ cup sliced pepperoncini salad peppers (from 1 [12-oz.] jar), plus more for garnish
  Fresh mint leaves

1. Preheat oven to 425°F. Line a large rimmed baking sheet with parchment paper; set aside.
2. Place panko and milk in a small bowl; let stand 10 minutes. Place ground chuck; sausage; grated garlic; 1 teaspoon of the salt; 1 teaspoon of the lemon zest; and ½ teaspoon each of the cumin, black pepper, and cinnamon in a large bowl. Add panko mixture and egg to meat mixture; gently mix together with hands just until ingredients are evenly dispersed (do not overmix).
3. Form meat mixture into 24 (2-tablespoon) balls; space evenly on prepared baking sheet, and spray with cooking spray. Bake in preheated oven until golden brown and a thermometer inserted into thickest portion of meatball registers 165°F, 18 to 20 minutes.
4. Meanwhile, heat marinara sauce; pepperoncini peppers; remaining 1 teaspoon lemon zest; remaining ½ teaspoon salt; and remaining ¼ teaspoon each cumin, black pepper, and cinnamon in a large saucepan over medium to let flavors meld, about 10 minutes. Reduce heat to low; keep warm.
5. Remove meatballs from oven; transfer to saucepan, and gently stir to coat. Garnish with fresh mint leaves and pepperoncini peppers.

Summer Garden Tart
ACTIVE 20 MIN. · TOTAL 1 HOUR, 25 MIN.
SERVES 8

- 1 (14.1-oz.) pkg. refrigerated piecrusts
  All-purpose flour, for dusting
- 4 oz. grated Parmesan cheese, divided (about 1 cup)
- 1 tsp. black pepper, divided
- 1 (12-oz.) container store-bought pimiento cheese (about 1½ cups)
- ¾ cup thinly sliced zucchini (from 1 small zucchini)
- ¾ cup thinly sliced yellow squash (from 1 small squash)
- ¾ cup thinly sliced red onion (from 1 small onion)
- ½ cup fresh corn kernels (from 1 ear)
- ½ tsp. kosher salt, divided
- 2 tsp. olive oil
- 1 large egg, lightly beaten
  Fresh basil leaves

1. Preheat oven to 400°F. Unroll 1 piecrust on a lightly floured piece of parchment paper. Lightly spray piecrust with cooking spray; sprinkle evenly with ⅓ cup of the Parmesan and ½ teaspoon of the pepper. Top with remaining piecrust. Using a rolling pin, press to seal the crusts together, and roll into a 14-inch circle. Transfer to a large baking sheet; freeze or refrigerate 10 minutes.
2. Remove baking sheet with piecrust from freezer or refrigerator. Spoon pimiento cheese into center of piecrust; spread in an even layer to within 1 inch of edges. Layer sliced zucchini, squash, and onion over pimiento cheese, overlapping as needed. Sprinkle with corn kernels and ¼ teaspoon each of the pepper and kosher salt.
3. Fold edges of piecrust up and over to overlap filling by about 1 inch, pleating dough as needed. Drizzle oil over vegetables in center of tart. Brush edges of tart lightly with egg; sprinkle crust and filling evenly with remaining ⅔ cup Parmesan and ¼ teaspoon each pepper and salt.
4. Bake in preheated oven until crust is golden brown, 28 to 30 minutes. Let cool at least 15 minutes or up to 3 hours. Garnish with basil leaves just before serving.

Smoky Grilled Corn Ribs
ACTIVE 25 MIN. · TOTAL 25 MIN.
SERVES 4 TO 6

- 4 ears fresh corn
- ¼ cup unsalted butter, melted
- 2 tsp. kosher salt
- 1 tsp. smoked paprika
- 1 tsp. black pepper
- ½ tsp. ground cumin
  Lime wedges
  Fresh cilantro leaves (optional)

1. Preheat grill to high (450°F to 500°F). Cut corn ears in half crosswise using a sharp knife. Trim about 1 inch from pointed ends; discard trimmed ends. Working with 1 half at a time, turn each piece of corn on its flattest, widest cut end, and carefully cut in half lengthwise. Turn corn halves cut sides down; cut in half lengthwise again. Repeat with remaining corn. Place corn ribs in an even layer on a large, rimmed baking sheet; set aside.
2. Stir together melted butter, salt, paprika, pepper, and cumin in a small bowl; brush evenly over corn. Place on oiled grates; grill, uncovered, turning often, until corn is charred and tender, 6 to 8 minutes. Squeeze lime wedges over corn ribs; sprinkle with cilantro, if desired.

Mixed Pickle Salad
ACTIVE 5 MIN. · TOTAL 5 MIN.
SERVES 4 TO 6

- 1½ cups sliced pickled peaches (from 1 [16-oz.] jar)
- 1½ cups sliced pickled okra (from 1 [16-oz.] jar)
- 1 cup sliced pickled red onion (from 1 [12-oz.] jar)
- 1 Tbsp. chopped fresh dill
- ¼ tsp. black pepper

Stir together peaches, okra, red onion, and dill in a medium bowl. Sprinkle with pepper.

GREEK DINER MEATBALLS, SUMMER GARDEN TART, MIXED PICKLE SALAD, AND SMOKY GRILLED CORN RIBS

FRIED-PICKLE CHICKEN TENDERS (PAGE 143)

FRIED-OKRA CORNBREAD (PAGE 140)

LIGHTEN UP

It's Peak Squash Season

This roasted riff on a classic side reduces the fat but keeps the crunchy topping

Sheet Pan Squash Casserole
ACTIVE 30 MIN. - TOTAL 55 MIN.
SERVES 8

- 9 small yellow crookneck squash (about 2¾ lb.), cut into ¼-inch-thick slices
- 2½ tsp. kosher salt, divided
- 1 tsp. black pepper
- ¾ tsp. smoked paprika
- ½ tsp. garlic powder
- ¼ tsp. cayenne pepper
- 3 oz. sharp white cheddar cheese, shredded (about ¾ cup)
- 2 oz. Parmesan cheese, finely shredded (about ¾ cup)
- 1 small red onion, thinly sliced
- 4 red sweet mini peppers, thinly sliced crosswise into rings
- 3 Tbsp. olive oil, divided
- 1 cup crushed saltine crackers (about 16 crackers)

1. Preheat oven to 400°F. Place squash in an even layer on paper towels; sprinkle lightly with ½ teaspoon of the salt. Let stand 15 minutes; pat dry.
2. Stir together black pepper, smoked paprika, garlic powder, cayenne pepper, and remaining 2 teaspoons salt in a small bowl. Stir together cheeses in a medium bowl.
3. Spray a large rimmed baking sheet with cooking spray. Sprinkle 1½ teaspoons of the salt mixture evenly in bottom of prepared baking sheet. Arrange half each of squash, onion, and pepper slices in an even layer; sprinkle with 1½ teaspoons of the salt mixture and ¾ cup of the cheese mixture. Repeat with remaining squash, onion, peppers, salt mixture, and cheese mixture. Drizzle top evenly with 1 tablespoon of the oil.
4. Toss crackers with the remaining 2 tablespoons oil in a small bowl; sprinkle over vegetables. Bake in preheated oven until vegetables are tender and crackers are golden brown, about 25 minutes.

Before Recipe Makeover:
CALORIES: **517** – CARB: **29 G** – FAT: **40 G**

After Recipe Makeover:
CALORIES: **182** – CARB: **15 G** – FAT: **11 G**

SNACK TIME

Ready to Roll

Forget those flat quesadillas—this pull-apart version is party perfect

Party Quesadillas
ACTIVE 40 MIN. • TOTAL 1 HOUR
SERVES 10 TO 12

- 3 cups shredded, cooked chicken (from 1 rotisserie chicken)
- ½ cup store-bought jalapeño pimiento cheese (4 oz.)
- ¼ cup coarsely chopped fresh cilantro, plus more for garnish
- 1 Tbsp. hot sauce (such as Cholula)
- ¾ tsp. kosher salt
- ½ tsp. black pepper
- 8 oz. pepper Jack cheese, shredded (about 2 cups)
- 6 oz. sharp cheddar cheese, shredded (about 1½ cups)
- 16 (6-inch) flour tortillas
- Avocado Dipping Sauce (recipe follows)

1. Preheat oven to 400°F. Line a large rimmed baking sheet with parchment paper. Place a 4-inch-wide ovenproof ramekin in center of prepared baking sheet; set aside.
2. Stir together chicken, pimiento cheese, cilantro, hot sauce, kosher salt, and black pepper in a large bowl; set aside. Stir together pepper Jack and cheddar cheeses in a medium bowl; reserve 1 cup cheese blend in a small bowl.
3. Cut tortillas in half. Working with one at a time, sprinkle 1 tablespoon of the remaining cheese blend in an even layer over a tortilla half; top with 1 tablespoon of the chicken mixture. Fold in one corner of tortilla to cover half the filling. Fold over again to enclose the filling and form a cone shape; place seam side down. Repeat the process with remaining tortilla halves, cheese blend, and chicken mixture.
4. Arrange half of tortilla cones, seam side down, in an even layer around ramekin on prepared baking sheet, with pointed ends against ramekin. Sprinkle half of the reserved cheese blend over cones. Repeat with remaining tortilla cones and cheese blend, arranging cones, seam side down, on top of first layer. Spray with cooking spray. Bake in preheated oven until cheeses are melted and edges are crispy and golden brown, about 20 minutes. Let cool for 5 minutes. Serve with Avocado Dipping Sauce; garnish with additional cilantro.

Avocado Dipping Sauce
ACTIVE 5 MIN. • TOTAL 5 MIN.
MAKES ABOUT 2 CUPS

Process 2 pitted and peeled **large avocados**, 1 stemmed **medium jalapeño**, ¾ cup **sour cream**, ½ cup **fresh cilantro**, ¼ cup **water**, 2 Tbsp. **fresh lime juice**, and 1½ tsp. **kosher salt** in a food processor until smooth, 1 to 2 minutes.

Wrap it up

(A) Add cheese blend and chicken mixture to tortilla half. **(B)** Fold in one corner of tortilla to cover half the filling. **(C)** Fold over again to form a cone shape.

A　　　B　　　C

2024 JUNE-JULY 149

IVY'S KITCHEN

Garden Party

Simple tricks for preserving produce—no canning required

AS A SOUTHERNER from the farming community of Moultrie, Georgia, I feel a sense of duty to be a canning expert. Maybe it's because I grew up in a house with an overflowing garden and graduated with a degree in home economics from the University of Georgia, where the National Center for Home Food Preservation is located. Or maybe it's because Colquitt County, where I'm from, has a canning plant that's open to the public during peak harvest season. But if I'm being honest, I'm no pro. In fact, I would go so far as to say I really don't like it.

The boiling water, the lava-hot glass jars, the super-slippery tongs, and the fears about food safety loom over the whole to-do. When harvest time comes for my own little garden, I will freeze, juice, and quick-pickle a vegetable 10 times before I'll can it. My recipe for freezer tomato sauce is much easier than the traditional method. Not only does it avoid the dreaded water bath, but it also calls for using whole tomatoes, skins and all, to make a fast, fuss-free sauce that works in so many recipes. For a girl who doesn't love "putting up," this recipe is can do.

Easy Freezer Tomato Sauce
ACTIVE 1 HOUR · TOTAL 1 HOUR, PLUS 30 MIN. COOLING
MAKES 5 CUPS

- 5 lb. ripe tomatoes
- 2 tsp. kosher salt

1. Working in 3 batches, place 5 lb. ripe tomatoes (about 10 medium tomatoes), quartered, in a food processor bowl, and pulse until finely chopped, about 15 pulses.
2. Transfer finely chopped tomatoes to a 4-quart Dutch oven, and cook over medium-high, stirring occasionally, until mixture has reduced by half, about 30 minutes.
3. Remove Dutch oven from heat. Using an immersion blender, process tomatoes until smooth, about 1 minute. (You can also use a regular blender, working in batches.)
4. Return Dutch oven to heat. Reduce the heat to medium, and cook until sauce is slightly thickened, about 10 minutes. Stir in 2 tsp. kosher salt. Ladle into freezer-safe airtight containers, and let cool completely, about 30 minutes. Store in freezer up to 1 year.

Quick-Pickled Jalapeños
ACTIVE 10 MIN. · TOTAL 40 MIN., PLUS 24 HOURS CHILLING
MAKES 1 (16-OZ.) JAR

Slice 5 **large jalapeños**; place in a heatproof (16-oz.) glass jar with 2 smashed **garlic cloves.** In a small saucepan, bring ½ cup each **water** and **white vinegar,** 1 Tbsp. **granulated sugar,** and 1 tsp. **salt** to a boil over high; cook until sugar and salt are dissolved, 1 to 2 minutes. Pour over jalapeños; secure lid. Let cool 30 minutes. Chill at least 24 hours (up to 1 week).

Cucumber Cooler
ACTIVE 10 MIN. · TOTAL 10 MIN.
MAKES 1

Place 1½ lb. chopped **cucumbers** and ½ cup **water** in a blender. Blend until very smooth. Pour through a fine mesh strainer into a bowl; discard solids. Stir together ½ cup of the cucumber juice, 2 Tbsp. **lemon juice,** 2 Tbsp. **simple syrup,** and 1½ oz. **gin, tequila, or vodka** in a Collins glass. Add **ice,** and top with **sparkling water.** Garnish with **fresh mint.** Store leftover cucumber juice in an airtight container in freezer up to 6 months.

CUCUMBER COOLER

QUICK-PICKLED JALAPEÑOS

EASY FREEZER TOMATO SAUCE

COOKING SCHOOL

TIPS AND TRICKS FROM THE SOUTH'S MOST TRUSTED KITCHEN

The Truth About Tomatoes
Here's how to store them the right way

CAN THEY BE REFRIGERATED?
To prolong their freshness, fully ripe tomatoes can be kept in the fridge for a few days without a lasting impact on their flavor or texture, but they taste best at room temperature. If they aren't as ripe as you'd like them to be, place them on the counter. Just make sure they're away from direct sunlight.

DOES THE "TAPE HACK" ACTUALLY WORK?
Some folks say that putting a piece of transparent tape over the stem will extend a tomato's shelf life—and they're right. The fruit can stay fresher for a longer period if it maintains its moisture, which can escape through the stem. We've found that storing them upside down works just as well and won't damage their thin skins.

PRO TIP: STEMS ARE IN
If you purchase tomatoes on the vine, keep them that way while they ripen to help lock in their moisture.

HOW LONG CAN YOU STORE CUT TOMATOES?
If you're not eating or cooking them within a few hours, sliced or chopped tomatoes must be refrigerated, as they can harbor potentially harmful bacteria. Pop them into a sealable container, and use them within a day or so.

152 2024 JUNE–JULY

August

154 Squash It Two tasty ways to enjoy the season's MVP

157 The Roots of Succotash While the South may claim this classic side as its own, the dish has a much longer history

158 Pretty as a Peach Salad Go beyond the usual cakes and cobblers, and pair the fruit with leafy greens and other flavorful ingredients

162 Dress to Impress Dinner is a cinch with these easy, breezy salads

169 Sundae Best Turn store-bought ice cream into something special with simple sauces and toppings

170 A Healthier Cobbler Peaches, plums, and cherries give this dessert a delicious makeover

171 The Morning Blend Fast and fruity smoothies for breakfast on the go

173 Chicken Little Take nuggets to the next level with a splash of dill pickle brine

174 Cooking School Our Test Kitchen professionals show you how to level up your knife skills–plus which knife is right for the task at hand

BOUNTY

Squash It
Two tasty ways to enjoy the season's MVP

EASY ZUCCHINI-BASIL PASTA

Easy Zucchini-Basil Pasta
ACTIVE 25 MIN. - TOTAL 25 MIN.
SERVES 4

- ½ tsp. kosher salt, plus more for salting water and to taste
- 1 (16-oz.) pkg. spaghetti
- ¼ cup extra-virgin olive oil
- 4 garlic cloves, thinly sliced (about 1 Tbsp.)
- 2 lb. zucchini (about 5 small zucchini), thinly sliced (8 cups)
- ½ tsp. coarsely ground black pepper, plus more for garnish
- ½ cup heavy whipping cream
- 3 Tbsp. unsalted butter, cut into pieces
- 1 cup loosely packed fresh basil leaves, plus more for garnish
- 4 oz. Parmesan cheese, grated (about 1 cup)

1. Bring a large pot of salted water to a boil over high. Add spaghetti; cook according to package directions for al dente.
2. While spaghetti cooks, heat oil in a large Dutch oven over medium. Add garlic, and cook, stirring often, until golden around the edges, about 3 minutes. Add zucchini, ½ teaspoon salt, and pepper; increase heat to high. Cook, stirring occasionally, until zucchini are just tender, about 8 minutes.
3. Using tongs, transfer cooked spaghetti to Dutch oven. Add ¾ cup of the pasta cooking water; reserve remaining pasta cooking water in pot. Stir cream and butter into Dutch oven; reduce heat to medium. Cook, stirring constantly with a wooden spoon, until slightly thickened, about 2 minutes. Remove from heat, and let cool 5 minutes, stirring occasionally.
4. Add basil and Parmesan to Dutch oven; stir constantly until cheese is melted and combined, about 2 minutes. Add a bit more pasta cooking liquid, ¼ cup at a time, if necessary, to achieve a creamy consistency. Season with kosher salt to taste. Garnish servings with additional basil and pepper.

SUMMER SQUASH SKILLET

Summer Squash Skillet
ACTIVE 25 MIN. - TOTAL 45 MIN.
SERVES 4

Preheat oven to 400°F. Heat 2 Tbsp. **olive oil** in a 12-inch cast-iron skillet over medium-high. Add 5½ cups sliced **zucchini**, 2½ cups sliced yellow **squash**, 2 cups thinly sliced **yellow onion**, 1 tsp. **kosher salt**, and ½ tsp. **black pepper**. Cook, covered, stirring occasionally, until squash mixture is mostly tender, about 10 minutes. Uncover and cook until most of the liquid has evaporated, about 5 minutes. Remove from heat; fold in ¼ tsp. **crushed red pepper** and 1 cup **Gruyère cheese**. Stir together ⅓ cup **panko breadcrumbs**, 1 tsp. **lemon zest**, and ¾ cup Gruyère in a small bowl; sprinkle evenly over squash mixture. Bake until topping is golden, about 18 minutes.

2024 AUGUST 155

THE WELCOME TABLE

The Roots of Succotash

While the South may claim this classic side as its own, the dish has a much longer history

SUMMER COMES EARLIER in the South than in the North, where I normally roost. I wait patiently for the arrival of tomatoes, corn picked so recently that it's still sweet, and plenty of beans—both shelled and in their pods. When I finally see all three of these ingredients at my farmers' market, the first thing I make is my favorite side: succotash.

The dish is traditionally prepared from the bounty of the "Three Sisters," a name for an ingenious way of growing things that's a testimony to the wisdom of Native American agriculture. In this method, corn, beans, and squash are planted together and live in symbiotic harmony. The corn stalks provide poles to support the squash and trailing beans (which add beneficial nutrients to the soil), and the broad squash leaves shade the young plants from the sun. When they all ripen, the whole harvest goes into a skillet. Even the word "succotash" reminds us of the dish's Native American origins; it comes from the Narragansett term "sahquttahhash," which means "broken corn kernels."

Over time, the side came to be associated with the South, though there is no clear answer as to why. I suspect it's because the region's fresh produce was irresistible to cooks, and this was a way to feature those summer standbys. Most of these succotash recipes include corn, tomatoes, okra, and field peas or lima beans. The version at right combines Southern and Native American elements—with yellow squash, corn, and pole beans plus tomatoes and pieces of thick-cut bacon. Kernels of fresh corn add color and provide a sweet counterpoint to the light acidity of the tomatoes, and the green beans supply a welcome tender-crisp texture. A hot cast-iron skillet will blister the vegetables a bit; let them cook for a while with minimal stirring to give them a nice char.

This flavorful mix pairs perfectly with fried chicken or fish—or just about any other main dish—and brings the abundance of the season straight to the table. –Jessica B. Harris

Three Sisters Succotash
ACTIVE 45 MIN. - TOTAL 45 MIN.
SERVES 6 TO 8

- 6 thick-cut bacon slices, cut into 1-inch pieces (about 1 cup)
- 1 cup chopped sweet onion (from 1 medium onion)
- 1 Tbsp. finely chopped garlic (about 3 cloves)
- 10 oz. fresh green beans, trimmed and cut into 2-inch pieces (2 cups)
- 1 medium-size yellow squash, halved lengthwise and cut into ¼-inch-thick slices (2½ cups)
- 2 cups fresh or frozen yellow corn kernels (from 4 ears)
- 1 (¾-oz.) habanero chile, pricked all over with a fork
- 1½ tsp. kosher salt
- ½ tsp. black pepper, plus more for garnish
- 1 cup halved cherry tomatoes
- 1 tsp. coarsely chopped fresh thyme leaves, plus more for garnish

1. Place bacon in a 12-inch cast-iron skillet. Cook over medium-high, stirring occasionally, until crispy, 12 to 15 minutes. Using a slotted spoon, transfer bacon to a paper towel–lined plate to drain, reserving 2 tablespoons drippings in skillet. Save remaining drippings for another use.
2. Add onion to reserved drippings in skillet; cook over medium, stirring often, until softened, about 5 minutes. Stir in garlic; cook, stirring constantly, until fragrant, about 30 seconds.
3. Increase heat to high; stir in green beans, squash, corn, habanero chile, salt, and black pepper. Cook, stirring mixture occasionally, until vegetables are slightly charred, about 8 minutes. Reduce heat to medium-high, and stir in ¼ cup water; cover and cook, undisturbed, until vegetables are tender, about 4 minutes. Remove and discard habanero. Stir in halved cherry tomatoes, fresh thyme, and cooked bacon. Garnish with additional thyme and black pepper.

Bring the Heat

SUCCOTASH REALLY SINGS when you add a little fire to the pot. I season mine by throwing in a pricked habanero (a whole chile that's been poked all over using a fork) with the vegetables as they cook. I remove and discard the pepper when the dish has just enough zing to suit my taste. A small jalapeño will also do the trick. If you like things on the spicier side, you can mince the chile and stir it in to cook with the other veggies in the skillet.

Pretty as a Peach Salad

Go beyond the usual cakes and cobblers, and pair the fruit with leafy greens and other flavorful ingredients

EAT A PEACH. Whenever this fruit comes into season, I can't help but think about the Allman Brothers Band and the late guitarist Duane Allman's famous quote: "Every time I'm in Georgia, I eat a peach for peace."

This is not a hard thing to do in the South during the summer. A bowl of ripe peaches will perfume your whole kitchen, driving you to eat them while standing over the sink—along with your tomato sandwich. Like tomatoes, peaches are seasonal and can be quite rare some years. The trees bloom in early spring, but a late frost can finish off most of a harvest. That's why a good season is so special.

Dessert is usually what comes to mind when they arrive, but this summer, consider a salad. Their balance of sweet and tart can pair nicely with things like bacon, chiles, and herby dressings. Your farmers' market offers an unlimited choice of other fruits and vegetables to add, as you'll see in these recipes.

"Green" Peach Salad was a favorite of our regulars at Crook's Corner in Chapel Hill, North Carolina, where I was head chef for 25 years. Every summer, I'd get bushels of peaches from my farmer friend Walter Atwater, and there would always be some unripe ones. Necessity is the mother of invention.

The Peach-Mango Salad with Avocados is a riff on some of the things my friends from Mexico have taught me about food. They often pair fruit with something picoso ("spicy" in Spanish).

The Peach-and-Tomato Salad was the result of a brainstorm between *Southern Living* Deputy Editor Lisa Cericola and me. I wasn't sure about putting peaches and tomatoes together, but I'll try anything once. After all, who first thought that peanuts would be good in a Pepsi? Similar to that classic combination, this pairing just works.

Before this season ends, remember Duane Allman's words. Then, buy a bunch of fruit at its peak, and surprise yourself with something deliciously different. —Bill Smith

Peach-Mango Salad with Avocados

Serrano peppers are a little spicy, but their heat fades quickly so it doesn't build up—select the amount that suits your taste. Here's a tip: If you cut both fruits into small cubes, this will make an excellent salsa or relish for grilled pork, chicken, or seafood.

ACTIVE 20 MIN. · TOTAL 50 MIN.

SERVES 6

- 1 Tbsp. olive oil
- 1 Tbsp. chopped fresh cilantro, plus torn cilantro for garnish
- 3 large firm-ripe mangoes, peeled and cut into 1-inch chunks (about 3½ cups)
- 3 large firm-ripe peaches, unpeeled and cut into ¾-inch wedges (about 3½ cups)
- 2 medium-size firm-ripe avocados, cut into ¾-inch chunks (about 2 cups)
- 3 Tbsp. fresh lime juice (from 2 limes), divided
- ¾ tsp. kosher salt, divided
- ½ tsp. granulated sugar
- 1 serrano chile, unseeded and thinly sliced crosswise
  Flaky sea salt

1. Stir together oil and chopped cilantro in a small bowl. Divide mixture evenly between 2 medium bowls. Add mangoes to 1 bowl, and toss to coat. Add peaches to remaining bowl, and toss to coat. Then cover bowls separately, and chill at least 30 minutes or up to 12 hours.
2. Place avocados in a medium bowl; gently stir in 1 tablespoon of the lime juice and ¼ teaspoon of the kosher salt until avocados are evenly coated. Set aside.
3. Stir together sugar, serrano chile, and remaining 2 tablespoons lime juice and ½ teaspoon kosher salt in a small bowl.
4. Arrange marinated peaches on a large platter; top with marinated mangoes and avocados. Spoon serrano-lime juice mixture over salad. Garnish with flaky sea salt and torn cilantro. Serve immediately.

Peach-and-Tomato Salad with Buttermilk-Herb Dressing

(Photo, page 161)

This summer-fresh take on ranch dressing is amped up with a handful of herbs. Use any combination you like, but stick to soft, leafy types instead of tougher ones like rosemary. Hold off on stirring in the lemon juice until just before serving to help the herbs keep their vibrant green color.

ACTIVE 20 MIN. · TOTAL 50 MIN.

SERVES 4

- ⅔ cup mayonnaise
- ½ cup whole buttermilk
- ¼ cup plain whole-milk strained (Greek-style) yogurt
- ½ cup finely chopped fresh herbs (such as basil, thyme, and/or parsley), plus more for garnish
- 1 Tbsp. fresh lemon juice (from 1 lemon)
- 1¼ tsp. kosher salt, divided
- ¼ tsp. black pepper
- 1 lb. mixed cherry and beefsteak heirloom tomatoes
- 1 (4-oz.) pkg. Little Gem lettuce or baby arugula
- 4 medium-size firm-ripe peaches, unpeeled and cut into 1-inch wedges
- 8 bacon slices, cooked and crumbled (about 1 cup)

1. Whisk together mayonnaise, buttermilk, and yogurt in a small bowl until well combined. Stir in herbs. Refrigerate, covered, until chilled, at least 30 minutes or up to 2 days. Just before time to serve, stir in lemon juice, ½ teaspoon of the salt, and pepper. Set aside.
2. Slice beefsteak tomatoes into 1-inch wedges, and cut cherry tomatoes in half. Sprinkle tomatoes evenly with remaining ¾ teaspoon salt. Set aside.
3. Divide lettuce evenly among 4 plates. Arrange tomatoes and peaches on top of lettuce. Sprinkle with crumbled bacon. Drizzle each salad with 2 tablespoons dressing, and garnish with additional fresh herbs. Serve immediately with remaining dressing.

158 2024 AUGUST

PEACH-
MANGO SALAD
WITH AVOCADOS

"Green" Peach Salad

Sometimes you end up coming home with some unripe peaches despite your best efforts, especially if you buy a whole bushel of them. This simple recipe solves that problem and will have you searching through the bin for the firmest ones you can find.

ACTIVE 10 MIN. · TOTAL 50 MIN.
SERVES 6

Toss together 6 cups thinly sliced underripe **peaches,** ¼ cup **granulated sugar,** and ½ teaspoon **kosher salt** in a large bowl until evenly combined. Let stand at room temperature for 10 minutes. Stir in 2 Tbsp. **extra-virgin olive oil,** 2 Tbsp. sliced **fresh mint,** and ½ tsp. **black pepper.** Chill, covered, at least 30 minutes or up to 3 hours. Serve.

PEACH-AND-TOMATO SALAD WITH BUTTERMILK-HERB DRESSING (PAGE 158)

SUPPERTIME

Dress to Impress

Dinner is a cinch with these easy, breezy salads

BLT SEVEN-LAYER SALAD

MAKE A STIR
No trifle dish? No problem! Mix all the ingredients together in a serving bowl.

BLT Seven-Layer Salad

ACTIVE 30 MIN. · TOTAL 30 MIN.
SERVES 6 TO 8

- 10 thick-cut bacon slices, cut into 1-inch pieces (about 1¾ cups)
- 2 cups quartered large cherry tomatoes (such as Campari)
- 1 tsp. kosher salt, divided
- ¾ tsp. black pepper, divided
- 4 cups torn baguette (from 1 baguette)
- ½ cup mayonnaise
- 2 Tbsp. apple cider vinegar
- 2 Tbsp. thinly sliced fresh chives, plus more for garnish
- ¼ cup olive oil
- 1 medium head iceberg lettuce, cored and sliced (about 10 cups), plus more for garnish
- 2 medium avocados, sliced
- 4 oz. shredded sharp cheddar cheese (about 1 cup)

1. Cook bacon in a large nonstick skillet over medium, stirring often, until crisp, about 15 minutes. Remove from heat. Transfer bacon to a plate lined with paper towels. Spoon 2 tablespoons of drippings into a large bowl; reserve remaining drippings in skillet. While bacon cooks, toss tomatoes with ¼ teaspoon each of the salt and pepper in a bowl; set aside.
2. Stir bread into drippings in skillet; sprinkle with ¼ teaspoon of the salt. Cook over medium, stirring often, until golden, about 6 minutes. Transfer croutons to plate with bacon.
3. Whisk mayonnaise, apple cider vinegar, chives, and remaining ½ teaspoon each of the salt and pepper into drippings in large bowl. Gradually whisk in oil until blended and creamy.
4. Place lettuce in a 5-quart trifle dish. Reserve 2 tablespoons mayonnaise mixture; drizzle remainder over lettuce. Layer tomato mixture, avocados, croutons, cheese, and bacon as desired. Top with additional lettuce, chives, and reserved dressing. Serve immediately.

Southern Niçoise Salad

(Photo, page 165)

Store-bought potato salad and hard-cooked eggs cut down the prep time for this filling option with roots in Southern France.

ACTIVE 20 MIN. · TOTAL 30 MIN.
SERVES 6

- 1 (8-oz.) pkg. microwavable haricots verts (French green beans)
- ⅓ cup finely chopped dill pickles plus 2 Tbsp. dill pickle juice (from 1 [16-oz.] jar)
- 4 tsp. Creole mustard
- 1 tsp. honey
- ¾ tsp. kosher salt, divided
- ½ tsp. black pepper, divided
- ⅔ cup olive oil
- 1 small romaine lettuce heart, leaves separated
- 1 cup multicolored cherry tomatoes, halved
- 3 hard-cooked eggs, peeled and halved lengthwise
- 2 cups prepared potato salad
- 1 (8-oz.) pkg. hot-smoked trout fillets, broken into large pieces (skin discarded)

1. Microwave green beans according to package directions. Spread cooked beans in an even layer on a large plate lined with paper towels. Refrigerate, uncovered, until cooled, about 15 minutes.
2. Meanwhile, whisk together chopped pickles, pickle juice, mustard, honey, ½ teaspoon of the salt, and ¼ teaspoon of the pepper in a small bowl until combined. Gradually whisk in oil until dressing is creamy.
3. Toss together lettuce and ¼ cup dressing in a large bowl until coated; arrange on a large platter with cooked green beans, cherry tomatoes, eggs, potato salad, and trout. Sprinkle evenly with remaining ¼ teaspoon each salt and pepper. Drizzle assembled salad with remaining ¾ cup dressing. Serve immediately.

Chicken Taco Pasta Salad

(Photo, page 164)

Omit the pasta, and serve the chicken mixture with tortilla chips as a hearty appetizer.

ACTIVE 15 MIN. · TOTAL 25 MIN.
SERVES 6 TO 8

- 1½ tsp. kosher salt, plus more for salting water
- 8 oz. uncooked small rigatoni pasta (about 2 cups)
- 2 ears fresh corn, shucked
- 1 small poblano chile, stemmed, seeded, and chopped (about ½ cup)
- 1 cup mayonnaise
- ½ cup loosely packed fresh cilantro leaves, plus more for garnish
- ⅓ cup chopped scallions (from 2 scallions)
- 2 Tbsp. fresh lime juice (from 1 lime)
- ½ tsp. smoked paprika
- ½ tsp. ground cumin
- ¼ tsp. black pepper, plus more for serving
- 3 cups shredded rotisserie chicken
- 2 cups shredded iceberg lettuce (from 1 small head)
- 2 cups cherry tomatoes, halved
  Blue corn tortilla chips

1. Bring a large pot of salted water to a boil over high. Add pasta; cook according to package directions for al dente. Add corn ears during final 5 minutes of cooking. Drain and rinse with cold water. Cut kernels from cobs, and set aside; discard cobs.
2. Process poblano, mayonnaise, cilantro, scallions, lime juice, salt, paprika, cumin, and black pepper in a blender until smooth, about 1 minute.
3. Place cooked pasta, corn kernels, chicken, lettuce, and tomatoes in a large bowl. Drizzle with poblano mixture. Sprinkle with additional black pepper; garnish with tortilla chips and additional cilantro.

2024 AUGUST **163**

CHICKEN TACO
PASTA SALAD
(PAGE 163)

SOUTHERN NIÇOISE SALAD (PAGE 163)

MUFFULETTA PANZANELLA

Muffuletta Panzanella

For crispier croutons, serve this sandwich-inspired bread salad immediately.

ACTIVE 20 MIN. · TOTAL 45 MIN.

SERVES 4

- 1 (18-oz.) loaf ciabatta, cut into 1-inch cubes
- ¼ cup, plus 3 Tbsp. olive oil, divided
- ¾ tsp. kosher salt, divided
- 2 large ripe tomatoes, divided
- 1 cup chopped pitted marinated olives
- 1 cup chopped giardiniera (mixed pickled vegetables), plus 2 Tbsp. brine (from 1 [16-oz.] jar)
- ½ cup roasted red bell pepper strips (from 1 [16-oz.] jar)
- 2 Tbsp. red wine vinegar
- 3 garlic cloves, finely grated (about 1½ tsp.)
- ⅓ lb. thinly sliced Italian deli meats (such as salami, hot capocollo, and mortadella), cut into bite-size pieces (about 1 cup packed)
- 4 oz. provolone cheese, cut into strips (about 1¼ cups)
- 2 cups packed baby arugula

1. Preheat oven to 350°F. Toss ciabatta with 3 tablespoons of the oil and ½ teaspoon of the salt on a large rimmed baking sheet; spread into an even layer. Bake until crisp, about 18 minutes, stirring halfway through baking time. Remove from oven. Let cool 15 minutes.
2. While bread bakes, cut 1 of the tomatoes in half. Place a box grater inside a large bowl. Grate tomato halves on largest holes of box grater; discard tomato skins. Stir in olives, giardiniera, brine, red bell pepper strips, vinegar, and remaining ¼ cup oil and ¼ teaspoon salt until combined.
3. Seed and roughly chop remaining tomato. Add toasted ciabatta, chopped tomato, sliced meats, and cheese to grated tomato mixture in bowl; toss to coat. Let stand until bread absorbs most of dressing, about 10 minutes, tossing occasionally. Stir in arugula just before serving.

SHRIMP-AND-FETA PASTA SALAD

Shrimp-and-Feta Pasta Salad

This recipe is great warm or cold; cover and refrigerate it overnight for even more flavor.

ACTIVE 20 MIN. · TOTAL 25 MIN.

SERVES 4

- ¾ tsp. kosher salt, plus more for salting water
- 1 cup uncooked orzo
- 1 large shallot, finely chopped (about ¼ cup)
- ⅓ cup extra-virgin olive oil
- ¼ cup drained and chopped sun-dried tomatoes in oil
- ¼ cup chopped fresh dill, plus more for garnish
- 2 Tbsp. white balsamic vinegar
- 2 Tbsp. fresh lemon juice (from 1 lemon)
- 1½ tsp. Dijon mustard
- ½ tsp. grated garlic (from 2 cloves)
- ¼ tsp. black pepper
- 1 lb. jumbo peeled and deveined cooked shrimp, tails removed
- 1 (8-oz.) block feta cheese, cut into ½-inch cubes
- 1 cup sliced English cucumber (from 1 small cucumber), cut into half-moons

1. Bring a medium saucepan of salted water to a boil over high. Add orzo; stir once, and cook according to package directions. Drain orzo; rinse under cold water to stop the cooking process, about 1 minute.
2. While orzo cooks, whisk together shallot, oil, sun-dried tomatoes, dill, vinegar, lemon juice, Dijon mustard, garlic, kosher salt, and pepper in a large bowl until combined.
3. Add cooked orzo, shrimp, feta, and cucumber to sun-dried tomato mixture in large bowl; toss to combine. Garnish with additional dill.

2024 AUGUST **167**

KEY LIME PIE SUNDAE

PIECE OF CAKE

Sundae Best

Turn store-bought ice cream into something special with simple sauces and toppings

Key Lime Pie Sundae

Place scoops of **vanilla ice cream** in a small bowl; drizzle with desired amount of **Lime Curd** (recipe follows). Top with **whipped cream,** crushed **graham crackers, lime zest,** and a **maraschino cherry.**

Lime Curd

ACTIVE 15 MIN. - TOTAL 15 MIN., PLUS 1 HOUR, 20 MIN. COOLING AND CHILLING
MAKES ABOUT 1½ CUPS

Whisk together 4 **large egg yolks,** 1 cup **granulated sugar,** and ½ cup **fresh lime juice** in a medium nonstick saucepan until smooth. Cook over medium, whisking often, until mixture coats the back of a spoon, about 8 minutes. Remove from heat; add ½ cup **butter** (cut into 8 pieces), 1 piece at a time, whisking until melted. Transfer Lime Curd to a small heatproof, airtight container, and place a piece of plastic wrap directly on surface to prevent a skin from forming. Let cool 20 minutes. Chill, covered with plastic wrap, at least 1 hour. Remove plastic wrap; serve chilled. Store leftover Lime Curd in an airtight container in refrigerator for up to 2 weeks.

Peach Melba Sundae

Place scoops of **vanilla or peach ice cream** in a small bowl. Top with **fresh raspberries and peach slices;** drizzle with desired amount of **Raspberry Sauce** (recipe follows). Top with **toasted sliced almonds** and **whipped cream.**

Raspberry Sauce

ACTIVE 10 MIN. - TOTAL 10 MIN., PLUS 50 MIN. COOLING AND CHILLING
MAKES ABOUT 1 CUP

Cook 4 cups **fresh raspberries,** ½ cup **granulated sugar,** and 1 Tbsp. **fresh lemon juice** in a saucepan over medium, stirring often, until sugar is dissolved and raspberries are completely broken down, 8 to 10 minutes. Remove from heat. Press sauce through a fine mesh strainer into a heatproof, airtight container, making sure to scrape mixture from bottom of strainer. Cool, uncovered, 20 minutes. Chill, covered, until cool, about 30 minutes. Serve chilled. Store leftover Raspberry Sauce in an airtight container in refrigerator for up to 1 week.

Turtle Sundae

Place scoops of **salted-caramel ice cream** in a small bowl. Drizzle with desired amount of **Hot Fudge** (recipe right). Top with **toasted chopped pecans** and **whipped cream.**

Hot Fudge

ACTIVE 5 MIN. - TOTAL 5 MIN.
MAKES ABOUT 1 CUP

Cook ½ cup **heavy whipping cream,** ¼ cup **butter,** and ½ tsp. **vanilla extract** in a medium saucepan over medium-high, whisking often, until butter is melted. Whisk in ⅓ cup **Dutch-process cocoa** and ¼ cup each **granulated sugar** and **dark brown sugar;** cook, whisking often, until mixture thickens slightly, 2 to 3 minutes. Serve immediately. Let leftover Hot Fudge cool 20 minutes. Store in an airtight container in refrigerator for up to 2 weeks. To reheat, microwave on HIGH in 30-second intervals, stirring between intervals.

TURTLE SUNDAE

PEACH MELBA SUNDAE

2024 AUGUST 169

LIGHTEN UP

A Healthier Cobbler

Peaches, plums, and cherries give this dessert a delicious makeover

GOOD FOR YOU!
To make fiber-rich oat flour, process a heaping cup of uncooked old-fashioned regular rolled oats in a food processor until a fine powder forms, 30 to 60 seconds. Store in an airtight container at room temperature for up to two months.

Before Recipe Makeover:
CALORIES: **322** – SUGAR: **46 G** – FIBER: **1 G**

After Recipe Makeover:
CALORIES: **254** – SUGAR: **30 G** – FIBER: **4 G**

Stone Fruit Cobbler
ACTIVE 20 MIN. · TOTAL 1 HOUR, 15 MIN.
SERVES 10

- 4 peaches, pitted and sliced (about 3 cups)
- 6 red plums, pitted and sliced (about 3 cups)
- 1 lb. fresh Bing cherries, pitted (about 2 cups)
- 1 tsp. grated lemon zest plus 1 Tbsp. juice (from 1 lemon)
- ½ tsp. ground cinnamon
- ¼ tsp. ground cardamom
- ¾ cup granulated sugar, divided
- 8 Tbsp. all-purpose flour, divided
- 1¼ tsp. kosher salt, divided
- 6 Tbsp. unsalted butter, melted
- ¼ cup whole milk
- 1 large egg
- ½ cup oat flour (see instructions right)
- 1 tsp. baking powder
- 2 Tbsp. toasted sliced almonds

1. Preheat oven to 375°F. Combine peaches, plums, cherries, lemon zest, lemon juice, cinnamon, cardamom, ¼ cup of the sugar, 2 tablespoons of the all-purpose flour, and ½ teaspoon of the salt in a large bowl; toss until fruit is well coated. Coat a 13- x 9-inch baking dish with cooking spray; arrange fruit mixture in an even layer in dish.
2. Whisk together melted butter and remaining ½ cup sugar. Whisk in milk and egg until smooth.
3. Whisk together oat flour, baking powder, and the remaining 6 tablespoons all-purpose flour and ¾ teaspoon salt in a medium bowl. Add oat flour mixture to butter mixture, stirring to combine. Dollop spoonfuls of batter over fruit, leaving some of the fruit mixture uncovered.
4. Bake in preheated oven until filling is bubbling and topping is golden brown, about 45 minutes. Remove from oven; let cool 10 minutes. Sprinkle with toasted almonds.

OVER EASY

The Morning Blend

Fast and fruity smoothies for breakfast on the go

Get a smooth start to your day with these cool, creamy, health-boosting beverages packed with fresh and frozen fruits and probiotic yogurt.

Mango-Kiwi Green Smoothie
ACTIVE 5 MIN. - TOTAL 5 MIN.
SERVES 2

Process 1½ cups sliced **frozen bananas** (from 2 medium bananas), 2 cups packed **fresh baby spinach**, 1 cup chopped **fresh or frozen mango** (from 1 medium mango), ⅔ cup chopped peeled **kiwis** (from 2 medium kiwis), ½ cup **vanilla whole-milk strained (Greek-style) yogurt**, ½ cup **unsweetened coconut milk or whole milk**, and 1½ tsp. chopped **fresh ginger** in a blender until smooth, about 1 minute. Pour into 2 glasses; garnish with **kiwi slices**.

Pineapple Blush Smoothie
ACTIVE 5 MIN. - TOTAL 5 MIN.
SERVES 2

Process 2 cups **frozen pineapple chunks**, 1¼ cups **frozen strawberries**, ½ cup **vanilla whole-milk strained (Greek-style) yogurt**, ½ cup **unsweetened almond or coconut milk**, ¼ cup **sweetened flaked coconut**, and 2 Tbsp. **fresh lime juice** in a blender until smooth, 1 minute. Pour into 2 glasses; garnish with **pineapple wedges**.

Brambleberry Smoothie
ACTIVE 5 MIN. - TOTAL 5 MIN.
SERVES 2

Process 2 cups **frozen blackberries**, 1 cup each **fresh or frozen raspberries and blueberries**, 1 cup **plain granola**, ½ cup **vanilla whole-milk strained (Greek-style) yogurt**, and ½ cup **pomegranate-cherry juice** in a blender until smooth, about 1 minute. Pour into 2 glasses; garnish with **berries**.

EASY RANCH

SNACK TIME

Chicken Little

Take nuggets to the next level with a splash of dill pickle brine

Extra-Crispy Chicken Nuggets
ACTIVE 40 MIN. - TOTAL 40 MIN.
SERVES 6 TO 8

- 4 large egg whites
- ½ cup dill pickle juice, plus dill pickle chips for serving
- 2 lb. boneless, skinless chicken breasts, cut into 1-inch pieces
- 1 cup all-purpose flour
- 1 cup panko breadcrumbs
- ¼ cup cornstarch
- 1 Tbsp. garlic powder
- 1 Tbsp. kosher salt, plus more to taste
- 2 tsp. black pepper
- 2 tsp. granulated sugar
- 1 tsp. smoked paprika
- Peanut oil, for frying
- Easy Ranch, Zesty Ketchup, or Hot-Honey Mustard (recipes right), for serving

1. Whisk egg whites in a medium bowl until foamy; whisk in pickle juice until combined. Add chicken pieces, stirring to coat. Let stand while preparing the rest of the ingredients.
2. Place flour, panko, cornstarch, garlic powder, salt, pepper, sugar, and paprika in a large ziplock plastic bag. Seal bag, and shake to combine.
3. Preheat oven to 200°F. Fill a large Dutch oven halfway with oil; heat over medium-high until a thermometer registers 375°F. Working in batches, remove chicken from egg mixture, letting excess drip off. Place chicken in bag with flour mixture; seal bag, and shake to coat evenly. Transfer coated chicken pieces to a parchment paper–lined baking sheet. Repeat with remaining chicken.
4. Working in batches, add chicken to hot oil; fry until golden brown, about 3 minutes. Transfer to a rimmed baking sheet lined with a wire rack; place in preheated oven to keep warm. Repeat with remaining chicken. Sprinkle with additional salt to taste. Serve with dill pickle chips and desired dipping sauces.

Easy Ranch
MAKES ABOUT ½ CUP

Stir together ½ cup **mayonnaise**, 2 Tbsp. chopped **fresh dill**, 1 Tbsp. **fresh lemon juice**, ½ tsp. **garlic powder**, and ¼ tsp. each **kosher salt** and **black pepper** in a small bowl until combined.

Zesty Ketchup
MAKES ABOUT ½ CUP

Stir together ½ cup **ketchup**, 2 Tbsp. **barbecue sauce**, and 1 tsp. **hot sauce** in a small bowl until combined.

Hot-Honey Mustard
MAKES ABOUT ½ CUP

Stir together ½ cup **stone-ground Dijon mustard** and 2 Tbsp. **hot honey** in a small bowl until combined.

ZESTY KETCHUP

HOT-HONEY MUSTARD

COOKING SCHOOL
TIPS AND TRICKS FROM THE SOUTH'S MOST TRUSTED KITCHEN

Sharpen Your Skills
Five essential knife cuts to cook with confidence

CHIFFONADE
Stack a handful of leaves (like mint, basil, or greens such as collards or spinach), gently roll them up into a tight cylinder, and then slice the bundle horizontally into ribbons.

CHOP
Less precise than dicing, this term refers to breaking down an item into pieces that are fairly equal in size. Consistency is key for even cooking.

MINCE
Place your non-dominant hand on the top of the knife; use your other hand to rock the blade back and forth over a chopped ingredient until pieces are about 1/8 inch or smaller.

DICE
Trim the item; cut it lengthwise into even planks. Flip the planks on their sides, and repeat to form sticks (like a julienne, at right). Slice the pieces horizontally to yield uniform cubes.

JULIENNE
Begin by trimming your chosen ingredient so that all sides are flat before slicing it lengthwise into thin rectangles of equal thickness. Slice each rectangle lengthwise again to form narrow strips.

GET A GRIP

Holding a knife improperly is more than just bad form—it can be dangerous. To be safe, curl your pinkie, ring, and middle fingers around the handle while pinching either side of the blade with your index finger and thumb.

Three Basic Knives You Need

CHEF'S
This kitchen workhorse is used for slicing, dicing, and more. It's sold in various sizes, so choose the length you're most comfortable with.

SERRATED
Best for cutting bread and tomatoes, this knife is crucial for many tasks, but it's tricky to sharpen. Buy an inexpensive one, and replace it when dull.

PARING
The smallest of the bunch, this is designed for precise tasks like deveining shrimp. Look for a lightweight version with a nonslip handle.

174 2024 AUGUST

September

176   **The Zing of Sumac**   This tart, vibrantly red spice grows wild all over our region

178   **A Well-Designed Game Plan**   Alabama-based designer Billy Reid is serious about tailgating

181   **Like Father, Like Son**   Emeril Lagasse and his son, E.J., are revisiting their Portuguese roots with an exciting new project

184   **The Mother of All Muscadines**   North Carolina's sweetest grapes likely started with an ancient plant that still thrives today

186   **Mushroom Magic**   Thanks to growers across the region, varieties such as maitake, oyster, and shiitake are practically at your fingertips.

194   **The Gift of Black Walnuts**   Growing in backyards across the South, this native ingredient is ripe for the fall harvest

200   **Apple of Your Eye**   This fast and flaky galette will be the star of your next get-together

203   **A Winning Chicken Dinner**   An easy, kid-approved meal that can be tailored for everyone's tastes

204   **What Time is Kickoff?**   No matter when the game starts, these tailgate menus will score big

219   **Notes From Home**   José Medina Camacho brings a taste of his native country to Alabama with unexpected cocktails rooted in Mexican flavors

220   **Our Daily Cornbread**   Cookbook author Anne Byrn traces the history and celebrates the art of this essential Southern baked good

222   **One & Done**   Single-pan recipes for busy back-to-school nights

227   **A Sweet Slice of Fall**   One versatile Bundt and three impressive glazes to change things up

228   **Good to the Core**   Break out your skillet for this quick dessert

230   **Cooking School**   Our Test Kitchen professionals show you how to make the best chicken stock you've ever tasted

BOUNTY

The Zing of Sumac
This tart, vibrantly red spice grows wild all over our region

OFTEN FOUND along highways, on dry hillsides, and in open fields, sumac is native to the South, and some kinds, such as smooth sumac, grow in all of the lower 48 states. North American varieties have long been part of Indigenous traditions, including the beverage sumac lemonade, made from steeping it in water. The bush features cone-shaped clusters of red berries, called drupes, which mature from late summer to fall. The fruits are harvested, dried, and ground into a spice. But leave the foraging to professionals, because types that produce white or gray berries are considered poisonous.

Instead, pick up a jar at your local spice store, and use its tart, citrus-like flavor in dinners, drinks, and even desserts. Our One-Pan Sumac Chicken Thighs (right), inspired by the Palestinian dish musakhan, adds a puckery punch to savory chicken and onions; the Sumac 75 (opposite) highlights the beautiful color the ingredient can impart; and Sumac Snacking Cake (opposite) balances sweetness with well-rounded sour notes. Give any of these a try, and this spice might just become your new favorite.

One-Pan Sumac Chicken Thighs
ACTIVE 20 MIN. - TOTAL 50 MIN.
SERVES 4

Stir together 1½ tsp. each **kosher salt** and **ground sumac**, 1 tsp. **garlic powder**, and ½ tsp. each **ground cumin** and **ground Aleppo pepper** in a small bowl. Pat 4 (8-oz.) **bone-in, skin-on chicken thighs** dry with a paper towel; rub spice mixture onto both sides of thighs. Add 2 Tbsp. **olive oil** to a large ovenproof skillet. Place chicken thighs, skin side down, in cold skillet. Cook over medium, undisturbed, until skin easily releases from skillet and is deeply golden brown, about 20 minutes. Flip thighs, and transfer skillet to oven; bake at 400°F until a thermometer inserted into thickest portion of thighs registers 165°F, 10 to 13 minutes. Stir together ½ cup **whole-milk strained (Greek-style) yogurt**, 1 Tbsp. **fresh lemon juice**, ¼ tsp. **kosher salt**, and 1 grated **medium garlic clove** in a small bowl. Spread yogurt mixture evenly over a platter, and top with chicken thighs. Garnish with thinly sliced red onion, chopped **fresh parsley**, grated **lemon zest**, and additional **ground sumac**.

Sumac Simple Syrup

ACTIVE 5 MIN. - TOTAL 1 HOUR, 35 MIN.
MAKES ABOUT 1¼ CUPS

Stir together 1 cup each **water** and **granulated sugar** in a medium saucepan; bring to a simmer over medium. Remove from heat; stir in 2 Tbsp. **ground sumac,** and cool completely, about 30 minutes. Strain syrup into a bowl, discarding solids. Chill, covered, until cold, about 1 hour.

Sumac Snacking Cake

ACTIVE 20 MIN. - TOTAL 2 HOURS, 20 MIN.
SERVES 9

Grease an 8-inch square baking pan with cooking spray; line bottom and sides with parchment paper, leaving a 1-inch overhang on all sides. Stir together 1¼ cups **granulated sugar** and 1 Tbsp. grated **lemon zest** in a large bowl, rubbing zest and sugar between fingers. Whisk in 2 Tbsp. **fresh lemon juice,** 1 cup **extra-virgin olive oil,** 1½ Tbsp. **ground sumac,** 2 tsp. **baking powder,** and 1 tsp. each **vanilla extract** and **kosher salt.** Whisk in 3 **large eggs** and 1 cup **whole-milk strained (Greek-style) yogurt** until smooth.

Whisk in 2 cups **all-purpose flour** until just combined. Spread batter evenly in prepared pan; bake at 325°F until a wooden pick inserted into center comes out clean, 45 to 50 minutes. Let cool in pan for 15 minutes. Remove cake from pan; transfer to a wire rack, and let cool 1 hour. Remove and discard parchment paper. Whisk together 1 cup **powdered sugar,** 2 Tbsp. **Sumac Simple Syrup** (recipe above right), ½ Tbsp. **water,** and ½ tsp. each **ground sumac** and **kosher salt** in a bowl until smooth, adding up to ½ tablespoon additional **water** for a thinner glaze, if desired. Spread over cooled cake. Sprinkle with additional **ground sumac.**

Sumac 75

ACTIVE 5 MIN. - TOTAL 5 MIN.
SERVES 1

Lightly coat the rim of a Champagne flute with **gin.** Stir together 1 tsp. each **ground sumac** and **granulated sugar** on a small plate. Dip rim in mixture; turn to coat. Stir together 3 Tbsp. **gin** and 1½ Tbsp. each **Sumac Simple Syrup** (recipe above) and **fresh lemon juice** in a cocktail shaker. Fill with **ice;** cover and shake vigorously until cold, about 30 seconds. Strain into prepared flute. Top with ¼ cup **Champagne;** garnish with a **lemon peel twist.**

2024 SEPTEMBER 177

A Well-Designed Game Plan

Alabama-based designer Billy Reid is almost as serious about tailgating as he is about his beloved Louisiana State University Tigers

WHEN JEANNE AND BILLY REID bought and renovated a lake house just outside Florence, Alabama, back in 2015, they had certain priorities. One, the couple was looking for a family getaway where they could unplug, especially on summer weekends and holidays. Two, they wanted something private and secluded, which isn't easy to find on Wilson Lake. And three, it had to be a place where they could entertain, especially during football season. For Billy, who grew up in Amite City, Louisiana, there are few things on the fall calendar more important than watching the Louisiana State University (LSU) Tigers play. "I've missed very few games," he said on the *Southern Living Biscuits & Jam* podcast. "I've either listened to it, watched it, or been there. I'm addicted." For Jeanne, who was raised here in Florence, it's all about Auburn University, her alma mater. That meant this house had to be designed to host a great tailgate party, and if you know anything about Billy Reid, you understand that design is something he takes very seriously.

Walk into a Billy Reid store—he has 12 of them now in cities all over the South and beyond—and it's hard not to feel right at home. When he opened his first clothing shops in Dallas, Houston, and Florence in 2004, he filled the spaces with antiques, family photographs, and comfortable furniture. There's always great music playing, and an employee will usually offer you a cold drink.

At the Reids' lake house, which is surrounded by hardwoods that go all the way down to Shoal Creek, he and Jeanne take the hospitality and design a step further. There's a dramatic chandelier that hangs over the living room, a fixture Billy had made with driftwood he collected from a little cove that juts into their property. The home is warm, casual, and open, with a big white sectional that almost begs you to sit down. "I can tell you where every single one of these pieces came from or how we made them," he says, pointing around the room. "Those wooden pews came out of a church in Vicksburg, Mississippi, that was built in 1851. The staircase was from my great-grandmother's house in Louisiana. A lot of these are sentimental things."

Billy gets even more sentimental when it comes to football. He has a collection of old LSU T-shirts and hats that go back decades, and he's used a tiger logo on some of his clothing lines. On the bar, which he made out of a couple of end tables and a slab of marble, there's a vintage LSU wine stopper sticking out of a bottle of bourbon. But he has a practical side too. "We arranged the televisions so there's one facing the kitchen and one facing the family room," he says. "You can see the TV from every angle in the house."

When it comes to fall Saturdays, their philosophy on entertaining is pretty simple. "We try to keep game days uncomplicated," he says. "We set up a self-service bar situation, mixing Bloody Marys ahead of time so everything is ready in the pitcher, and stock the bar and the fridge. We prep the night before so we're not scrambling the whole day."

For the food, Billy likes to bring a bit of Louisiana to the party. Sometimes he'll flash fry boudin balls or Jeanne will cook jambalaya, a perfect tailgate food because it doesn't have to be served hot. Lately, his go-to dish has been Cajun-rubbed pork chops that he cuts into little bites or a family-favorite Creole barbecue shrimp recipe.

The Reids clearly make a good team, but they joke that sometimes the football can get a little too serious, especially when LSU is playing Auburn. "If it's a game that doesn't mean a lot, we can hang together and watch it, but if both teams are good and the game means a lot, we'll separate," Billy says with a big laugh. Then there's the University of Alabama, which is something else entirely, especially when you're surrounded by Crimson Tide fans. "The LSU-Alabama game is one where we don't go to anyone's house. Nobody is coming over," he says.

There are plenty of games watched in person, too, either in Auburn or Baton Rouge. "When we go to Louisiana, it's so much about family," he says. "We have relatives who live 15 or 20 minutes from the stadium. We'll set up our tailgate near the Cow Palace. It's a little bit of a walk, but that's our spot."

Reid didn't attend LSU—he went to Southeastern Louisiana University and then the Art Institute of Dallas—so one might wonder why he's become such a hard-core fan. "It wasn't a choice," he says. "Even as I've moved all over, it never has left me. It's just part of my soul, part of who I am." —Sid Evans

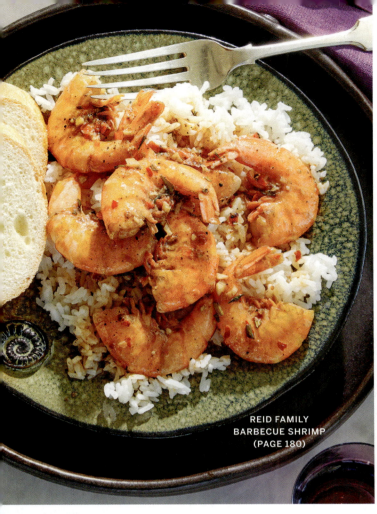
REID FAMILY
BARBECUE SHRIMP
(PAGE 180)

CITY GROCERY
BLOODY MARYS
(PAGE 180)

CAJUN-RUBBED
PORK CHOP BITES
(PAGE 180)

Reid Family Barbecue Shrimp

(Photo, page 179)

"We were in Baton Rouge at my sister-in-law's house, and she had cooked barbecue shrimp. It was phenomenal," Billy recalls. "Jeanne wrote down the recipe on the back of an envelope—which we still have, with stains all over it. This is the perfect tailgate food."

ACTIVE 20 MIN. - TOTAL 20 MIN.

SERVES 4

- ¾ cup unsalted butter
- ¾ cup (6 oz.) pilsner beer (such as Budweiser or Miller Lite)
- ½ cup shrimp stock
- 1½ tsp. minced garlic (from 3 garlic cloves)
- 1 tsp. Worcestershire sauce
- 1 tsp. cayenne pepper
- 1 tsp. black pepper
- 1 tsp. kosher salt
- ½ tsp. crushed red pepper
- ½ tsp. fresh thyme leaves
- ¼ tsp. chopped fresh rosemary
- ⅛ tsp. chopped fresh oregano
- 2 lb. jumbo unpeeled raw Gulf shrimp
  Hot cooked rice
  French bread

1. Melt butter in a large skillet over medium; add beer, stock, garlic, Worcestershire sauce, cayenne pepper, black pepper, salt, crushed red pepper, thyme, rosemary, and oregano. Cook, stirring constantly, until just beginning to simmer, 3 minutes.
2. Add shrimp to mixture in skillet; cook, stirring occasionally, until cooked through, 6 to 8 minutes. Remove skillet from heat; let stand 2 minutes. Serve over rice with bread.

Cajun-Rubbed Pork Chop Bites

(Photo, page 179)

The secret to these pork chops is to use a reverse sear. "You cook them on low for about an hour, real slow, and then just flame them," Billy says.

ACTIVE 20 MIN. - TOTAL 2 HOURS, 30 MIN., PLUS 12 HOURS CHILLING

SERVES 12

- 1 Tbsp. paprika
- 2¼ tsp. kosher salt, plus more to taste
- 2¼ tsp. garlic powder
- 2 tsp. black pepper
- 1¼ tsp. cayenne pepper
- 1⅛ tsp. onion powder
- 1 tsp. dried thyme
- 1 tsp. dried oregano
- ½ tsp. dried parsley flakes
- 4 (9- to 10-oz.) bone-in pork chops (about 1 inch thick)

1. Stir together paprika, salt, garlic powder, black pepper, cayenne pepper, onion powder, thyme, oregano, and parsley in a bowl until combined. Rub seasoning mixture on both sides of pork chops. Place pork chops on a wire rack over a rimmed baking sheet. Chill, uncovered, at least 12 hours or up to 24 hours.
2. Let pork chops come to room temperature, about 1 hour. Meanwhile, preheat a gas grill to low (250°F to 300°F) on 1 side or push hot coals to 1 side of a charcoal grill. Place pork chops on oiled grates over unlit side of grill. Grill, covered, until a thermometer inserted into thickest portion registers 130°F, about 1 hour, 5 minutes, rotating pork chops halfway through grilling time. Remove pork chops from grill.
3. Increase temperature of grill to high (450°F to 500°F). Place pork chops on lit side of grill. Grill, uncovered, until a thermometer inserted into thickest portion registers 145°F and pork chops are evenly seared, about 2 minutes per side. Transfer to a cutting board; tent with aluminum foil, and let rest for 5 minutes. Cut pork chops into bite-size pieces; sprinkle with additional salt to taste.

City Grocery Bloody Marys

(Photo, page 179)

"I use my good friend John Currence's recipe from City Grocery [a restaurant in Oxford, Mississippi] for one of my favorite Bloody Marys," says Billy. "I think it has 16 ingredients in it. That's the way he wants it—complicated, complex, and spectacular at the same time. It's a labor of love."

ACTIVE 10 MIN. - TOTAL 55 MIN.

SERVES 6

- 4 cups vegetable juice (such as V8)
- 1¾ cups (14 oz.) vodka (good quality but not top-shelf)
- 3 Tbsp. Worcestershire sauce
- 2 Tbsp. dill pickle juice
- 5 tsp. prepared horseradish
- 2½ tsp. finely grated shallot (from 1 large shallot)
- 2½ tsp. black pepper, plus more for serving
- 2 tsp. hot sauce (such as Tabasco)
- 2 tsp. grated lemon zest plus ¼ cup fresh juice (from 1 lemon)
- 1½ tsp. minced garlic (from 3 garlic cloves)
- 1½ tsp. kosher salt
- 1 tsp. grated lime zest plus 2 Tbsp. fresh juice (from 1 lime)
- ¾ tsp. celery seeds
  Ice
- 6 pickled okra pods
- 12 cocktail onions
- 6 good-quality pitted green olives (such as Castelvetrano)
- 6 lime wedges

1. Place vegetable juice, vodka, Worcestershire, pickle juice, horseradish, shallot, pepper, hot sauce, lemon zest, lemon juice, garlic, salt, lime zest, lime juice, and celery seeds in a large pitcher; stir well to combine. Chill in refrigerator for at least 45 minutes or up to 24 hours.
2. Fill 6 tumblers with ice. Thread 1 okra pod, 2 cocktail onions, and 1 olive on each of 6 skewers; add 1 skewer to each glass.
3. Pour chilled mixture over ice in glasses. Sprinkle each drink with additional pepper, and place 1 lime wedge on each rim.

Like Father, Like Son

Thirty-four years after opening his first restaurant, Emeril Lagasse is letting the next generation lead the kitchen. Together, he and his son, E.J., are revisiting their Portuguese roots with an exciting new project

GROWING UP, Emeril Lagasse found his calling in the kitchen by cooking alongside his mother, Hilda. Arms barely reaching the counter, he would peel vegetables from their small backyard garden—about as much as a 7-year-old could do to assist—while she made Portuguese staples like caldo verde, a comforting soup with greens, sausage, and potatoes. When he was 12, he began helping out at a family-owned bakery in his hometown (a Portuguese community near the eastern shore of Mount Hope Bay in Massachusetts), washing pots and pans until he was able to persuade the bakers to teach him how to make pastries and bread.

Stoked by his mother's culture and cuisine, he developed his passion at the bakeshop, which led him to culinary school and eventually to New Orleans, where, at age 23, he became executive chef at the legendary Commander's Palace. In 1990, he opened his own place, Emeril's, which just celebrated its 34th anniversary. "It's not easy staying open that long," he admits. "Now, we're looking toward the next 34 years."

In the newly renovated kitchen at the chef's namesake eatery, there's a growing legacy at work. Emeril is there (not every night, but sometimes), off to the side, watching orders come in and go out. In the middle of the flurry of plates and steam is someone else: his son, E.J. Lagasse, furrowing those same thick brows and wearing the same chef's coat as his father.

By the time E.J. was born, Emeril had been a celebrity chef for more than a decade. It wasn't long before that same passion for food grabbed hold of the younger Lagasse.

In a move that took the culinary world by surprise, E.J. stepped up to take the helm at Emeril's at just 19 years old, wielding skills honed from a well-seasoned childhood and from receiving his training at the same school as his father.

Just as Hilda had created a tether to Portuguese food with her son, Emeril did the same. "It was something that just seeped into me naturally through his and my grandmother's cooking," says E.J.

Portuguese favorites, like Hilda's stewed chicken with its rich, slowly simmered seasoned broth, make appearances on the family table and at holidays. So do the traditional tartlets of Emeril's pastry-shop days, which have a sweet and silky custard filling and a golden, bite-size crust.

The father-son duo is celebrating their ancestry even more with a new establishment called 34 Restaurant & Bar, expected to open this fall, that is entirely dedicated to Portuguese cuisine. Reminiscent of the lively, wood-fired kitchens found in Portugal, it features a menu of rotating daily tapas and is a romantic ode to their roots—and to Hilda, who passed away in 2016 after living in New Orleans for more than two decades.

"I've had the pleasure of watching my son take the lead and put his own spin on things," Emeril says. "It is not a given that you'll end up sharing a career with one of your children, so I cherish that."
—Kaitlyn Yarborough Sadik

HILDA'S PORTUGUESE STEWED CHICKEN

Hilda's Portuguese Stewed Chicken

For a shortcut, substitute 1 (14.5-ounce) can of petite diced tomatoes instead of prepping the fresh kind.

ACTIVE 45 MIN. - TOTAL 1 HOUR, 45 MIN.
SERVES 4

- ½ cup all-purpose flour
- 2 tsp. Emeril's Original Essence or Creole seasoning, plus more to taste
- 1 (4-lb.) whole chicken, cut into 8 pieces
- 3 Tbsp. olive oil
- 1 lb. Spanish chorizo, sliced into 2-inch pieces
- 2 cups large-diced red potatoes (from 3 medium potatoes)
- 1 medium-size yellow onion, diced (about 1½ cups)
- 1 medium-size red bell pepper, cut into thin strips (about 1 cup)
- 1 medium-size yellow bell pepper, cut into thin strips (about 1 cup)
- 2 cups peeled and diced fresh tomatoes
- 1 cup pitted kalamata olives (from 1 [8-oz.] jar), sliced
- 2 Tbsp. finely chopped shallot (from 1 medium shallot)
- 1 garlic head, skin removed and cloves left whole
- 1 cup dry white wine
- ½ cup finely chopped fresh flat-leaf parsley, plus more for garnish
- 2 cups chicken stock, divided
- Pinch of crushed red pepper
- ½ cup sliced scallions (from 2 scallions)
- ¼ tsp. kosher salt
- ⅛ tsp. black pepper
- 2 cups hot cooked white rice
- Freshly grated Parmesan cheese (optional)
- Crusty bread

1. In a large bowl, stir together flour and Emeril's Original Essence seasoning. Toss chicken pieces in seasoned flour to coat.
2. Heat olive oil in a large Dutch oven over medium-high until oil is shimmering. Working in batches, add chicken; sear until golden brown on all sides, 8 to 12 minutes per batch. Transfer chicken to a clean plate, and set aside. Add chorizo to skillet; cook until browned on both sides, about 3 minutes. Add potatoes, onion, and bell peppers. Cook, stirring occasionally, until softened, about 2 minutes. Add tomatoes, olives, shallot, and garlic cloves. Season vegetables with more Emeril's Original Essence seasoning to taste. Stir in wine, parsley, and 1 cup of the chicken stock; return chicken to pan.
3. Bring to a boil over medium-high. Reduce heat to low; cover and simmer until chicken is fall-off-the-bone tender, 1 hour to 1 hour, 15 minutes, adding desired amount of remaining 1 cup chicken stock as needed (stew is intended to be thick). Add crushed red pepper, scallions, salt, and black pepper.
4. Divide rice evenly among 4 bowls, mounding it in center of each. Spoon chicken-and-stew mixture around rice. If desired, garnish with cheese, parsley, and more Emeril's Original Essence seasoning. Serve with crusty bread.

Portuguese Custard Tartlets

Store-bought puff pastry varies in size and number of sheets per package. If buying a brand other than Dufour, be sure to purchase at least 28 ounces total to yield enough crusts for this recipe, using as many sheets as needed.

ACTIVE 1 HOUR - TOTAL 1 HOUR, 30 MIN.
MAKES 18

- Unsalted butter, softened
- All-purpose flour, for work surface
- 2 (14-oz.) pkg. frozen puff pastry (such as Dufour), thawed
- 1½ cups heavy whipping cream
- ¼ tsp. finely grated orange zest (from 1 orange)
- ½ vanilla bean, halved lengthwise and seeds scraped
- 6 large egg yolks
- ¾ cup granulated sugar
- 1 Tbsp. cornstarch
- Powdered sugar

1. Lightly grease 18 wells of a standard-size muffin tray with butter. On a lightly floured work surface, roll 1 puff pastry sheet into a 15-inch square (about ⅛ inch thick). Using a 5-inch round cookie cutter (or cutting around a 5-inch-diameter bowl), cut out 9 pastry rounds (the number of rounds per sheet may vary according to brand). Repeat with remaining puff pastry sheet. Tuck puff pastry rounds into prepared muffin wells; cover with plastic wrap, and chill at least 30 minutes or up to 1 day.
2. Heat heavy cream, orange zest, and vanilla bean and scraped seeds in a small saucepan over medium; bring just to a boil. Immediately remove from heat; cover with lid. Set aside, and let steep for 30 minutes.
3. Preheat oven to 425°F. In a medium bowl, whisk together yolks, granulated sugar, and cornstarch until thickened and pale yellow. Gradually add steeped cream, whisking constantly. Pour mixture through a fine mesh strainer into a bowl; discard solids. Set custard filling aside.
4. Place paper liners inside each pastry-lined muffin well. Add pie weights or dried beans to liners; bake in preheated oven until pastry is set around edges, 6 to 8 minutes. Remove from oven; carefully remove paper liners and pie weights from muffin tray, and return tray to oven. Bake at 425°F until bottoms of pastry become opaque and slightly firm, 2 to 3 minutes. Remove from oven, and reduce oven temperature to 350°F.
5. Divide custard filling evenly among pastry shells (about 2½ tablespoons per shell). Bake until lightly golden and custard is set, 20 to 25 minutes. Remove from oven; let cool in muffin tray 5 minutes. Transfer pastry shells to wire racks, and let cool 5 minutes. Sprinkle with powdered sugar; serve warm or at room temperature. Tartlets may be made up to 1 day in advance and stored in an airtight container in refrigerator for up to 3 days.

PORTUGUESE CUSTARD TARTLETS

HOMEGROWN

The Mother of All Muscadines

North Carolina's sweetest grapes likely started with an ancient plant that still thrives today

THE AROMA OF ripe muscadines is like a preview of coming attractions. These Southern grapes perfume the air with an unmistakable sweet, musky scent that wafts along balmy summer breezes. One taste confirms their syrupy, deep flavor that's unlike any other variety—and superior to most. We don't so much eat muscadines as experience them.

While experts have detailed criteria for categorizing each type, most people call the dark purple kinds muscadines and the light bronze ones scuppernongs.

Muscadines and scuppernongs are among a handful of fruits native to the Southeastern United States, where they thrive in our heat and humidity. In addition to foraging for them, Native Americans began cultivating these grapes more than 400 years ago. The earliest European explorers marveled at the profusion of vines and fruit growing all over the North Carolina coastal region we now call the Outer Banks. English sea captain Arthur Barlowe wrote that Roanoke Island was "so full of grapes...that I think in all the world the like abundance is not to be found."

There's a good chance that some of the plants they reported seeing sprang from the Mother Vine, considered to be the oldest cultivated grapevine in North America. Many historians believe the Croatoan people planted it long before any explorers came ashore, while others say it was grown by the settlers sent to replace the Lost Colony that disappeared mysteriously in the late 1500s. No matter its origin, no one disputes that it's very old and was once very big, with dense tangled vines covering acres and climbing 60 feet up into the treetops. At one point, the twisted, gnarled main root was nearly 3 feet in diameter and had shoots as thick as tree limbs.

A vestige of the Mother Vine persists today on the outskirts of Manteo, nestled in a homeowner's yard.

The Mother Vine is smaller and more fragile these days, as sometimes happens with venerable matriarchs, but in late summer, the signature perfume of ripe grapes always mingles with the salt air. It still produces a lush, verdant leaf canopy and a few buckets of bronze grapes, each one a taste of history. —Sheri Castle

Muscadine Dumplings

Make the most of these storied grapes by turning them into a jammy sauce that goes wonderfully with lemony dumplings and melty ice cream.
ACTIVE 1 HOUR, 15 MIN. - TOTAL 1 HOUR, 35 MIN.
SERVES 6

MUSCADINE SAUCE
- 2 lb. fresh purple muscadine grapes (about 6 cups)
- 1½ cups bottled red muscadine juice
- ⅓ cup granulated sugar
- 2 Tbsp. fresh lemon juice (from 1 medium lemon)
- 1 tsp. ground ginger
- 1 tsp. apple pie spice or pumpkin pie spice
- 2 (4-inch) rosemary sprigs, plus leaves for garnish
- ½ cup muscadine wine or juice
- 1 Tbsp. cornstarch

DUMPLINGS
- 1 cup all-purpose flour, plus more for rolling
- 2 Tbsp. granulated sugar
- 1½ tsp. grated lemon zest (from 1 medium lemon), plus more for garnish
- 1 tsp. baking powder
- ½ tsp. kosher salt
- 3 Tbsp. cold unsalted butter, cut into ½-inch cubes
- ⅓ cup half-and-half

ADDITIONAL INGREDIENT
Vanilla ice cream

1. Prepare the Muscadine Sauce: Cut each grape in half; remove seeds using tip of a skewer or paring knife. Set aside 4 cups grape halves for sauce; cut remaining halves in half, and reserve for serving.
2. Whisk together muscadine juice, sugar, lemon juice, ginger, and pie spice in a 6-quart Dutch oven or large, wide saucepan with a tight-fitting lid. Bring to a simmer over medium, whisking often. Stir in rosemary sprigs. Reduce heat to low, and keep warm over low.
3. Prepare the Dumplings: Whisk together flour, sugar, lemon zest, baking powder, and salt in a medium bowl. Cut in cold butter using a pastry cutter or 2 forks until mixture is crumbly. Slowly stir in half-and-half until a sticky dough that holds its shape forms. Transfer to a well-floured surface, and pat into a 6½- x 3½-inch rectangle; cut into about 1¾- x 1-inch rectangles. Brush off excess flour from bottoms of rectangles, if needed.
4. Stir together muscadine wine and cornstarch in a small bowl until smooth; whisk into juice mixture in Dutch oven. Bring to a low boil over medium-high, whisking often.
5. Stir in 4 cups reserved grape halves. Return mixture in Dutch oven to a low boil; drop dough rectangles evenly over top of bubbling mixture. Cover and reduce heat to medium (so mixture stays at an active simmer). Cover and simmer, undisturbed, for 10 minutes. (Do not lift lid while Dumplings are cooking.) Remove from heat; let stand, covered, for 10 minutes.
6. Discard rosemary sprigs; divide Muscadine Sauce and Dumplings evenly among 6 rimmed plates. Top servings with vanilla ice cream and reserved fresh grapes. Garnish with rosemary leaves and additional lemon zest.

Mushroom Magic

A decade ago, if you wanted "wild" mushrooms, you enlisted the help of a skilled forager or headed to the farmers' market at the crack of dawn and took your chances. These days—thanks to growers across the region—varieties such as maitake, oyster, and shiitake are practically at your fingertips

The Best Way to Clean Mushrooms

Avoid using excess water when washing these fungi, which are delicate and porous in nature. Most packaged varieties available at grocery stores are fairly clean and rarely require any special attention prior to cooking, but it's a good habit to inspect them. Wipe off excess soil and debris with a soft dish towel. If they're particularly dirty, briefly rinse with warm water before drying thoroughly. Use immediately after washing and drying, because moisture shortens their shelf life.

Chicken-Fried Mushrooms with Creamy Mushroom Gravy
ACTIVE 50 MIN. - TOTAL 1 HOUR, 10 MIN.
SERVES 4

CHICKEN-FRIED MUSHROOMS
- 2 cups Mushroom Stock (recipe, page 193)
- 1 lb. fresh oyster mushrooms, torn into 3- to 4-inch pieces (about 12 cups)
- 3 cups all-purpose flour
- 1 Tbsp. kosher salt, plus more to taste
- 2 tsp. black pepper, plus more to taste
- 1½ cups whole buttermilk
- 2 large eggs
- Vegetable oil, for frying

CREAMY MUSHROOM GRAVY
- 3 Tbsp. unsalted butter
- 3 Tbsp. all-purpose flour
- 1½ cups whole milk
- ½ cup Mushroom Stock (recipe, page 193)
- ¾ tsp. kosher salt
- ¾ tsp. black pepper
- Chopped fresh chives
- Cayenne pepper

1. Prepare the Chicken-Fried Mushrooms: Bring stock to a boil in a medium saucepan over medium-high. Place mushrooms in a large heatproof bowl. Pour hot stock over mushrooms, and gently stir to coat. Cover bowl tightly with plastic wrap, and let stand until mushrooms are mostly tender, 8 to 10 minutes.

2. Preheat oven to 200°F. Line a baking sheet with paper towels; then line a second baking sheet with parchment paper. Set both aside. Whisk together flour, salt, and pepper in a medium bowl until well combined. In a separate medium bowl, whisk together buttermilk and eggs until combined.

3. Remove mushrooms from stock; drain and transfer to prepared baking sheet lined with paper towels. Gently pat mushrooms dry. Working in batches, gently toss the mushrooms in flour mixture to coat. Dip mushrooms into buttermilk mixture, and dredge again in flour mixture until well coated, gently shaking off excess flour and egg mixture in between coats. Transfer dredged mushrooms to prepared baking sheet lined with parchment paper. Repeat process until all mushrooms are coated.

4. Line baking sheet with another layer of paper towels. Add oil to a depth of 3 inches in a large Dutch oven. Heat oil to 350°F. Working in batches, fry mushrooms, stirring and turning occasionally, until golden brown and crispy, 6 to 8 minutes per batch, adjusting heat as needed to maintain temperature. Transfer fried mushrooms to prepared baking sheet to drain; season to taste with salt and pepper. Keep mushrooms warm in preheated oven while preparing gravy.

5. Prepare the Creamy Mushroom Gravy: Melt butter in a medium saucepan over medium-low. Add flour, and cook, whisking constantly, until light golden brown, 2 to 3 minutes.

6. Whisk in milk and stock; cook, whisking constantly, until mixture thickens and begins to bubble, 4 to 5 minutes. Whisk in salt and black pepper. Remove saucepan from heat, and cover to keep warm until ready to use. Drizzle Chicken-Fried Mushrooms with Creamy Mushroom Gravy, and sprinkle with chives and cayenne pepper. Serve immediately.

PAN-SEARED RIB-EYE WITH MUSHROOM-HUNTER'S SAUCE (PAGE 190)

CRISPY ROASTED MUSHROOMS WITH CREAMY GRITS (PAGE 190)

Pan-Seared Rib-Eye with Mushroom-Hunter's Sauce

(Photo, page 188)

ACTIVE 45 MIN. · TOTAL 1 HOUR

SERVES 2

PAN-SEARED RIB-EYE

- 2 Tbsp. neutral oil (such as canola or vegetable)
- 1 (1½-lb.) boneless rib-eye steak (2 inches thick)
- 2 tsp. kosher salt
- 1 tsp. black pepper
- 4 Tbsp. unsalted butter
- 2 garlic cloves, crushed
- 5 (4-inch) thyme sprigs, plus leaves for garnish

MUSHROOM-HUNTER'S SAUCE

- ½ cup unsalted butter, cut into ½-inch pieces, divided
- 2 cups thinly sliced, stemmed fresh shiitake mushrooms (from 2 [3.5-oz.] pkg.)
- 1 small shallot, finely chopped (about 2 Tbsp.)
- ½ cup dry white wine
- ¼ cup tomato puree
- 1 cup Mushroom Stock (recipe, page 193)
- 2 tsp. chopped fresh thyme
- ½ tsp. kosher salt
- ¼ tsp. black pepper

1. Prepare the Pan-Seared Rib-Eye: Preheat oven to 400°F. Heat oil in a large cast-iron skillet over medium-high until shimmering and just beginning to smoke, 2 to 3 minutes. Pat steak dry with paper towels; sprinkle with salt and pepper. Add steak to skillet; cook, undisturbed, until evenly browned, 4 to 5 minutes. Reduce heat to medium, and flip steak. Add butter, garlic, and thyme. Cook, basting steak constantly with butter mixture, until garlic caramelizes and sides of steak are no longer pink, 4 to 5 minutes. Transfer skillet to preheated oven, and cook until a thermometer inserted into thickest portion of steak registers 130°F, 6 to 9 minutes. Transfer steak to a cutting board, and let stand, uncovered, 5 minutes.

2. Prepare the Mushroom-Hunter's Sauce: Melt 2 tablespoons of the butter in a large skillet over medium. Add mushrooms, and cook, stirring occasionally, until lightly browned, 5 to 6 minutes. Add shallot; cook, stirring constantly, until tender, about 1 minute. Add wine, and cook, undisturbed, until almost dry, about 2 minutes. Add tomato puree and stock; cook, stirring occasionally, until mixture bubbles and thickens, 8 to 10 minutes.

3. Remove skillet from heat. Add remaining 6 tablespoons butter to mushroom mixture, 1 tablespoon at a time, whisking constantly after each addition, until mixture is well combined and sauce is glossy. Stir in thyme, salt, and pepper; remove from heat.

4. Cut steak into ½-inch-thick slices. Spoon Mushroom-Hunter's Sauce over sliced steak; garnish with thyme leaves. Serve immediately.

Crispy Roasted Mushrooms with Creamy Grits

(Photo, page 189)

ACTIVE 35 MIN. · TOTAL 1 HOUR, 10 MIN.

SERVES 4

CRISPY ROASTED MUSHROOMS

- 2 lb. fresh maitake mushrooms, torn into 2- to 3-inch pieces
- 1 garlic head, halved crosswise
- ¾ cup olive oil
- 2 Tbsp. chopped fresh rosemary
- 2½ tsp. kosher salt
- ½ tsp. black pepper

CREAMY GRITS

- 2 cups half-and-half
- 2½ cups Mushroom Stock (recipe, page 193), divided
- 1 cup uncooked yellow stone-ground grits
- ½ cup (4 oz.) unsalted butter, cut into 1-inch pieces
- 2½ tsp. kosher salt
- ½ tsp. black pepper

ADDITIONAL INGREDIENT
Chopped fresh rosemary

1. Prepare the Crispy Roasted Mushrooms: Preheat oven to 400°F. Line a large rimmed baking sheet with parchment paper. Gently toss mushrooms, garlic, olive oil, rosemary, salt, and pepper in a large bowl until well combined. Arrange mushroom mixture in an even layer on prepared baking sheet. Place halved garlic cut sides down.

2. Roast mushrooms in preheated oven until tender and beginning to brown, about 30 minutes. Remove baking sheet from oven, gently toss mushrooms, and bake until crispy and golden brown, 35 to 40 minutes. Transfer mushrooms to a medium bowl, reserving garlic and oil on baking sheet. Squeeze cloves from each garlic half into bowl with mushrooms; discard skins. Transfer remaining mushroom oil mixture on baking sheet to a small bowl.

3. While mushrooms roast, prepare the Creamy Grits: Bring half-and-half and 2 cups of the stock to a gentle boil in a medium saucepan over medium-high. Immediately reduce heat to low; whisk in the grits; and cook, whisking frequently, until grits are tender, 20 to 25 minutes. Whisk in butter, salt, and pepper. Whisk in remaining ½ cup stock, if needed, to reach desired consistency. Remove saucepan from heat; cover to keep warm.

4. Divide Creamy Grits among 4 shallow bowls; top with Crispy Roasted Mushrooms. Garnish with a drizzle of reserved mushroom oil and chopped fresh rosemary. Serve immediately.

Shroom School
From dried to fresh, these are some of the most common varieties you'll see at the store

1. Dried shiitake, porcini, and morel — **2.** Cremini, also known as baby bella or baby portobello — **3.** Shiitake
4. King trumpet (a variety of oyster) — **5.** Portobello — **6.** Maitake (hen of the woods) — **7.** Golden and pink oyster

PORTOBELLO BOLOGNESE

Portobello Bolognese

ACTIVE 1 HOUR, 20 MIN. · TOTAL 1 HOUR, 30 MIN.
SERVES 4

- 4 (6-oz.) pkg. fresh portobello mushrooms, stems and gills removed, cut into ½-inch pieces
- 3 Tbsp. olive oil, divided
- 1 large yellow onion, finely chopped (about 2 cups)
- 1 large carrot, peeled and finely chopped (about 1 cup)
- 1 large celery stalk, finely chopped (about ½ cup)
- 2 tsp. finely chopped garlic (from 2 garlic cloves)
- 2 Tbsp. tomato paste
- 1 cup dry white wine
- 1 cup whole milk
- 2 cups Mushroom Stock (recipe, below right)
- 1 (14½-oz.) can crushed tomatoes
- 2 oz. Parmesan cheese, finely grated (about ½ cup)
- 2¼ tsp. kosher salt, plus more for salting water
- ½ tsp. black pepper
- 12 oz. uncooked tagliatelle, pappardelle, fettuccine, or linguine pasta
- Shaved Parmesan cheese
- Fresh basil leaves

1. Preheat oven to broil with rack about 6 inches from heat source. Line a large rimmed baking sheet with aluminum foil. Toss mushrooms and 2 tablespoons of the olive oil in a medium bowl to combine; arrange in an even layer on prepared baking sheet. Broil mushrooms until tender and very lightly charred, 10 to 12 minutes. Set aside.
2. Meanwhile, heat remaining 1 tablespoon oil in a large saucepan over medium until shimmering. Add onion, carrot, and celery; cook, stirring occasionally, until tender, 5 to 7 minutes. Add garlic, and cook, stirring constantly, until fragrant, about 1 minute. Add tomato paste, and cook, stirring constantly, until fragrant, 2 to 3 minutes. Add wine, and cook until liquid is almost completely reduced, 5 to 6 minutes. Add milk, stock, tomatoes, and broiled mushrooms to saucepan; bring to a boil over medium-high. Reduce heat to medium-low; simmer, stirring occasionally, until mixture thickens, 55 to 60 minutes. Remove from heat, and stir in grated Parmesan, salt, and pepper. Cover to keep warm until ready to serve.
3. Bring a large pot of salted water to a boil over high. Add pasta; cook according to package directions. Drain pasta, reserving 1 cup cooking water. Add cooked pasta to Portobello Bolognese along with ½ cup reserved cooking water, and stir gently to combine. Add more cooking water to reach desired consistency, if needed. Divide pasta among 4 bowls. Garnish with shaved Parmesan and fresh basil leaves, and serve immediately.

Mushroom Stock

ACTIVE 35 MIN. · TOTAL 1 HOUR, 50 MIN.
MAKES 2 QT.

- 2 Tbsp. olive oil
- 4 (8-oz.) pkg. sliced fresh cremini mushrooms
- 1 large yellow onion, chopped (about 3 cups)
- 1 large carrot, peeled and chopped (about 1 cup)
- 2 medium celery stalks, chopped (about ½ cup)
- 2 Tbsp. tomato paste
- 1 cup dry white wine
- 3 qt. water
- 4 oz. dried mushrooms (such as shiitake, porcini, oyster, lion's mane, or a mix)
- 1 Tbsp. black peppercorns
- 6 dried bay leaves
- 8 (6-inch) thyme sprigs
- 10 (6-inch) flat-leaf parsley sprigs

1. Heat oil in a large stockpot over high until shimmering, 1 to 2 minutes. Add cremini mushrooms, onion, carrot, and celery. Cook, uncovered, stirring occasionally, until mushroom mixture is tender and pan is dry, 20 to 25 minutes.
2. Add tomato paste to mushroom mixture, and cook, stirring constantly, until fragrant, about 2 minutes. Add wine, and cook, stirring frequently, until liquid has almost completely reduced, 3 to 4 minutes.
3. Add water, dried mushrooms, peppercorns, bay leaves, thyme, and parsley; bring to a boil over high. Reduce heat to low, and simmer, uncovered and undisturbed, until stock is fragrant and flavorful, about 1 hour.
4. Remove stockpot from heat, and carefully pour mixture through a fine mesh strainer into a medium saucepan; discard solids. Keep stock warm over low heat, uncovered, until ready to use. Or pour into a heatproof container, and let cool at room temperature 1 hour. Transfer to refrigerator, and chill completely. Store, covered, in refrigerator up to 5 days, or freeze up to 3 months.

The Gift of Black Walnuts
Growing in backyards across the South, this native ingredient is ripe for the fall harvest

BAM! K'TANG! If you've never been jarred awake by the ruckus of racquetball-size black walnuts plummeting from high up in a tree down to a tin roof, you've missed out on a quintessential Southern experience. It's a sound that's all too familiar to my husband, Patrick, whose family's South Mississippi property is graced by a large black walnut tree with limbs that shade an old chicken coop.

I didn't grow up eating black walnuts, other than in ice cream, but Patrick did. He enjoyed gathering those lime-green bombs that hurtled toward the ground every September and October and inhaling their scent, a spicy, citrusy aroma that always made him sneeze. The work of getting to the meat of the nuts deterred most folks from fooling with them—after cracking into an impossibly hard outer husk comes the chore of breaking through the bone-tough interior shell, both of which notoriously stain hands (and the mouths of enterprising squirrels).

Back in the day, you would have to really love them to crack them, and the reward was an unparalleled taste: profoundly earthy, tannic, bitter, and faintly sweet, with much more complexity than the traditional English walnuts. When I first tried a fresh one that Patrick had dissected for me— rather than just eating the ice-cream flavor—I was blown away.

Interestingly, those hard inner shells can be used in products ranging from abrasive cleaners to water filtration to even dynamite filler. But it's the meat, of course, that's the true prize. Since the shell is so hard to break into, you won't find intact walnut halves, as you do with English ones, but rather little nuggets and pieces. They're soft and rich with oil and have that distinctive taste that is nothing at all like the mildness of any other nut.

Because they are so unique and fragrant, black walnuts won't settle for a supporting role in a recipe. They are the defining ingredient in anything they make their way into, whether imbuing an apple pie with incomparable robustness, permeating banana bread with their distinctive depth, adding welcome savory notes to a fall salad, or peppering a pasta dish with flavor. And yes, when they're combined with heavy cream and some sweetened condensed milk, they can make an absolutely killer ice cream. –Ann Taylor Pittman

Black Walnut Banana Bread

Quick breads and walnuts have a long-standing friendship. This recipe takes it up a notch by including the nuts not only in the batter but also in the buttery streusel topping.

ACTIVE 35 MIN. • TOTAL 2 HOURS, 45 MIN.
SERVES 12

STREUSEL
- ¼ cup all-purpose flour
- ¼ cup packed light brown sugar
- ¼ tsp. kosher salt
- ¼ tsp. ground cinnamon
- 3 Tbsp. unsalted butter, softened
- ¼ cup toasted chopped black walnuts

BREAD
- 2 cups all-purpose flour
- 1 tsp. baking soda
- 1 tsp. ground cinnamon
- ¾ tsp. kosher salt
- 3 medium bananas
- 2 large eggs
- ⅔ cup granulated sugar
- ½ cup canola or vegetable oil
- ⅓ cup packed light brown sugar
- ⅓ cup whole buttermilk
- 2 tsp. vanilla extract
- ½ cup toasted chopped black walnuts

GLAZE
- ½ cup powdered sugar
- 1 Tbsp. whole buttermilk
- ¼ tsp. vanilla extract

1. Preheat oven to 350°F. Line bottom and sides of a 9- x 5-inch loaf pan with parchment paper, leaving a 1-inch overhang on all sides; set aside.
2. Prepare the Streusel: Whisk together flour, brown sugar, salt, and cinnamon in a medium bowl. Add softened butter, and stir together until crumbly; stir in walnuts until evenly distributed. Set aside.
3. Prepare the Bread: Whisk together flour, baking soda, cinnamon, and salt in a large bowl; set aside. Place bananas in a medium bowl; mash with a fork until almost smooth. Add eggs, granulated sugar, oil, brown sugar, buttermilk, and vanilla extract; whisk until smooth. Add banana mixture to flour mixture; stir until well combined. Stir in walnuts until evenly distributed.
4. Pour batter into prepared loaf pan, smoothing into an even layer with a spatula; sprinkle evenly with Streusel. Bake in preheated oven until a wooden pick inserted in center comes out with a few moist crumbs, 1 hour to 1 hour, 5 minutes. Let cool in pan on a wire rack 10 minutes; remove from pan. Let cool on wire rack 1 hour.
5. Prepare the Glaze: Whisk together powdered sugar, buttermilk, and vanilla in a small bowl until smooth. Drizzle over cooled Bread. Slice and serve.

BLACK WALNUT BANANA BREAD

STREUSEL-TOPPED
APPLE-WALNUT PIE
(PAGE 198)

Because they are so unique and fragrant, black walnuts won't settle for a supporting role in a recipe.

NO-CHURN BLACK
WALNUT ICE CREAM
(PAGE 198)

Streusel-Topped Apple-Walnut Pie

(Photo, page 196)

These rich nuts team up with tart Granny Smith and sweet Honeycrisp apples, warm spices, and a caramel-like filling to make the perfect fall pie.

ACTIVE 50 MIN. - TOTAL 2 HOURS, 5 MIN., PLUS 3 HOURS, 10 MIN. COOLING AND CHILLING

SERVES 8

PIE

- 1 (14.1-oz.) pkg. refrigerated piecrusts
  All-purpose flour, for work surface
- ¼ cup toasted finely chopped black walnuts
- 1⅔ lb. Granny Smith apples, peeled and sliced ¼ inch thick (about 6 cups)
- 1½ lb. Honeycrisp apples, peeled and sliced ¼ inch thick (about 5 cups)
- ⅔ cup granulated sugar
- ⅓ cup packed light brown sugar
- 3 Tbsp. cornstarch
- 1 Tbsp. apple cider vinegar
- 1 tsp. ground cinnamon
- ½ tsp. ground cardamom
- ¼ tsp. kosher salt
- 2 Tbsp. unsalted butter

STREUSEL

- ⅔ cup all-purpose flour
- ⅔ cup uncooked old-fashioned regular rolled oats
- ⅔ cup toasted chopped black walnuts
- ½ cup packed light brown sugar
- ½ tsp. ground cinnamon
- ½ tsp. kosher salt
- ½ cup unsalted butter, melted
  Ice cream, for serving (optional)

1. Prepare the Pie: Unroll 1 piecrust onto a lightly floured work surface; brush with a small amount of water. Top with remaining piecrust; gently press together to seal. Roll into a 13-inch circle. Transfer piecrust into a 9½-inch deep-dish pie plate; tuck edges of crust under, and crimp as desired. Prick bottom of piecrust all over with a fork. Chill, uncovered, in freezer at least 30 minutes or up to 12 hours.

2. Preheat oven to 350°F. Line bottom and sides of chilled piecrust with parchment paper; fill with pie weights. Bake until light golden brown, about 15 minutes. Remove parchment paper and weights; return crust to oven, and bake until bottom is lightly browned, about 5 minutes. Sprinkle walnuts evenly in bottom of crust, and let cool on a wire rack to room temperature, about 30 minutes. Increase oven temperature to 375°F, and place oven rack in lowest position. Line a thin baking sheet with aluminum foil; set aside.

3. While crust is cooling, place apples in a large bowl; sprinkle with granulated sugar, brown sugar, cornstarch, apple cider vinegar, cinnamon, cardamom, and kosher salt; toss well to coat. Melt butter in a large skillet or Dutch oven over medium. Add apple mixture; cook, stirring occasionally, until apples start to soften but are not yet tender and juices start to thicken, about 10 minutes. Remove skillet from heat, and let cool slightly at room temperature, about 10 minutes.

4. Meanwhile, prepare the Streusel: Stir together flour, oats, walnuts, brown sugar, cinnamon, and salt in a medium bowl. Drizzle with melted butter, and toss until evenly coated.

5. Spoon cooled apple mixture into cooled crust; sprinkle Streusel evenly over apple mixture. Place on prepared baking sheet. Bake in preheated oven on lowest rack until Streusel is crisp and filling is bubbly, about 45 minutes (loosely cover with foil after 25 minutes to prevent overbrowning). Transfer to a wire rack, and let cool to room temperature, 2 to 3 hours. Serve with ice cream, if desired.

No-Churn Black Walnut Ice Cream

(Photo, page 197)

Besides being blissfully simple to prepare, this dessert has a dreamy texture. Made with only a handful of ingredients, it comes out smooth and scoopable—and stays that way.

ACTIVE 25 MIN. - TOTAL 25 MIN., PLUS 6 HOURS FREEZING

SERVES 12

- 1½ cups toasted chopped black walnuts, divided
- 2½ cups heavy whipping cream
- 1½ tsp. vanilla extract
- ⅛ tsp. kosher salt
- 1 (14-oz.) can sweetened condensed milk

1. Place 1 cup of the walnuts in a blender; process on medium speed until a loose paste forms, 1 minute to 1 minute, 30 seconds, stopping to scrape down sides as needed. Scrape ¼ cup of the walnut paste into a large bowl. (Reserve remaining walnut paste for another use.) Gradually beat in cream with a hand mixer fitted with a whisk attachment on medium-low speed until well combined, about 1 minute, 30 seconds. Increase speed to medium-high, and beat until medium peaks form, 4 to 5 minutes. Beat in vanilla and salt on low speed until just combined. Gradually beat in sweetened condensed milk on medium-low speed until well combined, about 2 minutes.

2. Spoon half of cream mixture (about 2½ cups) into a 9- x 5–inch loaf pan; sprinkle evenly with ¼ cup of the walnuts. Top with remaining cream mixture; sprinkle evenly with remaining ¼ cup walnuts. Cover with plastic wrap, and freeze until firm enough to scoop, at least 6 hours or up to 12 hours. Keep covered in freezer up to 3 weeks.

Fall Salad with Candied Black Walnuts

(Photo, page 5)

You've had candied pecans on a salad, so why not try a different nut? Layered with sweet fall squash, a zippy dressing, and collards that are massaged until just tender, this is a showstopper.

ACTIVE 35 MIN. - TOTAL 55 MIN.

SERVES 6

ROASTED SQUASH

- 1 large (about 3-lb.) delicata squash
- 1 Tbsp. olive oil
- ½ tsp. kosher salt
- ¼ tsp. black pepper

CANDIED WALNUTS

- ½ cup toasted chopped black walnuts
- 2½ Tbsp. granulated sugar
- 1 Tbsp. unsalted butter
- ¼ tsp. kosher salt
- ¼ tsp. ground cumin
- ⅛ tsp. cayenne pepper

SALAD

- ¼ cup extra-virgin olive oil
- 2 Tbsp. white wine vinegar
- 1 Tbsp. honey
- 1 Tbsp. Dijon mustard
- ½ tsp. kosher salt

- ¼ tsp. black pepper
- 8 cups thinly sliced, stemmed collard greens (from 2 [9-oz.] bunches)
- ½ cup thinly sliced red onion (from 1 small onion)
- 1 oz. Parmesan cheese, shaved (about ½ cup)

1. Prepare the Roasted Squash: Preheat oven to 450°F. Cut squash in half lengthwise; scrape out and discard seeds and stringy flesh. Cut halves crosswise into ½-inch-thick slices. Place on a rimmed baking sheet; drizzle with oil, and sprinkle with salt and black pepper. Toss gently to coat; arrange in an even layer. Bake until lightly browned and tender, about 20 minutes, flipping halfway through cook time. Let stand at room temperature until ready to use.
2. While squash is baking, prepare the Candied Walnuts: Cook walnuts, sugar, butter, and salt in a medium-size nonstick skillet over medium, stirring often, until sugar is golden brown, 6 to 7 minutes. Quickly remove from heat, and stir in cumin and cayenne pepper. Immediately pour Candied Walnuts onto a sheet of parchment paper, breaking apart any large clumps. Let cool 5 minutes.
3. Prepare the Salad: Place oil, vinegar, honey, Dijon mustard, salt, and black pepper in a small jar; screw on lid, and shake well until dressing is combined, about 15 seconds. Place collard greens in a large bowl. Drizzle 2 tablespoons of the dressing over collard greens, and massage until greens are well coated and tender, about 30 seconds. Let stand 10 minutes. Add Roasted Squash, red onion, and remaining dressing to collard greens; toss gently to combine. Top with Parmesan and Candied Walnuts.

Garlicky Black Walnut-Breadcrumb Pasta

The spicy heat of garlic and red pepper flakes lifts up the flavor of the black walnuts in this fast-fix supper. Toasty panko, savory Parmesan, and bright lemon work their magic, yielding a crunchy yet creamy pasta that's both unexpected and extremely comforting.
ACTIVE 30 MIN. - TOTAL 35 MIN.
SERVES 6

- 1 (16-oz.) pkg. spaghetti
- 1¼ tsp. kosher salt, plus more for salting water

GARLICKY BLACK WALNUT-BREADCRUMB PASTA

- 3 Tbsp. unsalted butter
- 5 Tbsp. olive oil, divided
- ⅔ cup panko breadcrumbs
- ½ cup toasted chopped black walnuts
- 8 garlic cloves, finely chopped (about ¼ cup)
- ½ tsp. crushed red pepper
- 1½ oz. Parmesan cheese, grated with a Microplane grater (about 1 cup)
- 1½ tsp. grated lemon zest plus 3 Tbsp. fresh juice (from 1 lemon)
- ⅓ cup chopped fresh flat-leaf parsley

1. Bring a large pot of salted water to a boil over medium-high. Add spaghetti; prepare according to package directions, stirring occasionally.
2. Meanwhile, heat butter and 1 tablespoon of the oil in a large skillet over medium. Add panko; cook, stirring often, until browned and toasted, 3 to 4 minutes. Stir in walnuts; cook, stirring constantly, 1 minute. Remove panko mixture from skillet, setting aside in a small bowl (wipe skillet clean).
3. Reserve 1 cup of the cooking water; drain spaghetti, and set aside at room temperature. Heat remaining 4 tablespoons oil in skillet over medium-low. Add garlic and crushed red pepper; cook, stirring often, until garlic is light golden, about 2 minutes. Add drained spaghetti, ¾ cup of the reserved cooking water, Parmesan, lemon zest and juice, and salt; toss well to coat. Cook over medium-low, stirring constantly, until spaghetti is glossy and sauce clings to spaghetti, about 3 minutes. (Add additional cooking water, 1 tablespoon at a time, as needed, until sauce is silky.) Stir in parsley and panko mixture. Serve immediately.

HOSPITALITY

Apple of Your Eye

This fast and flaky galette will be the star of your next get-together

Caramel-Apple Galette

Whether you're hosting guests or traveling to a gathering, this impressive-looking dessert is simple to make and transport. The no-cook apple filling features store-bought caramel sauce, but the real hero is the Three-Ingredient Pie Dough. Flakier than anything you'll find at the supermarket, it comes together in minutes with a little help from your food processor.

ACTIVE 30 MIN. - TOTAL 1 HOUR, 40 MIN.
SERVES 8

- 3 Tbsp. sea salt caramel dessert sauce (such as Mrs. Richardson's), plus more for serving
- 1 Tbsp. fresh lemon juice (from 1 lemon)
- 2 tsp. cornstarch
- 1¼ tsp. apple pie spice
- ¼ tsp. kosher salt
- 4 medium Honeycrisp apples, unpeeled, cored, and cut into ¼-inch-thick slices (about 6 cups)
- Three-Ingredient Pie Dough (recipe, right)
- All-purpose flour, for surface
- 1 large egg, beaten
- 2 tsp. turbinado sugar
- 1 Tbsp. cold butter, cubed
- Vanilla ice cream
- Flaky sea salt

1. Whisk together caramel sauce, lemon juice, cornstarch, apple pie spice, and kosher salt in a large bowl until combined. Toss in apple slices until coated; set aside.
2. Roll dough into a 13-inch circle on a lightly floured surface. Transfer dough to a parchment paper-lined large baking sheet.
3. Arrange apple slices on dough in concentric overlapping circles, leaving a 2-inch border around edges. Drizzle any liquid remaining in bowl over apples. Fold edges of dough over apples, overlapping as needed. Freeze, uncovered, 15 minutes. Meanwhile, preheat oven to 400°F with oven rack in lower third position.
4. Brush edges of dough with beaten egg; sprinkle with turbinado sugar. Scatter butter cubes evenly over apples.
5. Bake in preheated oven until crust is golden brown and apples are tender, about 40 minutes. Cool on baking sheet 15 minutes. Drizzle with additional caramel sauce, and serve warm with ice cream and sea salt.

Three-Ingredient Pie Dough

ACTIVE 5 MIN. - TOTAL 2 HOURS, 5 MIN.
MAKES 1 DISK

- 1⅓ cups all-purpose flour
- ½ cup cold butter, cubed
- ⅓ cup cold sour cream

Pulse flour and butter in a food processor until butter forms pea-size pieces, 8 to 10 (1-second) pulses. Add sour cream; pulse until just combined and mixture is crumbly but holds together when pinched, 3 to 5 (1-second) pulses. Dump mixture onto a clean work surface, and knead just until dough comes together, 2 to 3 times. Shape into a disk, and wrap in plastic wrap. Refrigerate until firm, at least 2 hours or up to 3 days.

How To Assemble Our Caramel-Apple Galette

1. Layer the apples on the dough in concentric circles, shingling slices and leaving a 2-inch border around the outer edges.

2. Place the edges of the dough up over the fruit, overlapping slightly as needed to make a rustic circle.

3. Brush the folded edges with egg wash; sprinkle with turbinado sugar. Scatter butter over apples, and bake as directed.

CRISPY RANCH
CHICKEN CUTLETS

FAMILY STYLE

A Winning Chicken Dinner

An easy, kid-approved meal that can be tailored for everyone's tastes

MY 9-YEAR-OLD SON, THEO, is bright, sweet, and silly, but I don't have the patience for his hot takes on my cooking after a full day at work. So I often make dinner for my husband and me and cobble together a Theo Special if he doesn't like what's on that night's menu. (I can hear the parenting criticisms being formed as I write this.) I decided to turn one simple dish—a crispy piece of boneless chicken—into a customizable supper that everyone around the table could appreciate. To keep this meal from going into nugget territory, I turned to fellow parent and Test Kitchen Professional Anna Theoktisto. She pounded chicken breasts into thin cutlets and flavored the meat and the panko breading with ranch seasoning mix. The chicken is pan-fried until golden. Upon trying it, Theo uttered these four precious words: "Is there any more?" —Lisa Cericola

Crispy Ranch Chicken Cutlets
ACTIVE 35 MIN. · TOTAL 35 MIN.
SERVES 4 TO 6

- 6 (6-oz.) chicken breast cutlets
- 6 Tbsp. ranch seasoning mix, divided (from 2 [1-oz.] envelopes)
- 3 tsp. kosher salt, divided, plus more to taste
- 1 tsp. black pepper, divided
- 3 large eggs
- ½ cup all-purpose flour
- 3 cups panko breadcrumbs
- 1 cup canola oil, divided
- Hot buttered pasta
- Lemon wedges and chopped fresh dill, for topping (optional)

1. Preheat oven to 200°F. Place each cutlet between 2 sheets of plastic wrap or parchment paper. Using flat side of a meat mallet, pound each cutlet to an even ¼-inch thickness. Sprinkle cutlets with 2 tablespoons of the ranch seasoning mix, 2 teaspoons of the salt, and ½ teaspoon of the pepper.

2. Crack eggs into a large shallow bowl; beat until combined. Place flour in a second large shallow bowl. Place panko and remaining 4 tablespoons ranch seasoning mix, 1 teaspoon salt, and ½ teaspoon pepper in a third large shallow bowl.

3. Dredge each cutlet in flour, shaking off excess. Dip in egg to coat; place in panko mixture, pressing to coat both sides. Transfer cutlets to a parchment paper-lined baking sheet.

4. Heat ½ cup of the oil in a large skillet over medium-high. Add 2 cutlets; cook until golden brown on each side and a thermometer inserted in center registers 165°F, about 2 minutes per side. Transfer to a baking sheet lined with a wire rack; place in preheated oven to keep warm. Repeat procedure twice with remaining 4 cutlets, adding remaining ½ cup oil to skillet as needed. Sprinkle chicken with additional salt to taste. Serve over buttered pasta with lemon wedges and dill, if desired.

All Grown Up
Two adult-friendly ways to enjoy crispy fried chicken

Chicken Parm Sandwiches
ACTIVE 5 MIN. · TOTAL 5 MIN.
SERVES 2

Preheat oven to broil with rack about 4 inches from heat source. Spread cut sides of 2 **ciabatta rolls** with 2 Tbsp. softened **unsalted butter**. Place buttered sides up on an aluminum foil-lined baking sheet. Place half of 1 **Crispy Ranch Chicken Cutlet** on bottom half of each roll. Top each with 2 **fresh mozzarella cheese** slices; sprinkle with **Parmesan**. Broil until cheeses are melted, about 3 minutes. Spoon ¼ cup **marinara sauce** evenly over each; place remaining half of each roll on top.

Five-Minute Fried Chicken Salads
ACTIVE 5 MIN. · TOTAL 5 MIN.
SERVES 2

Toss together 4 cups torn **red leaf lettuce**, 1 cup halved **cherry tomatoes**, and ½ cup **pitted kalamata olives** in a large bowl, and divide mixture between 2 plates. Slice 2 **Crispy Ranch Chicken Cutlets**, and place 1 on top of each salad. Drizzle with your favorite **vinaigrette**.

What Time Is Kickoff?

No matter when the game starts, these tailgate menus will score big

GRAND MIMOSAS

11:00 A.M.
Rise & Shine
Start the day with a full spread of breakfast favorites made easier with a few smart shortcuts

Grand Mimosas
ACTIVE 10 MIN. - TOTAL 10 MIN.
SERVES 12

- 4 cups fresh orange juice (from 8 oranges)
- 1 cup (8 oz.) orange liqueur
- 2 (750-milliliter) bottles brut Cava, Prosecco, or other sparkling wine (chilled)
- Orange wheels, for garnish
- Fresh mint sprigs, for garnish

Combine juice and liqueur in a pitcher. Just before serving, pour in sparkling wine. Garnish with orange wheels and mint.

Bacon Pimiento Cheese
ACTIVE 20 MIN. - TOTAL 20 MIN.
MAKES 4 CUPS

- 8 thick-cut bacon slices, chopped
- 1½ cups mayonnaise
- 1 (4-oz.) jar diced pimientos, drained
- 1 tsp. Worcestershire sauce
- 1 tsp. onion powder
- 1 tsp. garlic powder
- ½ tsp. smoked paprika
- ¼ tsp. cayenne pepper
- 1 (8-oz.) block extra-sharp cheddar cheese, shredded (about 2 cups)
- 1 (8-oz.) block sharp cheddar cheese, shredded (about 2 cups)

1. Cook bacon in a skillet over medium, stirring occasionally, until crisp, 10 to 12 minutes. Transfer bacon to a paper towel–lined plate, and let cool completely, about 5 minutes. Discard drippings, or reserve for another use.
2. Stir together mayonnaise, pimientos, Worcestershire, onion powder, garlic powder, smoked paprika, and cayenne pepper in a medium bowl until combined.
3. Reserve 1 tablespoon cooked bacon. Fold cheeses and remaining cooked bacon into mayonnaise mixture until combined. Sprinkle with reserved bacon.

Cat-Head Biscuit Sandwiches
ACTIVE 20 MIN. - TOTAL 45 MIN.
SERVES 12

CAT-HEAD BISCUITS
- 6 cups all-purpose flour, plus more for dusting
- 3 Tbsp. baking powder
- 1 Tbsp. kosher salt
- 2 tsp. granulated sugar
- 2 cups unsalted butter, cut into ½-inch cubes, chilled
- 2 cups whole buttermilk, chilled

SANDWICHES
- 2 cups Bacon Pimiento Cheese (recipe, left)
- 12 fried chicken tenders
- ½ cup red pepper jelly
- 12 spicy dill pickle chips
- 12 wooden picks, for serving

1. Prepare the Cat-Head Biscuits: Preheat oven to 500°F. Line 2 large rimmed baking sheets with aluminum foil. Set aside. Combine flour, baking powder, salt, and sugar in a food processor; pulse until combined. Add butter; pulse until mixture is crumbly with small pieces of butter remaining, about 25 pulses. Drizzle buttermilk through food chute; pulse until just combined, about 8 pulses.

Continued on page 207

CAT-HEAD BISCUIT SANDWICHES

BACON PIMIENTO CHEESE

FRENCH TOAST DREAMS

SWEET-AND-SPICY SAUSAGE BITES

Continued from page 204

2. Turn dough out onto a lightly floured surface; gently flatten dough into a ¾-inch-thick (11- x 11-inch) square (dough will be very sticky). Cut out 9 rounds using a 3-inch round cutter dipped in flour. Reroll scraps to ¾-inch thickness; cut 3 more rounds. Divide dough rounds between prepared baking sheets, spacing 2 inches apart.
3. Bake biscuits in preheated oven until golden brown, 10 to 12 minutes. Let cool 5 minutes.
4. Prepare the Sandwiches: Using a fork, split biscuits in half; spread about 2 tablespoons Bacon Pimiento Cheese on cut side of each biscuit bottom. Top each with 1 chicken tender and 2 teaspoons pepper jelly. Cover with biscuit tops; place 1 pickle on each assembled sandwich, and secure with a wooden pick.

Sweet-and-Spicy Sausage Bites
ACTIVE 20 MIN. - TOTAL 20 MIN.
SERVES 10 TO 12

- 1 Tbsp. canola oil
- 2 lb. spicy hickory-smoked sausage (such as Conecuh), sliced diagonally into 1½-inch-thick pieces (about 6 cups)
- ½ cup pure cane syrup
- ⅓ cup packed dark brown sugar
- ¼ cup ketchup
- ¼ cup bourbon
- 2 Tbsp. spicy brown mustard
- 1 Tbsp. apple cider vinegar
- 1½ tsp. Worcestershire sauce

1. Heat oil in a large cast-iron skillet over medium-high. Add half of the sausage; cook, stirring occasionally, until browned, 4 to 5 minutes. Use a slotted spoon to transfer sausage to a paper towel-lined plate. Repeat with remaining sausage. Pour drippings into a small heatproof bowl, and set aside to cool before discarding; do not wipe skillet clean.
2. Whisk together cane syrup, brown sugar, ketchup, bourbon, spicy mustard, vinegar, and Worcestershire in a medium bowl until combined; pour into skillet. Bring to a boil over medium-high, stirring occasionally. Reduce heat to medium, and cook, stirring often, until sauce thickens slightly, 2 to 3 minutes.

3. Return sausage to skillet; stir until well coated. Cook over medium-low, stirring often, until heated through, about 1 minute.

French Toast Dreams
ACTIVE 30 MIN. - TOTAL 30 MIN.
SERVES 10 TO 12

- 1 (8-oz.) pkg. cream cheese, softened
- ¼ cup powdered sugar, plus more for dusting
- 1½ tsp. vanilla extract, divided
- 1 tsp. kosher salt, divided
- 12 (1-oz.) day-old white or brioche bread slices, crusts removed
- ⅔ cup whole milk
- 2 Tbsp. granulated sugar
- 1 tsp. ground cinnamon
- 4 large eggs
- Unsalted butter, for greasing
- Maple syrup, for serving

1. Beat cream cheese in a bowl with an electric mixer on medium speed until fluffy, about 1 minute. Add powdered sugar, ½ teaspoon of the vanilla, and ¼ teaspoon of the salt; beat on medium speed until fluffy, about 1 more minute, stopping to scrape down sides of bowl as needed.
2. Spread 2 tablespoons of the cream cheese mixture on half of bread slices, spreading to the edges; top with remaining bread slices. Cut each sandwich into 4 equal squares to yield 24 small sandwiches.
3. Whisk together whole milk, granulated sugar, ground cinnamon, eggs, and remaining 1 teaspoon vanilla and ¾ teaspoon salt in a shallow dish until just combined.
4. Heat a nonstick griddle to 325°F or a large nonstick skillet over medium. Lightly grease griddle or skillet with butter. Dip 12 sandwiches, 1 at a time, in milk mixture, quickly flipping to coat both sides; remove with a fork, letting excess liquid drip off. Place dipped sandwiches on prepared griddle or skillet, and cook until golden brown, 1 to 2 minutes per side. Transfer to a plate. Repeat with remaining sandwiches. Dust with more powdered sugar; serve warm with maple syrup for dipping.

2:30 P.M.

Let's Have Lunch

Whether you're traveling to the game or gathering at home, this menu is made to meet your needs

Chicken Wings Three Ways
ACTIVE 10 MIN. - TOTAL 50 MIN.
SERVES 10

- 3½ lb. chicken wings (about 14 whole wings), separated into drumettes and flats
- 4 tsp. kosher salt
- 1 Tbsp. baking powder
- 2 tsp. black pepper
- Honey-Bacon Topping, Chipotle-Barbecue Sauce, or Lemon-Pepper Crunch (recipes follow)

1. Preheat oven to 450°F with racks in top third and lower third positions. Pat wings dry with paper towels; place in a large bowl. Stir together salt, baking powder, and pepper in a small bowl. Sprinkle mixture evenly over wings; toss well to coat. Arrange, fatty sides down, in a single layer on 2 rimmed parchment paper-lined baking sheets.
2. Bake in preheated oven 25 minutes, rotating pans halfway through bake time. Turn wings over; continue baking until well browned and crispy, 17 to 20 minutes. Remove baking sheets from oven. Toss wings in desired sauce or topping to coat before serving.

Honey-Bacon Topping

Whisk together ½ cup warmed **honey** and 2 Tbsp. **apple cider vinegar** in a large bowl. Toss **cooked wings** in sauce to coat; sprinkle with ½ cup **crumbled cooked bacon**.

Chipotle-Barbecue Sauce

Whisk together ¾ cup **barbecue sauce** and 3 Tbsp. chopped **chipotle chiles in adobo sauce** (from 1 [7-oz.] can) in a large bowl. Toss **cooked wings** in sauce to coat; sprinkle with ¼ cup **fresh cilantro** leaves.

Lemon-Pepper Crunch

Cook ½ cup **panko** (Japanese-style breadcrumbs) in 2 Tbsp. **melted butter** in a skillet over medium until toasted, about 2 minutes. Stir in 1 Tbsp. grated **lemon zest**, 1 tsp. **black pepper**, and ¼ tsp. **kosher salt**. Sprinkle panko mixture evenly over **cooked wings**; serve with **lemon wedges**.

Greek Pasta Salad
ACTIVE 10 MIN. - TOTAL 20 MIN.
SERVES 10

- 1 lb. uncooked elbow macaroni
- 1½ tsp. kosher salt, plus more for salting water
- 2 Tbsp. red wine vinegar
- 1½ tsp. Dijon mustard
- ¼ tsp. dried oregano
- ¼ tsp. black pepper
- ¾ cup chopped pitted kalamata olives, plus 2 Tbsp. olive brine (from 1 [9.5-oz.] jar), divided
- ¼ cup extra-virgin olive oil
- 2 medium Persian cucumbers, unpeeled, halved lengthwise, and sliced ⅛ inch thick (about 1⅓ cups)
- ½ cup chopped sun-dried tomatoes
- ½ cup roughly chopped banana pepper rings (from 1 [16-oz.] jar)
- 5 oz. feta cheese, crumbled (about 1¼ cups)
- 2 Tbsp. chopped fresh dill, plus more for garnish

1. Cook elbow macaroni in a large pot of boiling salted water according to package directions for al dente. Drain and rinse under cold water until cool; set aside.
2. Meanwhile, whisk together vinegar, salt, mustard, oregano, black pepper, and olive brine in a large bowl. Gradually whisk in oil until smooth.
3. Add cooked macaroni to dressing, and toss to coat. Add cucumbers, sun-dried tomatoes, banana peppers, feta cheese, chopped dill, and olives; toss to combine. Transfer to a serving bowl; garnish with additional fresh dill.

TEAM SPIRIT
SUGAR COOKIES
(PAGE 210)

CHICKEN WINGS
THREE WAYS

GREEK PASTA
SALAD

Big-Batch BLTs

ACTIVE 10 MIN. - TOTAL 25 MIN.

SERVES 8

- 12 thick-cut bacon slices
- ½ cup mayonnaise
- 1 tsp. grated lemon zest (from 1 lemon)
- 1 garlic clove, grated (about ½ tsp.)
- ½ tsp. black pepper, divided
- 2 medium (8 oz. each) vine-ripened tomatoes
- ¼ tsp. kosher salt
- 2 (12-oz.) baguettes, sliced in half horizontally and toasted
- 8 butter lettuce leaves (from 1 [4-oz.] head), torn in half

1. Preheat oven to 400°F. Line a baking sheet with aluminum foil. Arrange bacon slices in an even layer on prepared baking sheet. Bake until crisp, 15 to 18 minutes. Drain bacon on a paper towel–lined plate, and set aside.
2. Stir together mayonnaise, lemon zest, grated garlic, and ¼ teaspoon of the pepper in a small bowl; set aside.
3. Cut tomatoes into ¼-inch-thick slices; cut slices into half-moons. Season with kosher salt and remaining ¼ teaspoon pepper. Roughly chop cooked bacon.
4. Spread about 2 tablespoons mayonnaise mixture over each of the cut sides of baguettes. Place lettuce on bottom halves of baguettes. Top with sliced tomatoes and bacon (about ¾ cup bacon per baguette). Cover with top halves of baguettes. Use a serrated knife to slice BLTs crosswise into 4-inch portions before serving.

Smoky Bacon Snack Mix

ACTIVE 30 MIN. - TOTAL 30 MIN.

SERVES 12

- 6 thick-cut bacon slices (about 7½ oz. total)
- ¼ cup unsalted butter, melted
- 1 Tbsp. smoked paprika
- 1 Tbsp. Worcestershire sauce
- 2 tsp. seasoned salt
- 4 cups corn cereal squares
- 2 cups smoked almonds

1. Preheat oven to 350°F. Place bacon in a large skillet, and cook over medium, turning often, until crisp, about

8 minutes. Remove bacon to a paper towel–lined plate; let cool, and then crumble. Pour bacon drippings into a heatproof bowl, and set aside.
2. Whisk together melted butter, smoked paprika, Worcestershire, seasoned salt, and 3 tablespoons of the warm bacon drippings in a large bowl. Add cereal; toss until well coated. Pour onto a parchment paper–lined baking sheet, and spread in an even layer.
3. Bake cereal mixture in preheated oven until crispy and dry, about 15 minutes, stirring every 5 minutes. Remove from oven, and return cereal mixture to large bowl. Add smoked almonds and crumbled bacon; toss to combine.

Tailgate Margaritas

ACTIVE 5 MIN. - TOTAL 5 MIN.

SERVES 12

- 4¼ cups blanco tequila
- 4 cups pure lime juice
- 1¼ cups light agave nectar
- 1¼ tsp. kosher salt
  Ice
  Sparkling water, sparkling wine, or orange soda, for serving
  Lime wheels (from 2 medium limes), for garnish

1. Stir together tequila, lime juice, agave, and salt in a pitcher. Cover and chill until ready to serve.
2. Divide margarita mixture evenly into cups filled with ice, and top each with a splash of sparkling water, wine, or orange soda. Garnish with lime wheels.

Team Spirit Sugar Cookies

(Photo, page 208)

ACTIVE 25 MIN. - TOTAL 2 HOURS

SERVES 16

- 1 cup unsalted butter, softened
- ½ cup packed light brown sugar
- 1⅔ cups granulated sugar, divided
- 2 large eggs, at room temperature
- 1 Tbsp. vanilla extract, divided
- ¼ tsp. almond extract (optional)
- 2¾ cups all-purpose flour
- 1 Tbsp. cornstarch
- 1½ tsp. baking powder
- 2½ tsp. kosher salt, divided

- 8 oz. cream cheese, softened
- 5 cups powdered sugar
- 2 tsp. meringue powder
- 1 tsp. whole milk
  Assorted colored sprinkles, for decorating

1. Preheat oven to 375°F with racks in top third and lower third positions. Line 3 large baking sheets with parchment paper, and set aside.
2. Beat softened butter, brown sugar, and 1⅓ cups of the granulated sugar in a stand mixer fitted with a paddle attachment on medium speed until light and fluffy, about 4 minutes, scraping down sides of bowl as needed. Add eggs, 1 at a time, beating on medium speed until just combined, about 30 seconds. Beat in 1½ teaspoons of the vanilla and almond extract, if desired.
3. Whisk together flour, cornstarch, baking powder, and 1½ teaspoons of the salt in a medium bowl. Gradually add flour mixture to sugar mixture, beating on low speed until just combined, scraping down sides and bottom of bowl as needed, about 30 seconds.
4. Scoop dough by 2-tablespoon portions; space 2 inches apart on prepared baking sheets. (If dough is too sticky to scoop, chill for 30 minutes.) Place remaining ⅓ cup granulated sugar in a medium bowl. Roll each dough portion into a ball, and then roll in sugar. Return to prepared baking sheets.
5. Bake until light golden brown around edges, 9 to 12 minutes, rotating pans halfway through bake time. Remove and let cool on pans 5 minutes. Transfer cookies to wire racks; let cool completely, about 20 minutes.
6. While cookies cool, beat cream cheese in a stand mixer fitted with a paddle attachment on medium-high speed until smooth and creamy, about 1 minute. Gradually add powdered sugar, and beat until smooth, 2 to 3 minutes. Add meringue powder, milk, and remaining 1½ teaspoons vanilla and 1 teaspoon salt. Beat until smooth, about 1 minute.
7. Spoon about 1 tablespoon of the frosting onto each cookie, and smooth with an offset spatula. Decorate cookies with desired sprinkles. Let frosting set 1 hour before serving.

PIMIENTO CHEESE CORNBREAD (PAGE 215)

GAME-DAY CHILI

WALKING TACOS BAR

6:30 P.M.

What's for Dinner?

For the main event, set up a grab-and-go buffet of crowd-pleasers

Game-Day Chili
ACTIVE 30 MIN. - TOTAL 3 HOURS, 30 MIN.
SERVES 10

- 2 lb. ground chuck
- 1 medium-size yellow onion, chopped (1¼ cups)
- 1 small green bell pepper, chopped (1 cup)
- 1 Tbsp. finely chopped garlic (from 1 large clove)
- 1½ Tbsp. chili powder
- 2 tsp. kosher salt
- 1½ tsp. black pepper
- 1 tsp. ground cumin
- 1 tsp. smoked paprika
- 2 (15-oz.) cans light red kidney beans, drained and rinsed
- 2 (14.5-oz.) cans diced tomatoes, undrained
- 2 (15-oz.) cans tomato sauce

1. Heat a large skillet over medium-high. Add ground chuck, onion, bell pepper, and garlic; cook, stirring occasionally, until beef is browned and crumbly, about 5 minutes. Stir in chili powder, salt, black pepper, cumin, and paprika. Cook, stirring constantly, until beef and vegetables are well coated, about 1 minute, and remove from heat.
2. Drain beef mixture. Add beef mixture, kidney beans, diced tomatoes, and tomato sauce to a 5-quart slow cooker; stir to combine. Cover and cook until heated through and thickened slightly, about 3 hours on HIGH or 6 hours on LOW. Serve from slow cooker, or transfer to a Dutch oven for serving, if desired.

Walking Tacos Bar
SERVES 12

Place toppings like **shredded cheddar cheese**, **salsa**, **sour cream**, **guacamole**, **pickled jalapeño slices**, chopped **fresh cilantro**, and sliced **fresh scallions** in small bowls. Lightly crush 12 (1-oz.) bags of **corn chips** (such as Fritos) without opening them. Open bags, and spoon about ½ cup **Game-Day Chili** into each bag of crushed chips. Top Walking Tacos as desired.

Pimiento Cheese Cornbread

(Photo, page 212)

ACTIVE 15 MIN. - TOTAL 50 MIN.

SERVES 12

- 2 Tbsp. canola oil
- 2 cups plain medium-grind yellow cornmeal (such as Bob's Red Mill)
- 1 cup all-purpose flour
- 1 Tbsp. baking powder
- 1¾ tsp. kosher salt
- 1¾ cups whole buttermilk
- 6 Tbsp. unsalted butter, melted
- 2 large eggs
- 1 cup Bacon Pimiento Cheese (recipe, page 204) or store-bought pimiento cheese (from 1 [10-oz.] container)
- 1 (4-oz.) jar diced pimientos (drained), divided
- 1 oz. sharp cheddar cheese, shredded (about ¼ cup)

1. Preheat oven to 425°F. Pour canola oil into a 10-inch cast-iron skillet, and place in preheated oven until oil is very hot, about 8 minutes.
2. Meanwhile, whisk together cornmeal, flour, baking powder, and salt in a large bowl until combined; make a well in center of cornmeal mixture. In a separate medium bowl, whisk together buttermilk, melted butter, and eggs until smooth. Pour buttermilk mixture into cornmeal mixture; gently fold until just combined. Fold in pimiento cheese and 6 tablespoons of the pimientos until combined.
3. Carefully remove skillet from oven; pour batter into hot skillet, gently spreading into an even layer. Sprinkle with shredded cheese and remaining 1 tablespoon pimientos. Bake in preheated oven until a wooden pick inserted in center comes out clean, 25 to 28 minutes. Immediately invert cornbread onto a plate; let cool about 10 minutes. Turn cheese side up; slice as desired.

Knock-Ya-Naked Brownies

ACTIVE 30 MIN. - TOTAL 3 HOURS, 45 MIN.

SERVES 16

- 1 (16-oz.) box fudge brownie mix
- ½ cup unsalted butter, melted
- 2 tsp. vanilla extract
- ¾ cup toasted chopped pecans, divided
- ¾ cup evaporated milk (from 1 [12-oz.] can), divided
- 60 individual caramel candies (from 2 [11-oz.] pkg.), unwrapped
- ½ tsp. kosher salt
- ¾ cup semisweet chocolate chips (from 1 [10-oz.] pkg.), divided
  Flaky sea salt (optional), for sprinkling

1. Preheat oven to 350°F. Lightly coat a 9-inch square baking pan with cooking spray. Line bottom and sides of pan with parchment paper, leaving a 1-inch overhang on all sides. Coat parchment with cooking spray; set aside.
2. Stir together brownie mix, melted butter, vanilla, ½ cup of the pecans, and ¼ cup of the evaporated milk until smooth (batter will be very thick). Press about 1½ cups of the brownie mixture into an even layer in prepared pan. Bake in preheated oven until just set and still a bit gooey, 7 to 8 minutes. Let cool 10 minutes.
3. Meanwhile, place caramels and remaining ½ cup evaporated milk in a microwave-safe bowl. Microwave on HIGH in 1-minute intervals, whisking after each interval, until caramels are melted and mixture is smooth, about 3 minutes total. Stir in salt until combined. Pour caramel sauce evenly over baked brownie layer. Sprinkle with ½ cup of the chocolate chips. Crumble and sprinkle remaining brownie batter evenly over caramel and chocolate (there will be caramel showing). Sprinkle evenly with remaining ¼ cup each pecans and chocolate chips.
4. Bake in preheated oven until edges are set, about 20 minutes. Sprinkle with flaky sea salt, if desired. Let cool to room temperature on a wire rack, about 1 hour, 30 minutes. Cover with plastic wrap, and chill until firm, about 1 hour. Using excess parchment as handles, remove brownies from pan; cut into squares. Store in an airtight container in refrigerator up to 2 weeks.

Bourbon Sunset Tea

ACTIVE 10 MIN. - TOTAL 3 HOURS, 10 MIN.

SERVES 12

- 8 single-serving black tea bags
- 6 single-serving peach herbal tea bags
- 2 to 3 cups (16-24 oz.) bourbon
- 1½ cups simple syrup
  Ice
  Lemon or lime wheels (optional), for serving

1. Place 12 cups water, black tea bags, and peach herbal tea bags in a 1-gallon (128-oz.) container or drink dispenser. Cover and place outside in direct sunlight, moving as necessary to keep in sunlight, until tea is desired strength, 3 to 4 hours.
2. Squeeze tea bags to extract excess tea; discard bags. Stir in bourbon and simple syrup. Serve over ice; garnish with lemon or lime wheels, if desired. Store in refrigerator up to 3 days.

Serve the Bourbon Sunset Tea in a beverage dispenser along with glasses, ice, and garnishes so everyone can craft their own drinks.

2024 SEPTEMBER **215**

10:00 P.M.

Late-Night Bites

Don't quit now—your team is counting on you! These dishes will keep you cheering till the clock runs out

Garlic Bread Pizzas
ACTIVE 10 MIN. - TOTAL 25 MIN.
SERVES 4

- 1 (16-oz.) loaf frozen garlic bread (about 15 inches long)
- 1 cup jarred marinara sauce (from 1 [24-oz.] jar)
- 1 Tbsp. extra-virgin olive oil
- ½ tsp. dried oregano
- 1 large garlic clove, grated (about ½ tsp.)
- 4 oz. mozzarella cheese, shredded (about 1 cup)
- 1 oz. fontina cheese, shredded (about ¼ cup)
- 1 oz. Parmesan cheese, grated (about ¼ cup)

1. Preheat oven to 425°F. Separate loaf into 2 halves. Place each half, cut side up, on a parchment paper-lined baking sheet.
2. Stir together marinara, olive oil, oregano, and garlic in a small bowl until combined. Spoon marinara mixture evenly over each bread half. Combine cheeses in a small bowl; sprinkle evenly over bread halves.
3. Bake in preheated oven until cheeses are melted and edges of bread are golden brown, 12 to 15 minutes. Increase oven temperature to broil, and broil until cheeses begin to brown, 2 to 3 minutes. Cut each pizza in half before serving.

Peach + Sausage + Red Onion Proceed as directed through Step 1. In Step 2, omit marinara sauce, olive oil, oregano, and garlic. Spread a thin layer of barbecue sauce over cut side of each bread half. Sprinkle with cheeses as directed; top with thinly sliced peaches, cooked smoked sausage, and red onion. Bake as directed.

Vidalia Onion + Pepperoni Proceed as directed through Step 2; top evenly with pepperoni slices and thinly sliced Vidalia onion. Bake as directed.

Mayo + Tomato + Basil Proceed as directed through Step 1. In Step 2, omit marinara sauce, olive oil, oregano, and garlic. Spread a thin layer of mayonnaise over cut side of each bread half. Sprinkle with cheeses as directed; top evenly with thinly sliced tomato. Bake as directed. Garnish with fresh basil.

Loaded Queso
ACTIVE 15 MIN. - TOTAL 15 MIN.
SERVES 12

- ½ lb. Mexican chorizo, casings removed
- 1 cup Mexican lager (such as Modelo)
- 1 lb. white processed cheese (such as Velveeta), cubed
- 2 oz. pepper Jack cheese, shredded (about ½ cup), plus more for garnish
- 1 (15-oz.) can black beans, drained and rinsed (about 1½ cups)
- 1 (10-oz.) can fire-roasted diced tomatoes with green chiles (such as Ro-Tel), undrained
- ¼ cup chopped fresh cilantro, plus more for garnish
- Pickled jalapeño slices, for garnish
- Tortilla chips, for serving
- Guacamole, for serving

1. Heat a medium-size nonstick skillet over medium-high. Add chorizo, and cook, stirring often, until cooked through and browned, about 6 minutes. Add beer, and scrape up any browned bits on bottom of skillet. Continue to cook, stirring occasionally, until liquid is almost evaporated, about 4 minutes. Add cheeses, and cook, stirring often, until melted, about 2 minutes.
2. Stir in black beans, diced tomatoes, and cilantro. Transfer to a serving bowl, and garnish with additional pepper Jack, additional cilantro, and pickled jalapeño slices. Serve with tortilla chips and guacamole.

Queso To Go Heat a medium-size nonstick skillet over medium-high. Add chorizo, and cook, stirring often, until cooked through, about 6 minutes. Add beer, and scrape up any browned bits on bottom of skillet. Continue to cook over medium, stirring occasionally, until liquid is almost evaporated, 4 to 6 minutes. Transfer to a 2-quart slow cooker. Add cheeses, black beans, and diced tomatoes. Cover and cook on LOW, stirring occasionally, until cheeses are melted, 1 to 2 hours. Stir in cilantro. Garnish with additional pepper Jack and cilantro and pickled jalapeños. Serve with tortilla chips and guacamole.

GARLIC BREAD PIZZAS

LOADED QUESO

RUM PUNCH (PAGE 218)

Chocolate-Peanut Butter Scotcheroos

ACTIVE 10 MIN. - TOTAL 10 MIN., PLUS 2 HOURS COOLING

SERVES 12

- 1 cup granulated sugar
- 1 cup light corn syrup
- 1 cup creamy peanut butter
- 6 cups crisp rice cereal (such as Rice Krispies)
- 1½ cups semisweet chocolate chips (from 1 [12-oz.] pkg.)
- 1 cup butterscotch chips (from 1 [11-oz.] pkg.)
- Sprinkles, for garnish
- Flaky sea salt (optional), for garnish

1. Line a 13- x 9-inch baking pan with parchment paper, and coat parchment with cooking spray; set aside.
2. Heat sugar and corn syrup in a small saucepan over medium, stirring constantly, until sugar is dissolved (do not boil), 3 to 4 minutes. Remove from heat. Stir in peanut butter until combined.
3. Place crisp rice cereal in a large bowl; stir in peanut butter mixture. Transfer to prepared pan, and press into an even layer with a spatula.
4. Place the chocolate and butterscotch chips in a microwavable bowl. Microwave on HIGH, stirring every 30 seconds, until melted, 1 to 2 minutes total. Spread melted chocolate mixture evenly over cereal mixture. Garnish with sprinkles and flaky sea salt. Let cool until chocolate has hardened, about 2 hours (chill, if needed). Cut into squares before serving.

Rum Punch

ACTIVE 10 MIN. - TOTAL 20 MIN.

SERVES 10

- ¾ cup granulated sugar
- 1 (2-inch) piece fresh ginger, peeled and thinly sliced
- 4 single-serving hibiscus tea bags
- 2 cups refrigerated lemonade (such as Simply Lemonade)
- 1½ cups (12 oz.) gold rum
- ¾ cup fresh lime juice (from 7 medium limes)
- ⅓ cup (2⅔ oz.) orange liqueur (such as Grand Marnier)
- Ice
- 2½ cups sparkling water
- Orange wheels, for garnish
- Cherries, for garnish

1. Bring 1 cup water, sugar, and ginger to a boil in a small saucepan over high. Stir until sugar is just dissolved, about 1 minute. Add tea bags to saucepan, and remove from heat. Let steep, covered, for 10 minutes. Remove and discard tea bags and ginger.
2. Stir together lemonade, rum, lime juice, orange liqueur, and tea mixture in a large pitcher until combined. Cover; refrigerate until ready to serve.
3. Serve over ice, and top each drink with ¼ cup sparkling water. Garnish with orange wheels and cherries.

MIX MASTER

Notes From Home

José Medina Camacho brings a taste of his native country to Alabama with unexpected cocktails rooted in Mexican flavors

JOSÉ MEDINA CAMACHO, mixologist and co-owner of Adiós bar in Birmingham, has spent his life in restaurants. At the age of 3, he moved with his family to the United States from Michoacán, Mexico. "My mom was a single parent of five kids, so to the oldest—me and my brother—she was like, 'Adiós!' My summer camp every year was at my uncle's restaurant."

After working every job in hospitality, he discovered a passion for bartending. Over the next few years, his mixology career blossomed. He became beverage director at the James Beard Award-winning restaurant Automatic Seafood and Oysters, and eventually opened a bar of his own.

Alongside business partner Jesús Méndez, Medina Camacho brought Adiós to downtown Birmingham in 2022. Two years later, it was named a Regional Top 10 Honoree for Best U.S. Cocktail Bar by the Spirited Awards. Adiós, inspired by the vibrancy of Mexico City during the 1968 Olympic Games, is Medina Camacho's way of sharing his heritage with the city and providing locals who have Latin roots a gathering spot for community.

Love Letter From Puebla

This variation on a spicy margarita pays homage to the aguas frescas that you'll find at any taqueria or Mexican market. You can sub in 3 tablespoons of pineapple juice and a dash of Angostura bitters for the tepache.
ACTIVE 5 MIN. - TOTAL 5 MIN.
SERVES 1

1. Stir together 1½ tsp. **honey** and 1½ tsp. **hot water** in a small bowl until honey dissolves, about 30 seconds. Set aside, and let cool.
2. Place 2 Tbsp. **chamoy sauce** and 2 Tbsp. **chili-lime seasoning** (such as Tajín) on separate small plates. Dip the rim of a collins glass in chamoy; then immediately dip in chili-lime seasoning, coating rim evenly.
3. Fill a cocktail shaker with **ice**, and add ¼ cup **blanco tequila**, 3 Tbsp. **tepache** (such as De La Calle Tropical), 1½ Tbsp. **fresh lime juice** (from 1 large lime), ½ Tbsp. **ancho chile liqueur** (such as Ancho Reyes), a pinch of **kosher salt**, and reserved honey mixture. Shake until well chilled, 20 to 30 seconds. Strain into prepared collins glass over **ice**. Garnish with a **lime wedge**.

All Roads Lead To Oaxaca

Medina Camacho says this riff on a black Manhattan channels the flavor profile of Mexican cola.
ACTIVE 5 MIN. - TOTAL 5 MIN.
SERVES 1

Place **ice** in a double old-fashioned glass; add 2 Tbsp. **Punt e Mes vermouth**, 1½ Tbsp. **añejo tequila**, 1½ Tbsp. **Cynar**, ½ Tbsp. **mezcal**, and 1 tsp. **crème de cacao**. Stir using a barspoon until well mixed and slightly chilled, 15 to 20 seconds. Garnish with an **orange peel twist**.

LOVE LETTER FROM PUEBLA

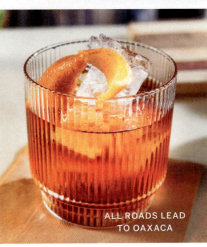

ALL ROADS LEAD TO OAXACA

STORIED RECIPES

Our Daily Cornbread

Cookbook author Anne Byrn traces the history and celebrates the art of this essential Southern baked good

BEFORE OVENS, wheat, yeast, dough paddles, bench scrapers, and all the other accouterments to bake bread, there was corn and fire. A little later, an iron skillet. So cornbread became the South's first daily bread.

When the European explorers ventured into the South, they found Indigenous People growing corn in fields. "Maize," as it was called, was a sacred grass farmed and stored for cooking and saved for next year's seed. While corn is native to the Americas, the Europeans introduced it to other parts of the world, including Africa. As Fred Opie wrote in his book *Hog and Homing,* travelers in Africa in the 1600s observed women in the Congo, Angola, and São Tomé grinding corn, wrapping corn mush in banana leaves, and baking it in the cinders of the fire. That same preparation is what the Choctaw people of Mississippi, Louisiana, and Oklahoma knew as bahana when they were interviewed by reporters with the 1935 Works Progress Administration (WPA).

Corn was easy to grow. It could be planted in small hills on uncleared land and required no plowing or animal power. Conveniently, it didn't need to be harvested at the same time as tobacco.

So in early Maryland, Virginia, North Carolina, Tennessee, and Kentucky, where the economic focus of the first colonists and settlers was on tobacco, corn had advantages over more labor-intensive wheat. Even in places where tobacco wasn't the center of the economy, people became fond of corn because they could grow a patch of it and have it milled or grind it themselves to feed their family.

Before long, in the small towns dotting the South, river currents powered mills and turned heavy millstones to grind the local corn into meal that tasted as sweet as the vegetable itself. It was a system of farming and food production rooted in necessity and feeding people. Cornmeal was scalded with boiling water and shaped into hoecakes and ashcakes, and it made its way into cornbread baked in a sizzling iron skillet. Regardless of socioeconomic status or race, cornbread was accessible.

But technology and change came to corn just as it did to cotton and other products of the Southern land. At the turn of the 20th century, steel roller mills could increase the shelf life of mass-produced cornmeal, but the flavorful germ—the heart of the corn— was removed. This new cornmeal was finer in texture than the older stone-ground, but the flavor of cornbread became less naturally sweet.

Yet in some remote places, like War Eagle Mill in northwestern Arkansas and The Old Mill in eastern Tennessee, progress didn't replace the old artisanal skill of grinding corn between stones. They've been quietly stone-milling corn and selling it to mail-order customers the way they've always done.

Today, we find cornmeal of all textures and colors—white, yellow, blue, red, and shades in between. We can choose cornmeal finely ground and silky to bake into creamy spoon bread or coarse and unbolted, meaning the flavorful hull and germ haven't been removed, to make into crispy hot-water corncakes.

Many Southern cooks have as strong a preference about cornbread as they do about politics or religion. Should cornmeal be yellow or white? Should cornbread be sweet? These questions are of existential importance in the South, something that philosophers and theologians might not discuss but families do. Inevitably, cornbread is about how your mama made it.

Linda Carman, who, as home economist for Nashville's Martha White Foods, taught much of the South to bake cornbread, tells the story of her predecessor, Alice Jarman, who put a teaspoon of sugar into cornbread because she thought it improved the flavor. Jarman and Tennessee Ernie Ford got into heated arguments, with the country music star saying, "I just do not want the sugar bowl anywhere close to my cornbread."

Where sugar does creep into cornbread, it might be because in warm climates, cornmeal could lose its freshness on the kitchen shelf. A little sugar made it taste better.

To much of the South, cornbread is simple and comforting, made from a recipe so basic you almost don't need one or by memory the way your family made it or just the one printed on the back of the cornmeal bag.

Editor's Note: Excerpted from the "Sizzling Cornbread" chapter of Byrn's *Baking in the American South,* which includes the following recipe and many other ways to prepare the Southern staple.

Molasses Cornbread for Zora Neale Hurston

The Harlem Renaissance novelist Zora Neale Hurston was born in the wintertime of 1891 in Notasulga, Alabama, back when Southerners harvested sweet potatoes and butchered hogs using the frigid temperatures as a natural refrigerator. At hog killings, the women made a hot lunch for the workers, wrote Fred Opie in his book Zora Neale Hurston on Florida Food, *roasting sweet potatoes and baking hot cornbread with molasses, which makes it sweet and dense like a square of pound cake. According to the late Valerie Boyd in her biography of Hurston,* Wrapped in Rainbows, *when Hurston was 9 months old, her mother gave her a piece of cornbread to placate her while she went down to the spring to wash collard greens. The door to the cabin was open, and in came a hungry sow lured by the smell of the child's cornbread. Pulling up to a chair to escape the sow, Hurston never crawled again. "I just took to walking and kept the thing a'going." Before modern ovens, molasses cornbread was steamed in an iron pot set over the hearth. This recipe, adapted from Opie's book and an 1892* Florida Agriculturalist *bulletin, blends old and new.*
ACTIVE 5 MIN. · TOTAL 40 MIN.
SERVES 12

AUTHOR AND FILMMAKER
ZORA NEALE HURSTON

Although the question of whether cornbread should be sweet can become an existential question in the South, this moist buttermilk cornbread made with molasses will inspire no arguments.

	Vegetable oil for greasing the pan
2	cups coarsely ground yellow cornmeal
2	cups whole-wheat flour
1	tsp. kosher salt
⅓	cup warm water (about 110°F)
1	Tbsp. baking soda
2	cups whole buttermilk
1	cup molasses
	Butter, for serving
	Flaky sea salt, for serving

1. Preheat the oven to 350°F with a rack in the middle. Brush a 9- x 13-inch baking pan with vegetable oil.
2. Whisk together the cornmeal, flour, and salt in a large bowl. Pour the warm water in a small bowl or cup, and stir in the baking soda to dissolve. Add to the cornmeal mixture, along with the buttermilk and molasses, stirring until just incorporated.
3. Pour the batter into the prepared pan, and bake until the edges of the cornbread are crisp and the center is firm, 33 to 37 minutes. Cut into squares, and serve with butter and flaky sea salt.

SUPPERTIME

One & Done

Single-pan recipes for busy back-to-school nights

CAST-IRON ROAST CHICKEN

Cast-Iron Roast Chicken

This impressive skillet dinner is a workhorse; use the leftovers to make the One-Pot Chicken Pasta on page 225.

ACTIVE 30 MIN. - TOTAL 2 HOURS, 50 MIN.

SERVES 6

- 1 (4-lb.) whole chicken
- ½ tsp. black pepper
- 1 Tbsp., plus ½ tsp. kosher salt, divided
- 1 (2-lb.) butternut squash, peeled, seeded, and chopped into 1½-inch pieces (6 cups)
- 1 fennel bulb, cut into 8 wedges, plus fronds for garnish
- 1 medium-size red onion, cut into 6 wedges
- 4 Tbsp. olive oil, divided
- 1 garlic head, cut in half crosswise
- 5 thyme sprigs, plus more for garnish
- 1 fresh sage sprig, plus ½ tsp. chopped fresh sage, divided

1. Place chicken, breast side up, on a baking sheet; pat dry. Sprinkle with pepper and 1 tablespoon of the salt.
2. Preheat oven to 425°F. Toss squash, fennel, and onion with 1 tablespoon of the oil and remaining ½ teaspoon salt in a 12-inch cast-iron skillet. Place 1 half of the garlic head in skillet. Stuff thyme sprigs, sage sprig, and remaining garlic half into cavity of chicken.
3. In a bowl, stir together 2 tablespoons of the oil with chopped sage. Spread under skin of chicken. Truss chicken; place in skillet breast side up. Brush chicken with remaining 1 tablespoon olive oil.
4. Transfer skillet to preheated oven; roast until a thermometer inserted into thickest portion of breast registers 155°F, 1 hour to 1 hour, 10 minutes. Remove from oven, and let stand 10 minutes. Garnish with fennel fronds and thyme. If preparing One-Pot Chicken Pasta (p. 225), reserve 1½ cups chicken, 1 cup roasted squash, ¼ cup roasted onion, and 6 roasted garlic cloves.

Sheet Pan Pork Chops

(Photo, page 224)

To round out this easy meal, serve it with a shortcut side such as heat-and-eat rice or mashed potatoes from the refrigerated section of your grocery store.

ACTIVE 15 MIN. - TOTAL 35 MIN.

SERVES 4

- 2 Tbsp. honey
- 2 Tbsp. stone-ground mustard
- 8 medium shallots, halved lengthwise
- 1 Tbsp. olive oil
- 2 medium apples, cut into 1-inch-thick slices
- 5 (4-inch) thyme sprigs, plus leaves for garnish
- 1½ tsp. kosher salt, divided
- 4 (6-oz., ¾-inch-thick) bone-in center-cut pork chops, at room temperature
- ½ tsp. black pepper

1. Preheat oven to broil with rack about 6 inches from heat source. Stir together honey and mustard until combined.
2. Toss together shallots and oil on a rimmed baking sheet until shallots are evenly coated, arranging shallots cut sides down. Broil for 5 minutes. Remove from oven.
3. Add apple slices, 1 tablespoon of the honey mixture, thyme sprigs, and ½ teaspoon of the salt to shallots; toss to combine. Turn shallots cut sides up; tuck thyme sprigs under apple mixture. Sprinkle pork chops evenly with black pepper and remaining 1 teaspoon salt. Brush pork chops with the remaining 2 tablespoons honey mixture, and place on top of apple mixture.
4. Broil until a meat thermometer inserted into thickest portion of pork chop registers 140°F, shallots are charred in spots, and apples are tender, 8 to 10 minutes. Remove from oven; let pork chops rest 5 minutes to finish cooking. Garnish with thyme leaves.

Our Best Stuffed Peppers

(Photo, page 224)

Red, orange, and yellow bell peppers are slightly sweeter, but less pricey green ones work fine in this comforting recipe.

ACTIVE 25 MIN. - TOTAL 1 HOUR

SERVES 6

- 6 large red, orange, yellow, or green bell peppers
- 1¾ tsp. kosher salt, divided
- 2 (15-oz.) cans tomato sauce
- 1 (1-oz.) envelope taco seasoning mix
- 1 lb. 90/10 lean ground beef
- 1 medium-size yellow onion, finely chopped (1¼ cups)
- 1 (15-oz.) can black beans, drained and rinsed
- 1 cup frozen corn, thawed
- 1 (8.8-oz.) pkg. precooked microwavable white rice
- 4 oz. shredded Mexican 3-cheese blend (about 1 cup)
- Fresh cilantro, for garnish

1. Preheat oven to 450°F. Cut tops off peppers, and set aside. Remove and discard seeds from peppers; sprinkle interiors of peppers with ¾ teaspoon of the salt. Stir together tomato sauce and taco seasoning.
2. Heat a large skillet over medium-high. Add beef, onion, and remaining 1 teaspoon salt; cook, stirring often, until beef is browned, 6 to 7 minutes. Stir in beans, corn, and 1 cup of the tomato mixture; reduce heat to medium. Simmer, stirring often, until flavors meld and sauce is mostly absorbed, about 2 minutes. Remove from heat; stir in rice until well combined.
3. Spoon about 1 cup of the rice mixture into each pepper. Spread remaining 2 cups sauce into skillet or a 13- x 9-inch baking dish. Add filled peppers to skillet or baking dish, tuck tops in between peppers, and cover tightly with foil.
4. Bake in preheated oven until peppers are fork-tender, 35 to 45 minutes. Remove foil, sprinkle with cheese blend, and bake until melted, 3 to 5 minutes. Garnish with cilantro and serve.

SHEET PAN
PORK CHOPS
(PAGE 223)

ONE-POT
CHICKEN PASTA

OUR BEST
STUFFED PEPPERS
(PAGE 223)

FOR A ZESTY KICK
Stir about 2 teaspoons of hot sauce or spicy barbecue sauce into the ketchup topping.

SHEET PAN MEATLOAF

One-Pot Chicken Pasta

You don't need to have leftovers to make this dish. Use any kind of cooked chicken, and substitute 1 pint halved cherry tomatoes for the roasted squash and onion.
ACTIVE 15 MIN. - TOTAL 20 MIN.
SERVES 6

- 4 cups chicken broth
- 4 cups uncooked cavatappi pasta
- 6 leftover roasted garlic cloves, mashed, or 3 garlic cloves, thinly sliced
- 1 tsp. kosher salt, plus more to taste
- 1 medium bunch kale, stemmed and torn into 2-inch pieces (6 cups)
- ¼ cup heavy whipping cream
- 2 oz. Parmesan cheese, grated (about ½ cup), plus more for serving
- 1½ cups chopped cooked chicken
- 1 cup leftover roasted butternut squash pieces, cut in half crosswise
- ¼ cup leftover roasted red onion wedges, chopped
- Crushed red pepper

1. Stir together broth, pasta, garlic, and salt in a large Dutch oven over medium-high, and bring to a boil. Reduce heat to medium, and simmer, stirring occasionally, 7 minutes. Add torn kale; cover and cook, stirring halfway through cook time, until pasta is tender, about 3 minutes.
2. Uncover and stir in cream and grated Parmesan; cook, stirring constantly, until sauce has thickened slightly, 1 to 2 minutes. Season with additional salt to taste.
3. Stir in cooked chicken, butternut squash, and onion. Cover and remove from heat. Let stand until chicken and squash are warmed through, about 5 minutes. Uncover and top with crushed red pepper. Serve with additional Parmesan.

Sheet Pan Meatloaf
ACTIVE 15 MIN. - TOTAL 50 MIN.
SERVES 6

- ½ cup whole milk
- 3 garlic cloves, grated with a Microplane grater (1 Tbsp.)
- 2 large eggs, beaten
- 2 Tbsp. dried Italian seasoning
- 3½ tsp. kosher salt
- 3 Tbsp. Worcestershire sauce, divided
- 1 cup panko breadcrumbs
- 4 oz. Parmesan cheese, grated (about 1 cup)
- ¾ cup finely chopped yellow onion (from 1 small onion)
- 3 lb. 85/15 lean ground beef
- ¾ cup ketchup
- Chopped fresh chives (optional)

1. Preheat oven to 350°F. Lightly coat a 13- x 9-inch rimmed baking sheet with cooking spray, and line with parchment paper; set aside.
2. Stir together milk, garlic, eggs, Italian seasoning, kosher salt, and 2 tablespoons of the Worcestershire sauce in a large bowl until combined. Stir in panko, Parmesan, onion, and beef until combined. Transfer meatloaf mixture to prepared baking sheet; press into an even layer. Stir together ketchup and remaining 1 tablespoon Worcestershire sauce in a small bowl until combined; evenly spread over meatloaf mixture.
3. Bake in preheated oven until a thermometer inserted into center registers 160°F, 30 to 35 minutes. Without removing meatloaf from oven, increase oven temperature to broil. Cook until glaze just starts to caramelize, 3 to 5 minutes. Remove from oven. Carefully pour fat from baking sheet into a heatproof container; discard when cooled. Let meatloaf stand 5 minutes before serving. Garnish with chives, if desired.

PIECE OF CAKE

A Sweet Slice of Fall

One versatile Bundt and three impressive glazes to change things up

Sweet Potato Bundt Cake

ACTIVE 30 MIN. - TOTAL 1 HOUR, 45 MIN.,
PLUS 1 HOUR, 40 MIN. COOLING AND SETTING
SERVES 12 TO 16

- Baking spray
- 3⅓ cups all-purpose flour
- 2 tsp. baking powder
- 1 tsp. ground cinnamon
- 1 tsp. kosher salt
- ½ tsp. baking soda
- ¼ tsp. ground nutmeg
- 1 cup unsalted butter, softened
- 1 cup packed light brown sugar
- ¾ cup granulated sugar
- 4 large eggs, at room temperature
- 1 Tbsp. vanilla extract
- 1¾ cups sweet potato puree (15 oz.)
- ¾ cup buttermilk, at room temperature
- Easy Chocolate, Salted-Caramel, or Vanilla-Buttermilk Glaze (recipes follow)
- ½ cup chopped toasted pecans (optional)

1. Preheat oven to 325°F. Coat a 10- to 12-cup Bundt pan with baking spray.
2. Whisk together flour, baking powder, cinnamon, kosher salt, baking soda, and nutmeg in a large bowl. Set aside.
3. Beat butter, brown sugar, and granulated sugar on medium speed with a stand mixer fitted with a paddle attachment until fluffy, about 3 minutes. Add eggs, 1 at a time, beating well after each addition, stopping to scrape down sides of bowl as needed, about 1 minute total. Add vanilla; beat until combined.
4. Whisk together sweet potato puree and buttermilk in a medium bowl. Add flour mixture alternately with sweet potato mixture to egg mixture, beginning and ending with flour mixture; beat on low speed just until ingredients are combined after each addition, about 2 minutes.
5. Transfer batter to prepared Bundt pan. Tap pan on counter to release any air bubbles. Bake in preheated oven until a wooden pick inserted into center of cake comes out clean, 1 hour, 15 minutes to 1 hour, 18 minutes. Let cake cool in pan for 10 minutes. Invert cake onto a wire rack; remove pan, and let cool completely, about 1 hour.
6. Pour preferred glaze over cooled cake; sprinkle evenly with pecans, if desired. Let set for 30 minutes before serving.

Easy Chocolate Glaze
MAKES 1¾ CUPS

Combine 1 (14-oz.) can sweetened condensed milk and 1 cup bittersweet chocolate chips in a saucepan over medium-low. Cook, stirring often, just until chocolate melts, about 5 minutes. Use glaze immediately.

Same Cake, Different Toppings
Two more amazing glazes

Salted-Caramel Glaze
MAKES 1 CUP

Cook ½ cup **butter** and ½ cup packed **light brown sugar** in a small saucepan over medium, whisking often, until sugar completely dissolves, about 5 minutes. Remove from heat; whisk in 1 Tbsp. **heavy whipping cream** and ¼ tsp. **kosher salt**. Let cool 15 minutes before using.

Vanilla-Buttermilk Glaze
MAKES ABOUT 1 CUP

Whisk together 2 cups sifted **powdered sugar**, 3 Tbsp. **buttermilk**, and 1 tsp. **vanilla extract** in a large bowl until smooth. Use glaze immediately.

IVY'S KITCHEN

Good to the Core

Break out your skillet for this 20-minute dessert

SOUTHERNERS REACH for their pie plates and cake pans long before their fall sweaters and boots. Once the seasons change, the annual bucket list of baking projects can seem endless: apple pie, pumpkin bread, pound cake—anything with cinnamon is fair game. But if you're like me, autumn happens to be one of the busiest times of year. I'm doing well if I can make dinner—let alone dessert! However, there are some nights when a hankering for something sweet just can't be ignored, and that's when I pull out a skillet and make this simple Apples Foster with Easy Granola. It takes only 20 minutes from start to finish (if you keep granola on hand like I do) and delivers everything you could want from a dessert: It's sweet, crunchy, hot, cold, and utterly decadent.

Apples Foster with Easy Granola

I haven't tried every type of apple (there are thousands), but Honeycrisp is definitely my go-to because it's available at most markets. The fruit has a great balance of sweetness and tartness—plus a super-crisp texture that holds up well during cooking and baking.

ACTIVE 20 MIN. - TOTAL 20 MIN.
SERVES 4

- 6 Tbsp. butter
- 2 lb. Honeycrisp apples, unpeeled, cored, and cut into 1-inch-thick wedges (about 8 cups)
- ¾ cup packed light brown sugar
- ¼ tsp. ground cinnamon
- ¼ tsp. kosher salt
- ½ cup bourbon
- 1 cup Easy Granola (recipe follows)
  Vanilla ice cream

1. Melt butter in a large nonstick skillet over medium until bubbly. Add apples, and cook, stirring occasionally, until apples are browned and slightly softened, about 5 minutes. Stir in brown sugar, cinnamon, and kosher salt until combined. Cook over medium, stirring often, until apples are tender and brown sugar mixture is slightly thickened, 6 to 8 minutes.
2. If using a gas cooktop, remove pan from heat before adding bourbon. Carefully add bourbon to skillet, and cook over medium, stirring often, until alcohol aroma dissipates, 2 to 3 minutes.
3. Using a slotted spoon, divide cooked apples evenly among 4 bowls. Reserve ¼ cup sauce; divide remaining sauce evenly among bowls. Top each bowl with ¼ cup granola and a scoop of ice cream; drizzle with reserved sauce. Serve immediately.

Easy Granola

ACTIVE 10 MIN. - TOTAL 55 MIN., PLUS 30 MIN. COOLING
SERVES 16

- 3 cups old-fashioned regular rolled oats
- ⅓ cup extra-virgin olive oil
- ⅓ cup pure maple syrup
- ⅓ cup packed light brown sugar
- 1 tsp. kosher salt
- ½ tsp. ground cinnamon
- ¼ tsp. ground cardamom
- 1 large egg white, beaten

1. Preheat oven to 300°F. Toss together oats, olive oil, syrup, brown sugar, salt, cinnamon, cardamom, and egg white in a large bowl until oats are well coated; spread in a single layer on a large parchment paper–lined baking sheet.
2. Bake in preheated oven until golden brown, crisp, and mostly dry, about 45 minutes,stirring every 15 minutes. Let cool completely on baking sheet on a wire rack, 30 to 45 minutes. (Granola will continue to crisp as it cools.) Store in an airtight container up to 10 days.

SLICE THEM RIGHT
If you own an old-fashioned corer/cutter, do yourself a favor and give it a rest. Here's a better method: Stand the fruit upright, and slice it vertically on one side along the core. Turn it 90 degrees, and repeat until you have four pieces. Then cut them as thin or thick as you prefer.

COOKING SCHOOL
TIPS AND TRICKS FROM THE SOUTH'S MOST TRUSTED KITCHEN

The Best Chicken Stock You've Ever Tasted
Homemade is always better. For the most robust flavor, use a batch of wings

1. ROAST THE CHICKEN
Browning in the oven will help create a richer final result. You can use any part of the bird—or skip this step if you have leftover carcasses, since they've already been roasted (you'll need two to three of them to replace the wings in the recipe at right).

2. ADD THE AROMATICS
A classic combination of onions, carrots, celery, garlic, and fresh herbs forms the base of our stock, but throw in whatever is in your crisper drawer (except starchy potatoes). Making a stock is a great way to use up vegetable scraps or produce that's past its prime.

3. SIMMER AND STRAIN
After it has cooked on the stovetop, pour the liquid through a fine mesh sieve. If you want it to look extra clear, line your strainer with a few layers of cheesecloth, which can be purchased at most kitchen-supply stores.

4. PORTION AND STORE
Let stock cool completely before putting it into airtight containers. It can be kept in the refrigerator for up to a week. If you're freezing it, leave at least ½ inch of space at the top of each container to allow for expansion. Smaller portions (1 to 2 cups) will thaw quicker.

Homemade Chicken Stock
ACTIVE 15 MIN. - TOTAL 3 HOURS, 20 MIN., PLUS 1 HOUR COOLING
MAKES 4½ TO 5½ QT.

Preheat oven to 450°F. Line a rimmed baking sheet with aluminum foil. Place 4 lb. **chicken wings** on foil, and drizzle with 2 Tbsp. **olive oil.** Bake until browned, about 35 to 40 minutes. Transfer wings to a large stockpot. Add 5 unpeeled **yellow onions**, 1 lb. unpeeled **carrots**, and 1 lb. **celery** (all cut into large chunks). Add 1 unpeeled **garlic head** (halved crosswise), 6 qt. **water**, 2 Tbsp. **whole black peppercorns**, 2 **bay leaves**, and 3 (½-oz.) pkg. **fresh herbs** (such as sage, thyme, parsley, or rosemary). Cover and bring to a boil over high. Reduce heat to maintain a simmer, and cook, partially covered, until stock is flavorful, about 2 hours, skimming as needed to remove any foam on top. Place a fine mesh strainer over a large bowl. Carefully pour stock through strainer into bowl; discard solids. Stir in 1½ Tbsp. **kosher salt**, if desired. Let stock cool completely, about 1 hour. Put into freezer-safe containers. Label with the date, and freeze up to 3 months. Or store in airtight containers in refrigerator up to 1 week.

October

233   **Perfect Pears**   Two savory ways to enjoy these autumn gems

235   **Oktober Feast!**   Skip the gory grub this year (though we love it!), and celebrate Halloween with festive fall snacks inspired by biergartens across the pond

236   **Super Fans**   We tracked down five football fanatics (who also happen to be award-winning chefs) to get their favorite game-day recipes.

244   **Super Bowls**   Fast and filling soups that are ready to serve in just 30 minutes

246   **Taking Root**   Turn the season's freshest beets, parsnips, sweet potatoes, carrots, and other vegetables into colorful fall side dishes

253   **French Twist**   Buttery croissants make the best breakfast sandwiches

254   **The Roast With the Most**   Embrace the changing seasons with a cozy pork supper

255   **Roll With It**   Company's coming? Bake a batch of these apple-stuffed delights

256   **Cooking School**   Our Test Kitchen shares step-by-step how-tos for making the fluffiest, most beautiful apple-cinnamon buns

PEAR, BACON, AND GORGONZOLA FLATBREAD

BOUNTY

Perfect Pears

Two savory ways to enjoy these autumn gems

SKILLET PORK CHOPS WITH CARAMELIZED PEARS

Pear, Bacon, and Gorgonzola Flatbread

ACTIVE 15 MIN. - TOTAL 35 MIN.
SERVES 4

Preheat oven to 450°F. Toss together 1 cup thinly sliced **pear (from 1 medium-size red Anjou pear)** and 2 tsp. **lemon juice** in a small bowl. Place 1 (16½- x 4½-inch) **flatbread** on a large parchment paper–lined baking sheet. Sprinkle with 1 cup shredded **fontina cheese;** top with pear and ⅓ cup sliced **shallot (from 1 shallot)**. Bake until cheese is melted, 12 to 15 minutes. Remove from oven, and sprinkle with ⅓ cup crumbled **Gorgonzola cheese,** ¼ tsp. **flaky sea salt,** and ⅛ tsp. **black pepper.** Drizzle with 1 Tbsp. **honey;** top with ½ cup loosely packed **baby arugula** and 2 Tbsp. **cooked crumbled bacon** (from two slices). Slice and serve immediately.

Skillet Pork Chops with Caramelized Pears

ACTIVE 30 MIN. - TOTAL 1 HOUR
SERVES 4

Sprinkle 4 (1¼-inch-thick) **bone-in center-cut pork chops** evenly with 1½ tsp. each **kosher salt, black pepper,** and **ground fennel seeds.** Let stand for 30 minutes. Heat 2 Tbsp. **olive oil** in a 12-inch cast-iron skillet over medium-high. Add pork; cook until golden brown, 3 to 5 minutes per side. Transfer to a plate. (Do not wipe skillet clean.) Add 3 cups (1-inch-thick) **pear wedges (from 3 medium-size green Anjou pears)** to skillet. Reduce heat to medium; cook, turning occasionally, until pears are caramelized, about 6 minutes. Stir in ⅓ cup **chicken stock,** 2 Tbsp. each **maple syrup** and **apple cider vinegar,** 2 tsp. **stone-ground mustard,** and 4 **thyme sprigs.** Nestle pork chops into skillet; simmer until an instant-read thermometer inserted into thickest portion of meat registers 140°F, 2 to 4 minutes. Transfer pork to a clean plate. Cook sauce until slightly thickened and pears are just softened, 2 to 3 minutes. Return pork to skillet, and spoon sauce over pork. Season with additional **salt** to taste; garnish with **fresh thyme leaves.**

SHINDIGS

Oktober Feast!

Skip the gory grub this year (though we love it!), and celebrate Halloween
with festive fall snacks inspired by biergartens across the pond

WHILE I RESPECT your right to serve spooky food in October, you won't find any gory grub at my house this month. Instead, I'm hosting a gathering that's inspired by biergartens across the pond. The focus of the menu is a fondue made with Gruyère cheese and crisp Riesling—like beer-cheese dip but more elevated. It's served with a smorgasbord of dippers such as smoked sausage, grapes, apples, and a few amped-up store-bought snacks, like Mustard-Glazed Pretzel Bites and Smoked Paprika Potato Chips. (Just one taste, and you'll want to add this spice to every bag you open.) Pour yourself a Cider Shandy, and get ready for a good time. Prost, y'all!
—Josh Miller

Mustard-Glazed Pretzel Bites

The aroma of freshly baked soft pretzels draws folks like the Pied Piper. Tossing them in spicy-sweet honey mustard makes them even more irresistible.

ACTIVE 5 MIN. - TOTAL 10 MIN.

SERVES 6 TO 8

Place 1 **(12-oz.) pkg. frozen soft pretzel bites** in an even layer on a rimmed baking sheet; reserve salt packet. Bake at 400°F until warmed through, 5 to 8 minutes. Meanwhile, stir together 2 Tbsp. **honey** and 1 Tbsp. **Dijon mustard** in a medium bowl until combined. Toss warm pretzels in mustard glaze until coated. Sprinkle with desired amount of reserved **salt packet**. Serve pretzel bites warm or at room temperature.

Riesling-Gruyère Fondue

Cheese dip just got a big upgrade. Gruyère—Swiss cheese's richer, nuttier cousin, teams up with crisp German white wine to deliver a comforting appetizer that's just the right amount of fancy. It's best served warm in a small skillet that you can reheat on the stove. Or set it out in a petite slow cooker or even an old-school fondue pot.

ACTIVE 25 MIN. - TOTAL 25 MIN.

SERVES 6 TO 8

16	oz. Gruyère cheese, shredded (4 cups)
2	Tbsp. all-purpose flour
1	cup dry Riesling
1	garlic clove, grated on a Microplane grater (¼ tsp.)
2	Tbsp. brandy
1	Tbsp. fresh lemon juice (from 1 lemon)
⅛	tsp. ground nutmeg
	Black pepper
	Grilled smoked sausage, cubed sourdough bread, apple wedges, and grapes, for serving

1. Toss together cheese and flour in a large bowl until evenly coated; set aside.
2. In a large saucepan, bring wine and garlic to a gentle simmer over medium, stirring occasionally. Reduce heat to medium-low; add ½ cup cheese mixture, stirring constantly, until melted, about 1 minute. Add remaining cheese mixture about ½ cup at a time, stirring constantly until fully melted after each addition, until smooth (about 8 minutes total).
3. Reduce heat to low; stir in brandy, lemon juice, and nutmeg until combined. Keep warm over low, or transfer to a small skillet or heated fondue pot. Garnish with pepper, and serve immediately with sausage, bread, apples, and grapes.

Cider Shandies

The shandy is a genius beverage for football season, when tailgating can last for hours on end. This refreshing drink typically combines light beer and citrusy soda or lemonade, but sparkling apple cider adds a seasonal twist. The recipe can be scaled up to serve in a pitcher.

ACTIVE 5 MIN. - TOTAL 5 MIN.

SERVES 2

Divide 1 chilled **(12-oz.) bottle hefeweizen or German pilsner** and 1½ cups chilled **sparkling apple cider** between 2 pint glasses. Divide 2 Tbsp. **fresh lemon juice** between the glasses; stir to combine. Garnish with **lemon wheels.**

Smoked Paprika Potato Chips

In and around Germany, sweet (not hot) paprika is a key player in many dishes. This easy recipe uses smoked paprika to give plain chips a boost of color and rich, savory flavor.

ACTIVE 15 MIN. - TOTAL 15 MIN.

SERVES 6 TO 8

Spread 1 **(8-oz.) pkg. plain kettle-cooked potato chips** in an even layer on a rimmed baking sheet. Bake at 300°F until chips are warm, about 5 minutes. Stir together 2 tsp. **smoked paprika,** 1 tsp. **light brown sugar,** and ¼ tsp. **black pepper** in a small bowl. Remove chips from oven, and sprinkle with paprika mixture, tossing to coat. Season with **kosher salt** to taste.

Super Fans

We tracked down five football fanatics (who also happen to be award-winning chefs) to get their favorite game-day recipes.

RON HSU
University of Georgia
Chef at Lazy Betty
Atlanta, Georgia

WHY ARE THESE WINGS IDEAL FOR TAILGATING? "They're very no fuss. I cook the rest of the week, so on game day I don't want to spend another six hours cooking. I'd rather spend six hours watching football."

Hoisin Barbecue Wings
ACTIVE 30 MIN. - TOTAL 1 HOUR, 10 MIN.
SERVES 4

- ½ cup hoisin sauce
- ¼ cup Southern-style unsweetened tea
- 1 Tbsp. apple cider vinegar
- 1 Tbsp. Worcestershire sauce
- 1 Tbsp. ketchup
- ½ Tbsp. Chinese five spice
- 1 tsp. lower-sodium soy sauce
- ½ tsp. minced fresh ginger (from 1 [1-inch] piece fresh ginger)
- ½ tsp. minced garlic
- 2½ lb. whole chicken wings (8 to 10 wings)
- Sliced green onions

1. Whisk together hoisin sauce, tea, vinegar, Worcestershire sauce, ketchup, Chinese five spice, soy sauce, ginger, and garlic in a large bowl.
2. Transfer ½ cup of the sauce mixture to a small bowl, and reserve for later use. Add chicken wings to the remaining ½ cup sauce mixture in large bowl, and toss until fully coated. Refrigerate for at least 30 minutes or up to 4 hours.
3. Preheat a gas grill to medium (350°F to 400°F) on 1 side, or push hot coals to 1 side of a charcoal grill. Place marinated chicken wings on oiled grates over lit side of grill; discard marinade. Grill, uncovered and turning occasionally, until nicely charred and grill marks appear, 5 to 7 minutes (rotating chicken wings as necessary to prevent burning).
4. Transfer chicken wings to unlit side of grill, placing wings skin side up. Brush with half of the reserved sauce mixture. Cook, covered, until a thermometer inserted into thickest portion of wings registers 175°F, 22 to 26 minutes. Brush chicken wings with remaining half of sauce mixture. Transfer wings to a platter; garnish with sliced green onions.

HUNTER EVANS
University of Mississippi
Chef at Elvie's and Mayflower Cafe
Jackson, Mississippi

WHY IS POACHED SHRIMP YOUR GO-TO? "They're so easy to throw together, and you can make them the night before; they get even better that way. Plus, shrimp are easy to pick up, and it's nice to have a cool, refreshing appetizer, especially at the beginning of the season when it can be pretty warm."

Poached Shrimp
(Photo, page 239)
ACTIVE 15 MIN. - TOTAL 1 HOUR, 10 MIN.
SERVES 8

- 1 cup dry white wine
- 2 Tbsp. kosher salt
- 2 dried bay leaves
- 1 tsp. crushed red pepper
- 1 medium-size yellow onion, halved lengthwise
- 1 large celery stalk, roughly chopped (about ¾ cup), plus leaves for garnish
- 1 Tbsp. liquid shrimp-and-crab boil seasoning (Zatarain's)
- 1 large lemon, halved, plus wedges for serving
- 2 lb. jumbo peeled raw Gulf shrimp, tail on
- Elvie's Rémoulade, for serving (recipe follows)

1. Combine 2 quarts water, wine, salt, bay leaves, crushed red pepper, onion halves, chopped celery, and shrimp-and-crab boil seasoning in a large stockpot. Squeeze lemon halves over mixture, and add lemon halves to stockpot. Bring to a boil over medium-high; reduce heat to medium, and simmer, stirring occasionally, until flavors meld, about 20 minutes.
2. Bring to a boil over medium-high; add shrimp. Cook, stirring occasionally, until shrimp are barely opaque in centers, 3 to 4 minutes. Using a spider skimmer or slotted spoon, transfer shrimp to a rimmed baking sheet. Spread shrimp in an even layer, and chill until cool, about 30 minutes. (The poaching liquid can be saved and used again for poaching.)
3. Transfer shrimp to a large platter. Serve with Elvie's Rémoulade and lemon wedges; garnish with celery leaves.

Elvie's Rémoulade
ACTIVE 10 MIN. - TOTAL 10 MIN.
SERVES 8

- ¼ cup finely chopped celery (from 1 medium stalk)
- ¼ cup thinly sliced scallions (from 2 medium scallions)
- ¼ cup white wine vinegar
- ¼ cup Creole mustard

Continued on page 240

HOISIN BARBECUE WINGS

APPLE JAM
BABY BACK RIBS
(PAGE 240)

POACHED SHRIMP (PAGE 236)

Continued from page 236

- 1 Tbsp. paprika
- ½ tsp. kosher salt, plus more to taste
- 1/16 tsp. cayenne pepper
- ½ cup vegetable oil
- Freshly ground black pepper, to taste

1. Place celery, scallions, vinegar, mustard, paprika, salt, and cayenne pepper in a blender. Process until smooth, about 1 minute, scraping down sides as needed.
2. With blender running, gradually add oil until combined and smooth. Pour rémoulade into a bowl; season with more salt and black pepper to taste. Serve with Poached Shrimp.

NICK WALLACE
Jackson State University
**Chef at Nissan Cafe by Nick Wallace and Hen & Egg
Jackson, Mississippi**

WHAT MAKES THESE RIBS GREAT FOR FOOTBALL SEASON? "They bring folks to your house that you didn't even invite—you can never cook enough. The only bad thing is that people want them all the time."

Apple Jam Baby Back Ribs
(Photo, page 238)
ACTIVE 1 HOUR - TOTAL 4 HOURS, 50 MIN.
SERVES 8

- Applewood chunks
- ½ cup apple juice
- ½ cup, plus 1 Tbsp. cider vinegar, divided
- 2 slabs baby back pork ribs (6 lb. total)
- 4 tsp. kosher salt
- ½ cup pork rub seasoning (such as Nick's 26)
- 1 cup Nick's Apple Jam (recipe follows), divided
- ½ cup unsalted butter, cut into pieces
- ½ cup barbecue sauce

1. Open bottom vent of a charcoal grill completely. Light charcoal chimney starter filled with charcoal. When charcoal is covered with gray ash, pour charcoal onto bottom grate of grill, and push to 1 side of grill; scatter 3 or 4 applewood chunks over hot coals. Cover grill, adjusting vents as needed to maintain a grill temperature of 250°F to 275°F.
2. Combine apple juice and ½ cup of the cider vinegar in a spray bottle. Spray ribs with juice mixture, and sprinkle evenly with salt. Let stand 10 minutes. Sprinkle ribs with pork rub seasoning; let stand 15 minutes.
3. Place ribs, meaty sides up, on lightly oiled grates over side without coals. Cover grill, and smoke ribs until surface darkens slightly, about 2 hours, spraying the ribs with juice mixture every 45 minutes.
4. Remove ribs to a clean work surface. Spray bone side of ribs with juice mixture. Brush meat side of ribs with ½ cup of Nick's Apple Jam, and top with butter pieces. Tightly wrap each slab of ribs separately in a double layer of heavy-duty aluminum foil. Set rib packets, meat side up, on grill over side without coals. Grill, covered, at 250°F to 275°F until meat is tender but not falling off the bone, 1 to 1½ hours. Remove ribs from grill.
5. Stir together barbecue sauce and remaining ½ cup Nick's Apple Jam and 1 tablespoon cider vinegar in a medium bowl until combined.
6. Remove ribs from foil, and place on a foil-lined baking sheet. Brush ribs all over with half of the barbecue sauce mixture. Set ribs, meat side up, on grill over side without coals. Grill, covered, at 250°F to 275°F until sauce sets, about 10 minutes.
7. Brush meaty sides of ribs with remaining barbecue sauce mixture. Cover and continue to grill until sauce sets and begins to caramelize, about 10 minutes. Remove ribs from grill, and slice.

Nick's Apple Jam
ACTIVE 15 MIN. - TOTAL 30 MIN.
MAKES 1 CUP

- 1 lb. Honeycrisp apples, peeled and cored
- 3 Tbsp. apple cider vinegar
- 1 (3-inch) cinnamon stick
- 1 whole star anise
- ¾ cup granulated sugar
- 1 tsp. vanilla extract
- ⅛ tsp. ground cinnamon, plus more to taste

1. Grate apples on the small holes of a box grater (you should have about 1½ cups grated apples). Add grated apples to a small heavy-bottomed saucepan. Stir in vinegar, 3 tablespoons water, cinnamon stick, and star anise.
2. Cover and cook over low, stirring occasionally, until apples are slightly softened, about 5 minutes. Stir in sugar, and continue to cook over low, stirring often, until thickened to a jam consistency, 15 to 18 minutes.
3. Remove from heat, and stir in vanilla and cinnamon to taste. Cool completely, about 1 hour. Store in a sealed jar in refrigerator for up to 1 week.

ERICA BLAIRE ROBY
Texas A&M University
**Founder of Blue Smoke Blaire's BBQ
Houston, Texas**

WHY DO YOU LOVE MAKING THIS DISH? "Brisket is a forgiving cut of meat, and you don't have to babysit it when you could be tailgating or watching the game. To me, barbecue is supposed to be like a welcome mat, and these burnt ends make sure that no one leaves hungry or unhappy."

Shortcut Brisket Burnt Ends
(Photo, page 243)
ACTIVE 15 MIN. - TOTAL 3 HOURS, 20 MIN.
SERVES 8

- 3 lb. trimmed brisket point (¼-inch-thick fat cap), cut into 1-inch cubes
- 3 Tbsp. barbecue rub
- 1 cup barbecue sauce (such as Stubb's), divided
- Kosher salt, to taste

1. Preheat oven to 300°F with rack in top third position. Line a large rimmed baking sheet with aluminum foil; place a wire rack on top of foil. Toss brisket

cubes and barbecue rub together until brisket is fully coated. Arrange cubes on wire rack 1 inch apart.
2. Bake in preheated oven until very tender, about 3 hours. Remove baking sheet from oven, and increase oven temperature to broil.
3. Toss cooked brisket and ½ cup of the barbecue sauce in a bowl until completely coated; return brisket to wire rack. Broil until sauce caramelizes, about 5 minutes. Remove from oven; transfer brisket to a large bowl. Add remaining ½ cup barbecue sauce, and toss until coated. Season with salt to taste. Transfer to a platter; let rest 5 minutes before serving.

DAVID BANCROFT
Auburn University
Chef at Acre and Bow & Arrow
Auburn, Alabama

WHAT MAKES THIS RECIPE TASTE SO GOOD? "It always goes great when you're playing LSU. It's a fun little jab. But everybody in Alabama loves Conecuh sausage, and everybody in Alabama loves a corn dog."

Conecuh Sausage Corn Dogs with Back Forty Beer Mustard

(Photo, page 242)
ACTIVE 25 MIN. - TOTAL 2 HOURS, 25 MIN.
SERVES 8

- 1¼ cups all-purpose flour
- ¾ cup fine yellow cornmeal
- 3 Tbsp. granulated sugar
- 2¼ tsp. baking powder
- 1¼ tsp. kosher salt
- 1 cup whole milk
- 2 large eggs, lightly beaten
- Peanut oil, for frying
- 16 (6-inch) wooden skewers
- 1 lb. Conecuh sausage, cut crosswise into 3-inch links
- Back Forty Beer Mustard, for serving (recipe follows)

1. Whisk together flour, cornmeal, sugar, baking powder, and salt in a large bowl. Whisk in milk and eggs until smooth. Cover and chill until batter thickens slightly, at least 2 hours but no longer than 4 hours.
2. Add peanut oil to a depth of 2 inches in a Dutch oven; heat oil to 350°F over medium. Insert skewers into sausage links so that at least 3½ inches of each skewer is still exposed on 1 end.
3. Working with 1 sausage skewer at a time, dip each into batter in a slow spinning motion. Using tongs, immediately place dipped sausage in hot oil, holding the skewer in the oil for 2 to 3 seconds before dropping fully into fryer (this will help prevent sausage from sticking to the bottom of the pot). Fry in batches of 3 or 4, turning constantly to ensure even browning, until golden brown and crispy, 4 to 5 minutes.
4. Transfer to a wire rack set over a rimmed baking sheet to drain, and repeat procedure with remaining sausage skewers and batter. Serve with Back Forty Beer Mustard while corn dogs are crispy and hot.

Back Forty Beer Mustard

ACTIVE 25 MIN. - TOTAL 2 HOURS, 25 MIN.
MAKES 1½ CUPS

- 6 Tbsp. yellow mustard seeds
- 1 (12-oz.) can Back Forty Truck Stop Honey brown ale
- ½ tsp. kosher salt, plus more to taste
- 6 Tbsp. honey, plus more to taste
- ⅔ cup spicy brown mustard (such as Gulden's)

1. Add mustard seeds, beer, and salt to a small saucepan; bring to a simmer over medium. Cook, stirring occasionally, until beer is reduced just beneath the top of the mustard seeds, about 20 minutes (if mixture is too soupy, the mustard will be runny and thin). Remove from heat; let cool 5 minutes.
2. Add honey, mustard, and mustard seed mixture to a medium bowl; whisk until combined. Cover and chill 2 hours. Add more honey and kosher salt to taste, if desired. Serve with Conecuh Sausage Corn Dogs.

How To Make Corn Dogs

1. Whisk together dry ingredients in a bowl until combined; then whisk in milk and eggs until smooth. Cover and chill until slightly thickened.

2. Skewer sausages, leaving a 3½-inch handle on one end. Dip each sausage in batter, slowly spinning to coat completely.

3. Using tongs, immediately lower dipped sausages in hot oil, waiting a few seconds before releasing them to prevent sticking.

4. Transfer fried corn dogs to a wire rack placed inside a rimmed baking sheet to drain. Keep warm in a 200°F oven, if desired.

CONECUH SAUSAGE CORN DOGS WITH BACK FORTY BEER MUSTARD (PAGE 241)

SHORTCUT BRISKET BURNT ENDS (PAGE 240)

SUPPERTIME

Super Bowls

Fast and filling soups that are ready to serve in just 30 minutes

WHITE CHICKEN CHILI

VEGETABLE-BEEF SOUP

CREAMY CHICKEN-AND-RICE SOUP

SMOKY PORK-AND-GREENS STEW WITH EASY BUTTERMILK CORNBREAD

White Chicken Chili

ACTIVE 30 MIN. - TOTAL 30 MIN.

SERVES 8

- 2 Tbsp. olive oil
- 1 large sweet onion, chopped (about 2 cups)
- 2 garlic cloves, finely chopped (2 tsp.)
- 4 cups shredded rotisserie chicken (from 2 rotisserie chickens)
- 2 (14½-oz.) cans chicken broth
- 2 (4-oz.) cans chopped green chiles
- 1 (1¼-oz.) pkg. white chicken chili seasoning mix
- 3 (15½-oz.) cans white beans (such as navy beans), drained, rinsed, and divided

  Toppings: Sour cream, shredded Monterey Jack cheese, fresh cilantro leaves, and chopped avocado

Heat olive oil in a large Dutch oven over medium-high. Add onion and garlic; cook, stirring often, until onion softens, about 4 minutes. Stir in chicken, broth, chiles, seasoning mix, and 2 cans of the beans. Coarsely mash remaining 1 can beans; stir into chicken mixture. Bring to a boil over high. Cover and reduce heat to low; simmer, stirring occasionally, until mixture thickens slightly and flavors meld, about 10 minutes. Serve with desired toppings.

Vegetable-Beef Soup

ACTIVE 30 MIN. - TOTAL 30 MIN.

SERVES 10

- ¼ cup olive oil
- 1 small yellow onion, chopped (about 1 cup)
- ½ cup chopped dried mushrooms (such as porcini or shiitake)
- 3 garlic cloves, chopped (1½ Tbsp.)
- 1 (6-inch) rosemary sprig
- 2 tsp. Italian seasoning
- 2 tsp. kosher salt, plus more to taste
- ½ tsp. black pepper
- 6 cups beef broth
- 2 (14½-oz.) cans diced tomatoes
- 2 (14½-oz.) cans diced new potatoes, drained
- 2 (15-oz.) pkg. refrigerated cooked beef pot roast with seasoned gravy
- 1 (15-oz.) pkg. frozen mixed vegetables

  Fresh thyme leaves (optional)

Heat oil in a large Dutch oven over medium-high. Add onion, mushrooms, garlic, rosemary, Italian seasoning, salt, and pepper. Cook, stirring often, until onion softens slightly, about 4 minutes. Add broth, tomatoes, and potatoes. Cover and bring to a boil over high. Uncover and add pot roast with gravy and frozen vegetables; cook over high until flavors meld, about 10 minutes. Discard rosemary sprig. Season with salt to taste. Garnish with thyme, if desired.

Creamy Chicken-and-Rice Soup

ACTIVE 30 MIN. - TOTAL 30 MIN.

SERVES 8

- 3 Tbsp. unsalted butter
- 1 large yellow onion, chopped (2 cups)
- 3 carrots, peeled and thinly sliced (¾ cup)
- 3 garlic cloves, finely chopped (1 Tbsp.)
- 1½ Tbsp. poultry seasoning
- 1¼ tsp. kosher salt, plus more to taste
- ⅓ cup all-purpose flour
- ¼ cup dry white wine
- 8 cups lower-sodium chicken broth
- 4 cups packed chopped fresh collard greens
- 3 cups shredded rotisserie chicken (from 1 rotisserie chicken)
- 1 cup heavy whipping cream
- 2 (8.8-oz.) pkg. precooked microwavable long-grain and wild rice (such as Ben's Original)
- 4 oz. grated Parmesan cheese (about 1 cup)

Melt butter in a large Dutch oven over medium-high. Add onion, carrots, garlic, poultry seasoning, and salt. Cook, stirring often, until softened, about 5 minutes. Add flour; cook, stirring constantly, 1 minute. Add wine; cook, stirring constantly, until some of the alcohol burns off, about 30 seconds. Add broth; cover and bring to a boil over high. Uncover and stir in collard greens, chicken, cream, rice, and cheese. Cook over high, stirring occasionally, until collard greens are just tender, about 5 minutes. Season with salt to taste.

Smoky Pork-and-Greens Stew

ACTIVE 30 MIN. - TOTAL 30 MIN.

SERVES 8

- 3 Tbsp. olive oil
- 1 medium-size yellow onion, chopped (about 1½ cups)
- 3 garlic cloves, chopped (1 Tbsp.)
- 1½ tsp. smoked paprika
- 1 tsp. ground cumin
- 6 cups lower-sodium chicken broth
- 6 (5-inch) corn tortillas, chopped (2 cups)
- 2 (15-oz.) cans hominy, drained and rinsed
- 2 (7-oz.) cans chopped green chiles
- 1 (15.7-oz.) jar tomatillo salsa
- 2 (12-oz.) pkg. hickory-smoked and seasoned pulled pork (such as Curly's)
- 6 cups chopped fresh turnip greens

  Easy Buttermilk Cornbread (recipe follows)

Heat oil in a large Dutch oven over medium-high. Add onion, garlic, smoked paprika, and cumin. Cook, stirring often, until onion softens slightly, about 4 minutes. Add broth, tortillas, hominy, chiles, and salsa. Cover and bring to a boil over high. Uncover and mash some of the hominy against side of Dutch oven to thicken stew. Pull pork into bite-size pieces; add to stew with turnip greens. Cook over high, stirring occasionally, until greens are just tender, about 5 minutes. Serve with Easy Buttermilk Cornbread.

Easy Buttermilk Cornbread

ACTIVE 8 MIN. - TOTAL 40 MIN.

SERVES 10

Preheat oven to 425°F. Place ¼ cup **bacon drippings** in a 9-inch cast-iron skillet, and heat in oven 5 minutes. Stir together 2 cups **cornmeal mix**, ½ tsp. **baking soda**, 2 **eggs**, and 1½ cups **buttermilk** in a bowl just until combined. Remove skillet from oven; stir drippings into batter. Pour batter into hot skillet. Bake until golden brown, about 27 minutes; cut into wedges, and serve.

Taking Root

Turn the season's freshest beets, parsnips, sweet potatoes, carrots,
and other vegetables into colorful fall side dishes

Miso-Honey Roasted Root Vegetable Medley

Miso is a traditional Japanese ingredient made from fermented soybeans. It adds a rich, savory flavor that balances the honey and naturally sweet vegetables in this recipe. Find it in the refrigerated section of your grocery store's produce department.

ACTIVE 35 MIN. - TOTAL 1 HOUR, 15 MIN.

SERVES 8

- 1 lb. small or medium-size red beets, peeled and cut into ½-inch wedges (2½ cups)
- 9 oz. medium parsnips, peeled (1 cup)
- 9 oz. medium carrots, peeled and cut diagonally into ½-inch slices (1 cup)
- 1 lb. sweet potatoes, unpeeled and cut into 1-inch pieces (3 cups)
- 12 oz. small or medium turnips, peeled and cut into ½-inch wedges (1½ cups)
- 1 medium-size red onion, cut into ½-inch wedges (2 cups)
- ¼ cup olive oil
- 1 tsp. kosher salt
- ½ tsp. black pepper
- 3 Tbsp. white miso
- 3 Tbsp. unsalted butter
- 2 Tbsp. honey
- 1 Tbsp. apple cider vinegar
  Flaky sea salt, for sprinkling

1. Preheat oven to 425°F with racks in top third and bottom third of oven. Line 2 baking sheets with parchment paper.
2. Place beets in bottom of a large microwavable bowl. Cut parsnips crosswise into 2- to 3-inch-long pieces; cut each piece lengthwise into ¼-inch-thick planks. Place a piece of parchment paper, as large as the bowl, over beets; arrange parsnips and carrots on parchment. Cover bowl tightly with plastic wrap; pierce once with a knife to vent. Microwave on HIGH for 3 minutes. Carefully uncover bowl, and lift out parsnips and carrots using parchment paper.

3. Drain beets on paper towels, if needed. Arrange beets on 1 side of 1 prepared baking sheet. Arrange parsnips and carrots on other side of same baking sheet. Arrange sweet potatoes, turnips, and onion on remaining baking sheet. Drizzle all vegetables evenly with olive oil, and sprinkle evenly with kosher salt and pepper. Roast in preheated oven for 20 minutes. Remove baking sheets from oven. Gently stir vegetables, and rotate baking sheets. Continue roasting until tender, about 20 minutes.
4. Meanwhile, stir together miso, butter, honey, and vinegar in a small saucepan over medium to combine. Cook, stirring occasionally, until butter melts and mixture is smooth, about 5 minutes. Remove pan from heat, and cover to keep warm while vegetables roast.
5. Remove roasted vegetables from oven. Transfer parsnips, carrots, sweet potatoes, turnips, and onion to a large bowl; drizzle with miso mixture, and toss to coat. Add beets to mixture; toss to coat. Sprinkle with flaky sea salt.

Creamy Root Vegetable Soup with Brown Butter Pecans

(Photo, page 249)

This silky, smooth soup calls on the heroes of the root cellar—namely sweet potatoes, rutabagas, and parsnips. Sprinkle on some brown butter–toasted pecans and fresh sage and add a dollop of gently spiced crème fraîche for a festive, elegant touch.

ACTIVE 30 MIN. - TOTAL 50 MIN.

SERVES 8

- 5 Tbsp. unsalted butter, divided
- 1 cup thinly sliced leek (from 1 leek)
- 2 garlic cloves, minced (about 1½ tsp.)
- 1 lb. rutabaga, peeled and coarsely chopped (2½ cups)
- 1 lb. sweet potatoes, peeled and coarsely chopped (3½ cups)
- 12 oz. parsnips, peeled and coarsely chopped (2½ cups)
- 2 dried bay leaves
- 4 cups lower-sodium vegetable broth
- ½ tsp. black pepper
- 2¼ tsp. kosher salt, divided
- ½ cup crème fraîche
- ¾ tsp. ground coriander
- ¼ cup pecans, chopped
- 1 Tbsp. chopped fresh sage, plus more sage leaves for garnish
- 1 cup heavy whipping cream

1. Melt 2 tablespoons of the butter in a Dutch oven over medium. Add leek and garlic; cook, stirring occasionally, until soft, 4 to 5 minutes. Add rutabaga, sweet potatoes, parsnips, bay leaves, broth, pepper, and 2 teaspoons of the salt. Bring to a boil over high. Reduce heat to medium-low; partially cover, and cook, undisturbed, until vegetables are tender, about 30 minutes.
2. Meanwhile, stir together crème fraîche, coriander, and remaining ¼ teaspoon salt in a small bowl to combine; set aside.
3. Melt remaining 3 tablespoons butter in a small skillet over medium. Cook until butter just starts to brown, about 2 minutes. Add pecans; cook, stirring often, until butter is browned and pecans are toasted, 2 to 3 minutes. Pour into a small bowl; stir in sage.
4. Remove bay leaves from vegetable mixture. Pour half of vegetable mixture into a blender. Secure lid on blender, and remove center piece to allow steam to escape. Place a clean towel over opening. Process until smooth, about 1 minute. Pour pureed soup into a large bowl. Repeat procedure with remaining vegetable mixture. Stir in whipping cream until thoroughly combined. Divide soup among 8 bowls. Top with crème fraîche mixture and pecans. Garnish with sage leaves.

246 2024 OCTOBER

MISO-HONEY ROASTED ROOT VEGETABLE MEDLEY

CIDER-GLAZED
RAINBOW CARROTS
(PAGE 252)

CREAMY ROOT
VEGETABLE SOUP
WITH BROWN
BUTTER PECANS
(PAGE 246)

DOUBLE BEET SALAD WITH HONEY-DIJON VINAIGRETTE (PAGE 252)

CHEESY TURNIP GRATIN (PAGE 252)

Cider-Glazed Rainbow Carrots

(Photo, page 248)

Simmered until thick and syrupy, apple cider complements these vibrant carrots with a hint of tartness. The veggies can be boiled, cooled, and refrigerated two days ahead of time. Before serving, finish them in a skillet with brown butter and the cider glaze.

ACTIVE 25 MIN. - TOTAL 25 MIN.

SERVES 8

- 1½ cups unfiltered apple cider
- 1 (2-lb.) pkg. multicolored carrots
- 3 Tbsp. unsalted butter
- 1 Tbsp. chopped fresh thyme
- 1 tsp. kosher salt, plus more for salting water

1. Bring cider to a boil in a large skillet over high. Reduce heat to medium; simmer, stirring occasionally, until it's syrupy and reduced to 2 tablespoons, about 15 minutes. Transfer to a small bowl, and set cider syrup aside. Wipe skillet clean.
2. While cider reduces, bring a large pot of lightly salted water to a boil over high. Cut carrots crosswise into 2- to 3-inch-long pieces; cut each piece lengthwise into ¼-inch-thick planks. Add carrots to boiling water; boil, undisturbed, until just softer than tender-crisp, about 4 minutes. Drain and rinse with cold water; drain well.
3. Melt butter in cleaned skillet over medium; cook, stirring often, until butter is browned and smells toasty, 3 to 5 minutes. Add carrots, chopped thyme, and 1 teaspoon salt to skillet; toss to coat with butter. Drizzle with cider syrup; cook, stirring occasionally, until carrots are heated through, about 2 minutes.

Double Beet Salad with Honey-Dijon Vinaigrette

(Photo, page 250)

Turn heads with this stunning salad of raw golden beets and roasted red ones. To keep the rosy juices of the cooked beets from saturating the yellow slices, toss them in the vinaigrette separately. Wait to combine them until you're plating the dish.

ACTIVE 15 MIN. - TOTAL 1 HOUR, 55 MIN.

SERVES 6

- 1½ lb. small or medium-size red beets (6 to 7 beets), trimmed
- ¼ cup roasted walnut oil or extra-virgin olive oil
- 2 Tbsp. Champagne vinegar or white wine vinegar
- 1½ tsp. honey
- 1 tsp. Dijon mustard
- ¾ tsp. kosher salt
- ½ tsp. black pepper
- 9 oz. small golden beets (about 2 beets), trimmed
- 3 oz. goat cheese, crumbled (about ¾ cup)
- ½ cup chopped black walnuts, toasted

1. Preheat oven to 400°F. Scrub red beets, and leave unpeeled. Arrange red beets on a large piece of heavy-duty aluminum foil, and wrap tightly. Bake until tender when pierced with a knife, about 1 hour, 30 minutes. Remove from oven. Unwrap foil, and allow red beets to cool slightly, about 10 minutes. Rub off and discard skins. Cut red beets into wedges (about ½ inch thick).
2. While red beets bake, combine oil, vinegar, honey, mustard, salt, and pepper in a small lidded jar; secure lid, and shake well to combine.
3. Peel golden beets; cut into very thin slices (about ⅛ inch thick) using a vegetable peeler or mandoline. Place golden beets in a medium bowl; drizzle with 2 tablespoons of the vinaigrette, and toss well to coat.
4. Place red beet wedges in a large bowl; drizzle evenly with remaining vinaigrette, and toss to coat. Arrange red and golden beets in a large, shallow bowl or platter; sprinkle evenly with goat cheese and chopped walnuts.

Cheesy Turnip Gratin

(Photo, page 251)

Heavy cream infused with fragrant garlic, rosemary, bay leaves, and a dash of white pepper transforms often-overlooked turnips into a bubbly and decadent dish that's layered with nutty Gruyère and sharp Pecorino Romano cheeses.

ACTIVE 25 MIN. - TOTAL 1 HOUR, 40 MIN.

SERVES 8

- 1 large garlic clove, halved
- 1¼ cups heavy whipping cream
- 1 tsp. kosher salt
- ¼ tsp. ground white pepper
- 2 dried bay leaves
- 1 (4-inch) rosemary sprig
- 2 lb. medium turnips, peeled and cut into ⅛-inch slices
- 4 oz. Gruyère cheese, shredded (about 1 cup)
- 1 oz. Pecorino Romano cheese, grated (about ¼ cup)

1. Preheat oven to 400°F. Rub cut sides of garlic clove firmly against bottom and sides of a 2-quart glass or ceramic baking dish. Coat dish with cooking spray.
2. Combine garlic halves, heavy cream, kosher salt, white pepper, bay leaves, and rosemary in a small saucepan; bring to a simmer over medium, stirring occasionally. Remove from heat; let stand 10 minutes. Using a slotted spoon, remove garlic, bay leaves, and rosemary. (It's okay if some rosemary leaves are left in the liquid.)
3. Layer one-third of turnip slices in prepared baking dish, overlapping slices; sprinkle evenly with ⅓ cup of the Gruyère, and drizzle evenly with ⅓ cup of the cream mixture. Repeat layers twice, using all remaining cream mixture on top layer.
4. Cover dish with aluminum foil, and bake in preheated oven for 45 minutes. Remove from oven; uncover and sprinkle gratin evenly with Pecorino Romano. Bake, uncovered, until top is browned and turnips are tender when pierced with a knife, about 15 minutes. Let stand 10 minutes before serving.

252 2024 OCTOBER

OVER EASY

French Twist

Buttery croissants make the best breakfast sandwiches

Bacon-Egg-and-Cheese Croissant Sandwiches
ACTIVE 20 MIN. - TOTAL 30 MIN.
SERVES 6

- 12 thick-cut bacon slices (from 1 [24-oz.] pkg.)
- 12 large eggs
- ½ cup whole milk
- 1 tsp. garlic powder
- ½ tsp. black pepper
- ½ tsp. kosher salt
- 2 Tbsp. unsalted butter
- 6 (3-oz.) croissants, split
- 6 (1-oz.) sharp cheddar cheese slices
- 3 cups loosely packed baby arugula (about 3 oz.)
- Hot sauce, for serving

1. Preheat oven to 400°F. Line a large rimmed baking sheet with aluminum foil. Arrange bacon in an even layer on foil; bake until browned and crisp, about 25 minutes. Transfer bacon to a paper towel–lined plate to drain. Discard foil; set baking sheet aside.

2. While bacon cooks, whisk together eggs, milk, garlic powder, black pepper, and salt in a large bowl. Melt butter in a large nonstick skillet over medium. Add egg mixture to skillet, and cook, stirring often, until fluffy and set, about 5 minutes. Remove from heat.

3. Arrange bottom halves of croissants on baking sheet. Top each with 1 cheese slice, about ½ cup scrambled eggs, and 2 bacon slices. Cover with top halves of croissants.

4. Bake at 400°F until croissant tops are toasted and cheese is melted, about 5 minutes. Remove croissant tops; place about ½ cup arugula on each sandwich. Replace tops, and serve with hot sauce.

THE WELCOME TABLE

The Roast With the Most

Embrace the changing seasons with a cozy pork supper

FOR YEARS, I've said that pork is the meat of my people and the words "swine" and "butter" will be engraved on my tombstone. I collect pigs—ceramic ones, painted ones, stuffed animals, and fridge magnets—and have been known to travel the back roads of Louisiana in search of cracklings. Nowhere, though, does pork come to the forefront of my life as much as it does on my fall and winter tables. Then, I serve it up proudly as a roast with a crackling crust and a condiment of my choosing.

My Virginia-born Grandma Jones could put a hurtin' on a roast. In my family, that talent seems to have been matrilineal, with my grandmother passing her skills to my mother. They both delighted in creating rubs, inserting slivers of garlic, basting, and generally making sure the meat emerged from the oven ready to command its place as the centerpiece of the meal.

I like to believe that, like the women who came before me, I can bring to the table a roast that will do the family proud—whether it's a crisp-skinned chicken or a juicy leg of lamb. However, I am particularly fond of the roast pork that I serve at least once a year when the weather turns chilly and again on New Year's Day.

Pork's sweet and succulent meat is my favorite introduction to fall cooking. After summer's corn on the cob, hot dogs, and burgers, the formality of an oven-roasted joint reminds me of the approach of autumn and the cocooning that those cooler months bring. The additional fillip of a crisp crackling crust only adds to the delight. It's all about putting away the grab-it-and-go eating habits of the hotter months; gathering my friends around a dining table set with freshly ironed linens, gleaming crystal, real silver, and the good china; and then settling in for a season full of celebrations to come. –Jessica B. Harris

Roast Pork with Crackling
ACTIVE 35 MIN. - TOTAL 4 HOURS
SERVES 8

- 1 (5- to 6-lb.) bone-in pork shoulder (Boston butt) with ½-inch fat cap
- 2 tsp. poultry seasoning
- 1 tsp. rubbed sage
- 1 tsp. black pepper
- 2 Tbsp. kosher salt, divided
- 1½ Tbsp. olive oil
- Applesauce or chutney

1. Preheat oven to 325°F. Lightly coat a roasting rack with cooking spray; place rack inside a roasting pan.
2. Place pork, fat cap side up, on a cutting board. Using a sharp knife, score fat cap in a crosshatch pattern about ¼ inch deep at 1-inch intervals. Excluding fat cap, sprinkle pork evenly with poultry seasoning, sage, pepper, and 1½ tablespoons of the kosher salt. Transfer pork, fat cap side up, to prepared roasting rack. Brush fat cap with olive oil, and sprinkle evenly with remaining ½ tablespoon salt.
3. Roast in preheated oven until a thermometer inserted into thickest portion of pork registers 145°F, about 2 hours, 30 minutes. (Do not remove from oven.)
4. Increase oven temperature to 450°F, and roast until fat cap is crispy and golden brown and a thermometer registers 160°F, about 30 minutes. Remove from oven, and cover with aluminum foil; let stand 20 minutes. Slice as desired; serve with applesauce or chutney.

JUST ADD APPLES
Roast pork always seems to call for some sort of condiment to set it off properly. It is most fortuitous, then, that my favorite time for eating it coincides exactly with the season when apples are at their peak and so many varieties (ranging from popular picks such as McIntosh and Granny Smith to heirloom ones like King David and Roxbury Russet) are available. Simple to prepare, applesauce is the classic partner for pork, but a chutney, a relish, or just plain baked apples will also work well.

HOSPITALITY

Roll With It

Company's coming? Bake a batch of these apple-stuffed delights

Apple Cinnamon Rolls

ACTIVE 1 HOUR · TOTAL 2 HOURS, 50 MIN., INCLUDING 1 HOUR, 30 MIN. RISING

SERVES 9

- 1 (¼-oz.) envelope instant yeast (about 2¼ tsp.)
- 3¼ cups all-purpose flour, plus more for work surface
- 1 cup packed light brown sugar, divided
- 1¼ tsp. kosher salt, divided
- 1 large egg plus 1 large egg yolk, at room temperature
- 5 Tbsp. unsalted butter, melted and cooled
- 1 cup apple cider, warmed (100°F to 110°F), divided, plus more as needed
- ½ cup heavy whipping cream, warmed (100°F to 110°F), divided
- 3 medium apples (such as Granny Smith), peeled and finely chopped (4 cups)
- 2 tsp. cornstarch
- 4½ tsp. apple pie spice, divided
- ¼ cup unsalted butter, softened
- 2 oz. cream cheese, softened
- 2½ Tbsp. powdered sugar

1. Stir together yeast, flour, ¼ cup of the brown sugar, and 1 teaspoon of the salt in the bowl of a stand mixer fitted with a paddle attachment until combined. Add egg and yolk, melted and cooled butter, ½ cup of the cider, and ¼ cup of the cream; beat on medium-low speed until an elastic dough forms, stopping to scrape down sides of bowl as needed, 10 to 12 minutes. (Dough will be soft and slightly sticky.) Coat inside of a large bowl with cooking spray; place dough in bowl, turning dough to grease top. Cover and let rise in a warm place (75°F) until dough is doubled in size, 1 hour to 1 hour, 30 minutes.

2. While dough is rising, stir together apples, cornstarch, 1½ teaspoons of the apple pie spice, ¼ cup of the brown sugar, and remaining ½ cup cider and ¼ teaspoon salt in a large skillet. Cook over medium, stirring often, until juices thicken to a syrupy consistency, 8 to 10 minutes. Transfer mixture to a heatproof bowl; set aside, and let cool to room temperature, about 45 minutes.

3. Stir together remaining ½ cup brown sugar and 3 teaspoons apple pie spice in a small bowl; set sugar-spice mixture aside. Coat a 9-inch square baking pan with cooking spray. Gently punch down dough; roll dough on a lightly floured work surface into a 14- x 10-inch rectangle. Spread softened butter evenly over dough, leaving a ½-inch border on 1 short side. Sprinkle sugar-spice mixture over butter. Drain apple mixture, reserving juices; set juices aside, and spoon apples over sugar-spice mixture.

4. Starting from short side without border, roll dough into a tight log, pinching seam to seal. Using a serrated knife, trim both ends of log, if needed; cut log into 9 even slices (about 1¼ inches thick). Arrange slices in prepared baking pan. Cover with plastic wrap, and let rise in a warm place (75°F) until nearly doubled in size, 30 to 45 minutes. Preheat oven to 350°F.

5. Drizzle remaining ¼ cup cream over rolls. Bake in preheated oven until tops are golden brown and rolls are cooked through, 25 to 28 minutes. Meanwhile, add 2 tablespoons reserved apple juices to a small bowl. Add cream cheese and powdered sugar; whisk together until glaze is smooth, adding more apple cider as needed to reach drizzle consistency.

6. Let rolls cool in baking pan on a wire rack for 10 minutes. Drizzle glaze over warm rolls. Serve immediately.

COOKING SCHOOL

TIPS AND TRICKS FROM THE SOUTH'S MOST TRUSTED KITCHEN

Rock Your Rolls

Make the Apple-Cinnamon Rolls (recipe on page 255) easier with these steps

1. LET IT RISE
Use the provided time ranges for proofing, but rely on visual cues. Mark the outside of a clear glass bowl with tape so you can see when the dough has doubled in size.

2. ROLL IT EVENLY
For a neat spiral, make sure the dough is the same thickness throughout. Move the rolling pin in one direction, going from the center out (not back and forth).

3. SPREAD THE FILLING
A small offset spatula makes this step a breeze. Remember to leave a ½-inch border on one short side for sealing the rolled dough log.

4. CUT CAREFULLY
A sharp serrated knife is a must for cleanly slicing through the log without squishing the beautiful swirl inside. Use a gentle sawing motion to keep it intact.

5. CHECK THE DOUGH
These buns require a second rise. Before baking, dip a finger in flour and lightly poke one. If the indent fills in slowly, they're ready. If it bounces back, they need more time.

6. TEST FOR DONENESS
Even when cinnamon rolls are golden brown, their middles might be undercooked. A thermometer inserted into the center should read at least 190°F.

November

258 Flower Power More than just a side, cauliflower shines as a main dish

261 Good Inside Through her handcrafted pies, Natasha Burton aims to bring people together one slice at a time

262 Chess Moves A double-chocolate filling makes this classic pie better than ever

264 The Unsung Hero When it's a please-all occasion, this dish will take off the pressure

266 Easier Than Pie Not in the mood to roll out dough? Bake a Bundt cake bursting with fall flavors

272 Let's Talk Turkey Teach that classic bird some tasty new tricks

277 More Peas, Please This tangy relish will transform everything on your plate

278 Spiced-Up Sides Southern chefs with global roots share their spins on holiday favorites

283 Go Big With Butternut Four fresh recipes for autumn's sweetest squash

286 Sip and Savor Serve this elegant duo to tide over your guests until the big feast

287 The Big Cheese Satisfy a full house with this savory bacon, egg, and cheddar casserole

288 Cooking School Our Test Kitchen professionals share tips and techniques for making a "darn good gravy"

BOUNTY

Flower Power

More than just a side, cauliflower shines as a main dish

FORGET FAST FOOD
These sandwiches rival those from a popular Southern chain.

Nashville Hot Fried Cauliflower Sandwiches
ACTIVE 55 MIN. - TOTAL 55 MIN.
SERVES 6

Whisk together 1½ cups **buttermilk**, ¼ cup **hot sauce**, 1 **large egg**, and ½ tsp. **kosher salt** in a large bowl. Cut 1 **head cauliflower** into 12 (2-inch) florets; add to buttermilk mixture, and stir to coat. Combine 2½ Tbsp. **light brown sugar**, 1½ Tbsp. **Cajun seasoning**, and ½ tsp. each **cayenne pepper** and **kosher salt** in a small heatproof bowl. Whisk together 1½ cups **all-purpose flour** and 2 Tbsp. of the brown sugar mixture in a separate shallow dish. Fill a Dutch oven with **canola oil** to a depth of 2 inches; heat over medium-high to 350°F. Stir ⅓ cup of the hot oil into the remaining 3 Tbsp. brown sugar mixture. Working in 3 batches, dredge florets in flour mixture, and fry, turning occasionally, until golden brown, about 5 minutes per batch. Transfer to a wire rack set over a baking sheet. Immediately brush florets with oil mixture, and sprinkle lightly with **kosher salt**. Place 2 fried florets on each of 6 split, toasted **potato hamburger buns** dressed with **prepared coleslaw** and **bread-and-butter pickles**.

Cauliflower Personal "Pizzas"
ACTIVE 15 MIN. · TOTAL 45 MIN.
SERVES 4

Cut 2 (2-lb.) **cauliflower heads** in half; slice to create 2 (¾-inch-thick) "steaks" from each head. Arrange cauliflower steaks on a foil-lined baking sheet. Whisk together ¼ cup **extra-virgin olive oil**, 2 Tbsp. each grated **Parmesan cheese** and minced **garlic**, ½ tsp. **dried Italian seasoning**, and ¼ tsp. **kosher salt**. Spoon mixture over cauliflower steaks. Bake at 425°F on oven rack in upper third position until golden brown and tender, 25 to 30 minutes. Remove from oven, and top steaks with ½ cup **jarred pizza sauce**. Sprinkle with ½ tsp. **kosher salt**, and top with 1 cup shredded **mozzarella cheese**, 2 Tbsp. each finely chopped **bell pepper** and **red onion**, and 2 Tbsp. quartered **pepperoni slices**. Increase oven temperature to 450°F. Return baking sheet to oven, and bake until mozzarella is melted, 5 to 6 minutes. Transfer steaks to a platter, and sprinkle with ¼ tsp. **dried Italian seasoning**. Serve warm with additional **Parmesan** and **pizza sauce**.

ROASTED WHOLE CAULIFLOWER WITH SMOKY MAYO

Roasted Whole Cauliflower with Smoky Mayo
ACTIVE 15 MIN. · TOTAL 55 MIN.
SERVES 4

Whisk together ¼ cup each **canola oil** and **water**, 3 Tbsp. **Creole seasoning**, 2 Tbsp. **honey**, 2 Tbsp. **Creole mustard**, and 1 tsp. **smoked paprika** in a small bowl. Remove leaves and trim stems from 2 (1½-lb.) **cauliflower heads**. Turn each head upside down; drizzle 3 Tbsp. oil mixture into each, rotating to coat the interiors. Flip heads right side up; brush exteriors with remaining oil mixture. Place both heads in a 12-inch cast-iron skillet. Fill a small baking dish halfway full with water. Place baking dish on rack in lower third of oven; place skillet on center rack. This creates steam, which helps cook the cauliflower evenly and thoroughly, not just around the outside. Bake at 450°F until each cauliflower core is tender when pierced with a knife, 50 minutes to 1 hour. Meanwhile, whisk together 1 cup **mayonnaise**; 1 Tbsp. each **canola oil** and **water**; ½ tsp. each **Creole seasoning**, **smoked paprika**, and **fresh lemon juice**; and 1 grated **garlic clove** until mostly smooth. Spread mayonnaise mixture on a serving platter. Transfer roasted cauliflower to platter, and garnish with thinly sliced **scallions**. Serve warm.

2024 NOVEMBER 259

HARVEST SUNRISE PIE

Good Inside

Through her handcrafted pies, Natasha Burton aims to bring people together one slice at a time

"**I STARTED** with an Easy-Bake Oven [and used it] until the light bulb burned out," says pastry chef Natasha Burton, the owner of Mixed Fillings Pie Shop in Jacksonville, Florida. It's fitting that her love of food began when she was a kid; Burton has a childlike playfulness that permeates her baking to this day.

Her offerings are as creative as their names: Cookies and Dreams (cream cheese, brown butter, Oreo crust, and whipped cream) or Peanut Butter and Jealous (peanut butter mousse, ganache, Oreo crust, and Butterfinger-flavored whipped cream), to name just two.

The bakery was a pandemic pivot born from her desire to build something for herself, by herself. A trained chef, she graduated from Le Cordon Bleu culinary school in Dallas and came up in the kitchen of renowned Texas chef Stephan Pyles before transitioning to the sweet side.

She was relegated to pie making at one of her first baking jobs. "I was banished to the pie department but turned it into my superpower," she jokes.

In 2019, Burton relocated to Jacksonville, where she had family. In March 2023, she brought Mixed Fillings to the Five Points neighborhood. It quickly became a gathering place with a menu that regularly sold out. Building issues led Burton to close the location and move the bakery to a historic cottage in Jacksonville that she hopes to open late this year. In the meantime, you can order her creations online.

For those who can't make it to Florida for a slice, Burton shared the recipe for her Harvest Sunrise Pie (right) that was inspired by her favorite part of Thanksgiving: cranberry sauce.

Aside from unforgettable desserts, Mixed Fillings also provides a sense of community that extends beyond the kitchen. The website includes a special section titled "Random Acts of Pi(e)ness" of suggestions for making the world a better place. Our suggestion? Bake Burton's fantastic, fall-flavored recipe for friends and family.

Harvest Sunrise Pie
ACTIVE 30 MIN. - TOTAL 3 HOURS, 20 MIN.
SERVES 8

OAT CRUMBLE CRUST
- 1½ cups old-fashioned regular rolled oats
- ½ cup all-purpose flour
- ½ cup packed light brown sugar
- ½ tsp. ground cinnamon
- ¼ tsp. kosher salt
- 6 Tbsp. unsalted butter, melted
- 1 tsp. vanilla extract

PUMPKIN FILLING
- 1 (15-oz.) can pumpkin puree
- 4 large eggs
- 1 cup packed light brown sugar
- 3 Tbsp. unsalted butter, melted
- 1 Tbsp. cornstarch
- 2 tsp. ground cinnamon
- 1½ tsp. ground ginger
- 1 tsp. vanilla extract
- ½ tsp. kosher salt

ADDITIONAL INGREDIENTS
- Spiced Cranberry Compote (recipe, right)
- Sweetened whipped cream

1. Prepare the Oat Crumble Crust: Preheat oven to 350°F. Coat a 9-inch pie plate with cooking spray; set aside. Stir together oats, flour, brown sugar, cinnamon, and salt in a large bowl. Pour melted butter and vanilla over oat mixture; stir together with a fork until mixture is crumbly. Transfer to prepared pie plate. Press firmly into bottom and up sides, using bottom of a measuring cup to help press mixture down and smooth out surface. Bake until it begins to brown slightly around edges, 10 to 12 minutes.

2. Meanwhile, prepare the Pumpkin Filling: Beat together pumpkin, eggs, brown sugar, butter, cornstarch, cinnamon, ginger, vanilla, and salt in a large bowl with a hand mixer on medium-low speed until well blended, about 1 minute. Remove crust from oven, and pour filling into crust.

3. Bake at 350°F until filling is set, about 45 minutes. Let cool completely on a wire rack, 2 to 3 hours. Spoon Spiced Cranberry Compote over cooled pie. Pipe or dollop with sweetened whipped cream.

Spiced Cranberry Compote
ACTIVE 25 MIN. - TOTAL 1 HOUR, 25 MIN.
MAKES 1¾ CUPS

- 1½ tsp. cornstarch
- ⅔ cup granulated sugar
- 3 Tbsp. honey
- 1½ tsp. pumpkin pie spice
- 1 (12-oz.) pkg. fresh or frozen cranberries (3 cups)

Whisk together ¼ cup water and cornstarch in a heavy-bottomed large saucepan until cornstarch is dissolved, about 30 seconds. Whisk in granulated sugar, honey, and pumpkin pie spice until combined. Stir in cranberries. Cook over medium-high, gently stirring occasionally to avoid breaking berries too much, until thickened, about 15 minutes. Remove from heat, and transfer to a medium-size heatproof bowl. Let cool, uncovered, until room temperature, about 1 hour. Store in an airtight container in refrigerator up to 5 days.

PIECE OF CAKE

Chess Moves

A double-chocolate filling makes this classic pie better than ever

CHOCOLATE CHESS PIE

Top It Off
Two more delicious options

Chocolate-Orange Chess Pie
Follow recipe as directed through Step 2. In Step 3, replace vanilla extract with 2 tsp. grated **orange zest.** Proceed with recipe as directed. Garnish with whipped cream and **orange peel strips.**

Turtle Chess Pie
Follow recipe as directed through Step 2. In Step 3, omit whipped cream. Stir together 6 Tbsp. jarred **salted caramel sauce** and 4 Tbsp. **pecan pieces** in a small bowl. Spoon over pie just before serving.

Chocolate Chess Pie
ACTIVE 15 MIN. - TOTAL 50 MIN., PLUS 1 HOUR, 30 MIN. COOLING
MAKES 1 (9-INCH) PIE

- ¼ cup unsalted butter
- ¼ cup semisweet chocolate chips
- 1 cup packed light brown sugar
- 3 large eggs, at room temperature
- ¼ cup heavy whipping cream
- 2 tsp. vanilla extract
- ½ tsp. kosher salt
- ¼ cup unsweetened cocoa
- 2 Tbsp. all-purpose flour or fine yellow cornmeal
- 1 frozen piecrust (such as Marie Callender's), parbaked according to pkg. instructions
- Whipped cream

1. Preheat oven to 350°F. Melt butter and chocolate chips in a large microwavable bowl on HIGH in 30-second intervals, stopping to stir between each, about 1 minute total.
2. Whisk brown sugar into chocolate mixture. Whisk in eggs, 1 at a time, until fully incorporated.
3. Stir whipping cream, vanilla, and salt into chocolate mixture. Sift in cocoa and flour (or cornmeal, if you prefer a little more texture); whisk just until combined. Pour mixture into parbaked piecrust; bake in preheated oven until center is puffed but still jiggles slightly, 35 to 40 minutes. Let cool completely before slicing, about 1 hour, 30 minutes. Serve with whipped cream.

FAMILY STYLE

The Unsung Hero

When it's a please-all occasion, this dish will take off the pressure

THANKSGIVING is one of the few times of the year when family members from near and far gather around a table, bringing with them a host of dietary preferences, strong opinions, and casseroles.

There are the traditionalists, who scan the buffet to make sure all of the usual recipes are present and accounted for—it's just not the holidays without creamed onions, you know. There are the adventurous types, who shock everyone with a dish that came out of left field. (I apologize for the short ribs with Swiss chard I made instead of turkey in 2010.) And then there are the precious children, who eat only beige and brown foods on a daily basis but then make an exception to this rule on holidays—when they reject a veritable sea of beige and brown options and just want dessert.

It may seem impossible to satisfy everyone, especially on Thanksgiving, but here's your secret weapon: dressing. Yes, it's as expected as pumpkin pie, but it's also infinitely adaptable. Load it up with butternut squash, mushrooms, and spinach to make it a vegetarian main. Stir in cheddar and bake it in muffin trays for a side that kids will devour. Adjust it to fit your needs: Use gluten-free bread, toss in toasted nuts, or spice it up with chorizo. The turkey may be the star, but the dressing will win the crowd. –Lisa Cericola

Sourdough Bread Dressing

ACTIVE 35 MIN. · TOTAL 1 HOUR, 20 MIN.
SERVES 8

- 1 (1½-lb.) day-old sourdough bread loaf, cut into ¾-inch cubes (about 12 cups)
- ¾ cup unsalted butter, divided, plus more for greasing dish
- 1 lb. sweet Italian sausage
- 1 medium-size sweet onion, thinly sliced (about 2½ cups)

- 4 large celery stalks, chopped (about 1½ cups)
- ¾ tsp. black pepper
- 1½ tsp. kosher salt, divided
- ¼ cup chopped fresh parsley, plus small leaves for garnish
- 2 Tbsp. chopped fresh sage, plus small leaves for garnish
- 1 Tbsp. fresh thyme leaves, plus more for garnish
- ¾ cup dry white wine
- 3 cups chicken stock
- 2 large eggs, beaten

1. Preheat oven to 375°F. Butter a large (3-quart) baking dish, and set aside. Place bread cubes in a large heatproof bowl.
2. Melt 4 tablespoons of the butter in a 12-inch skillet over medium-high. Add sausage; cook, stirring occasionally, until browned and crumbly, about 4 minutes. Transfer to bowl with bread. Place skillet over medium-high heat, and add 4 tablespoons of the butter. Add onion, celery, pepper, and ½ teaspoon of the salt; cook, stirring occasionally, until onion is golden brown, about 6 minutes. Stir in parsley, sage, and thyme; cook until fragrant, about 30 seconds. Transfer to bowl with bread and sausage.
3. Add wine to skillet, and increase heat to high. Cook, stirring occasionally, until wine is reduced to about ¼ cup, about 3 minutes. Add stock and remaining 4 tablespoons butter and 1 teaspoon salt; remove from heat, and stir until butter is melted, about 2 minutes. Pour over bread mixture, stirring to combine. Let cool slightly, about 5 minutes.
4. Gently stir beaten eggs into bread mixture. Transfer mixture to prepared baking dish. Bake, uncovered, in preheated oven until golden brown, about 40 minutes. Remove from oven; garnish with parsley, sage, and thyme. Serve immediately.

Two More Takes

Transform our basic recipe into something surprising

Veggie-Packed Sourdough Dressing

ACTIVE 30 MIN. · TOTAL 1 HOUR, 15 MIN.
SERVES 8

Prepare recipe as directed through Step 1. In Step 2, replace sausage with 8 oz. sliced **cremini mushrooms**; cook, undisturbed, until browned, about 4 minutes. Replace sweet onion with 1 sliced **red onion**; cook until softened, about 3 minutes. Stir in 5 oz. **baby spinach** and 1 (15-oz.) pkg. thawed **frozen chopped butternut squash**; cook until spinach wilts, about 2 minutes. Omit sage and thyme. In Step 3, replace chicken stock with 3 cups **vegetable stock**; proceed with recipe as directed. Garnish with **parsley**.

Cheesy Dressing Muffins

ACTIVE 25 MIN. · TOTAL 1 HOUR
MAKES 24

Prepare recipe as directed in Step 1, but **butter** the wells of 2 (12-cup) muffin trays. In Step 2, omit sausage, parsley, and sage. In Step 3, increase **butter** to ½ cup. In Step 4, stir 1 cup shredded **sharp white cheddar cheese** into bread mixture along with eggs. Divide mixture among wells of muffin trays. Top evenly with 1½ cups additional shredded **cheddar**. Bake at 375°F until golden brown, about 30 minutes. Garnish with **thyme**.

264 2024 NOVEMBER

SOURDOUGH BREAD DRESSING

Easier Than Pie

Not in the mood to roll out dough? Bake a Bundt cake bursting with fall flavors

APPLE CIDER–DOUGHNUT BUNDT CAKE (PAGE 270)

MAPLE-GLAZED
PUMPKIN BUNDT CAKE
(PAGE 270)

CHOCOLATE BUNDT
CAKE WITH PECANS
(PAGE 270)

SPICED CREAM CHEESE BUNDT CAKE (PAGE 271)

Apple Cider–Doughnut Bundt Cake

(Photo, page 266)

ACTIVE 30 MIN. · TOTAL 3 HOURS, 30 MIN.

SERVES 12

Baking spray
½ cup packed light brown sugar
1¼ cups granulated sugar, divided
1 cup unsalted butter, softened and divided
3 large eggs
2 tsp. vanilla extract
3 cups all-purpose flour
1½ tsp. baking powder
1 tsp. kosher salt
½ tsp. baking soda
2½ tsp. ground cinnamon, divided
1¼ tsp. ground ginger, divided
¾ tsp. grated fresh nutmeg, divided
1 cup apple cider
½ cup unsweetened applesauce

1. Preheat oven to 350°F. Coat a 10- to 12-cup Bundt pan with baking spray, and set aside.
2. Beat brown sugar, 1 cup of the granulated sugar, and ¾ cup of the butter in the bowl of a stand mixer fitted with a paddle attachment on medium-high speed until light and fluffy, 3 to 4 minutes. With mixer on low speed, add eggs, 1 at a time, beating well after each addition. Beat in vanilla until just combined.
3. Whisk together flour, baking powder, salt, baking soda, 2 teaspoons of the cinnamon, 1 teaspoon of the ginger, and ½ teaspoon of the nutmeg in a large bowl until combined. Stir together apple cider and applesauce in a small bowl until just combined.
4. With mixer on low speed, add flour mixture and apple cider mixture alternately to butter mixture, beginning and ending with flour mixture, beating until just combined after each addition and stopping to scrape down sides of bowl as needed. Transfer batter to prepared pan.
5. Bake in preheated oven until a wooden pick inserted in center comes out clean, 50 to 55 minutes. Let cool in pan on a wire rack 10 minutes. Invert cake onto wire rack, and remove pan.
6. Microwave remaining ¼ cup butter in a small heatproof bowl on HIGH until melted, about 30 seconds.

7. Stir together the remaining ¼ cup granulated sugar, ½ teaspoon cinnamon, and ¼ teaspoon each ginger and nutmeg in a small bowl until combined. Set cake on a wire rack over a large, rimmed baking sheet. Brush warm cake with melted butter. Sprinkle evenly with cinnamon-sugar mixture; repeat with any excess from baking sheet until all cinnamon-sugar mixture is used, pressing gently to adhere to cake. Let cool completely on wire rack, about 2 hours. Store cake in an airtight container in refrigerator or at room temperature up to 3 days.

Maple-Glazed Pumpkin Bundt Cake

(Photo, page 267)

ACTIVE 15 MIN. · TOTAL 3 HOURS, 20 MIN.

SERVES 12

CAKE

Baking spray
3 cups all-purpose flour
2 tsp. ground cinnamon
1½ tsp. baking soda
1½ tsp. ground nutmeg
1 tsp. ground allspice
¾ tsp. kosher salt
½ tsp. baking powder
1 cup vegetable oil
2½ cups granulated sugar
3 large eggs, at room temperature
1 tsp. vanilla extract
1 (15-oz.) can pumpkin puree (not pumpkin pie filling)

GLAZE

⅓ cup pure maple syrup
3 Tbsp. unsalted butter
¼ tsp. ground cinnamon
⅛ tsp. kosher salt
1 cup powdered sugar, sifted
1 tsp. vanilla extract
Chopped toasted walnuts (optional), for garnish

1. Prepare the Cake: Preheat oven to 350°F. Generously grease a 10- to 12-cup Bundt pan with baking spray; set aside.
2. Sift flour into a large bowl. Add the cinnamon, baking soda, nutmeg, allspice, salt, and baking powder; whisk to combine.

3. Whisk vegetable oil and granulated sugar together in a separate large bowl until fully combined. Whisk in eggs, 1 at a time, whisking well after each addition. Whisk in vanilla until incorporated.
4. Add flour mixture and pumpkin puree alternately to sugar mixture, beginning and ending with the flour mixture, whisking after each addition just until ingredients are combined. (Do not overmix.)
5. Pour batter into prepared pan, smoothing top into an even layer. Firmly tap pan on counter a few times to release any air bubbles. Bake in preheated oven until a wooden pick inserted into center of Cake comes out clean, 55 to 60 minutes. Let cool in pan on a wire rack 10 minutes. Invert onto wire rack; remove pan, and let cool completely, about 2 hours.
6. Prepare the Glaze: Heat maple syrup, butter, cinnamon, and salt in a medium saucepan over medium-low, stirring occasionally until butter is melted. Remove pan from heat; whisk in the powdered sugar and vanilla. Let cool until slightly thickened, 2 to 4 minutes. Spoon warm Glaze over cooled Cake. (If Glaze begins to set before drizzling over Cake, return pan to heat for a few seconds and whisk until smooth.) Garnish with walnuts, if desired. Store in an airtight container in refrigerator or at room temperature up to 4 days.

Chocolate Bundt Cake with Pecans

(Photo, page 268)

ACTIVE 25 MIN. · TOTAL 3 HOURS, 15 MIN.

SERVES 12

Baking spray
2¼ cups all-purpose flour
2 cups granulated sugar
¾ cup unsweetened cocoa
2 tsp. baking soda
1 tsp. kosher salt
½ tsp. baking powder
2 large eggs
1 cup whole buttermilk
1 cup strong brewed coffee, cooled
½ cup canola oil
2 tsp. vanilla extract
¾ cup heavy whipping cream

270 2024 NOVEMBER

1 cup semisweet chocolate chips
2 tsp. coffee liqueur (such as Kahlúa)
Chopped toasted pecans, for garnish

1. Preheat oven to 350°F. Coat a 10- to 12-cup Bundt pan with baking spray, and set aside.
2. Whisk together flour, sugar, cocoa, baking soda, salt, and baking powder in a large bowl.
3. Whisk together eggs, buttermilk, coffee, oil, and vanilla in a separate medium bowl until combined. Add oil mixture to flour mixture, stirring until combined. Pour batter into prepared pan.
4. Bake in preheated oven until a wooden pick inserted in center comes out clean, 45 to 55 minutes. Let cool in pan on a wire rack 10 minutes. Invert cake onto rack; remove pan, and let cool completely, about 2 hours.
5. Heat cream in a small saucepan over medium, stirring often, until it just begins to steam, about 3 minutes. Remove from heat, and immediately pour over chocolate chips in a medium-size heatproof bowl. (Do not stir.) Let stand 2 minutes; gently stir until chocolate is melted and mixture is smooth. Stir in coffee liqueur until combined. Place cake on a wire rack set inside a large rimmed baking sheet. Drizzle or pour chocolate mixture over top of cooled cake as desired. Before chocolate mixture sets, sprinkle with pecans. Store cake in an airtight container in refrigerator or at room temperature up to 3 days.

Spiced Cream Cheese Bundt Cake
ACTIVE 35 MIN. - TOTAL 3 HOURS, 45 MIN.
SERVES 12

Baking spray
1 (8-oz.) pkg. cream cheese, softened
¾ cup unsalted butter, softened
1½ cups granulated sugar
1 tsp. kosher salt
4 large eggs, at room temperature
1¼ tsp. vanilla extract, divided
2½ cups all-purpose flour
½ tsp. baking powder
⅓ cup whole milk
¼ cup packed light brown sugar
4 tsp. pumpkin pie spice, plus more for garnish
1¼ cups powdered sugar
1 Tbsp. heavy whipping cream

1. Preheat oven to 325°F. Coat a 10- to 12-cup Bundt pan with baking spray; set aside.
2. Beat cream cheese and butter in the bowl of a stand mixer fitted with a paddle attachment on medium-high speed until fluffy, about 4 minutes, stopping to scrape down sides of bowl as needed.
3. Add granulated sugar and kosher salt; beat on high speed for 5 minutes, stopping occasionally to scrape down sides of bowl. With mixer on low speed, add eggs, 1 at a time, beating well after each addition. Beat in 1 teaspoon of the vanilla until combined.
4. Stir together flour and baking powder in a medium bowl. With mixer on low speed, add flour mixture and milk alternately to butter mixture, beginning and ending with flour mixture, beating until just combined after each addition and stopping to scrape down sides of bowl as needed.
5. Transfer half of the batter (about 3 cups) to another medium bowl; stir in brown sugar and pumpkin pie spice until smooth. Spoon about 1 cup of the plain batter evenly into prepared pan; spoon about 1 cup of the spiced batter over top of plain batter in an even layer. Repeat process two more times, alternating with plain and spiced batters. Using a knife, pull the blade back and forth through the layered batters to create a swirled effect. Smooth the top with a spatula or the back of a spoon.
6. Bake in preheated oven until a wooden pick inserted in center comes out clean, about 1 hour. Let cool in pan on a wire rack 10 minutes. Invert onto wire rack; remove pan, and let cool completely, about 2 hours.
7. Whisk together the powdered sugar, 1½ tablespoons water, cream, and the remaining ¼ teaspoon vanilla in a medium bowl until smooth. Drizzle over cooled cake. Sprinkle pumpkin pie spice over the glaze to garnish, if desired.

SPICED CREAM CHEESE BUNDT CAKE

HOSPITALITY

Let's Talk Turkey

Teach that classic bird some tasty new tricks

Mayo-Roasted Turkey

ACTIVE 40 MIN. - TOTAL 4 HOURS, 40 MIN., PLUS 12 HOURS DRY BRINING
SERVES 8 TO 10

- 1 (12- to 14-lb.) turkey
- 2 tsp. poultry seasoning
- 5 Tbsp., plus ½ tsp. kosher salt, divided
- 2¼ tsp. black pepper, divided
- 1 cup mayonnaise, divided
- 1 Tbsp. minced fresh rosemary, plus 4 sprigs, divided
- 1 Tbsp. minced fresh sage, plus 4 sprigs, divided
- 1 Tbsp. minced fresh thyme, plus 4 sprigs, divided
- 6 garlic cloves, grated (1 Tbsp.), plus 1 garlic head, halved crosswise, divided
- 1 lemon, zested and quartered, divided
- 1 yellow onion, quartered
- Mixed herb sprigs and lemon halves and wedges (optional)

1. Remove giblets and neck from turkey; set aside for gravy, if desired. Pat turkey dry. Stir together poultry seasoning, 5 tablespoons of the kosher salt, and 2 teaspoons of the black pepper in a bowl. Sprinkle over turkey and in cavity. Place turkey on a rack set inside a rimmed baking sheet. Chill uncovered 12 to 36 hours.

2. Remove turkey from refrigerator 1 hour before cooking. Preheat oven to 425°F with rack in lower third position. Set a roasting rack inside roasting pan.
3. Stir together ¾ cup of the mayonnaise, minced herbs, grated garlic, lemon zest, and remaining ½ teaspoon salt and ¼ teaspoon black pepper in a medium bowl until combined.
4. Loosen skin from turkey breast and thighs; spread mayonnaise mixture under skin. Rub remaining ¼ cup mayonnaise all over turkey. Tuck wing tips under; transfer turkey to prepared roasting pan, breast side up. Stuff yellow onion quarters, garlic head, lemon quarters, and herb sprigs in turkey cavity. Tie legs together with kitchen twine.
5. Roast turkey in preheated oven for 30 minutes. Loosely cover with aluminum foil, and reduce heat to 350°F. Roast until a thermometer inserted into thickest portion registers 160°F, 2 hours to 2 hours, 30 minutes, uncovering turkey during last few minutes to crisp skin.
6. Transfer turkey to a cutting board; reserve drippings for gravy. Let turkey rest for 30 minutes before carving. Garnish with mixed herb sprigs and lemon halves and wedges, if desired.

Classic Gravy

ACTIVE 40 MIN. - TOTAL 1 HOUR, 15 MIN.
SERVES 8 TO 10

- 2 Tbsp. canola oil
- Neck and giblets from a whole turkey
- 1 yellow onion, chopped
- 2 carrots, chopped
- 2 celery stalks, chopped
- 4 garlic cloves, smashed
- ½ cup dry white wine
- 6 cups unsalted chicken stock, plus more if needed
- 4 flat-leaf parsley sprigs
- 4 thyme sprigs
- 2 fresh bay leaves
- ½ cup pan drippings from any roasted turkey, divided
- Butter, if needed
- ¼ cup all-purpose flour
- Kosher salt and black pepper to taste

1. Heat oil in a large pot or Dutch oven over medium-high. Add turkey neck and giblets, onion, carrots, celery, and garlic. Cook, stirring occasionally, until turkey pieces are browned, about 8 minutes. Add wine, scraping to release any browned bits. Cook, stirring often, about 1 minute.
2. Add stock, parsley, thyme, and bay leaves. Bring to a boil over medium-high; reduce heat to medium-low, and simmer, undisturbed, until reduced by about half, 30 minutes.
3. Pour stock mixture through a fine mesh strainer into a large heatproof bowl; discard solids. (Add more stock as needed to yield 3 cups.)
4. Strain drippings; discard solids. Let stand 5 minutes; spoon fat from liquid. Set aside fat and drippings separately.
5. Heat 3 tablespoons reserved fat in a saucepan over medium (add butter as needed to yield 3 tablespoons fat). Add flour, and cook, stirring constantly, until toasted, 2 to 3 minutes.
6. Gradually pour reserved stock into flour mixture in a thin, steady stream, whisking constantly. Whisk in reserved drippings. Cook, stirring often, until thick enough to coat the back of a spoon, 10 to 15 minutes. Season with salt and pepper to taste.

SMOOTH MOVE
Creamy mayo is much easier to slather on turkey than butter.

MAYO-ROASTED TURKEY WITH CLASSIC GRAVY

"I CAN'T BELIEVE IT'S NOT SMOKED" TURKEY (PAGE 276)

FRENCH ONION TURKEY (PAGE 276)

French Onion Turkey

(Photo, page 275)
ACTIVE 45 MIN. - TOTAL 4 HOURS, 45 MIN.,
PLUS 12 HOURS DRY BRINING
SERVES 8 TO 10

- 1 (12- to 14-lb.) turkey
- 3 Tbsp. kosher salt
- 1 Tbsp. black pepper
- 1 tsp. onion powder
- 1½ tsp. granulated sugar, divided
- 4 yellow onions, sliced into 12 (1-inch-thick) rounds, plus 1 yellow onion, quartered, divided
- 1 cup butter, softened
- 1 (1-oz.) envelope onion soup and dip mix
- ¼ cup crispy fried onions (such as French's), finely crushed
- 1 tsp. balsamic vinegar
- ½ tsp. garlic powder
- ¼ tsp. dry mustard
- 4 fresh thyme sprigs, plus more for garnish
- 2 red onions, cut into wedges
- 2 sweet onions, cut into wedges

1. Remove giblets and neck from turkey. Pat turkey dry. Stir together salt, black pepper, onion powder, and 1 teaspoon of the sugar in a small bowl. Sprinkle over turkey and in cavity. Place turkey on a wire rack set inside a rimmed baking sheet. Chill turkey, uncovered, at least 12 hours or up to 36 hours.
2. Remove turkey from refrigerator; let stand at room temperature 1 hour. Preheat oven to 425°F with rack in lower third position. Arrange yellow onion rounds in bottom of a large roasting pan.
3. Stir together butter, onion soup mix, crispy fried onions, balsamic vinegar, garlic powder, dry mustard, and remaining ½ teaspoon sugar in a medium bowl until smooth and creamy.
4. Loosen skin from turkey breast and thighs; spread butter mixture under skin and all over turkey. Tuck wing tips under; transfer turkey to prepared roasting pan, breast side up. Stuff yellow onion quarters and 4 thyme sprigs in turkey cavity. Tie legs together with kitchen twine. Pour 1 cup water into bottom of roasting pan.
5. Roast turkey in preheated oven for 30 minutes. Loosely cover with aluminum foil, and reduce heat to 350°F. Roast for 1 hour. Remove from oven, and nestle red and sweet onion wedges around turkey. Loosely cover with foil, and bake at 350°F until onions are tender and a thermometer inserted into thickest portion registers 160°F, 1 hour to 1 hour, 30 minutes.
6. Transfer turkey to a cutting board and onions to a serving platter; reserve drippings for gravy, if desired. Let rest for 30 minutes before carving. Transfer meat to platter with roasted onion wedges. Garnish with thyme.

"I Can't Believe It's Not Smoked" Turkey

(Photo, page 274)
ACTIVE 40 MIN. - TOTAL 4 HOURS,
PLUS 12 HOURS DRY BRINING
SERVES 8 TO 10

- 1 (12- to 14-lb.) turkey
- 5 Tbsp. kosher salt
- 1 Tbsp. granulated sugar
- 2 tsp. black pepper
- 1 tsp. garlic powder
- 2 Tbsp. smoked paprika, divided
- ¾ cup butter, softened, divided
- 3 garlic cloves, finely chopped (about 1 Tbsp.)
- 1 canned chipotle in adobo sauce, finely chopped, plus 2 Tbsp. adobo sauce from can, divided
- 1 tsp., plus ¼ cup maple syrup, divided
- 1 tsp. chopped fresh oregano, plus 2 sprigs, divided
- 1 tsp. chopped fresh sage, plus 2 sprigs, divided
- 2 Tbsp. canola oil
- 1 (8-oz.) smoked ham hock
- 1 tsp. Worcestershire sauce
- Fresh oregano and sage sprigs (optional)

1. Remove giblets and neck from turkey; set aside for gravy, if desired. Pat turkey dry. Stir together salt, sugar, pepper, garlic powder, and 1 teaspoon of the smoked paprika in a small bowl. Sprinkle over turkey and in cavity. Place turkey on a wire rack set inside a rimmed baking sheet. Chill, uncovered, at least 12 hours or up to 36 hours.
2. Remove turkey from refrigerator; let stand at room temperature 1 hour. Preheat oven to 350°F with rack in lower third position. Set a roasting rack inside a large roasting pan.
3. Stir together ½ cup of the butter; chopped garlic; 1½ teaspoons of the chopped chipotle; 1 teaspoon each of the maple syrup, chopped oregano, and chopped sage; and 2 teaspoons of the smoked paprika in a medium bowl until combined. Set aside. Stir together canola oil and 2 teaspoons of the smoked paprika in a small bowl until combined, and set aside.
4. Loosen skin from turkey breast and thighs; spread the butter mixture under skin, being careful to avoid tearing the skin. Rub oil mixture all over turkey. Tuck wing tips under; transfer turkey to prepared roasting pan, breast side up. Stuff ham hock and oregano and sage sprigs in cavity. Tie legs together with kitchen twine; loosely cover turkey with aluminum foil. Roast in preheated oven for 90 minutes.
5. Meanwhile, heat the Worcestershire sauce and remaining ¼ cup each butter and maple syrup, 2 tablespoons adobo sauce, and remaining 1 teaspoon smoked paprika in a small saucepan over medium-low. Cook, stirring occasionally, until butter is melted and mixture is smooth.
6. Uncover turkey; brush with butter mixture. Roast, uncovered, until a thermometer inserted into thickest portion registers 160°F, 1 hour to 1 hour, 30 minutes, brushing with butter mixture every 20 minutes.
7. Transfer turkey to a cutting board; reserve drippings for gravy. Let rest for 30 minutes before carving. Garnish with oregano and sage, if desired.

CRUNCH TIME
Crispy fried onions add a concentrated savoriness to your holiday bird.

IVY'S KITCHEN

More Peas, Please

This tangy relish will transform everything on your plate

WHEN I WAS a kid growing up in Georgia, my family didn't serve our Thanksgiving meal on fancy china at a table set with a stunning centerpiece, nor did we take turns saying what we were grateful for. If you were invited to our holiday lunch, you'd walk into a room bursting at the seams with people. Everyone would line up, waiting impatiently to fill their Chinet paper plates from the buffet of precariously parked CorningWare and Pyrex dishes. Among the classics—dressing, potatoes, casseroles—there would be an occasional green vegetable, which would most definitely be slow-cooked and swimming in a savory lake of pork-jowl–laden potlikker.

It may have been a fuss-free potluck, but our cooking skills were over-the-top. There would be deep-fried turkey, lacy cornbread, and a sideboard full of layer cakes and pies. Each person's signature dish could rival the next, but for me, the crown jewel was Nana's Marinated Pea Salad (recipe above right). Perched unassumingly in the middle of a sea of rich, starchy sides, it was a welcome addition of texture, flavor, and color. Often served from a humble repurposed plastic Country Crock tub, the simple mixture of canned sweet peas and corn with fresh bell pepper, celery, and onion got its sweet, zesty kick from a vinegar-and-oil dressing.

Nana has always known a thing or two about how to properly eat a plate of Southern food. The way she fixes herself a bite is pure magic—she tops every forkful of creamy casserole or greens with a little bit of the salad before popping it into her mouth. She knows that when the peas are added to the other dishes, the whole meal comes to life. If we were a family who went around the room sharing what we were thankful for, I would claim Nana's marinated peas and how they've taught me to season everything with a little tang and a lot of love.

Nana's Marinated Pea Salad
ACTIVE 25 MIN. - TOTAL 1 HOUR, 25 MIN.
MAKES ABOUT 5 CUPS

- 1 cup granulated sugar
- ¾ cup apple cider vinegar
- ⅓ cup vegetable oil
- 1 (15-oz.) can very young small sweet peas, drained and rinsed (such as Le Sueur)
- 1 (11-oz.) can white shoepeg corn, drained and rinsed
- 1 (4-oz.) jar diced pimientos, undrained
- 1 cup finely chopped green bell pepper (from 1 small pepper)
- 1 cup finely chopped sweet onion (from 1 small onion)
- ⅓ cup finely chopped celery (from 1 large stalk)
- 1 tsp. kosher salt
- ½ tsp. black pepper
- Fresh dill fronds and/or parsley leaves

1. Combine sugar, vinegar, and oil in a small saucepan over medium, and cook, undisturbed, until sugar is dissolved, about 6 minutes. Transfer mixture to a heatproof bowl to cool slightly, about 15 minutes.
2. Combine peas, corn, pimientos, bell pepper, onion, celery, salt, and black pepper in a large bowl. Add vinegar mixture, and toss to coat. Chill, covered, at least 1 hour or up to 3 days before serving. Serve, without draining marinating liquid. Garnish with fresh dill or parsley.

NEW TRADITIONS

Spiced-Up Sides

Southern chefs with global roots share their spins on holiday favorites

THE TURKEY doesn't always have to be the center of attention on Thanksgiving. We turned to five chefs—who are originally from all over the world but have come to call the South home—to prove that the sides steal the show. Their riffs on classics combine familiar ingredients with others that might be new to you. The green beans are made creamy with coconut milk instead of canned soup, the sweet potatoes are topped with chile-laced pecans rather than marshmallows, and the Cranberry Chutney (seasoned with ginger, mustard seeds, and cloves) is bound to upstage the typical canned sauce. Infused with bold flavors, these recipes are sure to liven up your feast and complement all your favorite standbys.

Cranberry Chutney

"The one thing that's never missing on my Thanksgiving menu is cranberry sauce, and since sauces are like chutneys, I make this recipe year-round. It has black mustard seeds, ginger, and other ground spices added to the cranberries; the brown sugar balances the tartness. The ingredients are simmered together until the pectin-rich cranberries burst open and the mixture develops a deep, jewellike color." —Palak Patel, chef and cookbook author in Atlanta

ACTIVE 15 MIN. - TOTAL 1 HOUR, 15 MIN.

MAKES 2 CUPS

- 1 lb. fresh or frozen cranberries
- 1 Tbsp. neutral cooking oil (such as canola oil)
- ¼ tsp. black mustard seeds
- ½ cup packed light brown sugar, plus more to taste
- ¼ cup apple cider vinegar
- ⅛ tsp. ground cloves
- ⅛ tsp. cayenne pepper
- 1 (1-inch) piece fresh ginger, peeled and grated (about 1 tsp.)
- ½ to 1 tsp. kosher salt, to taste

1. If using fresh cranberries, discard any stems or soft fruit. If using frozen berries, thaw and drain well.
2. Heat oil in a medium saucepan over medium until shimmering. Add mustard seeds, and cook until they sputter, 30 seconds to 1 minute. Stir in cranberries, brown sugar, ½ cup water, apple cider vinegar, cloves, cayenne pepper, and grated ginger. Cook, stirring occasionally, until cranberries burst and mixture thickens, 10 to 15 minutes. Taste and add sugar as desired.
3. Stir ½ teaspoon of the salt into cranberry mixture, and let cool to room temperature, about 1 hour. Taste chutney, and add more salt, if desired. Serve at room temperature, or transfer to an airtight container and store in refrigerator up to 2 weeks.

Trinidad and Tobago Macaroni Pie

"Macaroni pie is not a dish I would make frequently, mainly because it requires so much discipline to not devour the whole thing! It takes me back to my childhood, as it was a staple for all of our large family gatherings. It's truly the perfect addition to any holiday table." —Sedesh Boodram Wilkerson, chef at The Anvil Pub & Grill in Birmingham

ACTIVE 15 MIN. - TOTAL 55 MIN.

SERVES 6 TO 8

- 3 Tbsp. unsalted butter, divided
- 8 oz. yellow sharp cheddar cheese, grated (2 cups)
- 8 oz. low-moisture mozzarella cheese, grated (2 cups)
- 2 (12-oz.) cans evaporated milk
- 2 garlic cloves, minced (about 2 tsp.)
- 1 large egg, whisked
- ½ small yellow onion, finely diced (about ½ cup)
- ½ fresh Scotch bonnet chile, seeded (if desired) and finely minced (1 tsp.)

- 2 Tbsp. tomato paste
- 2 tsp. Dijon mustard
- 1 tsp. fresh thyme leaves, chopped, plus more for garnish
- 1 tsp. kosher salt, plus more for salting water
  Pinch of black pepper
- 1 lb. dried macaroni

1. Preheat oven to 350°F. Grease a 13- x 9-inch baking dish with 2 tablespoons of the butter.
2. Stir together cheddar and mozzarella in a medium bowl, and set aside. Whisk together evaporated milk, garlic, egg, onion, chile, tomato paste, mustard, thyme, salt, and a generous pinch of black pepper in a large bowl until very well combined. Set aside.
3. Bring a large saucepan of salted water to a boil over high. Cook macaroni according to package directions for al dente. Drain and return macaroni to saucepan. Add remaining 1 tablespoon butter, stirring until melted. Add half of cheese mixture, and stir until fully combined. Stir in reserved evaporated milk mixture until pasta is coated. Pour into prepared baking dish, spreading evenly, and sprinkle top with remaining cheese mixture.
4. Bake in preheated oven until top is golden brown, 30 to 35 minutes. Remove from oven, and let rest at least 10 minutes before serving. Garnish macaroni pie with thyme leaves, if desired.

CREAMED STRING BEANS

RAJAS POBLANAS WITH POTATOES

Braised Sweet Potatoes with Piri Piri Pecans

(Photo, page 279)

"The spices used in American Thanksgiving recipes are everyday ingredients in Cape Town, South Africa, where I'm from. Nutmeg, allspice, cinnamon, and cardamom give these sweet potatoes great depth of flavor. I opted to ditch the classic streusel topping while honoring its crunch with spiced pecans. The piri piri pepper is native to Mozambique, but any chile powder will do." —Dale Gray, cookbook author in Brookhaven, Mississippi

ACTIVE 15 MIN. · TOTAL 1 HOUR, 15 MIN.

SERVES 8

PIRI PIRI PECANS

- 1 Tbsp. extra-virgin olive oil
- 1 cup pecan pieces
- ½ tsp. kosher salt
- ¼ tsp. piri piri or ancho chile powder

BRAISED SWEET POTATOES

- 3 lb. medium-size white sweet potatoes (about 6), peeled and cut into ½-inch slices
- 1 (3-inch) cinnamon stick
- 1 whole star anise
- 8 Tbsp. butter
- 1 cup packed light brown sugar
- ½ cup fresh orange juice (from 1 orange)
- ½ cup fresh lemon juice (from 3 lemons)
- 1 Tbsp. minced fresh ginger
- 2 tsp. ground cinnamon
- 1 tsp. ground cardamom
- ½ tsp. ground allspice
- ½ tsp. kosher salt
- ¼ tsp. ground nutmeg

1. Prepare the Piri Piri Pecans: Heat olive oil in a small skillet over medium. Add pecans, salt, and piri piri; cook, stirring often, until nuts are toasted, 1 to 2 minutes. Transfer to a bowl.
2. Prepare the Braised Sweet Potatoes: Preheat oven to 400°F. Place sliced sweet potatoes, cinnamon stick, and star anise in bottom of a 13- x 9-inch baking dish. Melt butter in a medium saucepan over medium. Add brown sugar, orange juice, lemon juice, ginger, ground cinnamon, cardamom, allspice, salt, and nutmeg; cook, stirring often, until sauce starts to bubble, about 2 minutes.
3. Pour brown sugar mixture over sweet potatoes in baking dish. Gently stir to coat sweet potatoes with sauce. Cover with aluminum foil. Bake in preheated oven until potatoes are fork-tender, about 1 hour, stirring once halfway through baking time. Sprinkle with Piri Piri Pecans. (Leave whole spices for presentation, if desired, but remove before serving.)

Rajas Poblanas with Potatoes

"Thanksgiving is all about sides—with potatoes always taking center stage! I love this dish because it perfectly fits the very American tradition, which I have adopted as an excuse to hang out with friends and share a bit of my roots." —Ana Castro, chef and owner of Acamaya in New Orleans

ACTIVE 30 MIN. · TOTAL 45 MIN.

SERVES 8

- 3 lb. fingerling potatoes
- 5 Tbsp. kosher salt, divided, plus more to taste
- 3 poblano chiles (about 11 oz.)
- ¼ cup unsalted butter
- 1 medium-size yellow onion, thinly sliced (about 2 cups)
- 6 large garlic cloves, thinly sliced (about 3 Tbsp.)
- 1½ (8-oz.) pkg. cream cheese
- ½ serrano chile, stemmed and chopped (about 1 tsp.)
- ½ cup fresh parsley leaves
- ¾ cup heavy whipping cream, warmed
- 1 cup (about 4 oz.) shredded mozzarella cheese (optional)

1. Bring potatoes, 3 quarts water, and 3 tablespoons of the salt to a boil in a large saucepan over high; cook until potatoes are tender, about 18 minutes.
2. While potatoes cook, preheat oven to broil with rack 6 inches from heat source. Place poblanos on a large rimmed baking sheet lined with foil. Broil until charred, 12 to 15 minutes, turning once. Place charred poblanos in a bowl, and cover with a lid or plastic wrap; let steam 10 minutes.
3. Meanwhile, melt butter in a large cast-iron skillet over medium. Add onion, garlic, and 1 tablespoon of salt; cook until onion is softened, about 5 minutes. Remove from heat; set aside.
4. Using a paper towel, rub off charred skin from peppers; remove stems and seeds. Cut 2 poblanos into strips; set aside. Place remaining poblano in a blender along with cream cheese, serrano, and parsley. Add warm cream; process until smooth, about 30 seconds. Pour into skillet with onion mixture; fold in reserved poblano strips. Simmer over medium, stirring often, about 2 minutes.
5. Drain potatoes; return to pan. Using a wooden spoon, smash potatoes; sprinkle with remaining 1 tablespoon salt. Transfer to poblano mixture in skillet; stir to combine. Season with additional salt to taste. Sprinkle with mozzarella (if using). Broil in preheated oven until top is golden and crispy, 2 to 3 minutes.

Creamed String Beans

"I grew up hating vegetables in the Philippines, but for some reason, I love any vegetables that are cooked in coconut milk—especially in this dish. It reminds me of how life can be simple yet amazing. My family was poor, but my siblings and I spent our childhood making lots of fun memories." —Nikko Cagalanan, chef and owner of Kultura in Charleston, South Carolina

ACTIVE 20 MIN. · TOTAL 20 MIN.

SERVES 8

- 2 Tbsp. canola oil
- 5 garlic cloves, crushed
- 1 large white onion, thinly sliced (about 3 cups)
- 1 (4-inch) piece fresh ginger, peeled and cut into thin strips (about ½ cup)
- 2 lb. fresh green beans, trimmed
- 1 (13⅝-oz.) can unsweetened coconut milk, well shaken
- 1 Tbsp. chicken bouillon granules
- 1 tsp. fish sauce, plus more to taste
- 1 tsp. kosher salt, plus more to taste
- ¼ tsp. black pepper, plus more to taste
- 3 scallions, cut into 2-inch pieces
- Cooked rice

1. Heat oil in a large skillet over medium-high. Add garlic, onion, and ginger; cook, stirring often, until onion is softened, about 5 minutes.
2. Add beans to skillet; cook, stirring often, 1 minute. Add coconut milk, bouillon, fish sauce, salt, and pepper. Simmer over medium-high, stirring often, 8 minutes. Add scallions; cook, covered, until beans are tender, about 3 minutes.
3. Season with additional fish sauce, salt, or pepper to taste. Serve with cooked rice.

BUTTERNUT SQUASH SALAD WITH COLLARDS AND RADICCHIO

Go Big With Butternut

Four fresh recipes for autumn's sweetest squash

Butternut Squash Salad with Collards and Radicchio

ACTIVE 25 MIN. - TOTAL 35 MIN.

SERVES 8

- 1 medium butternut squash, peeled, halved lengthwise, seeded, and cut crosswise into ½-inch-thick slices (about 6 cups)
- 5½ Tbsp. olive oil, divided
- 1 tsp. kosher salt, divided
- 10 cups stemmed and torn fresh collard greens (from 1 large bunch)
- 2 tsp. granulated sugar
- ¼ cup red wine vinegar
- 1 Tbsp. Dijon mustard
- 1 garlic clove, minced (about 1 tsp.)
- 2 tsp. pure maple syrup
- 1 tsp. dried oregano
- ½ tsp. black pepper
- 1 cup torn radicchio (from 1 small head)
- ¼ cup thinly sliced red onion (from 1 small onion)
- 1½ cups plain or cornbread croutons
- ½ oz. Parmesan cheese, shaved (about ¼ cup)

1. Preheat oven to 425°F with racks in upper third and lower third positions. Line 2 large rimmed baking sheets with parchment paper. Toss butternut squash, 1 tablespoon of the oil, and ½ teaspoon of the salt in a large bowl until coated. Divide squash evenly among prepared baking sheets, spreading in an even layer. Bake until squash is tender and lightly browned, rotating baking sheets from front to back and top to bottom halfway through, 25 to 30 minutes total. Let cool on pan 5 minutes.
2. While squash is roasting, place collard greens and 2 tablespoons of the oil in the same large bowl. With clean hands, scrunch and crush collard greens thoroughly until leaves turn dark green and are slightly wilted, 2 to 3 minutes. Stir in sugar and remaining ½ teaspoon salt. Let stand, covered, 20 minutes.
3. Whisk together red wine vinegar, mustard, and garlic in a medium bowl. Whisking constantly, gradually drizzle remaining 2½ tablespoons oil into bowl. Whisk in maple syrup, oregano, and pepper until mixture is slightly creamy, about 1 minute. Add to collard greens along with radicchio, onion, and croutons; toss to combine. Add roasted squash; toss gently until coated with dressing. Transfer to a large bowl or platter; top with shaved Parmesan just before serving.

Butternut Squash–and–Fennel Gratin

ACTIVE 25 MIN. - TOTAL 1 HOUR, 25 MIN.

SERVES 8

- 3 Tbsp. unsalted butter
- 1 large fennel bulb, trimmed, cored, and thinly sliced (about 4 cups), fronds reserved
- ¼ cup finely chopped yellow onion (from 1 small onion)
- 1 garlic clove, minced (about 1 Tbsp.)
- 1¼ tsp. kosher salt, divided
- 3 Tbsp. all-purpose flour
- 1½ cups heavy whipping cream
- 1 cup whole milk
- 2 tsp. Dijon mustard
- 1 tsp. black pepper
- ⅛ tsp. ground nutmeg
- 1 large butternut squash, peeled and sliced crosswise into ⅛-inch-thick rounds, seeds removed (about 12 cups)
- 4 oz. Parmesan cheese, grated (about 1¼ cups), divided
- ¼ cup dry breadcrumbs

BUTTERNUT SQUASH–AND–FENNEL GRATIN

1. Preheat oven to 450°F. Melt butter in a 12-inch cast-iron skillet over medium; stir in fennel, onion, garlic, and ½ teaspoon of the salt. Cook, stirring occasionally, until onion is translucent, 3 to 4 minutes.
2. Stir in flour; cook, stirring constantly, until flour coats vegetables, about 1 minute. Stir in cream, milk, mustard, pepper, nutmeg, and remaining ¾ teaspoon salt. Bring to a simmer over medium; cook, stirring occasionally, until mixture thickens slightly, about 2 minutes. Remove from heat; transfer 2 cups of the cream mixture to a medium bowl. Set aside.
3. Layer half of butternut squash rounds over remaining cream mixture in skillet, overlapping slices slightly. Top with 1 cup of the reserved cream mixture and ¼ cup of the Parmesan. Repeat with remaining cream mixture and squash and ¼ cup of the Parmesan. Loosely cover skillet with aluminum foil; bake in preheated oven until squash is tender, 35 to 40 minutes.
4. Reduce oven temperature to 400°F. Remove and discard aluminum foil; top evenly with breadcrumbs and remaining ¾ cup Parmesan. Bake until sauce is bubbling and cheese is golden brown around the edges, 20 to 25 minutes. Remove from oven, and let stand 15 minutes to allow the sauce to absorb and the gratin to settle. Garnish with reserved fennel fronds just before serving.

WHIPPED BUTTERNUT SQUASH WITH BACON CRUMBLE

Whipped Butternut Squash with Bacon Crumble

ACTIVE 30 MIN. · TOTAL 1 HOUR
SERVES 8

- 2 (3-inch) rosemary sprigs, plus 1 tsp. chopped fresh rosemary, divided
- 2 medium unpeeled butternut squash, halved lengthwise and seeds removed
- 6 bacon slices
- 6 Tbsp. butter
- ½ cup whole smoked almonds, chopped
- ¼ cup heavy whipping cream
- 2 Tbsp. dark brown sugar
- 1 tsp. pumpkin pie spice
- ¾ tsp. kosher salt
- ½ tsp. ground allspice

1. Preheat oven to 450°F with racks in upper third and lower third positions. Place rosemary sprigs on a large rimmed baking sheet; place squash over rosemary, cut sides down. Bake on upper rack until very tender, 40 to 45 minutes, rotating pan halfway through. Remove from oven; let stand until squash are cool enough to handle, 15 minutes.

2. While squash are cooking, arrange bacon in a single layer on an aluminum foil–lined baking sheet. Bake in preheated oven on lower rack until bacon is crisp, 12 to 15 minutes. Transfer bacon to a paper towel–lined plate, and set aside.

3. Heat butter in a medium saucepan over medium until melted, about 2 minutes. Cook over medium, stirring occasionally, until foamy, about 1 minute. Reduce heat to low, and cook until lightly browned, about 2 minutes. Transfer ¼ cup butter to a large heatproof bowl; set aside. Stir almonds and chopped rosemary into remaining butter in saucepan. Cook over medium-low, stirring often, until lightly toasted, about 1 minute. Remove from heat.

4. Scoop out squash flesh; discard skins and rosemary sprigs. Place squash in a food processor with reserved ¼ cup butter, cream, brown sugar, pumpkin pie spice, salt, and allspice; blend until smooth, 1 to 2 minutes. Transfer to a large serving bowl.

5. Chop bacon into small pieces, and stir into almond mixture. Sprinkle squash mixture with 2 tablespoons of the bacon topping. Serve with remaining topping.

Rice-and-Poblano-Stuffed Butternut Squash

ACTIVE 20 MIN. · TOTAL 1 HOUR, 20 MIN.
SERVES 8

- 2 medium unpeeled butternut squash with stems trimmed, cut lengthwise with seeds left intact
- 5 Tbsp. olive oil, divided
- 2½ tsp. kosher salt, divided
- 1 cup long-grain and wild rice mix
- 2 cups chopped fresh shiitake mushrooms (from 1 [8-oz.] pkg.)
- ½ cup finely chopped yellow onion (from 1 small onion)
- 1 medium poblano chile, chopped (about ¾ cup)
- 3 garlic cloves, chopped (about 1 Tbsp.)
- 1 tsp. ground cumin
- ¼ tsp. black pepper
- ½ cup dried cranberries
- ¼ cup raw unsalted pumpkin seed kernels (pepitas)
- Chopped fresh cilantro, for garnish

1. Preheat oven to 450°F. Brush cut sides of butternut squash with 1 tablespoon of the oil, and sprinkle cut sides evenly with 1 teaspoon of the salt. Arrange squash cut sides down on a large rimmed baking sheet. Bake until tender, 40 to 45 minutes, rotating pan from front to back halfway through.

2. Remove from oven. Carefully turn squash over, and let stand 15 minutes. Keeping squash halves on baking sheet, scoop out and discard seeds with a spoon. Leaving a ½-inch border, scoop flesh from neck portion of each squash; cut into ½-inch cubes. Transfer to a medium bowl.

3. While squash are cooking, rinse rice in a fine mesh strainer under running water. Place rice, 1⅔ cups water, 1 tablespoon of the oil, and ½ teaspoon of the salt in a medium saucepan; bring to a boil over high. Reduce heat to low; cover and cook until rice is cooked through, about 45 minutes. Remove from heat; let stand, covered, 10 minutes. Fluff rice with a fork. Cover and set aside.

4. Heat remaining 3 tablespoons oil in a large nonstick skillet over medium. Add mushrooms, onion, and poblano; cook, stirring often, until softened and browned in spots, about 5 minutes. Stir in garlic, cumin, black pepper, and remaining 1 teaspoon salt. Cook, stirring constantly, until fragrant, about 30 seconds. Stir in cooked rice and roasted squash cubes. Remove from heat; stir in cranberries and pumpkin seeds.

5. Spoon rice mixture into each squash half; cover loosely with aluminum foil, and bake in preheated oven until heated through, 5 to 7 minutes. Transfer to a platter, and garnish with cilantro.

RICE-AND-POBLANO-STUFFED BUTTERNUT SQUASH

SNACK TIME

Sip and Savor

Serve this elegant duo to tide over your guests until the big feast

Spicy Pear-and-Cheddar Bites
ACTIVE 15 MIN. - TOTAL 20 MIN.
SERVES 8

Stir together 3 Tbsp. each **extra-virgin olive oil** and melted **unsalted butter**, 2 tsp. minced **garlic**, 1½ tsp. finely chopped **fresh thyme**, and ¼ tsp. each **garlic powder** and **kosher salt** in a medium bowl. Arrange 24 **large round buttery crackers** (such as Breton) in a single layer on 2 rimmed baking sheets lined with parchment paper; brush with olive oil mixture. Bake at 350°F with racks in top third and lower third positions until golden brown, about 6 minutes. Transfer crackers to a platter; top each with a slice of **smoked sharp white cheddar cheese** and a thin slice of **red Anjou pear**. Spoon ½ tsp. **hot pepper jelly** over each pear slice; garnish with **fresh thyme**.

Bourbon Sparkler
ACTIVE 5 MIN. - TOTAL 5 MIN.
SERVES 1

Place 1 **brown sugar cube** in the bottom of a coupe glass; add 5 dashes of **whiskey barrel-aged bitters** (such as Fee Brothers). Pour in 1 Tbsp. **bourbon**, and gently stir to combine. (Sugar will not be completely dissolved.) Top with ½ cup **Champagne**; garnish with a **lemon twist**.

OVER EASY

The Big Cheese

Satisfy a full house with this savory bacon, egg, and cheddar casserole

BREAD WINNER
If you can't find brioche, use a loaf of King's Hawaiian sliced bread.

Cheese Dreams Breakfast Casserole

ACTIVE 20 MIN. - TOTAL 1 HOUR, 10 MIN.
SERVES 8

- Cooking spray
- 4 oz. extra-sharp yellow cheddar cheese, finely shredded (about 1 cup)
- ½ cup unsalted butter, softened
- ¼ tsp. smoked paprika
- 1½ tsp. Worcestershire sauce, divided
- 1¼ tsp. dry mustard, divided
- ½ tsp. cayenne pepper, divided
- 14 (½-inch-thick) slices brioche, crusts trimmed, lightly toasted (from 1 [14-oz.] loaf)
- 8 large eggs
- 2 cups half-and-half
- 1 tsp. kosher salt
- 6 thick-cut bacon slices, cooked and crumbled
- 1 Tbsp. finely chopped chives

1. Preheat oven to 350°F. Grease a 13- x 9-inch baking dish with cooking spray. Set aside.
2. Beat cheese and butter in a medium bowl with an electric mixer on medium speed until blended, about 15 seconds. Add smoked paprika, ½ teaspoon of the Worcestershire, and ¼ teaspoon each of the dry mustard and cayenne; beat until incorporated, about 10 seconds.
3. Spread 1 tablespoon of the cheese mixture on 1 side of toasted bread slices to cover completely. Cut each slice into 4 squares. Starting in one corner, shingle 14 of the bread squares down the length of prepared dish, overlapping slices slightly. Repeat process with remaining squares to create 4 rows of 14 (alternate directions with rows, if desired).
4. Whisk together eggs, half-and-half, salt, remaining 1 teaspoon each Worcestershire and dry mustard, and remaining ¼ teaspoon cayenne in same medium bowl. Pour egg mixture over bread in baking dish. Sprinkle with bacon, and cover with aluminum foil.
5. Bake until cheese is melted and egg mixture is puffed, about 30 minutes. Remove foil; bake until lightly browned and filling is set, 10 to 15 minutes more. Let casserole stand 10 minutes before slicing. Sprinkle with chives.

COOKING SCHOOL

TIPS AND TRICKS FROM THE SOUTH'S MOST TRUSTED KITCHEN

How To Make a Darn Good Gravy

Perfect our richest, silkiest sauce ever (page 272) with these steps

1. SAUTÉ
Brown the turkey neck, giblets, onion, carrots, celery, and garlic. This creates flavorful bits (known as "fond") in the bottom of the pan that will add depth to the base of the gravy.

2. DEGLAZE
Pour in wine (or water) to release the brown bits, scraping the bottom of the pan with a wooden spatula to loosen any stubborn spots. Cook until the liquid has almost evaporated.

3. INCLUDE HERBS
Add chicken stock along with parsley, thyme, and bay leaves. Simmer, undisturbed, until reduced by about half to help concentrate and enrich the mixture. Strain, discard solids, and set aside stock.

4. SEPARATE
While the turkey rests, strain the drippings. Pour them into a fat separator, and let sit for 5 minutes; use the fat for the roux. Or chill the drippings, and skim the solids off the top with a spoon.

5. MAKE A ROUX
Heat 3 tablespoons of the fat in a saucepan over medium heat. Add flour, and cook, whisking constantly, until toasted. Don't rush this process, or your gravy will taste like raw flour.

6. FINISH
Gradually pour the reserved stock into the roux, whisking constantly. Add the strained drippings. Cook, stirring often, until the mixture coats the back of a spoon. Season with salt and pepper to taste before serving.

December

290 Precious Persimmons Savor this tart fruit during its short-but-sweet harvest season

292 The Gift of Fudge Re-creating a family recipe is a true labor of love

293 Get In the Spirit Mix and mingle with three easy cocktails

295 Party Like It's 1984 Entertaining is quite different than it was forty years ago, but our recipes stand the test of time

298 Elegant Made Easy Tender braised short ribs are fancy enough for Christmas dinner or any special occasion. Bonus: They're make-ahead!

300 Festival of Bites Few people can turn down the fabulous fried foods that grace Hanukkah tables

304 Just Heavenly Yeast is the secret to biscuits so light they almost float off your plate

305 A Cake for Every Baker This delicious-yet-doable dessert can be made three different ways

312 Orange Crush Stunning citrus desserts to wow your crowd

320 The Ultimate *Southern Living* Cookie Tin Looking for a spectacular (but simple) recipe for this year's swap? These recipes are anything but cookie-cutter

330 Thumbs Up Three twists on the classic chocolate-filled cookie

332 Made With Love Turn gift-giving into something more meaningful and less stressful, Southern style

334 The Delicious Mystery of Court Bouillon Jessica B. Harris unravels the origin of this famous Louisiana dish with French and Caribbean roots

336 The Legend of the Lasagna Ivy Odom shares how family recipes can get a little lost in translation

338 Rosalynn Carter's Traveling Pimiento Cheese Memories of the former First Lady and her beloved family recipe

339 Baking School Our Test Kitchen professionals highlight how pudding mix is the secret to a rich chocolate fudge and a tender chocolate chip cookie

340 Cooking School Our Test Kitchen professionals share how to make crispy, never-greasy, golden-brown latkes

BOUNTY

Precious Persimmons

Savor this tart fruit during its short-but-sweet harvest season

Spiced Persimmon Quick Bread
ACTIVE 25 MIN. - TOTAL 2 HOURS
SERVES 10

Coat an 8½- x 4½-inch loaf pan with **baking spray**. Line with **parchment paper**, leaving a 2-inch overhang on long sides. Stir together ¾ cup **Hachiya persimmon puree** (below right) and 1 tsp. **baking soda** in a large bowl until combined. Sift together 1¼ cups **all-purpose flour**, 1 tsp. **ground cinnamon**, and ¾ tsp. **ground ginger** in a bowl. Whisk 2 **large eggs**, 1 cup packed **light brown sugar**, ⅓ cup melted **unsalted butter**, 2 tsp. **vanilla extract**, and ¾ tsp. **kosher salt** into persimmon mixture until combined; gradually stir in flour mixture until just combined. Spread batter evenly into prepared loaf pan; top with 6 very thin slices of unpeeled ripe **Fuyu persimmon**, overlapping slightly as needed. Bake at 350°F until a wooden pick inserted into center of bread comes out clean, 55 minutes to 1 hour, 10 minutes, loosely covering with foil to prevent overbrowning, if needed. Let bread cool in pan 10 minutes. Using parchment paper as handles, remove from pan and transfer to a wire rack. Stir together 1 Tbsp. warmed **honey** and ⅛ tsp. **ground ginger** in a bowl; brush over top and sides of bread. Let cool 30 minutes before serving.

Persimmon-and-Arugula Salad
ACTIVE 15 MIN. - TOTAL 15 MIN.
SERVES 4

Whisk together ¼ cup **olive oil**, 3 Tbsp. **Champagne vinegar**, 1 Tbsp. finely chopped **red onion**, 2 tsp. **honey**, 2 tsp. **Dijon mustard**, ½ tsp. **kosher salt**, and ¼ tsp. **black pepper** in a bowl until smooth. Place 6 cups **arugula**, 3 cups thinly sliced **Fuyu persimmons** (from 1 lb. halved ripe persimmons), and 3 Tbsp. chopped **roasted salted pistachios** in a large bowl; toss with desired amount of dressing until coated. Sprinkle with ½ cup **pomegranate arils** and ¼ cup crumbled **goat cheese**. Serve with remaining dressing on the side.

SPICED PERSIMMON QUICK BREAD

HOW TO MAKE PERSIMMON PUREE
Pureed persimmons give this bread flavor and moisture. To prepare, simply peel and quarter 3 (4-oz.) ripe Hachiya persimmons; then puree in a blender until smooth, about 45 seconds. We recommend using Hachiyas, which are widely available and are soft when ripe.

PERSIMMON-AND-ARUGULA SALAD

HOSPITALITY

The Gift of Fudge

Re-creating a family recipe is a true labor of love

HIS NAME was James Bray, Jimmy to friends and Papaw to me. To the employees of his doctors' offices, our church, and the salon where my grandmother got her hair done every week, he was the man who brought peanut butter fudge at Christmas.

During the holidays, my grandfather always had a CorningWare dish filled with fudge tucked away in the refrigerator. He wanted to make sure there were plenty of pieces on hand for anyone who came by—and, of course, for himself. Then, just before workplaces would close for the winter break and everyone would depart for the end-of-year respite, he'd make batch after batch for these important people, delivering the sweet cubes of candy in humble plastic containers to their desks.

The grateful recipients would tell him how they looked forward to this moment all year, how they circled his appointments on the calendar so they could be present. No one wanted to miss out. They said his peanut butter fudge, edged with a hint of cocoa, was richer and smoother than any other they'd ever had.

Fudge is a gift. Or, rather, making it is a gift. It's not the simplest confection. It requires patience and persistence, and you must be observant to the slightest shifts in texture and color. Perhaps that's why no one else in my family had been eager to learn. No one, except me.

Every time my grandfather made his fudge, I stood watch. He'd bring out the recipe card, one written by his mother many decades before and updated in his thin scrawl, and he'd have me follow along as he brought the sugar and evaporated milk to a boil. He had made this recipe so many times he no longer bothered with a candy thermometer. He didn't need a timer either. After stirring and swirling his way through hundreds of batches, he knew the fudge by feel, and it rarely failed him.

The first batches I made after he died, however, failed me. Without him, the recipe was nothing but a jumble of words. He'd updated ingredients and amounts as products changed over time, and I forgot his clarifications, ones left unwritten on the index card, stained and soiled with decades of use. My first attempt burned. Scorched, even. The molten sugar had nearly become one with the cast-iron skillet, scarring the requisite wooden spoon that he had approved for use.

But I became better, and the batches of candy did too. Now, my family will tell others that I know how to make Papaw's fudge, and they'll request it, eager to recapture that moment of bliss they felt with the first bite.

I make the recipe so infrequently I have to concentrate like I'm taking a college admissions test, but an unspoken entreaty comes out with the index card, a nudge from my grandfather to make another batch and keep trying. "It took me years to get it right too," he told me—and then he'd pass me the peanut butter and wooden spoon and say try again.
—Kimberly Holland

Papaw's Peanut Butter Fudge
ACTIVE 20 MIN. · TOTAL 4 HOURS, 20 MIN.
SERVES 20

- 2 cups granulated sugar
- 2 Tbsp. unsweetened cocoa
- 1 (5-oz.) can evaporated milk
- 1 Tbsp. unsalted butter, plus more for greasing baking pan
- 1¼ cups creamy peanut butter
- 1 tsp. vanilla extract

1. Grease an 8-inch square baking pan with butter; set aside.
2. Stir together sugar and cocoa powder in a medium saucepan; stir in evaporated milk, 4 teaspoons water, and the 1 tablespoon butter. Heat over medium, stirring often, until sugar is dissolved. Bring to a boil over medium, stirring often. Boil, stirring often, until a thermometer registers 226°F to 227°F, about 3 minutes, 30 seconds.
3. Remove from heat, and immediately stir in peanut butter and vanilla. Stir vigorously until peanut butter is fully incorporated and mixture thickens slightly. Quickly pour into prepared baking pan, and smooth into an even layer. Set aside, and let cool completely, about 4 hours. (Alternatively, let cool slightly at room temperature, about 30 minutes; chill, uncovered, in refrigerator until fully chilled, about 1 hour.) Once cooled, cut into 1-inch squares.

BAR CART

Get In the Spirit

Mix and mingle with three easy cocktails

White Cranberry Cosmo
ACTIVE 5 MIN. - TOTAL 5 MIN.
SERVES 2

Place 6 tablespoons (3 oz.) **vodka**, 6 tablespoons **white cranberry juice**, 2 tablespoons (1 oz.) **elderflower liqueur** (such as St-Germain), and 2 tablespoons fresh **lemon juice** in a cocktail shaker filled with **ice.** Cover, and shake until chilled, about 15 seconds. Strain into 2 chilled martini glasses, and garnish with fresh or frozen **cranberries,** if desired.

Satsuma Margarita
ACTIVE 5 MIN. - TOTAL 5 MIN.
SERVES 2

Place 6 tablespoons (3 oz.) **añejo tequila,** 6 tablespoons fresh **satsuma or orange juice,** ¼ cup (2 oz.) **orange liqueur** (such as Cointreau), and 3 tablespoons fresh **lime juice** in a cocktail shaker filled with **ice.** Cover, and shake until chilled, about 15 seconds. Strain into 2 coupe glasses. Garnish each drink with a **satsuma slice** dipped in margarita salt, if desired.

Pomegranate French 75
ACTIVE 5 MIN. - TOTAL 5 MIN.
SERVES 2

Place 6 tablespoons (3 oz.) **gin,** ¼ cup refrigerated **pomegranate juice,** 2 tablespoons **lemon juice,** and 2 tablespoons **simple syrup** in a cocktail shaker filled with **ice.** Cover, and shake until chilled, about 15 seconds. Strain into 2 glasses; gradually pour ¼ cup chilled **Champagne** into each glass. Garnish each drink with a **lemon twist** and **pomegranate arils,** if desired.

CHRISTMAS RELISH TREE WITH CHUNKY ONION DIP

CRAB PUFFS
(PAGE 297)

REFRESHING CHAMPAGNE PUNCH (PAGE 297)

Party Like It's 1984

Entertaining is quite different than it was forty years ago, but our recipes stand the test of time

IT STARTED with a missing salad. Back in 2021, a reader named Susan posted this message to the 30,000+ members of our "What's Cooking With *Southern Living*" Facebook group: "I am missing page 325 from my 1984 SL annual cookbook and it has my favorite salad (oranges, bacon, nuts) on it. Ugh!! If anyone has that page could you please post a photo of the front and back? Thank you."

If you think that this is a long shot request (A salad? From the 1980s?), you don't know our readers. They came to Susan's rescue immediately, sharing images from their 1984 *Southern Living Annual Recipes* cookbook. These hardcover recipe archives occupy a special place on many people's shelves. Often handed down through the generations, these books are not only a helpful reference, they are a time capsule of how Southerners ate and entertained. As a commenter named Dotty replied to Susan: "So glad to know I'm not the only one holding onto all those old annual cookbooks! '83 and '84 were the best!" (We love them all.)

After that, we noticed other mentions of 1984 here and there on our social media channels. Commenters shared beloved recipes and photos of their tattered books flagged with paper clips and missing covers from so much use. Others purchased used copies and joined the bandwagon. One wrote: "I'm sitting here reading the book like a novel and so happy that I bought it!"

What was it about 1984 that was so special? We decided to find out. The *Southern Living* food team prepared several recipes from the November and December issues and gathered to enjoy them together. Forty years later, they still held up. Our menu of appetizers and snacks, like Crab Puffs and onion dip, felt nostalgic but still right for a modern-day party. (Although Senior Food Editor Josh Miller couldn't resist making the holiday relish tree with a Styrofoam cone and lots of crudités—a trend that has surprisingly resurfaced on Instagram.)

Cooks in 1984 could never have imagined today's world, where you can search for any recipe in the palm of your hand, find it in seconds, share it with others instantly, and get feedback from people all over the world. Staying true to the theme, we kept the internet and smartphones out of our holiday celebration—not an easy task for editors. But distraction-free, we were able to focus on the tasty spread of food and the good company. The Party Cheese Ball wasn't the most beautiful dish in the world, but no one felt the need to post a photo of it on Facebook. We were too busy eating it, anyway.

Christmas Relish Tree

Originally submitted by Margaret Long, Forsyth, GA
ACTIVE 45 MIN. - TOTAL 1 HR.
SERVES 12

1. Remove and discard stems from 2 bunches **curly kale.** Begin to form the tree by attaching leaves to the bottom of 1 **Styrofoam cone,** about 1½ feet tall, with **florist picks,** and move upward, completely covering the cone with kale.
2. Attach 12 **cooked and peeled medium shrimp,** 1 carton **cherry tomatoes,** 1 sliced **zucchini,** ½ head **cauliflower,** separated into florets, and 4 **carrots,** cut into 2-inch sticks to kale-covered cone with **wooden picks,** arranging in desired pattern to resemble a decorated Christmas tree.
3. Using a small paring knife, trim the stem and root end of each **radish.** Working your way around the radish from bottom to top, make a series of shallow cuts to create "petals" all around the radish. Place radish roses in a bowl of ice water for 15 minutes.
4. Place tree on a tray or cake stand; arrange radish roses and extra vegetables around the base, if desired.

2024 DECEMBER 295

PARTY CHEESE BALL

CHOCOLATE VELVETS

CHEESE-BACON CRISPIES

HARVEST POPCORN

Chunky Onion Dip

(Photo, page 294)

Originally submitted by
Mary Linda Brooks, Hayes, VA
ACTIVE 5 MIN. - TOTAL 5 MIN.
SERVES 8

Combine 1 (8-oz.) package **cream cheese**, softened, ½ cup **mayonnaise**, ¼ cup **chili sauce** (such as Heinz), ¼ tsp. **Worcestershire** sauce, and ¼ tsp. **salt** in a bowl; beat at medium speed with an electric mixer until smooth. Stir in ¾ cup finely chopped **green onions**, blending well. Chill if desired. Garnish with additional chopped green onions; serve with **raw vegetables**.

Refreshing Champagne Punch

(Photo, page 295)

Originally submitted by
Susan Laubacher, Marietta, GA
ACTIVE 15 MIN. - TOTAL 2 HOURS, 15 MIN.
SERVES 12

Bring 2 cups **water** to a boil in a large saucepan; add 1 **family-size tea bag**. Remove from heat; let stand 3 minutes. Remove tea bag. Add 1⅓ cups **granulated sugar**, 1 cup **lemon juice**, and 1 cup **lime juice**, stirring until sugar dissolves. Transfer to punch bowl; refrigerate 2 hours. Stir in 3 cups **club soda** and 2 (750-milliliter) bottles **Champagne**. Garnish with **lemon and lime slices**, if desired.

Party Cheese Ball

Originally submitted by
Mrs. J. D. McMullen, Georgetown, KY
ACTIVE 15 MIN. - TOTAL 15 MIN.
SERVES 12

Combine 12 oz. softened **cream cheese**, 1 (4.25-oz.) can **deviled ham spread**, 2 cups (8 oz.) shredded **sharp cheddar cheese**, 2 Tbsp. finely chopped **pimiento-stuffed olives**, 2 Tbsp. fresh chopped **chives**, 1 Tbsp. prepared **mustard**, ¼ tsp. **celery salt**, ¼ tsp. **dry mustard**, and ¼ tsp. **crushed red pepper**; mix well. Cover and chill 30 minutes. Shape into a ball; roll in 1 cup chopped **pecans**. Wrap and chill. Serve with **crackers**.

Chocolate Velvets

Originally submitted by
Cynthia Kannenberg, Brown Deer, WI
ACTIVE 40 MIN. - TOTAL 9 HOURS, 40 MIN.
SERVES 18

Position knife blade in food processor bowl. Break 12 oz. **milk chocolate** into pieces, and place in bowl; process until finely chopped. Heat ¾ cup **whipping cream** and ¼ cup unsalted **butter** in a small saucepan over medium, stirring occasionally, until butter is melted, about 3 minutes. With processor running, add hot cream mixture; continue processing 1 minute. Stir in 1½ tablespoons **Kahlúa**. Pour mixture into a bowl; cover and chill overnight. Shape mixture into ¾-inch balls, and roll in **chocolate-flavored sprinkles**. Freeze 1 hour or until firm.

Cheese-Bacon Crispies

Originally submitted by
Lynn Bartlett, Jacksonville, FL
ACTIVE 15 MIN. - TOTAL 45 MIN., PLUS 8 HOURS CHILLING
SERVES 12

Combine ½ cup softened **unsalted butter** or margarine, 2 cups (8 oz.) shredded sharp **cheddar cheese**, ¼ tsp. **salt**, ¼ tsp. **dry mustard**, 1 tsp. **Worcestershire** sauce, and 3 drops **hot sauce** in a large bowl; mix well. Stir in 1¼ cups all-purpose **flour** and 1 cup cooked, crumbled **bacon**. Shape dough into 2 rolls, 1½ inches in diameter. Wrap in plastic wrap; chill overnight. Preheat oven to 375°F. Unwrap rolls; cut into ¼-inch-thick slices. Place slices on lightly greased baking sheets; bake for 10 to 13 minutes or until lightly browned. Let cool on pans 5 minutes, then cool completely on a wire rack.

Harvest Popcorn

Originally submitted by
Joyce Andrews, Washington, VA
ACTIVE 10 MIN. - TOTAL 30 MIN.
SERVES 12

Preheat oven to 350°F. Combine 8 cups freshly popped unsalted **popcorn**, 2 (1.75-oz.) cans **potato sticks**, and 2 cups salted **mixed nuts** on a large rimmed baking sheet. Combine 6 Tbsp.

unsalted **butter**, melted, 1 tsp. **lemon pepper seasoning**, 1 tsp. dried whole **dill weed**, 1 tsp. **Worcestershire** sauce, ½ tsp. **garlic powder**, and ½ tsp. **onion powder**; pour over popcorn mixture, stirring until evenly coated. Bake until toasted, about 8 minutes, stirring mixture once halfway through. Let cool on baking sheet slightly, about 10 minutes, before transferring to a serving bowl. Sprinkle with **salt** to taste.

Crab Puffs

(Photo, page 294)

Originally submitted by
Eileen Wehling, Austin, TX
ACTIVE 30 MIN. - TOTAL 1 HOUR, 20 MIN.
SERVES 12

Preheat oven to 400°F. Combine 1 cup **water**, ½ cup unsalted **butter** or margarine, and ½ tsp. **salt** in a medium saucepan; bring mixture to a boil. Reduce heat to low; add 1 cup all-purpose **flour**, and stir vigorously until mixture leaves sides of pan and forms a smooth ball. Remove saucepan from heat, and allow mixture to cool slightly, about 10 minutes. While mixture is cooling, stir together 1 (8-oz.) pkg. fresh **lump crab meat**, drained and flaked, ½ cup (2 oz.) shredded **sharp cheddar cheese**, 3 chopped **green onions**, 1 tsp. **dry mustard**, and 1 tsp. **Worcestershire** sauce in a medium bowl until combined. Gradually add 4 large **eggs** to flour mixture, beating with a wooden spoon after each addition until smooth. Add crab mixture; stir well. Drop batter by heaping teaspoonfuls onto 2 parchment-lined baking sheets. Bake in batches in preheated oven for 15 minutes; reduce heat to 350°F, and bake 10 minutes more. Garnish with chopped fresh **chives**.

SUPPERTIME

Elegant Made Easy

Tender braised short ribs are fancy enough for Christmas dinner or any special occasion. Bonus: They're make-ahead!

Bourbon-Braised Short Ribs

Fall-apart tender and blessedly easy, the beef tastes even better the next day.

ACTIVE 40 MIN. · TOTAL 2 HOURS, 40 MIN.

SERVES 6 TO 8

- 5 lb. beef short ribs (about 8 to 10 short ribs)
- 1½ Tbsp. kosher salt
- 1 tsp. black pepper
- 3 Tbsp. canola oil
- 1 yellow onion, finely chopped (1½ cups)
- 4 celery stalks, finely chopped (1 cup)
- 4 garlic cloves, peeled and smashed
- 3 dried bay leaves
- 2 Tbsp. tomato paste
- 2½ cups lower-sodium beef broth
- 1 cup bourbon
- 3 Tbsp. molasses
- 2 Tbsp. Worcestershire sauce
- 3 Tbsp. whole-grain mustard, divided

   Chopped fresh tender herbs (such as parsley or tarragon)

1. Preheat oven to 325°F. Sprinkle short ribs with salt and pepper on a baking sheet. Heat oil in a large Dutch oven over medium-high until shimmering. Working in batches, sear ribs, turning occasionally, until deeply browned on all sides, 10 to 15 minutes. Return to baking sheet, reserving 2 tablespoons drippings in Dutch oven. Discard remaining drippings.

2. Add onion, celery, garlic, and bay leaves to Dutch oven; cook over medium, stirring often, until onion is lightly browned, about 8 minutes. Add tomato paste; stir until vegetable mixture is coated, about 1 minute. Stir in broth, bourbon, molasses, Worcestershire, and 2 tablespoons of the mustard.

3. Nestle ribs into Dutch oven, meaty sides down. Bring liquid to a simmer over medium. Cover and transfer to preheated oven; bake until short ribs are tender, 2 hours to 2 hours and 15 minutes.

4. Using a slotted spoon, gently transfer short ribs to a serving platter. Pour braising liquid through a fine mesh strainer into a large bowl or measuring cup. Gently press on solids to extract any liquid; discard solids. Skim and discard any fat. Stir remaining

1 tablespoon mustard into braising liquid. Transfer braising liquid to a bowl; spoon over short ribs just before serving. Garnish with herbs.

Slow Cooker Bourbon-Braised Short Ribs

If you have the time, prepare these short ribs in your slow cooker for equally tasty results.

Prepare recipe as directed through Step 2. Omit Step 3; spoon onion mixture into a 6-quart slow cooker. Stir in broth, molasses, Worcestershire, and 2 tablespoons of the mustard. Nestle short ribs into broth mixture in slow cooker, meaty side down. Cover and cook on LOW until short ribs are tender, 8 to 9 hours. Proceed with Step 4 as directed.

Smoked Gouda Grits

Thanks to quick-cooking grits, this side dish comes together in less than half an hour. You can make this recipe up to three days ahead; simply reheat in a large saucepan over medium-low, stirring in a splash or two of milk for a creamy consistency, if needed.

ACTIVE 25 MIN. · TOTAL 25 MIN.

SERVES 8

- 4 cups whole milk
- 3 garlic cloves, peeled and smashed
- 2 fresh bay leaves
- 1 Tbsp. kosher salt
- ½ tsp. black pepper, plus more for garnish
- 2 cups uncooked regular grits
- 12 oz. smoked Gouda, mozzarella, or cheddar cheese, shredded (about 3 cups)
- ¼ cup unsalted butter, cut into pieces, plus more for serving

1. Bring milk, 4 cups water, garlic, bay leaves, salt, and black pepper to a simmer in a large saucepan over medium-high, stirring occasionally. Reduce heat to medium-low; remove and discard garlic and bay leaves.

2. Gradually whisk in grits. Cook, whisking constantly, until mixture starts to thicken, 2 to 3 minutes. Cover, reduce heat to low, and cook, stirring and scraping bottom of saucepan often, until grits are tender and creamy, about 15 minutes.

3. Remove from heat; stir in cheese and butter until melted and combined, about 1 minute. If making ahead, transfer grits to a resealable container, and refrigerate for up to 3 days. To serve, transfer grits to a large bowl. Garnish with additional black pepper; top with a pat of butter while grits are still warm, if desired. Serve immediately.

Winter Salad with Fennel and Oranges

With rich dishes like beef short ribs and cheesy grits on the menu, this fresh, citrus-filled salad is just what you need to perk up your palate. Customize this recipe to suit your family's tastes by trading the fennel for thinly sliced red onion, or using sweetened dried cranberries in lieu of the cherries.

ACTIVE 20 MIN. · TOTAL 20 MIN.

SERVES 8

- 3 Tbsp. apple cider vinegar
- 3 Tbsp. orange marmalade
- 2 tsp. Dijon mustard
- 1 tsp. kosher salt
- ½ tsp. black pepper
- ⅓ cup olive oil
- 1 bunch fresh collard greens, stemmed and chopped (5 packed cups)
- 1 bunch rainbow chard, stemmed and chopped (6 cups)
- 1 fennel bulb, cored and very thinly sliced (2 cups)
- ½ cup dried cherries, divided
- ½ cup chopped smoked almonds, divided
- 2 oz. Parmesan cheese, shaved (about ½ cup), divided
- ½ cup orange segments (from 1 lb. oranges)

1. Whisk together vinegar, marmalade, mustard, salt, and pepper in a large bowl until combined. Gradually add oil in a thin, steady stream, whisking until smooth and combined.

2. Add collard greens, chard, and fennel to vinegar mixture in bowl. Massage greens and vinegar mixture with clean hands until greens are wilted and softened, 1 to 2 minutes. Add ¼ cup each of the cherries, almonds, and cheese; toss to combine.

3. Transfer to a large platter, and sprinkle evenly with orange segments and remaining ¼ cup each cherries, almonds, and cheese.

SHINDIGS

Festival of Bites

Few people can turn down the fabulous fried foods that grace Hanukkah tables

EASY LATKES

APPLE CIDER BUTTER

AS A NOD to the miracle of the long-burning menorah, greet guests with a platter of crispy latkes and fun toppings so folks can build their perfect bites. Nothing pairs better with fried foods than sparkling wine, and our DIY drink station (page 302) allows partygoers to customize cocktails with spiced syrups and boozy cherries. Since no party is complete without dessert, cap off the evening with a tower of sufganiyot (Jewish donuts; page 303) topped with honey and pistachios. Whether you say "cheers," "l'chaim," or both, this menu will guarantee all a good night. —Josh Miller

Easy Latkes
ACTIVE 1 HOUR, 15 MIN. - TOTAL 1 HOUR, 15 MIN.
SERVES 12

- 1½ lb. russet potatoes, scrubbed
- 1 medium white onion, peeled
- 3 large eggs, beaten
- ¾ cup all-purpose flour
- 1½ tsp. baking powder
- 1 Tbsp. kosher salt, plus more to taste
- Vegetable oil
- Apple Cider Butter, Smoky Tomato Butter, and Fancy Ranch (recipes follow), smoked salmon, chopped fresh chives, fresh parsley, pickled onions, pimiento cheese, cornichons

1. Preheat oven to 200°F. Place a wire rack on a rimmed baking sheet; set aside. Grate potatoes and onion on largest holes of box grater. Working in batches, place grated potato and onion in a kitchen towel; squeeze firmly to remove excess liquid. Place squeezed potato and onion in a large bowl; repeat with remaining potato and onion. Stir eggs, flour, baking powder, and 1 tablespoon of the salt into potato mixture until combined.

2. Add oil to a large skillet, filling to a depth of ¼ inch. Heat over medium-high until shimmering, about 5 minutes. Scoop batter in 1-tablespoon portions; carefully add to oil (do not overcrowd pan). Using the back of a spoon, gently flatten each portion to about ¼ inch thick. Cook until golden brown and crispy, 6 to 8 minutes per batch, turning once halfway through cook time. Use a slotted spatula to transfer latkes to prepared baking sheet. Sprinkle with salt to taste; keep warm in preheated oven. Repeat with remaining batter, adding more oil to skillet as needed.

Apple Cider Butter
ACTIVE 5 MIN. - TOTAL 5 MIN.
MAKES ABOUT 1 CUP

Stir together 1 cup jarred **apple butter**, 2 Tbsp. **apple cider vinegar**, and ½ tsp. grated **fresh ginger** in a small bowl until combined. Garnish with chopped fresh **apples** and **flaky sea salt**, as desired.

Smoky Tomato Butter
ACTIVE 20 MIN. - TOTAL 20 MIN.
MAKES ABOUT ¾ CUP

Cook 1 pint **cherry tomatoes** in a medium nonstick skillet over medium-high, stirring often, until skins are blistered, about 8 minutes. Reduce heat to medium; stir in 1 Tbsp. **olive oil**, 1 Tbsp. thinly sliced **garlic**, and ½ tsp. **smoked paprika**. Using back of spoon, press tomatoes to break down; stir well until combined. Stir in 2 Tbsp. **white balsamic vinegar**; cook, stirring often, until slightly thickened, about 5 minutes. Remove from heat; stir in 2 Tbsp. salted **butter** until melted. Garnish with chopped fresh **parsley**, as desired.

Fancy Ranch
ACTIVE 5 MIN. - TOTAL 5 MIN.
MAKES ABOUT 1 CUP

In a medium bowl, whisk together 1 cup **crème fraîche**, ½ cup whole **buttermilk**, and 1 Tbsp. **ranch dressing and seasoning mix** (from 1 [1-oz. envelope]) until smooth.

FANCY RANCH

TOP IT OFF
Store-bought smoked salmon and pimiento cheese are smart shortcuts.

SMOKY TOMATO BUTTER

SET UP A BUBBLY BAR
Let your guests spike their favorite sparkling wines with sugar, spice, and everything nice.

GINGER-CITRUS SPARKLER

CHERRY BOMB COCKTAIL

CRANBERRY-SPICE SPRITZ

BOURBON CHERRIES

Ginger-Citrus Sparkler
Pour 3 tablespoons of the **Ginger-Citrus Mixer** (recipe follows) into a glass; top with ½ cup (4 ounces) chilled **sparkling wine**; garnish with an **orange zest strip**.

Cherry Bomb Cocktail
Place 1 Tbsp. **Bourbon Cherries liquid** and 3 **Bourbon Cherries** (recipe follows) in a glass; top with about ½ cup (4 ounces) chilled **sparkling wine**.

Cranberry-Spice Spritz
Pour 2 Tbsp. **Spiced Cranberry Mixer** (recipe follows) into a glass; top with about ½ cup (4 ounces) chilled **sparkling wine**; garnish with skewered **cranberries**.

Ginger-Citrus Mixer
ACTIVE 5 MIN. - TOTAL 35 MIN.
MAKES ABOUT 2¼ CUPS

Stir together 1½ cups **orange juice** and 1½ tsp. grated **fresh ginger** in a 2-cup measuring cup with a spout; chill 30 minutes. Pour through a fine mesh strainer into a small pitcher; discard solids. Stir in ¾ cup **orange liqueur** (such as Grand Marnier); use immediately, or cover and store in refrigerator up to 1 week.

Bourbon Cherries
ACTIVE 5 MIN. - TOTAL 5 MIN., PLUS 24 HOURS CHILLING
MAKES ABOUT 2 CUPS

Place 1 drained (15-ounce) can **dark sweet cherries** or 1½ cups thawed frozen sweet cherries, ½ cup (4 ounces) **bourbon**, ¼ cup **water**, and 1 (6-inch) split and scraped **vanilla bean** in a heatproof glass jar. Cover with lid; store in refrigerator until infused, at least 24 hours or up to 1 month.

Spiced Cranberry Mixer
ACTIVE 10 MIN. - TOTAL 1 HOUR, 10 MIN.
MAKES ABOUT 1⅓ CUPS

Bring 1½ cups **cranberry juice cocktail**, 3 **cinnamon sticks**, 1 Tbsp. lightly crushed **cardamom pods**, and 1 tsp. whole **allspice** to a simmer in a saucepan over medium. Remove from heat; cover and let steep 30 minutes. Pour through a fine mesh strainer into a small pitcher; discard spices. Cover and refrigerate 30 minutes to 2 weeks.

Pistachio-Honey Donut Tower

ACTIVE 50 MIN. - TOTAL 50 MIN.
SERVES 12

Heat 1½ inches **oil** in a large Dutch oven over medium-high until a deep-fry thermometer registers 350°F. Stir together ½ cup granulated **sugar**, 2 tsp. **cinnamon**, 1 tsp. **cardamom**, and ¼ tsp. **kosher salt** in a medium bowl; set aside. Cut 16 **refrigerated biscuits** (from 2 [16.3-oz.] cans, such as Grands!) into quarters; roll each quarter into a ball. Working in batches, add doughballs to oil. Cook, turning occasionally, until golden brown, about 3 minutes per batch. Remove from oil using a slotted spoon; place in sugar mixture, tossing to coat. Transfer to a baking sheet. Drizzle 2 Tbsp. **honey** on a serving plate; arrange about 25 donut holes in a circle in an even layer. Drizzle with 1 tablespoon honey. Repeat with remaining donut holes and about 5 Tbsp. **honey**, layering to form a tower. Drizzle with 2 Tbsp. **honey**; sprinkle with ¼ cup chopped **salted roasted pistachios**.

BREAD BASKET

Just Heavenly

Yeast is the secret to biscuits so light they almost float off your plate

LITTLE ANGELS
Tuck the dough rounds into the pan tightly so they'll give each other an extra lift as they bake.

Heavenly Angel Biscuits
ACTIVE 30 MIN. - TOTAL 2 HOURS, 50 MIN.
MAKES 2½ DOZEN

- ½ cup warm water (110°F)
- 1 (¼-oz.) envelope active dry yeast
- 1 tsp., plus 3 Tbsp. granulated sugar, divided
- 5 cups all-purpose flour
- 1 Tbsp. baking powder
- 1½ tsp. kosher salt
- 1 tsp. baking soda
- ½ cup cold butter, cubed
- ½ cup shortening, cubed
- 2 cups whole buttermilk
- ¼ cup butter, melted and divided

1. Stir together warm water, yeast, and 1 teaspoon of the sugar in a small bowl. Let stand 5 minutes.
2. Stir together flour, baking powder, salt, baking soda, and remaining 3 tablespoons sugar in a large bowl. Using a pastry blender or 2 forks, cut in cold butter and shortening until mixture is crumbly.
3. Add yeast mixture and buttermilk to flour mixture, stirring just until dry ingredients are moistened.
4. Cover bowl with plastic wrap; chill at least 2 hours or up to 5 days.
5. Preheat oven to 400°F. Turn dough out onto a lightly floured surface, and knead 3 or 4 times. Gently roll into a ½-inch-thick circle. Fold in half; reroll to ½-inch thickness.
6. Cut dough with a 2-inch round cutter. Reroll remaining scraps; cut with cutter. Place rounds with sides touching in a 10- or 12-inch cast-iron skillet or on a parchment paper–lined baking sheet. (If using a 10-inch skillet, place remaining biscuits on a baking sheet.) Brush biscuits with 2 tablespoons of the melted butter.
7. Bake in preheated oven until golden brown, 15 to 20 minutes. Brush with remaining 2 tablespoons melted butter just before serving.

A Cake for Every Baker
This delicious-yet-doable dessert can be made three different ways

WHITE POINSETTIA LAYER CAKE WITH CRANBERRY-ORANGE FILLING (PAGE 309)

THE BIG WHITE CAKE, as it's referred to at the *Southern Living* office, is a big deal to us. These beautiful desserts that've graced every December cover since 1995 involve dozens of meetings, months of planning, and a village of creative folks (recipe developers and testers, photographers, prop and food stylists, and a team of designers and editors) to bring them into the world. It's a true labor of love. But one person deserves extra gifts from Santa this year: Senior Test Kitchen Recipe Developer Tricia Manzanero Stuedeman. She took all of our ideas, hopes, and dreams and transformed them into an elegant and absolutely delicious cake that any baker can pull off. "This project basically lived in my mind rent-free for four months," Stuedeman says. "Me and my husband would go for walks at night, and all I would talk about was the Big White Cake."

This year's showstopper had an additional challenge—we wanted readers to be able to use the same components to make a layer cake, cupcakes, or a sheet cake. "It took a lot of math to figure that out," Stuedeman says with a laugh. "In the end, I was able to make it work with no waste. I'm pretty proud of that!" After she got the rich Brown Butter Cake just right and perfected the sweet-tart cranberry filling, she turned to the frosting, which is made with whipped cream and a surprise ingredient— white chocolate pudding mix. "The pudding stabilizes the whipped cream, so it spreads and pipes like a dream," Stuedeman says. "It can be easily made two days before and refrigerated. It's kind of awesome." No cover cake is complete without a topper, and our candy poinsettias are surprisingly approachable. "I don't consider myself a white chocolate savant by any means," Stuedeman admits. "If I can do it, anyone can." And you don't have to tackle them by yourself. "Make it a project for you and friend," she suggests. "Invite a buddy over to help you, and then catch up over a cup of coffee. Share the work, and share the love."

WHITE POINSETTIA CUPCAKES WITH CRANBERRY-ORANGE FILLING (PAGE 310)

WHITE POINSETTIA SHEET CAKE WITH CRANBERRY-ORANGE FILLING (PAGE 311)

White Poinsettia Layer Cake with Cranberry-Orange Filling

(Photo, page 305)

This is the sum of thoughtfully composed parts. Flavored and fortified with white chocolate pudding, the whipped cream frosting surrounds brown butter–infused cake layers. Crimson cranberry filling is hidden inside like a last-minute gift, bringing just the right amount of brightness.

ACTIVE 45 MIN. - TOTAL 1 HOUR, 15 MIN.
SERVES 12

- Brown Butter Cake (recipe, right)
- Whipped Cream Frosting (recipe, page 310), divided
- Cranberry-Orange Filling (recipe, page 310)
- White Chocolate Candy Leaves (recipe, page 310)
- Gold dragées
- Fresh bay leaves

1. Prepare Brown Butter Cake as directed. Using a serrated knife, trim domed tops of cake layers; discard trimmings. Remove and discard parchment.

2. Place 1 cake layer on a serving plate, trimmed side up; spread ¼ cup of the frosting evenly over top. Spoon 1¼ cups of the frosting into a piping bag or ziplock plastic bag; cut a ½-inch hole in tip or corner. Pipe a ½-inch-tall border of frosting around edge of cake. Spread half of the filling (about ¾ cup) evenly within border. Repeat layers once (set aside frosting in piping bag). Top with remaining cake layer, cut side down. Spread a very thin layer of frosting over top and sides of cake to form a crumb coat. Chill, uncovered, 30 minutes.

3. Spread remaining frosting in bowl or container over top and sides of cake using an offset spatula. Using reserved piping bag, pipe two small mounds of frosting on top of cake about 6 inches apart to serve as bases for the poinsettia flowers. Tuck candy leaves into mounds in a star shape, layering leaves as desired and piping additional frosting on back of leaves as needed. Pipe a small dot of frosting in center of each poinsettia; arrange gold dragées in centers. Tuck in fresh bay leaves as desired. Remove dragées and fresh bay leaves before eating. (Cake components can be prepared in advance; assemble and decorate cake the day you plan to serve it for best results.)

Brown Butter Cake

The key ingredient in this versatile batter is high-quality butter, which is cooked until it is nutty and browned.

ACTIVE 35 MIN. - TOTAL 3 HOURS, 35 MIN.
MAKES 3 (8-INCH) ROUND CAKE LAYERS, 1 (13- X 9-INCH) SHEET CAKE, OR 3 DOZEN CUPCAKES

- 10 Tbsp. unsalted European-style butter (such as Kerrygold)
- 2⅔ cups granulated sugar
- 1 tsp. orange zest (from 1 medium orange)
- ½ cup vegetable oil
- 2½ tsp. vanilla extract
- 5 large eggs, at room temperature
- 3½ cups all-purpose flour
- 1½ Tbsp. cornstarch
- 1½ tsp. ground cinnamon
- 1 tsp. baking powder
- ¾ tsp. kosher salt
- ½ tsp. baking soda
- 1¼ cups whole buttermilk, at room temperature
- ¼ cup heavy whipping cream, at room temperature
- Baking spray

1. Preheat oven to 325°F. Cook butter in a small saucepan over medium, stirring often, until butter solids are golden brown and nutty in aroma, 5 to 8 minutes. Add brown butter to a large heatproof bowl. Chill in freezer, uncovered, until butter is just set, 20 to 30 minutes.

2. Beat chilled butter with an electric mixer on medium-low speed until creamy, about 1 minute. Add sugar and orange zest; beat on medium speed until fluffy, 3 to 4 minutes. Beat in oil and vanilla until smooth. Add eggs, 1 at a time, beating until combined after each addition, stopping to scrape down sides of bowl as needed.

3. Whisk together flour, cornstarch, cinnamon, baking powder, salt, and baking soda in a medium bowl. Combine buttermilk and cream in a medium bowl. With mixer on low speed, add flour mixture to butter mixture, alternately with buttermilk mixture, beating just until combined, about 2 to 3 minutes total.

4. Coat 3 (8-inch) round cake pans with baking spray; line bottoms of pans with parchment paper. Divide batter among

Continued on page 310

Continued from page 309

prepared pans (about 2⅓ cups each), spreading evenly. Tap pans on counter several times to release any air bubbles.
5. Bake in preheated oven until a wooden pick inserted in centers comes out clean, 30 to 32 minutes. Let cool in pans on wire racks 10 minutes. Remove from pans; let cool completely on wire racks, about 2 hours. (To make ahead, wrap cooled cakes tightly with plastic wrap. Refrigerate up to 2 days or freeze up to 1 month.)

Cranberry-Orange Filling
ACTIVE 45 MIN. - TOTAL 45 MIN., PLUS 4 HOURS CHILLING
MAKES ABOUT 1½ CUPS

- 2½ cups fresh or frozen cranberries
- 2 tsp. orange zest, plus 3 Tbsp. fresh juice (from 1 large orange)
- ⅛ tsp. kosher salt
- 1 cup granulated sugar, divided
- 2¼ tsp. cornstarch
- 2 large eggs
- 1 large egg yolk
- 2 Tbsp. unsalted European-style butter (such as Kerrygold), cubed
- ¼ tsp. vanilla extract

1. Stir together cranberries, orange zest and juice, salt, and ¾ cup of the sugar in a medium saucepan; cook over medium, stirring often, until sugar is dissolved and cranberries have mostly burst, 10 to 12 minutes.
2. Pour cranberry mixture into a blender. Secure lid on blender, and remove center piece to allow steam to escape. Place a clean towel over opening. Process until smooth, about 1 minute. Strain cranberry mixture through a fine mesh strainer into a medium bowl, pressing firmly with back of a spoon to yield about 1¼ cups; discard solids. Whisk together cornstarch and remaining ¼ cup sugar in a large bowl; whisk in eggs and egg yolk. Gradually whisk in cranberry mixture until combined.
3. Return mixture to saucepan; cook over medium-low, whisking constantly, until bubbles just start to break the surface, 5 to 15 minutes. Continue cooking, whisking constantly, until mixture is thickened, 3 to 4 minutes. Remove from heat; whisk in butter and vanilla until combined.

4. Transfer cranberry mixture to a medium-size heatproof bowl. Place plastic wrap directly on surface of mixture; chill until cooled and set, at least 4 hours or up to 3 days.

Whipped Cream Frosting
ACTIVE 10 MIN. - TOTAL 10 MIN.
MAKES ABOUT 6 CUPS

- 3¾ cups heavy whipping cream
- 1 cup powdered sugar
- ⅓ cup white chocolate instant pudding and pie filling mix (such as Jell-O) (from 1 [3.3-oz.] pkg.)
- ¼ tsp. kosher salt

Combine whipping cream, powdered sugar, pudding mix, and salt in a large bowl. Beat with an electric mixer on medium-low speed until mixture is smooth and just starting to thicken, about 5 minutes, stopping to scrape down sides of bowl often. Increase speed to medium; beat until medium-stiff peaks form, 1 to 2 minutes more. (Frosting will continue to thicken slightly as it stands.) Use immediately, or store in an airtight container in refrigerator up to 2 days. Stir before using, if needed.

White Chocolate Candy Leaves
Fresh bay leaves work best, due to their pliability. Although the recipe calls for 20 leaves, you can also work in batches with however many you have on hand.
ACTIVE 35 MIN. - TOTAL 1 HOUR, 5 MIN.
MAKES 20 LEAVES

- 20 (¾- to 3-inch) fresh bay leaves (see note following recipe), washed and thoroughly patted dry
  Cooking spray
- 2 cups white vanilla melting wafers (from 1 [10-oz.] pkg.)

1. Coat bottom side of each bay leaf with cooking spray, wiping away any excess.
2. Place wafers in a medium heatproof bowl; microwave on HIGH in 30-second intervals, stirring between each interval, until melted and smooth, 90 seconds to 2 minutes.
3. Carefully dip coated side of each leaf into melted mixture in bowl. Using your fingers, spread mixture in a thin, even layer; wipe excess from edges as needed. Place leaves, coated sides up, on a parchment paper–lined baking sheet.

Let stand at room temperature until set, about 15 minutes.
4. Carefully peel away bay leaves; set aside candy leaves. If making additional leaves, wipe off and reuse bay leaves and repeat process until desired number of leaves is reached, reheating mixture as needed.
Note: We used 2¾- to 3-inch bay leaves for large poinsettias, 1¾-to 2½-inch bay leaves for medium poinsettias, and ¾- to 1-inch bay leaves for small poinsettias. Once set, candy leaves can be trimmed to desired sizes, if needed.

White Poinsettia Cupcakes with Cranberry-Orange Filling
(Photo, page 307)
ACTIVE 1 HOUR, 30 MIN. - TOTAL 3 HOURS, 20 MIN.
SERVES 36

- **Brown Butter Cake batter (recipe, page 309)**
- **Cranberry-Orange Filling (recipe, left)**
- **Whipped Cream Frosting (recipe, left)**
- **White Chocolate Candy Leaves (recipe, left)**
- **Fresh bay leaves**
- **Gold dragées**

1. Preheat oven to 325°F. Make Brown Butter Cake through Step 3. Line 3 (12-cup) muffin trays with paper liners. Spoon about 3 tablespoons batter into each liner.
2. Bake 2 muffin trays in preheated oven until a wooden pick inserted in centers comes out clean, 16 to 22 minutes. Let cupcakes cool in muffin trays on wire racks 10 minutes. Remove from muffin trays; let cool completely on wire racks, about 1 hour. Repeat with remaining muffin tray.
3. Scoop out about 2 teaspoons from center of each cupcake, keeping pieces as intact as possible; reserve cake pieces. Spoon filling into a piping bag or ziplock plastic bag; cut a small hole in tip or corner. Pipe filling into centers of cupcakes (about 1½ teaspoons each); use reserved cake pieces to cover.
4. Spoon frosting into a piping bag or ziplock plastic bag; cut a small hole in tip or corner. Pipe frosting over tops of cupcakes (about 2½ tablespoons each). Garnish with candy leaves, bay leaves, and dragées. (See steps for creating a poinsettia shape at right.) Remove dragées and fresh bay leaves before eating.

White Poinsettia Sheet Cake with Cranberry-Orange Filling

(Photo, page 308)

If the idea of decorating a layer cake gives you the jitters, try this easy 13- x 9-inch version. You can leave it in the pan to transport it with ease.

ACTIVE 40 MIN. - TOTAL 1 HOUR, 45 MIN., PLUS 2 HOURS COOLING

SERVES 18

- Baking spray
- Brown Butter Cake batter (recipe, page 309)
- Whipped Cream Frosting (recipe, opposite), divided
- Cranberry-Orange Filling (recipe, opposite)
- White Chocolate Candy Leaves (recipe, opposite)
- Fresh bay leaves
- Gold dragées

1. Preheat oven to 325°F. Coat a 13- x 9-inch baking pan with baking spray; line bottom and sides of pan with parchment paper, leaving a 2-inch overhang on long sides.
2. Make Brown Butter Cake through Step 3; spread batter evenly in prepared pan. Tap pan on counter a few times to get rid of any bubbles.
3. Bake in preheated oven until center bounces back when lightly pressed and a wooden pick inserted in center comes out clean, 50 to 55 minutes. Let cool in pan on a wire rack 15 minutes. Remove from pan; let cool completely on wire rack, about 2 hours. (Center may dip slightly as it cools.)
4. Using a serrated knife, trim domed top of cake. Place cake on a serving plate, cut side down; discard parchment. Spread ½ cup of the frosting evenly in a very thin layer over top. Spoon ½ cup frosting into a piping bag or ziplock plastic bag; cut a ½-inch hole in tip or corner.
5. Pipe a ½-inch-tall border of frosting around cake edge. Dollop and spread filling evenly within border. Reserve ¼ cup frosting to decorate sides of cake, if desired. Pipe some of remaining frosting over top of cake, smoothing as desired. Pipe three small mounds of frosting on top of frosted cake about 6 inches apart to serve as bases for the poinsettia flowers. Tuck candy leaves into mounds in a star shape, layering leaves and piping additional frosting on back of leaves as needed. Pipe a small dot of frosting in center of each poinsettia; arrange gold dragées in centers. Tuck in fresh bay leaves as desired. Remove dragées and fresh bay leaves before eating.

How To Make White Chocolate Candy Leaves

1. Spray. Coat the bottom sides of bay leaves with cooking spray, or brush with oil to coat.

2. Dip. Dip coated sides of leaves into white chocolate. Spread coating using your finger, if needed.

3. Cool. Let leaves cool on a parchment paper–lined baking sheet until set, about 15 minutes.

4. Peel. Gently pull the bay leaves away from white chocolate. Trim candy leaves as desired.

How To Make a Poinsettia

1. Build a base. Pipe a small mound of frosting onto the center of frosted cupcake or on top of layer or sheet cake to serve as a base for the leaves.

2. Tuck in leaves. Carefully insert leaves into frosting mound to create a flower shape. Pipe more frosting in center, if needed.

3. Finish the bloom. Carefully press gold dragées (in varying sizes, if desired) into the frosting at the center of the poinsettia.

Orange Crush

Stunning citrus desserts to wow your crowd

BLOOD ORANGE UPSIDE-DOWN CAKE

Blood Orange Upside-Down Cake

A surprisingly easy mosaic of blood orange slices makes this typically humble dessert a showstopper for holiday parties.

ACTIVE 45 MIN. - TOTAL 1 HOUR, 40 MIN.

SERVES 9

- 2½ cups granulated sugar, divided
- 2 medium blood oranges
  Baking spray
- 6 Tbsp. unsalted butter, cubed
- 2 large eggs, at room temperature
- ¾ cup sour cream, at room temperature
- ½ cup packed light brown sugar
- ¾ tsp. blood orange zest, plus 4 Tbsp. fresh juice (from 2 medium oranges)
- 2 Tbsp. neutral oil (such as canola oil or vegetable oil)
- 2 tsp. vanilla extract
- 2 cups bleached cake flour (such as Swans Down)
- 2½ tsp. baking powder
- ½ tsp. kosher salt

1. Combine 2 cups water and 2 cups of the granulated sugar in a large, wide saucepan; bring to a boil over medium-high, stirring occasionally. Meanwhile, trim and slice blood oranges crosswise into 14 to 16 slices (about ¼ inch thick) using a serrated knife. Add orange slices to boiling sugar mixture; reduce heat to low. Gently simmer, turning occasionally, until slices start to turn translucent, about 25 minutes. Remove from heat, and transfer slices to a wire rack placed over a rimmed baking sheet; reserve syrup in saucepan. Set aside.

2. Preheat oven to 350°F. Spray a 9-inch square baking pan with baking spray.

3. Heat butter in a small saucepan over medium, stirring frequently, until browned and nutty in aroma, 5 to 7 minutes. Transfer butter to a large heatproof bowl; let cool 10 minutes.

4. Whisk eggs, sour cream, brown sugar, orange zest and juice, oil, vanilla, and remaining ½ cup granulated sugar into browned butter until combined. Sift together flour, baking powder, and salt into a medium bowl. Gradually whisk flour mixture into egg mixture until combined.

5. Cut candied orange slices in half; arrange in prepared pan as desired, trimming or cutting slices to fit. Reserve any remaining slices for another use. Spread batter evenly over orange slices using a small spatula. Gently tap pan on counter a few times to get rid of any large air bubbles.

6. Bake in preheated oven until a wooden pick inserted in center comes out clean, 30 to 35 minutes. Remove cake from oven; prick all over using a fork. Brush cake with ¼ cup of reserved syrup.

7. Let cake cool in pan on a wire rack 10 minutes. Invert cake onto a serving plate; prick all over using a fork. Generously brush top of cake with ¼ cup reserved syrup; save any remaining syrup for another use. Serve cake warm or at room temperature.

Flourless Chocolate-Orange Cake with Grand Marnier Whipped Cream

(Photo, page 314)

This fudgy single-layer cake is not only incredibly delicious—it's also gluten free, thanks to the almond flour. If you can't find any at the store, pulse blanched almonds in your food processor until very finely ground.

ACTIVE 40 MIN. - TOTAL 3 HOURS, 15 MIN.

SERVES 8

- 8 oz. (60% cacao) bittersweet chocolate bars, finely chopped (about 1⅓ cups)
- 1 cup unsalted butter, cubed
- 2 tsp. instant espresso powder
- ¼ tsp. kosher salt
- 1¼ cups blanched almond flour
- 2 Tbsp. unsweetened cocoa, sifted
- 1 tsp. ground cinnamon
- ⅛ tsp. ground cloves
- 3 Tbsp. orange liqueur (such as Grand Marnier), divided
- 5 large eggs, at room temperature
- ¼ cup packed light brown sugar
- 2 tsp. orange zest (from 1 navel orange)
- 1 cup, plus 1 Tbsp. granulated sugar, divided
- 1 cup heavy whipping cream
  Candied Orange Peel, for garnish (optional; recipe on page 319)

1. Preheat oven to 350°F. Spray a 9-inch springform pan with cooking spray; line bottom with a round of parchment paper and sides with a separate strip of parchment paper.

2. Fill a medium saucepan with water to a depth of 1 inch; bring to a boil over medium-high, and then reduce heat to a simmer over medium-low. Combine chocolate, butter, espresso powder, and salt in a medium heatproof bowl; place over simmering water in pan. (Make sure bottom of bowl does not touch water.) Cook over medium-low, stirring often, until chocolate mixture is melted and smooth, about 6 minutes. Remove from heat. Whisk in almond flour, cocoa, cinnamon, cloves, and 2 tablespoons of the liqueur until combined.

3. Beat eggs, brown sugar, orange zest, and 1 cup of the granulated sugar in a stand mixer fitted with the whisk attachment on medium-high speed until mixture is increased in volume and falls from whisk attachment in a ribbon, about 5 minutes. Gradually fold chocolate mixture into egg mixture just until combined. Spread chocolate mixture evenly in prepared pan using a small offset spatula.

4. Bake in preheated oven until a wooden pick inserted in center comes out with some moist crumbs attached, about 35 minutes. Let cool in pan on a wire rack about 30 minutes. Loosen sides of cake using a butter knife; remove pan sides. Let cool completely on pan base on wire rack, 1 hour, 30 minutes to 2 hours.

5. Whisk cream and remaining 1 tablespoon each granulated sugar and liqueur in a large bowl until stiff peaks form, 2 to 3 minutes. Dollop whipped cream over cake; top with Candied Orange Peel, if desired.

FLOURLESS CHOCOLATE-ORANGE CAKE WITH GRAND MARNIER WHIPPED CREAM (PAGE 313)

ORANGE-AND-WHITE CHOCOLATE CRÈME BRÛLÉE (PAGE 319)

ORANGE-BOURBON BUNDT CAKE (PAGE 318)

ORANGE PAVLOVA WREATH (PAGE 318)

Take Your Pick

Kumquats
Native to China but grown in Florida, these small olive-shaped fruits are in season from October to February. Unlike their larger cousins, kumquats have a thin, edible skin, which surrounds intensely sweet-and-sour flesh. They are typically eaten whole.

Blood Oranges
From the outside, they have a faint blush; inside, the flesh is a striking blackberry hue and tastes like raspberries with a hint of bitterness. Likely native to the Mediterranean, they are also grown in Florida, Texas, and California and are in season from December to April.

Navel Oranges
The workhorse of American oranges, these have a thick peel that's easy to remove and fruit with a sweet, tangy flavor. Their name comes from a second, smaller orange under the peel, which causes a slight bulge that some say resembles a belly button.

Orange-Bourbon Bundt Cake

(Photo, page 316)

This sticky-sweet Bundt got top marks from the Southern Living *Test Kitchen. A sprinkle of toasted pistachios adds a festive finishing touch.*

ACTIVE 50 MIN. - TOTAL 3 HOURS, 55 MIN.
SERVES 10

CAKE

- 1 2/3 cups granulated sugar
- 1 1/4 cups unsalted butter, softened
- 1/3 cup packed light brown sugar
- 1 Tbsp. packed orange zest (from 1 orange)
- 5 large eggs, at room temperature
- 3 cups bleached cake flour
- 1 tsp. kosher salt
- 1/2 tsp. baking soda
- 1/2 tsp. ground cinnamon
- 3/4 cup sour cream, at room temperature
- 1/4 cup (2 oz.) bourbon
- 1/2 cup chopped toasted pistachios, plus more for garnish
- Baking spray

BOURBON SYRUP

- 2/3 cup granulated sugar
- 1/2 cup unsalted butter, softened
- 1/2 cup (4 oz.) bourbon
- 1/4 cup packed light brown sugar
- 1/4 cup fresh orange juice (from 1 orange)
- 1/4 tsp. kosher salt

1. Prepare the Cake: Preheat oven to 350°F. Beat granulated sugar, butter, brown sugar, and zest with a stand mixer fitted with a paddle attachment on medium speed until fluffy, 3 to 4 minutes, stopping to scrape down sides of bowl. Gradually add eggs, 1 at a time, beating just until combined after each addition.

2. Sift together flour, salt, baking soda, and cinnamon into a medium bowl. Whisk together sour cream and bourbon in a second medium bowl until combined. With mixer on medium-low speed, gradually add flour mixture to butter mixture alternately with sour cream mixture, beating just until combined after each addition. Fold in pistachios just until incorporated.

3. Generously coat a 12- to 15-cup Bundt pan with baking spray. Add batter to prepared pan; forcefully tap pan on countertop several times to spread batter and get rid of any large bubbles. Bake in preheated oven until a wooden pick inserted in center comes out clean, 50 to 55 minutes.

4. Prepare the Bourbon Syrup: Bring granulated sugar, butter, bourbon, brown sugar, orange juice, and salt to a boil in a medium saucepan over medium-high, stirring occasionally. Cook, undisturbed, until mixture is thickened to a loose syrup consistency, 5 to 7 minutes.

5. Let Cake cool in pan on a wire rack 15 minutes. While Cake cools, poke top of Cake all over using a fork. Generously brush half of Bourbon Syrup over Cake. Invert Cake onto a wire rack placed over a rimmed baking sheet; remove pan, and poke Cake all over using a fork. Brush remaining Bourbon Syrup over top. Garnish with additional pistachios. Let cool completely on a wire rack before serving.

Orange Pavlova Wreath

(Photo, page 317)

Crunchy, sweet clouds of meringue are flavored with hints of ginger and citrus and then topped with cardamom whipped cream, rosemary, and colorful fruit.

ACTIVE 45 MIN. - TOTAL 4 HOURS, 15 MIN., INCLUDING 2 HOURS, 30 MIN. COOLING
SERVES 8

- 5 large egg whites, at room temperature
- 1/4 tsp. cream of tartar
- 1 1/4 cups, plus 2 1/2 Tbsp. granulated sugar, divided
- 3/4 tsp. ground ginger
- 1/2 tsp. orange zest (from 1 navel orange)
- 1/4 tsp. kosher salt
- 1 1/4 tsp. vanilla extract, divided
- 1 3/4 cups heavy whipping cream
- 1/2 tsp. ground cardamom
- 1/4 cup orange marmalade
- 1 navel orange, sectioned (about 1/3 cup)
- Candied Kumquats (recipe, opposite)
- Candied Blood Oranges (recipe, opposite)
- Pomegranate arils
- Fresh rosemary leaves

1. Preheat oven to 250°F. Beat egg whites and cream of tartar with a stand mixer fitted with a whisk attachment on medium speed until frothy, 1 to 2 minutes. Increase the speed to medium-high; with mixer running, gradually add 1¼ cups of the sugar and beat until stiff peaks form, about 10 minutes. Add ginger, zest, salt, and ¾ teaspoon of the vanilla; fold in by hand until just combined.

2. Line a large baking sheet with parchment paper. Spoon 8 dollops of meringue (each about the size of an orange) onto the parchment in a 9-inch ring, leaving a 4-inch round space in the center and allowing dollops to touch on the sides. Slightly flatten each dollop using the back of a spoon.

3. Bake in preheated oven until set and dry to the touch, 1 hour to 1 hour, 10 minutes. Turn off oven; let cool in oven at least 2 hours. Remove from oven, and let cool completely on baking sheet on a wire rack before assembling, 30 minutes to 1 hour.

4. Whisk cream, cardamom, remaining 2½ tablespoons sugar, and remaining ½ teaspoon vanilla by hand in a large bowl until stiff peaks form, 2 to 3 minutes. Spread cream mixture over cooled pavlova. Stir marmalade in a small bowl to loosen; drizzle over cream mixture as desired.

5. Top pavlova with fresh navel orange sections, Candied Kumquats, Candied Blood Oranges, pomegranate arils, and rosemary leaves. Serve immediately.

Orange-and-White Chocolate Crème Brûlée

(Photo, page 315)

Few desserts feel more special than a properly prepared crème brûlée. Creamy white chocolate brings buttery richness, and fragrant orange zest provides a sweet, floral lift.

ACTIVE 40 MIN. • TOTAL 3 HOURS, 45 MIN.
SERVES 8

- 3 cups heavy whipping cream
- 1 (4-oz.) white chocolate bar, finely chopped (about ⅔ cup)
- ¼ cup packed light brown sugar
- ¼ tsp. kosher salt
- 2 tsp. packed orange zest, plus ¼ cup fresh juice (from 2 navel oranges), divided
- 9 large egg yolks
- ⅓ cup, plus 3 Tbsp. granulated sugar, divided
- 4 tsp. vanilla bean paste
- Candied Kumquats and quartered Candied Navel Orange Slices (recipes, right)
- Fresh mint leaves

1. Preheat oven to 325°F. Place cream, chocolate, brown sugar, salt, and orange zest in a medium saucepan; cook over medium-low, stirring frequently, until mixture is steaming, 8 to 12 minutes. Remove from heat.

2. Whisk together egg yolks and ⅓ cup of the granulated sugar in a large bowl until well combined. Gradually add cream mixture to egg yolk mixture, whisking constantly, until combined. Strain egg yolk mixture through a fine mesh strainer back into saucepan; whisk in vanilla bean paste and orange juice. Divide egg mixture evenly among 8 (7- to 8-oz.) ramekins.

3. Place ramekins in a large roasting pan. Add boiling water to pan to come halfway up sides of ramekins. Bake in preheated oven until egg mixture is just set but still jiggles, 30 to 35 minutes.

4. Carefully transfer ramekins to a wire rack. Let cool 30 minutes. Refrigerate, uncovered, until chilled, about 2 hours. (Cover with plastic wrap, and refrigerate for up to 3 days, if desired.)

5. Sprinkle remaining 3 tablespoons sugar over crème brûlées. Toast sugar using a kitchen torch until sugar is caramelized. (Alternatively, broil on the top rack, watching closely, until the sugar is caramelized, 3 to 5 minutes.) Let stand until sugar is set, about 10 minutes. Garnish with Candied Kumquats, Candied Navel Orange Slices, and mint leaves.

Candied Citrus

ACTIVE 1 HOUR • TOTAL 2 HOURS, 45 MIN.
MAKES 12 TO 14 CANDIED ORANGE SLICES, ½ CUP CANDIED KUMQUATS, OR 1 CUP CANDIED ORANGE PEEL

Bring 12 to 14 (¼-inch-thick) **navel or blood orange** slices, 1 cup (⅛-inch-thick) **kumquat** slices, or about 1 cup (¼-inch) slices **orange peel** and 1 inch **water** to a boil over medium-high in a large, wide saucepan; drain using a fine mesh strainer (to remove bitterness from citrus). Repeat once. Using the same saucepan, bring 2½ cups **granulated sugar** and 2¼ cups **water** to a boil over medium-high, stirring often. Add citrus; reduce heat to medium-low, and bring to a simmer. Cook, turning occasionally, until peels are slightly translucent, 45 to 60 minutes for orange slices and peels, and 20 to 30 minutes for kumquats. For a sugary coating, spread citrus on a wire rack. Let stand until dry but still sticky, about 12 hours. Sprinkle both sides with **granulated sugar**; press to coat. Alternatively, arrange citrus in a single layer on an oven-safe wire rack set over a baking sheet and bake at 200°F until citrus is slightly dried, about 1 hour for orange slices and peels, and 40 minutes for kumquats. Let cool 30 minutes. Store in an airtight container at room temperature for up to 1 week. (Reserve citrus syrup for another use, if desired; refrigerate in an airtight container up to 1 month.)

The Ultimate *Southern Living* Cookie Tin

Looking for a spectacular (but simple) recipe for this year's swap?
These recipes are anything but cookie-cutter

STAINED GLASS SNOWFLAKES

Stained Glass Snowflakes

ACTIVE 55 MIN. - TOTAL 2 HOURS, 25 MIN., PLUS 2 HOURS CHILLING
MAKES ABOUT 2 DOZEN

- 1¼ cups unsalted butter, at room temperature
- 1 cup granulated sugar
- 2 large egg yolks
- 1 tsp. almond extract
- 3½ cups all-purpose flour, plus more for surface
- 1 tsp. kosher salt
- Hard candies (such as Jolly Rancher), finely crushed
- 1 large egg white, beaten
- Sparkling sugar

1. Beat butter and granulated sugar in a large bowl with an electric mixer on medium speed until light and fluffy, about 3 minutes. Beat in egg yolks and almond extract until just combined, about 30 seconds. Add flour and salt; beat on low speed just until combined, about 30 seconds. Divide dough in half. Shape each half into a 6-inch-wide x ¾-inch-thick disk; wrap each disk tightly with plastic wrap. Chill until firm, at least 2 hours or up to 3 days.

2. Preheat oven to 350°F. Let dough stand at room temperature 10 minutes. Roll each dough half on a lightly floured surface to ¼-inch thickness. Cut dough using a 4-inch snowflake cookie cutter. Working in batches, transfer cookies to parchment paper–lined baking sheets, spacing about 1 inch apart (about 8 cookies per baking sheet). Using a 2-inch snowflake cookie cutter, cut centers out of each larger cookie. Reroll and cut scraps twice; chill if dough becomes too soft to work with.

3. Sprinkle about ½ teaspoon crushed candies in center of each cutout cookie. (Don't worry about spreading to edges, candies will melt and fill in.) Brush tips of dough with egg white and sprinkle with sparkling sugar.

4. Bake in preheated oven, 1 baking sheet at a time, until lightly browned around edges and candies have melted, 10 to 12 minutes. Let cool slightly on baking sheets, about 5 minutes. Transfer to a wire rack, and let cool completely, about 20 minutes. Transfer to a resealable container, and store at room temperature up to 4 days.

Peppermint Meringues

ACTIVE 55 MIN. - TOTAL 1 HOUR, 50 MIN, PLUS 3 HOURS COOLING
MAKES ABOUT 45

- 2 large egg whites
- ¼ tsp. cream of tartar
- ½ cup superfine sugar
- 1½ tsp. cornstarch
- ⅛ tsp. peppermint extract
- Red food coloring gel

1. Preheat oven to 225°F with racks in middle and lower third positions. Line 2 large baking sheets with parchment paper; set aside.

2. Beat egg whites with a stand mixer fitted with a whisk attachment on medium-high speed until foamy, about 1 minute. Add cream of tartar, and beat 30 seconds. Stir together sugar and cornstarch in a small bowl until combined. With mixer on medium-high speed, gradually add sugar mixture, 1 teaspoon at a time. Beat on medium-high speed until glossy, sugar is mostly dissolved, and medium-stiff peaks form, about 5 minutes. Beat in peppermint extract until just combined, about 15 seconds.

3. Using a small paintbrush, brush 3 to 4 strips of food coloring gel down the length of the inside of a piping bag. Fill three-quarters full with meringue. Cut a ½-inch hole at the tip of the bag.

4. Pipe 1-inch-wide x 1-inch-tall kisses onto prepared baking sheets, about 1 inch apart. (The first meringues piped will be very red, but color fades as you continue to pipe.) Repeat food coloring gel brushing process with new piping bags until all meringue is piped.

5. Place baking sheets in middle and lower third positions of preheated oven; reduce oven temperature to 200°F. Bake at 200°F until meringues are dry to the touch and hollow sounding when tapped, 1½ to 2 hours. Turn oven off, and let cool completely in closed oven for at least 3 hours or up to 8 hours. Store in a sealed container at room temperature for up to 1 week.

PEPPERMINT MERINGUES

RUGELACH
(PAGE 324)

CHECKERBOARD
COOKIES
(PAGE 325)

Rugelach

(Photo, page 322)

ACTIVE 45 MIN. · TOTAL 3 HOURS, 35 MIN.

MAKES 32

- 2 cups all-purpose flour, plus more for surface
- ½ tsp. kosher salt
- 1 cup unsalted butter, at room temperature and cubed
- 4 oz. cold cream cheese, cubed
- 2 (4-oz.) semisweet chocolate bars, chopped (about 1⅓ cups)
- ⅓ cup packed light brown sugar
- 1 tsp. instant espresso powder
- 1 large egg white, beaten
  Sparkling sugar

1. Pulse flour and salt in a food processor until combined, about 5 pulses. Add butter and cream cheese; pulse until dough forms, 15 to 20 pulses. Transfer to a lightly floured surface; knead until smooth dough forms, about 12 times. Divide dough into 3 equal portions. Shape each portion into a round (4-inch-wide x ½-inch-thick) disk, and wrap each in plastic wrap. Refrigerate until chilled and firm, about 1 hour, 30 minutes or up to 3 days.

2. Preheat oven to 350°F. Line 3 large baking sheets with parchment paper; set aside. Working with 1 disk at a time, roll on a lightly floured surface into a 10-inch circle (⅛ to ¼ inch thick). Repeat process with remaining disks; set aside.

3. Microwave chocolate in a medium-size microwavable bowl on HIGH, in 30-second intervals, stirring after each interval, until melted, about 1 minute, 30 seconds. Stir in brown sugar and espresso powder until combined. Spread ⅓ cup of the chocolate mixture onto 1 circle of dough, leaving a ½-inch border. Using a knife or pizza cutter, cut each circle of dough into 12 wedges (like cutting a pizza). Starting at wide end, roll each triangle up. Transfer to prepared baking sheets, spacing about 2 inches apart. Repeat process with remaining 2 dough circles and ⅔ cup chocolate mixture. Brush tops with egg white, and sprinkle with sparkling sugar.

4. Bake 1 baking sheet at a time in preheated oven until golden, 20 to 25 minutes. Let cool completely on baking sheet, about 20 minutes. Repeat process with remaining cookies. Store in a sealed container at room temperature for up to 5 days.

Eggnog Snickerdoodles

(Photo, page 323)

ACTIVE 50 MIN. · TOTAL 2 HOURS, 20 MIN.

MAKES ABOUT 3 DOZEN

- 1 cup unsalted butter, softened
- 1¾ cups granulated sugar, divided
- 2 large eggs, at room temperature
- 1 tsp. rum extract
- ½ tsp. vanilla extract
- 2¾ cups all-purpose flour
- 1 tsp. baking powder
- ¾ tsp. kosher salt
- ½ tsp. cream of tartar
- ¾ tsp. ground nutmeg, divided, plus more for sprinkling
- ⅛ tsp. ground cinnamon
- ⅔ cup white chocolate chips

1. Preheat oven to 400°F. Beat butter and 1½ cups of the granulated sugar with a stand mixer fitted with a paddle attachment on medium speed until light and fluffy, 3 to 4 minutes, stopping to scrape down sides as needed. Add eggs, rum extract, and vanilla; beat on medium speed until just combined, 15 to 30 seconds.

2. Whisk together flour, baking powder, salt, cream of tartar, and ½ teaspoon of the nutmeg in a medium bowl until combined. Add flour mixture to butter mixture in 3 additions, beating on low speed until just incorporated after each addition and stopping to scrape down sides as needed, 1 to 2 minutes. Cover bowl with plastic wrap, and chill until firm, about 30 minutes.

3. Whisk together cinnamon, remaining ¼ cup sugar, and remaining ¼ teaspoon nutmeg in a small bowl. Scoop about 1½ tablespoons of dough per cookie, and roll into balls. Roll in cinnamon mixture until evenly coated. Arrange on parchment paper–lined baking sheets at least 2½ inches apart (about 8 per baking sheet).

4. Bake cookies, 1 baking sheet at a time, in preheated oven until edges are set but centers are still slightly soft, 7 to 8 minutes. Let cool on baking sheet 5 minutes; transfer to wire racks, and let cool completely, about 20 minutes.

5. Microwave white chocolate chips in a medium microwave-safe bowl on HIGH in 15-second intervals until melted, about 1 minute, stirring between each interval. Place melted white chocolate in a small ziplock plastic bag; cut a ¼-inch hole in corner. Drizzle cookies with white chocolate; let stand until set, about 5 minutes. Sprinkle with nutmeg. Store in a sealed container at room temperature for up to 3 days.

Hot Cocoa Cookies

(Photo, page 323)

ACTIVE 50 MIN. · TOTAL 3 HOURS

MAKES 3 DOZEN

- ½ cup unsalted butter, softened
- 3 cups semisweet chocolate chips, divided
- 1½ cups all-purpose flour
- ¼ cup unsweetened cocoa, plus more for dusting
- 1 tsp. baking powder
- ½ tsp. kosher salt
- 1 cup packed light brown sugar
- 3 large eggs, at room temperature
- 1 tsp. vanilla extract
- 18 marshmallows, halved crosswise

1. Heat butter and 2 cups of the chocolate chips in a medium saucepan over medium, stirring often, until melted and combined, about 5 minutes. Remove from heat, and let cool 10 minutes.

2. Whisk together flour, cocoa, baking powder, and salt in a medium bowl until combined. Whisk together brown sugar, eggs, and vanilla in a large bowl until well combined. Add cooled chocolate mixture to brown sugar mixture in 3 additions, whisking vigorously until completely incorporated. Whisk in flour mixture. Fold in ¾ cup of the remaining chocolate chips. Cover, and chill dough until very firm, about 1 hour.

Cookie swaps are a fun and social way to trade traditions and load up your cookie platters with a wide variety of cookies you wouldn't otherwise have time to make.

3. Preheat oven to 325°F with racks in top third and lower third positions. Line 3 large baking sheets with parchment paper. Scoop dough into 36 portions (about 1 heaping tablespoon each); roll into balls. Place 12 doughballs on each prepared baking sheet at least 2 inches apart.
4. Place 2 baking sheets in preheated oven, and bake until tops are cracked but centers still seem soft, about 10 minutes, rotating baking sheets from top to bottom and front to back halfway through bake time.
5. Remove cookies from oven; immediately press 3 of the remaining chocolate chips into center of each cookie. Place a marshmallow, cut side down, over chocolate chips and press gently to adhere (cookies will crackle and spread slightly). Let cool on baking sheets 5 minutes. Transfer to a wire rack; let cool completely, about 45 minutes. Repeat with remaining cookies, chocolate chips, and marshmallows. Lightly dust cocoa over cooled cookies. Store in a sealed container at room temperature for up to 3 days.

Checkerboard Cookies
(Photo, page 322)
ACTIVE 1 HOUR • TOTAL 2 HOURS, 50 MIN.
MAKES ABOUT 2 DOZEN

- ¾ cup cold unsalted butter, cubed
- ¾ cup powdered sugar
- 1 tsp. orange zest (from 1 orange)
- 1 large egg yolk
- 1 tsp. vanilla extract
- ½ tsp. kosher salt
- 1⅓ cups, plus 2 Tbsp. all-purpose flour, divided
- 3 Tbsp. unsweetened cocoa
- 1 large egg white, beaten

1. Beat butter, powdered sugar, and orange zest with a stand mixer fitted with a paddle attachment on medium speed until light and fluffy, about 3 minutes. Beat in egg yolk and vanilla until just combined, about 30 seconds. Add salt and 1⅓ cups of the flour; beat on low speed just until combined, about 1 minute. Remove and reserve half of dough from mixer. Beat 2 tablespoons flour into remaining dough until just combined; remove from mixer, and set aside.
2. Return reserved dough to mixer. Add cocoa, and beat on low speed until just combined, about 30 seconds. Wrap each dough half separately in plastic wrap, and refrigerate until chilled, at least 30 minutes or up to 2 days.
3. Preheat oven to 350°F. Line 2 large rimmed baking sheets with parchment paper; set aside. Divide each chilled portion of dough in half. Roll each portion of dough on a lightly floured surface to form 4 (⅜-inch-thick, 4- x 4-inch) squares (2 vanilla and 2 chocolate). Brush top of 1 chocolate square evenly with egg white. Top with a vanilla square, and brush with egg white. Repeat process with remaining egg white, chocolate, and vanilla dough squares for a total of 4 layers. Wrap dough stack in plastic wrap, and freeze until firm, about 15 minutes.
4. Unwrap chilled dough stack, and cut into 10 (⅜-inch-thick) slices. Stack 4 of the slices on top of each other, cut sides down, alternating to form a checkerboard pattern, brushing with egg white between layers. Repeat process with 4 of the slices to form a second block of checkerboard dough. Cut remaining 2 slices in half crosswise; repeat process, brushing with egg white and stacking as directed, to form a third, smaller half-block of checkerboard dough. Wrap each dough block in plastic wrap, and freeze until firm, about 15 minutes.
5. Unwrap all dough, and cut crosswise into 25 (⅜-inch-thick) slices. Arrange slices 1 inch apart on prepared baking sheets.
6. Bake cookies, 1 baking sheet at a time, in preheated oven until lightly browned around edges, about 12 minutes. Let cool on baking sheets set on a wire rack 5 minutes. Transfer cookies directly to wire rack, and let cool completely, about 15 minutes. Meanwhile, repeat process with remaining cookies. Store in an airtight container at room temperature up to 1 week.

Checkerboard Cheatsheet

1. Stack 1 chocolate square with a vanilla square, and brush with egg white. Repeat the process for a total of four layers.

2. Cut the dough block into 10 slices.

3. Stack four of the slices on top of each other, cut sides down, to form a block of checkerboard dough.

4. Cut blocks crosswise into 25 (⅜-inch-thick) slices.

CRANBERRY-PISTACHIO BISCOTTI

CHERRY ICEBOX COOKIES (PAGE 328)

ICED OATMEAL COOKIES

We bake cookies all year, but there's something special about the ones we make this season. They usher in Christmas with each sweet bite.

Cranberry-Pistachio Biscotti

ACTIVE 45 MIN. - TOTAL 1 HOUR, 55 MIN.
MAKES ABOUT 2 DOZEN

- 2 cups all-purpose flour, plus more for surface
- ¾ tsp. baking soda
- ¾ tsp. kosher salt
- ½ cup packed light brown sugar
- ¼ cup granulated sugar
- ¼ cup unsalted butter, softened
- 1 tsp. vanilla extract
- 3 large eggs, at room temperature
- ¾ cup sweetened dried cranberries, coarsely chopped
- ½ cup unsalted roasted pistachios, coarsely chopped
- 1 cup white chocolate chips

1. Preheat oven to 350°F. Line a baking sheet with parchment paper; set aside. Whisk together flour, baking soda, and salt; set aside.

2. Beat brown sugar, granulated sugar, and butter with a stand mixer fitted with a paddle attachment on medium speed until light and fluffy, 3 to 4 minutes. Add vanilla and 2 of the eggs; beat on low speed until combined, about 1 minute. With mixer on low speed, gradually add flour mixture; beat until no streaks remain, about 45 seconds. Add cranberries and pistachios; beat on low speed until evenly distributed, about 10 seconds.

3. Turn dough out onto a lightly floured surface. Divide dough half; shape each half into a 12-inch-long log (about 1½ inches wide x 1 inch thick). Place logs 3 inches apart on prepared baking sheet. Whisk together water and remaining egg. Brush logs with egg mixture.

4. Bake in preheated oven until golden brown and firm on top, 25 to 30 minutes. Let cool on baking sheet 5 minutes; transfer to a cutting board while still warm. Carefully cut logs crosswise into ¾-inch-thick slices. Place slices, cut sides down, on same parchment-lined baking sheet, spacing evenly.

5. Bake in preheated oven until mostly firm in center and slightly browned, 8 to 12 minutes, flipping biscotti once halfway through bake time. Transfer biscotti to a wire rack; let cool completely, about 25 minutes.

6. Microwave white chocolate in a medium microwave-safe bowl on HIGH in 30-second intervals, stirring between each interval, until melted and smooth, 1 to 2 minutes. Dip bottoms of biscotti into melted white chocolate; shake gently to remove excess. Transfer, chocolate side down, to a parchment paper–lined wire rack. Let stand until chocolate is set, 5 to 8 minutes. Store in a sealed container at room temperature for up to 5 days.

Iced Oatmeal Cookies

ACTIVE 45 MIN. - TOTAL 1 HOUR
MAKES 2 DOZEN

- ½ cup unsalted butter, softened
- ½ cup packed light brown sugar
- ⅓ cup granulated sugar
- 1 large egg, at room temperature
- 1 Tbsp. unsulphured light molasses (such as Grandma's Original)
- ½ tsp. vanilla extract
- 1 cup, plus 2 Tbsp. all-purpose flour
- 1½ cups uncooked old-fashioned regular rolled oats
- ¼ cup toffee bits (such as Heath)
- ½ tsp. kosher salt
- ½ tsp. ground cinnamon
- ¼ tsp. baking soda
- ¼ tsp. baking powder
- ⅛ tsp. ground allspice
- 2 cups powdered sugar
- ⅓ cup heavy whipping cream

1. Beat butter, brown sugar, and granulated sugar in a stand mixer fitted with the paddle attachment on medium speed until light and fluffy, 3 to 4 minutes. Add egg, molasses, and vanilla; beat on medium until combined, 15 to 30 seconds.

2. Stir together flour, oats, toffee bits, salt, cinnamon, baking soda, baking powder, and allspice in a medium bowl. Reduce mixer to low speed, and add flour mixture, about ½ cup at a time, beating until just combined, about 1 minute. Cover bowl with plastic wrap, and chill until firm, about 30 minutes.

3. Preheat oven to 375°F. Line 2 large baking sheets with parchment paper. Scoop dough into 24 portions (about 2 tablespoons each), and roll into balls (about 1¼ inches in diameter). Arrange on prepared baking sheets at least 2 inches apart.

4. Bake in preheated oven, 1 baking sheet at a time, until tops appear dry but centers are still soft, 10 to 12 minutes. Remove from oven, and place on a wire rack; let cool completely, about 20 minutes.

5. While cookies are cooling, stir together powdered sugar and cream in a medium microwave-safe bowl until combined (mixture will be very thick). Microwave on HIGH for 30 seconds; stir until smooth.

6. Lightly dip tops of cookies into icing until partially coated; lift up, and shake gently to remove excess. Transfer cookies, icing side up, to a wire rack. Let stand until icing is set, about 10 minutes. Store in a sealed container at room temperature for up to 5 days.

Cherry Icebox Cookies

(Photo, page 326)
ACTIVE 25 MIN. - TOTAL 2 HOURS, 20 MIN., PLUS 2 HOURS CHILLING
MAKES ABOUT 4 DOZEN

- 1 cup unsalted butter, softened
- 1 cup granulated sugar
- 1 large egg, at room temperature
- 1 tsp. vanilla extract
- ¼ tsp. almond extract
- 2⅔ cups all-purpose flour, plus more for surface
- ½ tsp. kosher salt
- ¾ cup red and green candied cherries, patted dry and roughly chopped
- Red and green sanding sugars

1. Beat butter and sugar with a stand mixer fitted with a paddle attachment on medium speed until light and fluffy, about 3 minutes. Add egg, vanilla, and almond extract; beat on medium speed until just combined, 15 to 30 seconds.
2. Whisk together flour and salt in a medium bowl. Reduce mixer to low speed; add flour mixture in 3 additions, beating until just combined, 1 to 2 minutes. Add cherries, and beat on low speed just until evenly distributed, about 15 seconds.
3. Divide dough in half on a lightly floured surface. Shape each half into a 12-inch log (about 1½ inches in diameter); wrap each log in plastic wrap. Chill in freezer at least 2 hours or up to 24 hours.
4. Preheat oven to 375°F. Place red and green sanding sugars in 2 separate large shallow dishes.
5. Unwrap 1 dough log; let stand at room temperature until slightly softened, about 20 minutes. Roll log in red sanding sugar to adhere. Cut log crosswise into ⅜-inch-thick slices. Place slices on parchment paper–lined baking sheets at least 1½ inches apart.
6. Bake cookies, 1 baking sheet at a time, in preheated oven until tops appear dry but centers are still slightly soft, 10 to 12 minutes. Let cookies cool on baking sheets 5 minutes; transfer to wire racks, and let cool completely, about 30 minutes. Repeat Steps 5 and 6 with remaining dough and green sanding sugar. Store in a sealed container at room temperature for up to 5 days.

Jam Pinwheels

ACTIVE 40 MIN. - TOTAL 1 HOUR, 50 MIN., PLUS 12 HOURS CHILLING
MAKES 3 DOZEN

- 3¼ cups all-purpose flour, plus more for surface
- 1 cup cold unsalted butter, cubed
- ½ cup granulated sugar
- 1 tsp. grated lemon zest (from 1 lemon)
- ½ tsp. kosher salt
- 1 (8-oz.) pkg. cold cream cheese, cubed
- 6 Tbsp. apricot or seedless raspberry jam
- 1 large egg white, beaten
- Powdered sugar

1. Place flour, butter, sugar, lemon zest, and salt in a food processor; pulse until mixture is crumbly, about 10 pulses. Add cream cheese; pulse until dough clumps together, 15 to 20 pulses. Transfer dough to a lightly floured surface, and knead gently just until dough is smooth, 15 to 30 seconds. Divide dough into 3 equal portions. Shape each portion into a disk, and wrap in plastic wrap. Chill at least 12 hours or up to 2 days.
2. Preheat oven to 350°F. Line 3 large rimmed baking sheets with parchment paper; set aside. Let dough stand at room temperature until slightly softened, about 10 minutes.
3. Working with 1 disk of dough at a time, roll dough to about 1/16-inch thickness on a lightly floured surface. Using a 3¼-inch square cutter, cut dough, and place on 1 prepared baking sheet. Reroll and cut scraps twice.
4. Repeat process with remaining 2 disks and baking sheets. On each square of dough, make 4 (1-inch) cuts at corners diagonally toward center. Place ½ teaspoon jam in center of each square of dough. Dab corners of dough squares with egg white; fold every other tip over toward center, forming a pinwheel. Chill, uncovered, 10 minutes.
5. Bake in preheated oven, 1 baking sheet at a time, until edges are light golden brown, 13 to 15 minutes. Let cool completely on pans, about 15 minutes. Dust with powdered sugar, if desired. Store in a sealed container at room temperature for up to 3 days.

Pinwheel Pointer

1. Make 4 cuts at each corner of the dough square diagonally toward the center.

2. Place ½ teaspoon of jam in the center of each square. Dab the corners with egg white.

3. Fold every other tip over toward the center, onto the jam, forming a pinwheel.

4. Bake the cookies until lightly golden brown. After cooling, dust with powdered sugar for a festive touch.

JAM
PINWHEELS

PIECE OF CAKE

Thumbs Up

Three twists on the classic chocolate-filled cookie

Chocolate Kiss Cookies
ACTIVE 20 MIN. - TOTAL 1 HOUR, 15 MIN.
MAKES 3 DOZEN

- ½ cup unsalted butter, softened
- ½ cup packed light brown sugar
- 1 cup granulated sugar, divided
- 1 large egg, at room temperature
- 2 Tbsp. half-and-half
- 1 tsp. vanilla extract
- 2 cups all-purpose flour
- ½ cup unsweetened cocoa
- 1 tsp. baking soda
- ½ tsp. kosher salt
- 36 milk-chocolate kisses

1. Preheat oven to 375°F. Line a large rimmed baking sheet with parchment paper.
2. Beat butter, brown sugar, and ¾ cup of the granulated sugar with a stand mixer fitted with a paddle attachment or an electric hand mixer on medium speed until fluffy, about 2 minutes.
3. Add egg, half-and-half, and vanilla; beat on medium-high speed until fully combined and fluffy, about 1 minute.
4. Whisk together flour, cocoa, baking soda, and salt in a medium bowl until combined; add to butter mixture, beating on low speed until just combined, about 1 minute.
5. Roll dough into 36 (1-inch) balls (about 1 tablespoon each). Place remaining ¼ cup granulated sugar in a bowl; roll balls in sugar to coat. Arrange 12 dough balls on prepared baking sheet, spacing 2 inches apart.
6. Bake in preheated oven for 8 minutes. Remove from oven; immediately press 1 chocolate kiss into center of each cookie. Return to oven; bake at 375°F for 2 more minutes. Remove from oven; cool on baking sheet for 3 minutes. Transfer cookies to a wire rack. Repeat with remaining 24 balls and chocolate kisses. Let cookies cool completely on wire rack, about 20 minutes.

Peppermint Kiss Cookies
Prepare recipe as directed through Step 1. In Step 2, reduce granulated sugar to ½ cup. In Step 3, substitute vanilla with 1½ tsp. **peppermint extract.** In Step 4, increase all-purpose flour to 2½ cups and omit cocoa; proceed as directed. In Step 5, omit granulated sugar; roll balls in **red and green nonpareils** to coat. Bake and cool as directed in Step 6.

Molasses-Spice Kiss Cookies
Prepare recipe as directed through Step 1. In Step 2, reduce granulated sugar to ½ cup, and add 2 Tbsp. **molasses.** Continue with Step 3 as directed. In Step 4, increase all-purpose flour to 3 cups, omit cocoa, and add 2 tsp. **pumpkin pie spice;** proceed as directed. In Step 5, omit granulated sugar; roll balls in ⅓ cup **turbinado sugar** to coat. Bake and cool as directed in Step 6.

How To Shape and Bake Kiss Cookies

1. Roll each ball in sugar, making sure not to flatten them. Arrange doughballs 2 inches apart on the prepared baking sheet.

2. Bake cookies for 8 minutes, then remove from oven. Working quickly, gently press a candy into the center of each cookie.

3. Return cookies to oven to finish baking. Let cool on the baking sheet for 3 minutes before transferring to a wire rack to cool completely.

FAMILY STYLE

Made With Love

Turn gift-giving into something more meaningful and less stressful, Southern style

ONE OF MY favorite Southern traditions is the "happy" (some call it a *surcee*), which is a small, unexpected gift designed to make someone smile. A good happy shouldn't cost much money or even require wrapping. It could be as simple as a box of tea left on a coworker's desk, a cookie from a bakery for your child, or a pack of seeds tucked inside a card for a faraway friend. It's a caring gesture that's worth more than the item itself, a way to say "I'm thinking of you" when life gets tough—or for no reason at all.

While I enjoy this type of gift-giving, holiday shopping sends me into a tizzy. As soon as Santa makes his appearance at the end of the Macy's Thanksgiving Day Parade, I feel my anxiety start to rise. Choosing presents for family members is easy (Dad, you're getting a "coupon" for a dinner out with me… again), but figuring out something for teachers, neighbors, and coworkers stumps me. Not to mention our lawn guy, Secret Santa at the office, postal workers, babysitters, that nice lady at the library, and probably several others I am forgetting about.

I can hear you now: "Just buy a bunch of gift cards!" And yes, that is often my plan. But this year, I'm embracing the homemade happy. This caramel corn is inexpensive, make-ahead, and customizable in so many fun ways (like our Mexican hot chocolate version). Plus, if you can recruit a young helper, they will also experience the joy that a happy can bring.

A special treat along with a note (plus money or a gift card for service workers) is better than anything you could buy at the last minute. The point of all of this giving isn't to add another holiday mug to someone's collection. It's about the warm, fuzzy feeling that comes from being seen and appreciated.
—Lisa Cericola

Classic Caramel Corn
ACTIVE 1 HOUR - TOTAL 1 HOUR, 30 MIN.
SERVES 18

- 18 cups popped plain popcorn (from 1 [8-oz.] bag)
- 1 cup packed light brown sugar
- ½ cup unsalted butter
- ½ cup light corn syrup
- 1 tsp. kosher salt
- 1 Tbsp. bourbon (optional)
- 1 tsp. vanilla extract
- ½ tsp. baking soda

1. Preheat oven to 250°F with racks in top third and lower third positions. Line 2 large rimmed baking sheets with parchment paper; set aside.
2. Place popcorn in a large heatproof bowl. Place brown sugar, butter, corn syrup, and salt in a medium saucepan; bring to a boil over medium. Boil, stirring often, until mixture reaches 260°F, about 6 minutes. Remove from heat; add bourbon (if desired), vanilla, and baking soda, stirring vigorously until incorporated (mixture will bubble up). Pour over popcorn in bowl, and stir well to coat popcorn. Spread in an even layer on prepared baking sheets.
3. Bake in preheated oven, stirring every 10 to 15 minutes, until caramel is set, about 50 minutes. Let cool completely on baking sheets, about 30 minutes. Break into pieces before serving or packaging. Store in an airtight container at room temperature for up to 1 week.

Mexican Hot Chocolate Caramel Corn
ACTIVE 1 HOUR - TOTAL 1 HOUR, 30 MIN.
SERVES 18

Prepare recipe as directed through Step 1. In Step 2, omit bourbon and add ½ teaspoon ground **cinnamon** and ¼ teaspoon **cayenne pepper** to caramel mixture. Proceed with Step 3. After popcorn has cooled, microwave 2 ounces chopped **dark chocolate** with ½ teaspoon **coconut oil** in a small microwavable bowl on HIGH until melted, stirring every 15 seconds. Drizzle over popcorn. Let stand until set, about 1 hour. Break into pieces before serving or packaging.

Cheesy Caramel Corn
ACTIVE 1 HOUR - TOTAL 1 HOUR, 30 MIN.
SERVES 18

Prepare recipe as directed through Step 1. In Step 2, replace plain popcorn with **cheddar popcorn**; add 2 cups whole plus ½ cup crushed **cheddar crackers** (such as Cheez-It) before tossing with caramel. Proceed with recipe as directed.

CLASSIC
CARAMEL CORN

THE WELCOME TABLE

The Delicious Mystery of Court Bouillon

Jessica B. Harris unravels the origin of this famous Louisiana dish with French and Caribbean roots

AS A FOOD HISTORIAN, I am always attempting to find the genesis of one recipe or another. Where did peanut brittle originate? How did the Huguenot torte get its name? Usually, tracing a dish's source is a tortuous road that has many twists and turns, and more often than not, there are varying stories. As an expert in the cuisine of the African diaspora, I am often struck by how frequently the African hand in the pot is overlooked when folks are attributing origins.

Take court bouillon, a Creole specialty, for example. If you look it up, you will find that it is a French term for a seasoned broth used as a poaching liquid. (There are several variants of spelling. You can find it in classic cookbooks spelled court-bouillon, court bouillon, coubillon, coubion, or even couvillon.) In Louisiana, it's typically a tomato-based stew with seafood that is served over rice. All sorts of recipes will tell you that it's a poached fish dish that's essentially a Provençal bouillabaisse adapted to the Gulf Coast. But there seems to be no relationship other than the name to the classic French court bouillon.

How does this happen? The tomato does bring hints of the Mediterranean, and in many ways the recipe is like Marseille's famed fish stew, but without the shellfish and the rascasse (red scorpion fish) that is essential in a traditional bouillabaisse. While there are certainly echoes of the South of France in the dish, I suggest looking in a different direction: to the French-speaking Caribbean.

In Guadeloupe, one can discover another possible connection to the court bouillon that is a New Orleans favorite. I was introduced to it there by my "Maman Guadeloupe," the late Carmélita Jeanne, a Creole second-generation chef and stalwart member of the Cuisinières, the group of women chefs who are the guardians of the culinary traditions of that island. At her table and in her restaurant kitchen, she made me a spicy, tomato-based fish stew that is a closer match to the Louisiana version than the much-touted bouillabaisse. In fact, it is a culinary fraternal twin that even goes by the same name: court bouillon.

The stew's brightness might make some think of summer, so it was a surprise to discover that it is traditionally eaten by many Creole families in New Orleans this time of the year. For that reason, I included it in my 1995 book, *A Kwanzaa Keepsake*, that has just been reissued with a new foreword by Carla Hall. Celebrate the recipe's origins and the holidays by serving it with a playlist of Louisiana jazz and Guadeloupean beguine along with the seasonal classics.

Red Snapper in Creole Court Bouillon
ACTIVE 1 HOUR · TOTAL 1 HOUR
SERVES 8

- 1 Tbsp. olive oil
- 2 Tbsp. all-purpose flour
- 1 medium-size yellow onion, finely chopped (about ¾ cup)
- ⅓ cup finely chopped green bell pepper (from 1 bell pepper)
- 3 Tbsp. finely chopped celery (from 2 large stalks)
- 2 Tbsp. finely chopped scallions (from 2 scallions), plus more for garnish
- 1 Tbsp. minced garlic (from 3 garlic cloves)
- ¼ tsp. ground allspice
- ½ cup dry white wine
- 8 large tomatoes, peeled, seeded, and chopped (6 cups)
- 2 fresh bay leaves
- 1 Tbsp. finely chopped fresh flat-leaf parsley
- 1 tsp. fresh thyme leaves
- 8 (4-oz.) red snapper fillets
- ½ tsp. black pepper
- 2¼ tsp. kosher salt, divided, plus more to taste
- 2 Tbsp. fresh lemon juice (from 1 lemon)
- 1 to 2 tsp. minced hot chile (from 1 chile, such as Scotch bonnet), plus more to taste
- Hot cooked white rice

1. Heat olive oil in a large, heavy nonreactive deep-sided skillet over medium-low. Slowly sprinkle flour in skillet; cook, stirring constantly, until a tan paste forms (the roux), about 2 minutes. Add onion, bell pepper, celery, scallions, garlic, and allspice; cook, stirring constantly, until fragrant and onion is translucent, about 3 minutes. Add white wine; cook, scraping up any browned bits from bottom of skillet, until mixture is smooth, about 1 minute. Add tomatoes, bay leaves, 2 cups water, parsley, and thyme; bring slowly to a boil over medium. Cook, stirring often, until tomatoes are cooked down and thickened into a gravy consistency, 30 to 40 minutes.

2. Sprinkle fish fillets with black pepper and 1¼ teaspoons of the salt. Nestle fillets in a single layer in tomato sauce in skillet, spooning sauce over the top to fully cover. Reduce heat to low. Cover and simmer until fillets are cooked through, 5 to 8 minutes. Transfer fillets from skillet to a heated platter to keep warm. Stir lemon juice, chile, and remaining 1 teaspoon salt into sauce in skillet; cook until flavors meld, about 3 minutes. Season with additional salt and chile to taste. Spoon sauce over fish fillets. Garnish with additional scallions; serve hot with rice.

Big Easy Flavor

THIS IS A VARIATION on the redfish court bouillon that is traditionally served in many of the Black Creole homes of New Orleans at Christmastime. Here, though, instead of the entire baked fish, snapper fillets are poached in the Creole court bouillon, which is more like a sauce than like the classic French court bouillon poaching liquid. You may wish to serve this as an entrée or as an alternative main dish along with the more traditional roasts that usually appear on the holiday table.

IVY'S KITCHEN

The Legend of the Lasagna

Ivy Odom shares how family recipes can get a little lost in translation

SOME FOLKS like to change up their holiday menus from year to year, but not the Odoms. When Christmas Eve rolls around, we know exactly what's going to be on our table—Mémère's lasagna. Like all the best family recipes, this keeper was passed down by word of mouth, to my dad from his Mémère, my great-grandmother. In her thick French Canadian-in-Connecticut accent, she would say the layers out loud as she assembled them. Eager to learn the secret to her famous dish, my dad would listen to her chant, "meat sauce, cottage cheese, cheese, noodles." For my entire childhood this is how we made lasagna, until one year my Mama pointed out–to our chagrin–that most recipes use ricotta.

In search of the truth, we called my Great-Aunt Bobbie (Mémère's daughter). Either due to her mother's strong accent or my dad's foggy memory, somewhere along the line "ricotta" became "cottage." Regardless of whose ears were to blame, Aunt Bobbie claimed our cheese choice wasn't authentic. My dad tried making it Mémère's way, but we missed the way the cottage cheese curds didn't fully melt, creating a supercreamy layer that grainy ricotta just couldn't deliver. Since that experiment, we've always assembled our night-before-Christmas dish the way we like it. While it may not be my great-grandmother's exact recipe, the story of "her" lasagna reminds us that when we make special dishes our own, new memories are made. I think she would be proud of that.

Christmas Eve Lasagna
ACTIVE 40 MIN. - TOTAL 1 HOUR, 35 MIN.
SERVES 8

- 2 tsp. extra-virgin olive oil
- ¾ lb. ground round (85/15 ground beef)
- ½ lb. hot Italian pork sausage
- ½ cup finely chopped sweet onion (from 1 small onion)
- ½ cup finely chopped red bell pepper (from 1 small pepper)
- 2 Tbsp. minced garlic (from 6 cloves)
- ¼ cup tomato paste (from 1 [6-oz.] can)
- 1 (28-oz.) can crushed tomatoes
- 2 tsp. Italian seasoning
- 1¾ tsp. kosher salt
- ¾ tsp. granulated sugar
- ½ tsp. freshly ground black pepper
- ½ tsp. Worcestershire sauce
- 9 lasagna noodles (from 1 [16-oz.] pkg.)
- 18 (¾-oz.) slices low-moisture part-skim mozzarella
- 1 (16-oz.) container whole milk small curd cottage cheese
- ½ cup freshly grated Parmesan cheese (about 2 oz.)

1. Heat oil in a large Dutch oven over medium-high. Add ground beef and sausage; cook, stirring to break into small crumbles, until meat starts to brown, 2 to 3 minutes. Add onion and bell pepper; cook, stirring often, until vegetables are soft and meat is browned, about 4 more minutes. Stir in garlic until fragrant, about 1 minute.

2. Stir tomato paste into meat mixture until well coated. Cook, stirring often, until tomato paste starts to caramelize, about 3 minutes. Stir in crushed tomatoes, Italian seasoning, salt, sugar, and black pepper. Bring to a boil; reduce heat to medium-low, and simmer 20 minutes. Stir in Worcestershire, and remove from heat.

3. Preheat oven to 350°F. Cook noodles according to package directions in heavily salted water. Drain noodles well. Spoon ½ cup meat sauce in an even layer in the bottom of a 9- x 13-inch baking dish. Layer 3 noodles on top of the meat sauce; top with about 1½ cups meat sauce. Spread ⅓ of the cottage cheese (about ½ cup) evenly over the meat sauce, then top with 6 slices mozzarella. Repeat layers 2 more times, topping the last layer of mozzarella with Parmesan. Cover with aluminum foil lightly greased with cooking spray. Bake in preheated oven until bubbling around the edges, about 30 minutes. Uncover and continue baking until edges are bubbly and the cheese is browned in some spots 25 to 30 minutes more. Remove from oven, and let stand 10 minutes before serving.

MAKE IT AHEAD
Prepare recipe through Step 2; let cool 30 minutes at room temperature before transferring meat sauce to an airtight container and refrigerating for up to 3 days before using, or freeze for up to 4 months. Thaw completely before using. Proceed with recipe as directed.

SIGNATURE DISH

Rosalynn Carter's Traveling Pimiento Cheese

Memories of the former First Lady and her beloved family recipe

FOR JASON CARTER, one simple dish evokes special Christmas memories of his late grandmother, former First Lady Rosalynn Carter. Instead of reflecting on her numerous social and political accomplishments, Jason chooses to remember Rosalynn as he saw her: a humble Southern grandma with a healthy appreciation for mayonnaise. She was the type of woman who always packed a lunch—with enough to spare. And like most Georgia-bred ladies of her generation, Rosalynn had a killer pimiento cheese recipe.

"My grandmother was like everyone else's grandmother in a lot of ways: She was kind, loving, and almost all of her recipes call for mayonnaise," says Jason, chairman of The Carter Center and eldest grandson of President and Mrs. Carter.

He fondly recalls how his grandparents used to take the whole family on a big trip at Christmas—and the time when his grandmother's famous spread came along with them. "We were all in the back of the plane together," he says. "After takeoff, we looked over and my grandmother had taken out a Tupperware of her pimiento cheese and a loaf of bread and started making sandwiches." If that wasn't enough, once all the kids in her family were fed, she shared with the other people on board. "I still remember the surprised looks on folks' faces as they watched a former First Lady pass out those sandwiches!" he says. "That moment is a perfect reflection of my grandmother: practical, down-to-earth, and selfless."

Carter Family Pimiento Cheese

Many Southerners stir in "secret" ingredients to make their version of the spread stand out. Rosalynn Carter added cream cheese for tanginess and savory onion powder to complement the subtle sweetness of the grated fresh onion.

ACTIVE 15 MIN. · TOTAL 15 MIN.
SERVES 8

16	oz. extra-sharp cheddar cheese, shredded (about 4 cups)
1	(8-oz.) pkg. cream cheese, softened
½	cup mayonnaise of your choice
1	(4-oz.) jar diced pimientos, drained
1	Tbsp. grated yellow onion
¼	tsp. onion powder
¼	tsp. kosher salt
⅛	tsp. black pepper
	White bread, for serving

In a medium bowl, stir together the first 8 ingredients until combined. Serve on white bread (even to strangers on an airplane).

BAKING SCHOOL
TIPS AND TRICKS FROM THE SOUTH'S MOST TRUSTED KITCHEN

Easiest Fudge Ever
ACTIVE 10 MIN.
TOTAL 2 HOURS, 10 MIN.
SERVES 16

1. Grease an 8x8-inch square baking pan with **butter**; line with parchment. Cook ⅔ cup **milk** and ½ cup **unsalted butter** in a saucepan over medium, stirring often, until butter is melted, about 1 minute.

2. Whisk in 2 (5-oz.) pkg. **chocolate cook-and-serve pudding and pie filling** and 1 tsp. each **vanilla** and **salt**. Cook, whisking often, until thickened, about 1 minute. Remove from heat. Stir in 1 lb. **powdered sugar** and ⅓ cup **Dutch-process cocoa**.

3. Spread fudge evenly into pan. Press plastic wrap directly onto fudge; chill until firm, about 2 hours. Remove from pan; cut into squares.

Chocolate Chip Pudding Cookies
ACTIVE 20 MIN.
TOTAL 1 HOUR, 5 MIN.
MAKES ABOUT 32 COOKIES

Preheat oven to 350°F. Sift together 2 cups **all-purpose flour**, 1 tsp. **baking powder**, ¾ tsp. **kosher salt**, and ½ tsp. **baking soda**. Beat 1 cup **unsalted butter**, ¾ cup packed **dark brown sugar**, and ¼ cup **granulated sugar** with an electric mixer on medium-high speed until light and fluffy, about 3 minutes. Add 1 (3.4-oz.) pkg. **vanilla instant pudding and pie filling**, 2 large **eggs**, and 1 tsp. **vanilla extract**; beat on medium speed until well combined, about 1 minute. With mixer on low speed, gradually add flour mixture, beating just until combined, about 1 minute. Fold in 2 cups **semisweet chocolate chips**. Scoop dough in 2-tablespoon portions; spaced 2 inches apart on 3 parchment paper-lined baking sheets. Sprinkle with **flaky sea salt**. Bake, 1 baking sheet at a time, until edges of cookies are lightly golden, 10 to 12 minutes. Let cool 10 minutes before serving.

The Proof Is In the Pudding Mix
A secret ingredient that improves all sorts of sweets, from fudge to cookies

UNLIKE THE Argo or Clabber Girl in your pantry, the cornstarch in instant pudding is formulated to thicken without using heat. Instead of turning the powdered mix into a quick dessert, you can use it as a stabilizing ingredient in recipes like the Whipped Cream Frosting (page 310) used on our cover cake. The starch in the white chocolate pudding mix keeps the whipped cream from deflating on the cake.

But pudding mixes are good for more than whipped cream. They can improve the texture of many desserts. In chocolate chip cookies, the starch helps create a soft center and a more tender crumb. In our ultra-easy fudge recipe, the cook-and-serve pudding mix, which contains both regular and modified cornstarch, quickly sets the candy (no need to get out a thermometer and heat the mixture to a specific temperature).

COOKING SCHOOL
TIPS AND TRICKS FROM THE SOUTH'S MOST TRUSTED KITCHEN

Grate Expectations
How to make the ultimate golden-brown latkes (page 300)

1. SQUEEZE
Water is the enemy of crispy fried foods, so it's crucial to remove excess moisture. Place the grated potatoes and onion in a clean tea towel, and squeeze to remove as much liquid as possible.

2. MIX
Add the eggs, flour, salt, and baking powder to the potato mixture. Stir just until the flour is evenly moistened and no dry spots remain. A fork is a great tool for this job; it helps distribute the ingredients evenly.

3. SCOOP
Spoon about 1 tablespoon of the batter into hot oil. Working quickly, use the side of the spoon to spread batter into an even layer (about ¼-inch-thick). Don't crowd the pan—this will cause them to steam rather than brown.

4. FRY
Cook, flipping once halfway through, until evenly browned and crispy (adjust heat as needed for even color). Remove them from the pan; place on a wire rack set inside a baking sheet. Immediately sprinkle with salt.

Our Favorite Soups & Stews Recipes

When you're in need of pure comfort, these recipes feed body and soul. If time is short, stir up a pot of Chicken-and-Prosciutto Tortelloni Soup (page 342) in just 20 minutes. Looking for something light and fresh? Try Lemony Chicken Soup with Sweet Potatoes (page 343). In need of a company-worthy dinner? Seafood Gumbo (page 354) made with from-scratch seafood broth will rise to the occasion. From Old-Fashioned Chicken and Dumplings (page 353) to modern Mediterranean Kale and Cannellini Stew with Farro (page 354), our (and your!) best bowls are here.

Soups

Sausage Minestrone

ACTIVE 25 MIN. - TOTAL 14 HOURS, 55 MIN., INCLUDING 8 HOURS SOAKING
SERVES 5

- ¾ cup dried navy beans (about 5 oz.)
- ¾ cup dried butter beans or baby limas (about 5 oz.)
- 8 oz. smoked sausage, cut into ¼-inch slices
- 1 cup chopped yellow onion (from 1 onion)
- 3 garlic cloves, chopped
- 6 cups chicken stock
- 1 cup chopped carrots (from 3 carrots)
- 1 cup chopped celery (from 3 stalks)
- 1 cup fresh corn kernels (from 2 ears)
- ¾ tsp. kosher salt
- ½ tsp. black pepper
- 3 cups thinly sliced collard greens (from 1 bunch)
- 1 cup uncooked large elbow macaroni

1. Place dried beans in a large bowl, and cover with 3 to 4 inches of water. Soak beans 8 hours or overnight. Drain and place in a 6-quart slow cooker.
2. Heat a large nonstick skillet over medium-high. Add sausage slices; cook

until lightly browned, about 6 minutes. Using tongs, add sausage to slow cooker. Add onion and garlic to skillet; cook over medium-high, stirring often, until onions are slightly softened, 4 to 5 minutes. Transfer to slow cooker.
3. Add chicken stock, carrots, celery, corn, salt, and pepper to slow cooker; stir to combine. Cover and cook on HIGH until beans are tender, about 6 hours. Stir in collard greens and pasta; cover and cook until collards and pasta are tender, about 30 minutes. Serve immediately.

Southern Wedding Soup

ACTIVE 50 MIN. - TOTAL 1 HOUR, 20 MIN.
SERVES 10

MEATBALLS
- 12 oz. raw andouille sausage, diced
- 1¼ lb. ground pork
- ½ cup finely chopped, stemmed fresh collard greens (about 1 oz.)
- 3 garlic cloves, smashed
- 1 cup finely chopped yellow onion
- 1½ oz. Asiago cheese, grated
- ⅓ cup ricotta cheese
- 2 Tbsp. extra-virgin olive oil
- 1 large egg, beaten
- 1 cup dry breadcrumbs
- ½ tsp. kosher salt

SOUP
- 2 Tbsp. olive oil
- 1½ cups finely chopped yellow onion

- 3 garlic cloves, minced
- ½ cup dry white wine
- 12 cups chicken stock
- 8 oz. uncooked pipette pasta
- 6 cups coarsely chopped, stemmed collards
- 1 (15-oz.) can black-eyed peas, drained and rinsed
- 1 Tbsp. kosher salt
- 1½ Tbsp. fresh lemon juice
- 3 oz. Asiago cheese, grated

1. Prepare the Meatballs: Preheat oven to 400°F with oven rack 6 inches from the heat.
2. Process andouille in a food processor until finely crumbled, about 20 seconds. Add pork, collard greens, garlic, and onion to food processor; pulse until combined, 5 to 6 times. Transfer mixture to a large bowl, and stir in Asiago cheese, ricotta cheese, olive oil, egg, breadcrumbs, and salt, stirring gently to combine. Shape mixture into 54 (1½-inch) meatballs, and place on 2 parchment paper–lined rimmed baking sheets. Bake in preheated oven for 10 minutes. Without removing baking sheets from oven, increase temperature to broil, and broil until browned, 4 to 5 minutes, stirring after 2 minutes.
3. Prepare the Soup: Heat oil in a large Dutch oven over medium-high. Add onion and garlic; cook, stirring occasionally, until softened, about 5 minutes. Stir in wine, and cook until

Continued on page 342

Continued from page 341

slightly reduced, about 3 minutes. Stir in chicken stock, and bring to a boil over high. Add pasta, and cook until al dente, about 8 minutes. Reduce heat to medium; stir in collards and black-eyed peas; cook until greens are just wilted and peas are heated through, about 3 minutes. Stir in salt and lemon juice. Ladle soup into 10 bowls, and sprinkle each with 2 tablespoons Asiago cheese.

Shepherd's Pie Soup

ACTIVE 45 MIN. - TOTAL 2 HOURS
SERVES 12

SOUP

- 2 Tbsp. olive oil
- 2 cups chopped onion
- 4 carrots, cut into small cubes (2¾ cups)
- 6 garlic cloves, minced
- 1 Tbsp. chopped fresh thyme
- 1½ lb. ground lamb
- 1 tsp. kosher salt
- ½ tsp. black pepper
- ¼ cup dry white wine
- 3 Tbsp. all-purpose flour
- 3 Tbsp. tomato paste
- 1 Tbsp. Worcestershire sauce
- 11 cups beef broth
- 3 cups frozen peas, thawed
- 2 cups frozen pearl onions, thawed
- 1 (15-oz.) can corn kernels, drained

MASHED POTATOES

- 2 lb. russet potatoes, cubed
- 1 Tbsp., plus ¾ tsp. kosher salt, divided
- 6 cups cold water
- ⅓ cup heavy cream
- 8 Tbsp. (4 oz.) unsalted butter, cut into pieces, divided
- 2 large egg yolks
- ¼ tsp. black pepper

1. Prepare the Soup: Heat oil in a Dutch oven over medium-high. Add chopped onion and carrots; sauté 7 minutes. Add garlic and thyme; sauté 1 minute. Add lamb, salt, and pepper. Sauté until meat is browned, 13 minutes.
2. Add wine, stirring to deglaze. Stir in flour. Whisk in tomato paste, Worcestershire, and broth. Bring to a boil; reduce to a simmer. Cook until thickened, about 20 minutes. Skim fat from surface. Stir in peas, pearl onions, and corn. Cook 2 minutes.

3. Prepare the Mashed Potatoes: Preheat oven to 425°F. Bring potatoes, 1 tablespoon salt, and 6 cups water to a boil in a saucepan over high. Reduce heat. Simmer, uncovered, until fork-tender, 12 minutes; drain. Cool 5 minutes. Press through a food mill or ricer into the pan.
4. Heat cream and 6 tablespoons butter in a small saucepan over medium, stirring until melted (do not boil), about 3 minutes. Stir mixture into potatoes. Add yolks, pepper, and remaining ¾ teaspoon salt.
5. Spoon potatoes into 3-inch mounds on a parchment-lined baking sheet. Melt remaining 2 tablespoons butter; brush mounds. Bake until golden, 20 to 25 minutes. Divide soup and potato puffs among 12 bowls.

King Ranch Chicken Soup

ACTIVE 35 MIN. - TOTAL 35 MIN.
SERVES 8 TO 10

- 2 Tbsp. butter
- 1 cup chopped yellow onion
- 1 cup chopped green bell pepper
- 1 garlic clove, minced
- 2 (10-oz.) cans diced tomatoes and green chiles
- 1 (10¾-oz.) can cream of mushroom soup
- 1 (10¾-oz.) can cream of chicken soup
- 5 cups chicken broth
- 1 (1½- to 2½-lb.) whole deli-roasted chicken, skin removed and meat shredded
- 1 tsp. dried oregano
- 1 tsp. ground cumin
- 1 tsp. chili powder
- 8 (6-inch) fajita-size corn tortillas, cut into ½-inch strips and halved
  Kosher salt
  Shredded cheddar or Monterey Jack cheese, for garnish

1. Melt butter in a large Dutch oven over medium-high. Add onion and bell pepper, and sauté until tender, 6 to 7 minutes. Add garlic, and sauté 1 minute. Stir in tomatoes, cream of mushroom soup, and cream of chicken soup; combine thoroughly. Stir in broth, chicken, oregano, cumin, and chili powder.
2. Increase heat to medium-high, and bring to a boil. Reduce heat to low, and simmer, stirring occasionally, 5 minutes.

Stir in tortilla strips, and simmer 2 more minutes. Add salt to taste. Garnish servings with shredded cheese.

Chicken-and-Prosciutto Tortelloni Soup

ACTIVE 20 MIN. - TOTAL 20 MIN.
SERVES 4 TO 6

- 1 (8-oz.) pkg. fresh chopped onions, peppers, and celery
- 1 Tbsp. olive oil
- ½ tsp. Italian seasoning
- 1 (14½-oz.) can diced tomatoes with roasted garlic
- 5 cups lower-sodium chicken broth
- ¼ tsp. kosher salt
- ½ tsp. black pepper
- 1 (9-oz.) pkg. refrigerated chicken-and-prosciutto tortelloni
- 1 (6-oz.) pkg. fresh baby spinach
  Cheesy Garlic French Bread, for serving (recipe follows)

Sauté onions, peppers, and celery in hot oil in a Dutch oven over medium-high 3 minutes; add Italian seasoning, and sauté 1 minute. Stir in tomatoes, broth, salt, and pepper. Increase heat to high; bring to a boil. Stir in tortelloni, and return to a boil. Reduce heat to low, and simmer 8 minutes or until tortelloni are tender. Remove from heat, and stir in spinach. Serve with Cheesy Garlic French Bread.

Cheesy Garlic French Bread

ACTIVE 5 MIN. - TOTAL 15 MIN.
SERVES 6 TO 8

Preheat oven to 375°F. Stir together ¼ cup **butter**, melted, and 1 **garlic** clove, pressed. Split 1 (12-oz.) **French bread** loaf; spread with butter mixture. Top with 3 Tbsp. grated **Parmesan cheese**. Place halves together on a baking sheet. Bake 8 to 10 minutes or until cheese is melted. Slice and serve warm.

Creamy Chicken-and-Rice Soup with Collard Greens

ACTIVE 35 MIN. - TOTAL 35 MIN.
SERVES 8

- 3 Tbsp. unsalted butter
- 2 large leeks, thinly sliced (white and light green parts only; 4 cups)

2 medium carrots, thinly sliced (1 cup)

2 celery stalks, finely chopped (½ cup)

2 large garlic cloves, minced

¼ cup all-purpose flour

8 cups lower-sodium chicken broth

3 cups shredded rotisserie chicken (from 1 whole chicken)

1 Tbsp. chopped fresh thyme, plus more for garnish

4 cups chopped collard greens (from 1 bunch)

2 cups cooked white rice

½ cup heavy whipping cream

1 Tbsp. kosher salt

¼ tsp. black pepper

Melt butter in a large Dutch oven over medium. Add leeks, carrots, celery, and garlic. Cook, stirring often, until softened, about 5 minutes. Add flour; cook, stirring constantly, 1 minute. Add broth, chicken, and 1 tablespoon thyme. Bring to a boil over medium–high. Reduce heat to medium–low, and simmer 10 minutes. Stir in collard greens; cook until just tender, about 5 minutes. Remove from heat; stir in cooked rice, cream, salt, and pepper. Garnish servings with additional thyme.

Lemony Chicken Soup with Sweet Potatoes

ACTIVE 15 MIN. · TOTAL 40 MIN.

SERVES 6

1 large lemon

2 Tbsp. olive oil

3 large shallots, thinly sliced (about 1 cup)

2 tsp. chopped fresh rosemary

8 cups unsalted chicken stock

2 medium sweet potatoes, peeled and cut into ¾-inch cubes (about 4 cups)

3 (8-oz.) boneless, skinless chicken breasts

2¾ tsp. kosher salt

¾ cup uncooked orzo

¼ cup chopped fresh flat-leaf parsley

1. Using a vegetable peeler, remove 6 (2-inch) lemon peel strips from lemon. Squeeze lemon to equal 2 tablespoons juice. Set aside.
2. Heat oil in a large Dutch oven over medium–high. Add shallots and rosemary. Cook, stirring occasionally,

until translucent, 4 to 5 minutes. Add lemon peel strips, stock, and potatoes. Bring to a boil over high; reduce heat to medium. Add chicken and salt, and cook 10 minutes. Add orzo, and cook until a thermometer inserted in thickest part of chicken registers 165˚F and potatoes and orzo are tender, about 10 minutes more.
3. Remove and discard lemon peel strips. Remove and shred chicken; return to soup. Stir in lemon juice. Ladle soup into bowls; sprinkle with chopped parsley.

Creamy Chicken Noodle Soup

ACTIVE 25 MIN. · TOTAL 25 MIN.

SERVES 4

¼ cup unsalted butter

1 medium yellow onion, finely chopped (about 1 cup)

3 medium carrots, sliced into ½-inch rounds (about ¾ cup)

2 medium celery stalks, chopped (about ½ cup)

1½ tsp. kosher salt, divided

¼ cup all-purpose flour

4 garlic cloves, finely chopped

¼ tsp. smoked paprika

6 cups chicken stock

8 oz. old-fashioned wide egg noodles

12 oz. cooked chicken, torn into bite-size pieces (4 cups)

½ cup heavy whipping cream

1 Tbsp. sherry vinegar

Fresh thyme leaves, for garnish

1. Melt butter in a large pot over medium–high. Add onion, carrots, celery, and ½ teaspoon of the salt. Cook, stirring occasionally, until softened, about 5 minutes. Add flour, garlic, and paprika. Cook, stirring constantly, until mixture is fragrant and flour turns light brown, about 1 minute.
2. Add stock to flour mixture, and increase heat to high. Bring to a boil, stirring occasionally. Add egg noodles. Cook, stirring occasionally, until tender and just cooked through, about 10 minutes. Reduce heat to medium–low. Add chicken. Cook, stirring constantly, until chicken is heated through, about 1 minute. Remove from heat. Stir in cream, sherry vinegar, and remaining 1 teaspoon salt. Divide soup evenly among 4 bowls; top with thyme leaves.

Green Chile–Chicken Soup

ACTIVE 20 MIN. · TOTAL 20 MIN.

SERVES 6

1 Tbsp. olive or canola oil

1 large poblano chile, seeded and chopped (about ½ cup)

1 medium sweet onion, chopped

4 garlic cloves, finely chopped

4 cups unsalted chicken broth

2 (15½-oz.) cans Great Northern beans, drained and rinsed

1 (15-oz.) can green enchilada sauce

1 tsp. kosher salt

1 tsp. ground cumin

½ tsp. ground coriander

3 cups coarsely shredded cooked chicken

¼ cup chopped fresh cilantro, plus more for garnish

Thinly sliced radishes, for garnish

Sour cream, for garnish

Heat oil in a large Dutch oven over medium–high. Add poblano and sweet onion; cook, stirring occasionally, until tender, about 5 minutes. Add garlic; cook, stirring constantly, until fragrant, about 30 seconds. Stir in broth, beans, enchilada sauce, salt, cumin, and coriander. Bring to a simmer, and cook, stirring occasionally, about 5 minutes. Using back of spoon, gently mash beans. Stir in chicken; continue simmering until heated through, about 5 minutes. Stir in cilantro. Garnish servings with radishes, sour cream, and additional cilantro.

Poblano Chile–Chicken Soup

ACTIVE 20 MIN. · TOTAL 1 HOUR

SERVES 8

2 Tbsp. olive oil

2¼ lb. bone-in, skinless chicken thighs (about 6 thighs)

2 tsp. kosher salt, divided

1½ cups chopped white onion

1½ cups chopped poblano chiles

8 fresh tomatillos, husked and chopped

3 garlic cloves, minced

1 Tbsp. ground cumin

2 tsp. dried thyme

4 cups chicken broth

Continued on page 344

2024 OUR FAVORITE SOUPS & STEWS RECIPES **343**

Continued from page 343

2 (15-oz.) cans white hominy, drained and rinsed

Toppings: sliced radishes, fresh cilantro, hot sauce, sour cream

1. Heat oil in a large Dutch oven over medium-high. Sprinkle chicken with 1 teaspoon of the salt. Cook until browned, 4 minutes per side. Transfer to a plate; reserve drippings in pan. Add onion, poblanos, and tomatillos to hot drippings. Cook, stirring, until softened, 3 minutes. Stir in garlic, cumin, and thyme; cook 1 minute. Stir in broth and remaining 1 teaspoon salt.
2. Add chicken; cover and cook over medium-low until tender, about 40 minutes. Transfer chicken to a cutting board; cool 5 minutes. Remove bones. Chop chicken; return to Dutch oven.
3. Stir in hominy and heat through. Serve with desired toppings.

Southern Italian Chicken Soup

ACTIVE 45 MIN. · TOTAL 50 MIN.
SERVES 8

1 large onion, diced

1 celery rib, thinly sliced

2 carrots, chopped

1 garlic clove, minced

3 Tbsp. olive oil, divided

6 cups chicken broth

1 (14½-oz.) can diced tomatoes

1 tsp. dried Italian seasoning

¼ tsp. dried crushed red pepper

4 (6- to 8-oz.) boneless, skinless chicken breasts

½ tsp. kosher salt

½ tsp. black pepper

2 cups sliced fresh okra

1 (15½-oz.) can black-eyed peas, drained and rinsed

1 (9-oz.) pkg. refrigerated cheese-filled tortellini

Freshly grated Parmesan cheese

1. Sauté onion, celery, carrots, and garlic in 2 tablespoons hot oil in a large Dutch oven over medium-high heat 3 to 5 minutes or until tender. Stir in broth, tomatoes, Italian seasoning, and crushed red pepper; bring to a boil, stirring occasionally. Reduce heat to medium, and simmer, stirring occasionally, 10 minutes.

2. Meanwhile, sprinkle chicken with salt and black pepper. Cook in remaining 1 tablespoon hot oil in a large nonstick skillet over medium-high heat until lightly browned, about 5 minutes. Cool slightly (about 5 minutes); cut into 1-inch pieces.
3. Add okra, black-eyed peas, and chicken to Dutch oven. Simmer, stirring occasionally, 10 minutes or until okra is tender. Add tortellini, and cook, stirring occasionally, 3 minutes or until tortellini is done. Serve with Parmesan.

Soulful Chicken Soup

ACTIVE 20 MIN. · TOTAL 8 HOURS, 20 MIN.
SERVES 6 TO 8

2 lb. bone-in chicken thighs, skinned and trimmed

3 medium carrots, cut into ½-inch pieces (1¼ cups)

1 celery root, peeled, trimmed, and cut into ½-inch pieces (2 cups)

1 medium leek (white and light green parts), cleaned and chopped

2 garlic cloves, peeled and smashed

2 thyme sprigs

2 sage sprigs

1 rosemary sprig

1 bay leaf

1½ tsp. kosher salt

1 tsp. black pepper

8 cups chicken broth

2 cups wide egg noodles

3 Tbsp. finely chopped fresh parsley, divided

1 Tbsp. fresh lemon juice

1. Place chicken, carrots, celery root, leek, garlic, thyme, sage, rosemary, bay leaf, salt, pepper, and broth in a 6-quart slow cooker. Cover and cook on LOW 6 hours or until chicken and vegetables are tender and chicken separates from bone.
2. Remove chicken from slow cooker. Dice meat, discarding bones. Return meat to slow cooker. Stir in noodles and nearly all of the parsley. Cover and cook on HIGH 15 to 20 minutes or until noodles are tender. Stir in lemon juice. Garnish servings with reserved parsley.

Lemon Chicken Soup

ACTIVE 15 MIN. · TOTAL 4 HOURS, 30 MIN.
SERVES 9

9 cups lower-sodium chicken broth

4 cups shredded cooked chicken (from 1 rotisserie chicken)

¾ cup chopped sweet onion (1 small onion)

¾ cup thinly sliced peeled carrots (2 large carrots)

½ cup thinly sliced celery (3 celery stalks)

½ cup dry white wine

2½ tsp. kosher salt

8 oz. uncooked orzo pasta

¾ cup frozen English peas, thawed

¼ cup chopped fresh flat-leaf parsley

1 Tbsp. lemon zest, plus ¼ cup fresh juice (from 2 lemons)

1. Combine broth, chicken, onion, carrots, celery, wine, and salt in a 6-quart slow cooker. Cover and cook on LOW until vegetables are tender, about 4 hours.
2. Increase heat to HIGH; stir in orzo. Cover and cook until orzo is tender, about 15 minutes. Stir in peas, parsley, zest, and juice.

Quick Chicken Noodle Bowls

ACTIVE 20 MIN. · TOTAL 45 MIN.
SERVES 6

6 cups chicken broth

4 boneless, skinless chicken thighs

⅓ cup sliced fresh ginger

2 garlic cloves, sliced

⅛ tsp. Chinese five spice

1 (9½-oz.) pkg. soba noodles or 8 oz. angel hair pasta

1 Tbsp. soy sauce

2 to 3 Tbsp. fresh lime juice

Toppings: sugar snap peas, fresh cilantro and mint, thinly sliced green onions, sliced red chile peppers

1. Bring broth, chicken, ginger, garlic, and seasoning to a boil in a large saucepan over medium heat. Cover, reduce heat to low, and simmer 6 to 8 minutes or until chicken is done.
2. Remove chicken, garlic, and ginger with a slotted spoon, reserving broth in saucepan. Discard garlic and ginger. Let chicken cool slightly (10 to 15 minutes); shred chicken.

3. Return broth to a boil over medium heat. Add noodles and soy sauce; cook, stirring to separate noodles, just until softened, 4 to 5 minutes. Remove noodles from broth using tongs, and divide among 6 bowls. Place chicken on noodles. Return broth to a boil over medium heat; remove from heat, and stir in lime juice. Divide broth among bowls. Serve with desired toppings.

Smoked Chicken Tortilla Soup

ACTIVE 25 MIN. - TOTAL 1 HOUR, 20 MIN.
SERVES 8 TO 10

- 1 large onion, diced
- 1 large jalapeño, seeded and chopped
- 3 Tbsp. olive oil
- 3 garlic cloves, chopped
- 8 cups chicken broth
- 1 (15¼-oz.) can whole kernel corn, drained
- 1 (15-oz.) can black beans, drained
- 1 (14½-oz.) can fire-roasted diced tomatoes
- 1 (14½-oz.) can diced tomatoes with chiles
- 3 Tbsp. ground cumin
- 1½ Tbsp. New Mexico chile powder
- 1½ tsp. kosher salt
- 1 tsp. Worcestershire sauce
- 5 cups shredded cooked chicken (from 2 rotisserie chickens)

    Toppings: tortilla strips, fresh cilantro, avocado slices, lime slices, crumbled queso fresco

1. Sauté onion and jalapeño in hot oil in a Dutch oven over medium-high 5 to 6 minutes. Add garlic, and sauté 1 to 2 minutes.
2. Stir in broth, corn, beans, fire-roasted tomatoes, diced tomatoes with chiles, cumin, chile powder, salt, and Worcestershire sauce. Bring to a boil; reduce heat, and simmer 40 minutes.
3. Remove from heat, and stir in chicken. Let stand 10 minutes before serving. Serve with desired toppings.

Curried Chicken Chowder

ACTIVE 40 MIN. - TOTAL 1 HOUR
SERVES 8 TO 10

- 1 large sweet onion, diced
- 1 cup diced celery
- 1 cup diced carrots
- 2 Tbsp. canola oil
- 2 garlic cloves, minced
- 6 cups chicken broth
- 1 lb. Yukon gold potatoes, peeled and cubed
- 1 lb. sweet potatoes, peeled and cubed
- 4 cups shredded cooked chicken
- 3 cups fresh yellow corn kernels (about 6 ears)
- 2 cups uncooked frozen shelled edamame
- 1 (13½-oz.) can unsweetened coconut milk
- 1 Tbsp. curry powder
- 2 tsp. kosher salt
- 1 tsp. black pepper

    Toppings: toasted coconut, green onions, peanuts, lime wedges

Sauté onion, celery, and carrots in hot oil in a large Dutch oven or stockpot over medium-high heat until tender, about 5 minutes; add garlic, and sauté 1 minute. Add broth, Yukon gold potatoes, sweet potatoes, chicken, corn, edamame, coconut milk, curry powder, salt, and pepper; bring to a boil, stirring often. Reduce heat to medium, and simmer, stirring occasionally, until vegetables are tender, 20 to 25 minutes. Add more salt and pepper to taste. Serve with desired toppings.

Chicken, Sweet Potato, and Corn Chowder

ACTIVE 25 MIN. - TOTAL 4 HOURS, 55 MIN.
SERVES 10

- 8 cups chicken broth
- 1½ lb. sweet potatoes, peeled and cut into ¼-inch pieces (about 4½ cups)
- 2 (1-lb.) bone-in chicken breasts, skinned
- 2 cups fresh corn kernels (from 4 ears)
- 2 yellow onions, chopped
- 1 large red bell pepper, chopped
- 1 large yellow bell pepper, chopped
- 3 stalks celery, chopped
- 2 tsp. kosher salt
- 1 tsp. black pepper
- 1 cup heavy whipping cream
- 5 Tbsp. cornstarch
- ¼ cup chopped fresh flat-leaf parsley

    Toppings: hot sauce, finely chopped fresh chives, fresh parsley

1. Combine broth, sweet potatoes, chicken, corn, onions, bell peppers, celery, salt, and black pepper in a 6-quart slow cooker. Cover and cook on HIGH until chicken and sweet potatoes are tender, about 4 hours. Remove chicken from slow cooker. Coarsely shred, discarding bones; set aside.
2. Whisk together cream and cornstarch in a bowl until smooth; stir into soup. Cover and cook until slightly thickened, about 30 minutes. Stir in chicken and parsley. Serve with desired toppings.

Turkey Posole Verde

ACTIVE 20 MIN. - TOTAL 5 HOURS, 20 MIN.
SERVES 8

- 1 Tbsp. olive oil
- 1 (8-oz.) container refrigerated prechopped yellow onion
- ¾ cup chopped poblano chile (from 1 large chile)
- 1 Tbsp. ground cumin
- 1 tsp. dried oregano
- 3 cups unsalted chicken stock
- 3 (15-oz.) cans white hominy, drained and rinsed
- 1 cup jarred salsa verde
- 2 (12-oz.) bone-in turkey thighs, skin removed

    Toppings: lime wedges, sliced radishes, shredded cabbage

1. Heat oil in a medium skillet over medium-high. Add onion and poblano; cook, stirring often, until tender and beginning to brown, about 6 minutes. Stir in cumin and oregano; cook, stirring constantly, about 1 minute. Transfer to a 5- to 6-quart slow cooker; stir in stock, hominy, and salsa verde. Nestle turkey thighs into mixture in cooker. Cover and cook on LOW until turkey is tender and done, 5 to 6 hours.
2. Remove turkey from cooker. Shred turkey meat, and return to cooker; discard bones. Serve with desired toppings.

2024 OUR FAVORITE SOUPS & STEWS RECIPES **345**

Shrimp–and–New Potato Chowder

ACTIVE 25 MIN. - TOTAL 50 MIN.

SERVES 4 TO 6

- 2 Tbsp. butter
- 3 bunches green onions, sliced
- 1½ lb. new potatoes, diced
- 2 cups lower-sodium chicken broth
- 1½ cups heavy whipping cream
- ½ cup dry white wine
- 1 tsp. kosher salt
- ¼ tsp. black pepper
- ½ lb. medium raw shrimp, peeled and deveined
- 2 tsp. hot sauce

1. Melt butter in a medium Dutch oven over medium heat. Add green onions, and cook, stirring often, 1 minute.
2. Add potatoes, broth, cream, wine, salt, and pepper, and increase heat to high. Bring to a boil. Reduce heat to medium-low, and cook, stirring occasionally, 25 minutes or until potatoes are tender.
3. Stir in shrimp and hot sauce, and cook 3 minutes.

Black Bean Soup

ACTIVE 10 MIN. - TOTAL 6 HOURS, 10 MIN.

SERVES 6

- 2 (15-oz.) cans black beans, rinsed and drained
- 2 (4½-oz.) cans chopped green chiles
- 1 (14½-oz.) can Mexican stewed tomatoes, undrained
- 1 (14½-oz.) can diced tomatoes, undrained
- 1 (11-oz.) can whole kernel corn, drained
- 4 green onions, sliced
- 2 carrots, sliced
- 2 to 3 Tbsp. chili powder
- 1 tsp. ground cumin
- 2 garlic cloves, minced

Combine beans, chiles, stewed tomatoes, diced tomatoes, corn, green onions, carrots, chili powder, cumin, and garlic in a 5-quart slow cooker. Cover and cook at HIGH 5 to 6 hours.

Italian White Beans with Cauliflower

ACTIVE 15 MIN. - TOTAL 7 HOURS, 15 MIN.

SERVES 4

- 3 cups lower-sodium vegetable broth
- 2 (15-oz.) cans cannellini beans, rinsed and drained
- 3 cups cauliflower florets
- 2 cups cherry tomatoes, divided
- 4 shallots, peeled and halved
- 4 garlic cloves, minced
- 2 tsp. dried Italian seasoning, crushed
- ½ tsp. salt
- ¼ tsp. black pepper
- 1 Tbsp. balsamic vinegar
- ½ cup chopped toasted hazelnuts
- ¼ cup chopped fresh basil

Combine broth, beans, cauliflower, 1 cup of the tomatoes, the shallots, garlic, Italian seasoning, salt, and pepper in a 5-quart slow cooker. Cover and cook on LOW 6 to 7 hours or HIGH 3 to 3½ hours. Cut remaining 1 cup tomatoes in half; stir tomatoes and vinegar into soup. Top servings with hazelnuts and basil.

Smoky Lentil Soup

ACTIVE 1 HOUR, 35 MIN. - TOTAL 1 HOUR, 35 MIN.

SERVES 8

- 2 Tbsp. olive oil
- 1 (12-oz.) pkg. center-cut bacon, cut into 1-inch pieces (about 14 slices)
- 1 medium yellow onion, chopped
- 3 medium carrots, chopped
- 9 garlic cloves, minced
- 2 Tbsp. tomato paste
- 1 Tbsp. smoked paprika
- 2 tsp. ground cumin
- 2 Tbsp. chopped fresh thyme
- 2 cups dried brown lentils (16 oz.)
- 2 tsp. kosher salt
- 6 cups vegetable broth
- 3 cups crushed tomatoes (from 1 [28-oz.] can)
- 1 large (6-oz.) bunch lacinato kale, stemmed and thinly sliced (about 4 cups)
- 1 Tbsp. sherry vinegar

1. Heat oil in a Dutch oven over medium. Add bacon, cook, stirring occasionally, until lightly browned but still tender, 8 to 10 minutes. Stir in onion, carrots, and garlic, and cook, stirring occasionally, until softened, 3 to 4 minutes. Stir in tomato paste, paprika, cumin, thyme, lentils, and salt; cook, stirring often, until tomato paste darkens and spices are fragrant, 3 to 4 minutes. Stir in broth, and bring to a boil. Reduce heat to low, and simmer, uncovered, stirring occasionally, until lentils are tender, about 1 hour; stir in tomatoes. Remove from heat.
2. Transfer half of lentil mixture to a blender. Remove center piece of blender lid (to allow steam to escape); secure lid on blender, and place a clean towel over opening (to prevent splatters). Process until smooth, about 2 to 3 minutes. Return pureed lentil mixture to Dutch oven, and stir to combine.
3. Bring lentil mixture to a simmer over medium-high. Stir in kale; cook, stirring occasionally, until wilted, 2 to 3 minutes. Remove from heat; stir in sherry vinegar.

French Onion Soup

ACTIVE 1 HOUR - TOTAL 2 HOURS

SERVES 10

- 3 lb. chicken wings (15 to 16 wings)
- 12 cups chicken broth
- 5 Tbsp. (2½ oz.) unsalted butter, cut into pieces
- 5 lb. yellow onions, thinly sliced (about 6 large onions)
- 1½ tsp. kosher salt, divided
- 3 thyme sprigs, plus more for garnish
- 1 tsp. black peppercorns
- 1 bay leaf
- 3 flat-leaf parsley sprigs
- ½ cup dry sherry
- 10 oz. Asiago cheese, grated (about 2½ cups)
- 10 oz. Gruyère cheese, shredded (about 2½ cups)
- 10 (½-inch-thick) baguette slices, toasted
- 1 large garlic clove, halved

1. Combine wings and chicken broth in a large stockpot. Boil over high; reduce to medium, and simmer about 40 minutes. Pour through a fine wire-mesh strainer into a large bowl. Set aside.

346   2024 OUR FAVORITE SOUPS & STEWS RECIPES

2. Heat butter in a large Dutch oven over medium until foamy, about 3 minutes. Stir in onions and 1 teaspoon of the salt. Partially cover, reduce heat to medium-low, and cook, stirring, until softened, 20 minutes. Uncover and cook, stirring often, until golden brown, about 1 hour and 15 minutes.

3. Meanwhile, place a 5-inch square of cheesecloth on a flat surface. Arrange thyme, peppercorns, bay leaf, and parsley in center of square. Gather edges together; tie with kitchen twine. Set aside.

4. Stir sherry into onions, stirring to deglaze. Stir in prepared chicken stock. Add herb bundle. Bring to a boil over high; reduce to medium-low. Simmer, about 10 minutes. Stir in remaining salt.

5. Preheat broiler to high with oven rack 6 inches from heat. Stir together Asiago and Gruyère cheeses in a medium bowl.

6. Rub toasted baguette slices with cut sides of garlic. Remove and discard herb bundle. Ladle about 1¼ cups soup into a broiler-safe soup bowl on a rimmed baking sheet. Sprinkle ¼ cup cheese mixture over soup, and place a baguette slice in the center. Top with ¼ cup cheese mixture. Place in oven, and broil until cheese is melted, about 2 minutes. Garnish with additional thyme sprigs, if desired.

Broccoli-Potato Soup

ACTIVE 30 MIN. - TOTAL 5 HOURS, 30 MIN.
SERVES 6

- 5 cups peeled and chopped russet potatoes
- 1 (32-oz.) carton lower-sodium chicken broth
- 1 cup chopped carrots
- 1 cup chopped onion
- 1 to 2 tsp. curry powder
- 5 cups broccoli florets
- 1 cup half-and-half
- ½ tsp. kosher salt
- ¼ tsp. black pepper
- Toppings: plain low-fat Greek yogurt, sliced green onions, shredded sharp cheddar cheese, crumbled crisp-cooked bacon, rye bread croutons

1. In a 5- to 6-quart slow cooker combine potatoes, broth, carrots, onion, and curry powder. Cover and cook on LOW 5 to 6 hours or HIGH 2½ to 3 hours. If using LOW, turn to HIGH. Stir in

broccoli. Cover and cook 30 minutes or until broccoli is tender.

2. Using an immersion blender, blend vegetable mixture as desired until slightly chunky or smooth. (Or cool slightly and, working in batches, transfer to a food processor or blender; cover and process or blend as desired. Return to cooker.)

3. Stir in half-and-half, salt, and pepper. Cover and cook on HIGH 10 minutes more. Serve with desired toppings.

Hearty Tomato Soup

ACTIVE 15 MIN. - TOTAL 6 HOURS, 15 MIN.
SERVES 5

- 2 (28-oz.) cans whole plum tomatoes
- 2 (15-oz.) cans lower-sodium chicken broth or vegetable broth
- 1 medium sweet onion, diced
- 4 carrots, diced
- 2 stalks celery, chopped
- 2 Tbsp. unsalted butter, cubed
- 2 garlic cloves, minced
- 1 tsp. dried Italian seasoning
- 1 tsp. kosher salt
- ½ tsp. black pepper
- 1 bay leaf
- ¼ cup thinly sliced fresh basil, plus more for garnish
- 1 Tbsp. red wine vinegar

1. Add tomatoes to a 5½- to 6-quart slow cooker, coarsely crushing them with a spoon or with hands. Add broth, onion, carrots, celery, butter, garlic, Italian seasoning, salt, pepper, and bay leaf; stir to combine.

2. Cook on LOW until vegetables are very tender, about 6 hours. Remove bay leaf. Stir in basil and vinegar. Garnish servings with additional basil.

Tomato-and-Red Pepper Soup

ACTIVE 15 MIN. - TOTAL 15 MIN.
SERVES 4 TO 6

- 1 (28-oz.) can whole tomatoes
- 1 (12-oz.) jar roasted red peppers, drained
- ¼ cup half-and-half
- 1½ tsp. kosher salt
- 1 tsp. granulated sugar
- ½ tsp. black pepper
- 2 garlic cloves

Combine tomatoes, red peppers, half-and-half, salt, sugar, pepper, garlic, and ¼ cup water in a food processor until smooth, stopping to scrape down sides as needed. Transfer mixture to a medium saucepan, and cook over medium-high, stirring often, until hot, about 8 minutes.

Mushroom Bisque

ACTIVE 30 MIN. - TOTAL 6 HOURS, 30 MIN.
SERVES 8

- 16 oz. fresh cremini mushrooms, stem ends trimmed, halved
- 8 oz. fresh shiitake mushrooms, stemmed and halved
- 2 Tbsp. olive oil
- ½ tsp. kosher salt
- ¼ tsp. black pepper
- 2½ cups vegetable broth or lower-sodium chicken broth
- 1 cup chopped onion
- ¼ cup dry sherry or dry white wine
- 4 garlic cloves, minced
- 2 Tbsp. all-purpose flour
- 2 Tbsp. butter, softened
- 1 (8-oz.) carton crème fraîche
- 1 Tbsp. chopped fresh dill
- 1½ tsp. lemon zest

1. Place mushrooms in a 3½- or 4-quart slow cooker. Drizzle with oil, and sprinkle with salt and pepper; toss to coat. Stir in broth, onion, sherry, and garlic. Cover and cook on LOW 6 to 7 hours or HIGH 3 to 3½ hours.

2. Using an immersion blender, blend mushroom mixture until nearly smooth, leaving some coarse mushroom pieces. (Or cool slightly and transfer, half at a time, to a food processor or blender; cover and process or blend until nearly smooth.)

3. If using LOW, turn to HIGH. Stir together flour and butter; whisk into mushroom mixture. Cover and cook until thickened and bubbly, 30 to 45 minutes more. Whisk in crème fraîche. Garnish servings with dill and lemon zest.

Wild Mushroom Soup

ACTIVE 45 MIN. - TOTAL 1 HOUR, 30 MIN.
SERVES 12

- 10 cups vegetable broth
- 8 cups dried shiitake mushrooms (4 oz.)
- 6 Tbsp. (3 oz.) unsalted butter, cut into pieces
- 1 medium yellow onion, chopped
- 10½ cups assorted fresh wild mushrooms, sliced (1 lb., 9 oz.)
- 7 garlic cloves, chopped
- 1 Tbsp. chopped fresh thyme, plus more for garnish
- ½ tsp. black pepper
- 1 tsp. kosher salt
- ½ cup (4 oz.) brandy
- 1 cup heavy whipping cream
- ¼ cup chopped fresh chives

1. Bring broth and dried mushrooms to a boil in a large saucepan over high. Remove from heat, and let stand at room temperature until mushrooms soften, about 30 minutes.
2. Meanwhile, melt butter in a Dutch oven over medium-high, without stirring, until butter begins to foam, 2 to 3 minutes. Continue to cook, stirring constantly with a wooden spoon to loosen brown bits from bottom of Dutch oven, until butter is golden brown and has a nutty aroma, 4 to 6 minutes. Stir in onion and fresh mushrooms; cook, stirring often, until softened and lightly browned, 10 to 12 minutes. Remove and reserve 1 cup browned mushrooms for serving. Stir garlic, thyme, pepper, and salt into mushroom mixture; cook, stirring often, until fragrant, about 1 minute. Add brandy; cook, stirring constantly, until liquid evaporates, 2 to 3 minutes. Stir in softened mushrooms and broth. Bring to a boil over high; reduce heat to low, and simmer, stirring occasionally, until thickened, 15 to 20 minutes.
3. Transfer half of mushroom mixture to a blender. Remove center piece of lid (to allow steam to escape); secure lid on blender, and place a clean towel over opening. Process until very smooth, about 1 to 2 minutes. Transfer to a large bowl. Repeat procedure with remaining mushroom mixture. Return mushroom mixture to Dutch oven, and stir in heavy cream. Cook over high, stirring occasionally, until hot, about 2 minutes.
4. Garnish servings with chives, thyme, and reserved mushrooms.

Loaded Cauliflower Soup

ACTIVE 15 MIN. - TOTAL 4 HOURS, 15 MIN.
SERVES 6

- 6 bacon slices, chopped
- 1 cup chopped leek
- ½ cup chopped celery
- 4 garlic cloves, minced
- 8 cups chopped cauliflower florets and stems (from 1 [2½-lb.] head)
- 3 cups unsalted chicken stock
- 1 tsp. kosher salt
- ¼ tsp. black pepper
- ¾ cup half-and-half
- 2 oz. sharp cheddar cheese, shredded (about ½ cup)
- 3 Tbsp. chopped fresh chives

1. Cook bacon in a skillet over medium, stirring often, until crisp, 5 to 7 minutes. Using a slotted spoon, transfer bacon to paper towels to drain. Reserve 1 tablespoon drippings in pan; discard remaining drippings.
2. Combine reserved drippings, leek, celery, garlic, cauliflower, stock, salt, and pepper in a 6-quart slow cooker. Cover and cook on LOW until tender, about 4 hours.
3. Remove 1 cup vegetables with a slotted spoon; finely chop.
4. Pour remaining mixture into a blender; add half-and-half. Remove center piece of blender lid (to allow steam to escape); attach lid, and place a clean towel over opening in lid. Process, starting slowly and increasing speed, until very smooth, 1 minute and 30 seconds to 2 minutes. Return mixture to slow cooker with chopped vegetables; cook until warmed through, about 2 minutes. Ladle soup into bowls; top with bacon, cheese, and chives.

Creamy Pumpkin Soup

ACTIVE 30 MIN. - TOTAL 1 HOUR
SERVES 10

- 1 whole star anise
- 1 cinnamon stick
- ¼ tsp. whole allspice
- 1 tsp. black peppercorns
- 2 bay leaves
- 5 thyme sprigs
- 9 Tbsp. unsalted butter, cut into pieces, divided
- 1 medium onion, chopped
- 1¾ cups chopped Honeycrisp apples (from 2 apples)
- 2 (15-oz.) cans pumpkin
- 5 cups vegetable broth
- 1¼ tsp. kosher salt, divided
- 1 cup raw pepitas
- ¼ tsp. cayenne pepper
- ½ tsp. granulated sugar
- 1 cup heavy whipping cream

1. Place a 5-inch square of cheesecloth on a flat surface. Place star anise, cinnamon stick, allspice, peppercorns, bay leaves, and thyme sprigs in the center of the square. Gather the edges together; tie securely with kitchen twine. Set the spice bundle aside.
2. Melt 8 tablespoons of the butter in a Dutch oven over medium until foamy, 2 to 3 minutes. Cook, stirring constantly to loosen brown bits from the bottom of the skillet, until butter is golden brown with a nutty aroma, 5 to 7 minutes. Stir in onion and apples; cook, stirring often, until softened, 6 minutes. Add pumpkin, broth, and 1 teaspoon of the salt; stir to combine. Add the spice bundle. Bring the pumpkin mixture to a boil over medium-high; reduce heat to low. Simmer, uncovered, 25 to 30 minutes.
3. Meanwhile, heat remaining 1 tablespoon butter in a medium skillet over medium-high until foamy, 2 to 3 minutes. Add pepitas, and cook, stirring occasionally, 3 minutes. Sprinkle with cayenne, sugar, and remaining ¼ teaspoon salt; cook, stirring, until pepitas are toasted, about 3 minutes. Transfer to a paper towel–lined plate.
4. Remove spice bundle from pumpkin mixture, and discard. Transfer half of mixture to a blender. Remove center of lid (to allow steam to escape); secure lid on blender, and place a clean towel over opening. Process until smooth, 30 seconds. Transfer to a large bowl. Repeat process with remaining mixture. Return soup to Dutch oven; stir in cream. Garnish servings with pepitas.

Spicy Pumpkin Soup with Avocado Cream

ACTIVE 55 MIN. - TOTAL 55 MIN.

SERVES 6 TO 8

- 1 cup diced yellow onion
- 3 Tbsp. olive oil, divided
- 1½ tsp. kosher salt, divided
- 2 garlic cloves, chopped
- 1 Tbsp. ground cumin
- 1 (29-oz.) can pumpkin
- 6 to 6½ cups lower-sodium chicken broth
- 1 canned chipotle pepper in adobo sauce, plus 1 Tbsp. adobo sauce from can
- 1 medium avocado, peeled and diced
- ½ cup whole buttermilk
- 2 Tbsp. fresh lime juice
- 2 Tbsp. extra-virgin olive oil
- 8 oz. smoked sausage, sliced
- 1 cup canned black beans, drained and rinsed
- ½ tsp. smoked paprika

1. Place onions, 2 tablespoons olive oil, and 1 teaspoon salt in a Dutch oven over medium; cover and cook until translucent, 5 to 6 minutes. Stir in garlic and cumin; cook 2 minutes. Whisk in pumpkin and 6 cups broth; add chipotle pepper and 1 tablespoon adobo sauce. Increase heat to medium-high, and simmer, stirring occasionally, 12 minutes.
2. Process soup, in batches, in a food processor or blender 1 minute. Add up to ½ cup broth, 2 tablespoons at a time, to reach desired consistency.
3. Process avocado, buttermilk, lime juices, and remaining ½ teaspoon salt in a blender until smooth. Add up to ¼ cup water, 1 tablespoon at a time, to reach desired consistency.
4. Cook smoked sausage in remaining 1 tablespoon olive oil in a large skillet over medium, stirring occasionally, 3 minutes. Stir in black beans and paprika, and cook 1 minute. Top servings with sausage mixture and avocado cream.

Carrot-Apple Soup

ACTIVE 30 MIN. - TOTAL 1 HOUR, 45 MIN.

SERVES 4 TO 6

- 1½ lb. carrots, peeled and chopped (about 8 large)
- 3 tart apples (such as Granny Smith) or creamy apples (such as McIntosh), peeled and chopped (about 1 lb.)
- 1 large yellow onion, chopped
- 2 cups heavy whipping cream
- 1½ cups unsalted chicken stock
- 1¼ cups apple cider
- 3 thyme sprigs
- 1 tsp. kosher salt
- ½ tsp. black pepper
  Sour cream and diced apples (optional)

1. Combine carrots, apples, onion, cream, stock, cider, thyme, salt, and pepper to a boil in a Dutch oven over medium-high heat; reduce heat to low, and simmer, stirring occasionally, 50 to 60 minutes or until carrots are tender. Remove from heat, and cool 15 minutes.
2. Remove thyme sprigs. Process soup, in batches, in a blender or food processor until smooth. (For a thinner soup, stir in more broth, 1 tablespoon at a time.) If desired, top servings with sour cream and additional diced apples.

Stews

Peppery Beef Stew with Root Vegetables

ACTIVE 25 MIN. - TOTAL 7 HOURS, 25 MIN.

SERVES 6

- 1 Tbsp. olive oil
- 2 lb. trimmed chuck roast (about 2⅓ lb. untrimmed)
- 2 tsp. black pepper, divided
- 1½ tsp. kosher salt, divided
- 6 garlic cloves, chopped
- 1 cup dry red wine
- 2 cups unsalted beef stock
- 3 Tbsp. all-purpose flour
- 2 Tbsp. unsalted tomato paste
- 4 thyme sprigs
- 2 bay leaves
- 1 lb. small turnips, peeled and cut into wedges (about 3 cups)
- 1 lb. carrots, peeled and cut into 2-inch pieces (about 3 cups)
- 1¼ lb. celery root, peeled and cut into cubes (about 2 cups)
- 2 cups fresh pearl onions, peeled, or thawed frozen pearl onions (about 8 oz.)
- 1 cup water
- 2 Tbsp. chopped fresh flat-leaf parsley

1. Heat olive oil in a skillet over medium-high. Sprinkle roast with ½ teaspoon pepper and ½ teaspoon salt. Add roast to skillet; cook until browned, about 5 minutes per side. Remove roast from skillet. Add garlic to pan; cook, stirring constantly, 1 minute. Add wine; cook until reduced by half, about 2 minutes, scraping bottom of pan to loosen browned bits.
2. Place roast and wine mixture in a 6-quart slow cooker.
3. Stir together stock and flour; pour over roast. Stir in tomato paste, thyme, bay leaves, remaining 1½ teaspoons pepper, and remaining 1 teaspoon salt. Add turnips, carrots, celery root, onions, and the water. Cover and cook on LOW until roast is tender, about 7 hours.
4. Coarsely shred beef; discard thyme and bay leaves. Garnish with parsley.

Pesto Meatball Stew

ACTIVE 10 MIN. - TOTAL 5 HOURS, 10 MIN.

SERVES 6

- 2 (14½-oz.) cans Italian-style stewed tomatoes, undrained
- 1 (16-oz.) pkg. (32) frozen cooked Italian-style meatballs, thawed
- 1 (15- to 19-oz.) can cannellini (white kidney) beans, rinsed and drained
- ½ cup water
- ¼ cup basil pesto
- ½ cup finely shredded Parmesan cheese (2 oz.)
  Fresh basil, for garnish

1. In a 4-quart slow cooker, combine tomatoes, meatballs, drained beans, water, and pesto.
2. Cover and cook on LOW 5 to 7 hours or on HIGH 2½ to 3½ hours. Sprinkle servings with cheese. Garnish with basil.

Brisket Chili

ACTIVE 20 MIN. - TOTAL 9 HOURS, 20 MIN.
SERVES 10

- 3 Tbsp. all-purpose flour
- 2 Tbsp. ancho chile powder
- 1 Tbsp. ground cumin
- 1 Tbsp. kosher salt
- 1 tsp. dried oregano
- 2 lb. beef brisket, trimmed and cut into 1-inch cubes
- 2 (15-oz.) cans black beans
- 1 (15-oz.) can fire-roasted diced tomatoes, drained
- 1 red bell pepper, chopped
- 1 medium red onion, chopped
- 3 garlic cloves, minced
- ¾ cup beef broth
- 4 Tbsp. olive oil, divided

1. Stir together flour, ancho chile powder, cumin, salt, and oregano in a small bowl. Sprinkle spice mixture evenly on each side of beef brisket cubes, and set aside.
2. Combine black beans, tomatoes, bell pepper, onion, garlic, and beef broth in a 6- to 7-quart slow cooker.
3. Heat 2 tablespoons of the oil in a large skillet over medium-high. Add half of brisket cubes; cook, stirring often, until browned on all sides, 5 to 7 minutes. Transfer beef to slow cooker. Repeat procedure with remaining oil and brisket.
4. Cover and cook on LOW 8 hours. Uncover and cook until slightly thickened, about 1 hour.

Beef–and–Butternut Squash Chili

ACTIVE 20 MIN. - TOTAL 1 HOUR, 30 MIN.
SERVES 8

- ½ small butternut squash, peeled and cubed (about 1½ cups)
  Vegetable cooking spray
- 1 lb. ground beef
- 1 green bell pepper, chopped
- 1 medium onion, chopped
- 2 garlic cloves, minced
- 2 (14½-oz.) cans Mexican-style stewed tomatoes, chopped
- 1 (16-oz.) can chili beans
- 1 cup lower-sodium beef broth
- 1½ tsp. ground cumin
- 1½ tsp. chili powder
- 1 cup frozen corn kernels

1. Place squash in a large microwave-safe bowl. Cover tightly with plastic wrap, folding back a small edge to allow steam to escape. Microwave on HIGH 8 minutes or until squash is tender, and drain. Lightly grease a 4- to 5-quart slow cooker with cooking spray. Arrange squash in bottom of slow cooker.
2. Cook beef, bell pepper, onion, and garlic in a skillet over medium-high heat until meat crumbles and is no longer pink, 5 to 6 minutes; drain well. Add to slow cooker.
3. Stir in tomatoes, chili beans, broth, cumin, chili powder, and corn. Cover and cook on HIGH 1 hour.

Louisiana Gumbo

ACTIVE 40 MIN. - TOTAL 40 MIN.
SERVES 8 TO 10

- ½ cup peanut oil
- ½ cup all-purpose flour
- 1 cup chopped sweet onion
- 1 cup chopped green bell pepper
- 1 cup chopped celery
- 2 tsp. Creole seasoning
- 2 garlic cloves, minced
- 3 (14-oz.) cans lower-sodium chicken broth
- 4 cups shredded cooked chicken
- ½ lb. andouille sausage, cut into ¼-inch-thick slices
- 1½ cups frozen black-eyed peas, thawed
- 1 lb. jumbo raw shrimp, peeled and deveined

1. Heat oil in a large Dutch oven over medium-high heat; gradually whisk in flour, and cook, whisking constantly, 5 to 7 minutes or until flour is chocolate colored. (Do not burn mixture.)
2. Reduce heat to medium. Stir in onion, bell pepper, celery, Creole seasoning, and garlic, and cook, stirring constantly, 3 minutes. Gradually stir in chicken broth; add chicken, sausage, and black-eyed peas. Increase heat to medium-high, and bring to a boil. Reduce heat to low, and simmer, stirring occasionally, 20 minutes. Add shrimp, and cook just until shrimp turn pink, about 5 minutes.

Chicken-Andouille Gumbo with Roasted Potatoes

ACTIVE 45 MIN. - TOTAL 3 HOURS, 10 MIN., INCLUDING POTATOES
SERVES 6 TO 8

- 1 lb. andouille sausage, cut into ¼-inch-thick slices
- ½ cup peanut oil
- ¾ cup all-purpose flour
- 1 large onion, coarsely chopped
- 1 red bell pepper, coarsely chopped
- 1 cup thinly sliced celery
- 2 garlic cloves, minced
- 2 tsp. Cajun seasoning
- ⅛ tsp. cayenne pepper (optional)
- 1 (48-oz.) carton chicken broth
- 2 lb. boneless, skinless chicken breasts
  Roasted Potatoes (recipe follows)
  Toppings: chopped fresh parsley, cooked and crumbled bacon, hot sauce

1. Cook sausage in a large skillet over medium heat, stirring often, until browned, about 7 minutes. Remove sausage; drain and pat dry with paper towels.
2. Heat oil in a stainless-steel Dutch oven over medium heat; gradually whisk in flour, and cook, whisking constantly, 18 to 20 minutes or until flour is caramel colored. (Do not burn mixture.) Reduce heat to low, and cook, whisking constantly, until mixture is milk chocolate-colored and texture is smooth (about 2 minutes).
3. Increase heat to medium. Stir in onion, bell pepper, celery, garlic, Cajun seasoning, and cayenne, if using. Cook, stirring constantly, 3 minutes. Gradually stir in chicken broth; add chicken and sausage. Increase heat to medium-high, and bring to a boil. Reduce heat to low, and simmer, stirring occasionally, 1 hour and 30 minutes to 1 hour and 40 minutes or until chicken is done. Shred chicken into large pieces using 2 forks.
4. Place Roasted Potatoes in serving bowls. Spoon gumbo over potatoes. Serve immediately with desired toppings.

Roasted Potatoes

ACTIVE 10 MIN. - TOTAL 50 MIN.
SERVES 6 TO 8

- 3 lb. baby red potatoes, quartered
- 1 Tbsp. peanut oil
- 1 tsp. kosher salt

Preheat oven to 450°F. Stir together potatoes, oil, and salt in a large bowl. Place potatoes in a single layer in a lightly greased 15- x 10-inch rimmed baking pan. Bake until tender and browned, stirring twice, 40 to 45 minutes.

White Bean, Sausage, and Turnip Green Stew

ACTIVE 30 MIN. - TOTAL 50 MIN.
SERVES 4 TO 6

- ¼ cup, plus 1½ tsp. kosher salt, divided
- 1 (1-lb.) pkg. fresh chopped turnip greens
- 2 cups diced smoked sausage
- 2 Tbsp. olive oil
- 3 medium turnips (about 1 lb.), chopped
- 2 leeks, chopped
- 1 red bell pepper, chopped
- 3 garlic cloves, minced
- 2 (15-oz.) cans white beans, drained and rinsed
- 1 (32-oz.) carton lower-sodium chicken broth
- ¼ cup grated Parmigiano-Reggiano cheese
- 1 tsp. black pepper

1. Bring 2 quarts water and ¼ cup kosher salt to a boil in a large stockpot over high. Add turnip greens, and boil 5 minutes or until tender. Drain.
2. Cook sausage in hot oil in a large Dutch oven over medium, stirring often, until browned, about 5 minutes. Stir in turnips, and cook 5 minutes. Add leeks, bell pepper, garlic, and beans, and cook, stirring often, until leeks are tender, about 5 minutes.
3. Increase heat to high. Add turnip greens and chicken broth, and bring to a boil. Reduce heat to medium, and simmer, stirring occasionally, 10 minutes. Stir in cheese, black pepper, and remaining 1½ tsp. salt.

Chicken Sausage–and–White Bean Stew

ACTIVE 11 MIN. - TOTAL 8 HOURS, 11 MIN.
SERVES 4

- 1 (12-oz.) pkg. spinach-and-feta chicken sausage, sliced
- 3 carrots, coarsely chopped
- 1 medium onion, chopped
- ½ tsp. kosher salt
- ½ tsp. dried rosemary
- ¼ tsp. black pepper
- 1 (14½-oz.) can fire-roasted diced tomatoes, undrained
- 2 (15.8-oz.) cans Great Northern beans, undrained
- 4 bacon slices, cooked and crumbled (optional)

1. Cook sausage in a large skillet over medium-high until browned, about 4 minutes.
2. Place carrots and onion in a 4- to 5-quart slow cooker; sprinkle with salt, rosemary, and pepper. Layer tomatoes and beans over carrot mixture. Top with sausage. Cover and cook on LOW 8 hours or until vegetables are tender. Sprinkle with crumbled bacon before serving, if desired

Stovetop Red Beans and Rice

ACTIVE 15 MIN. - TOTAL 2 HOURS, 45 MIN.
SERVES 6 TO 8

- 1 lb. dried red kidney beans
- ½ lb. andouille smoked chicken sausage, thinly sliced
- 3 celery ribs, chopped
- 1 green bell pepper, chopped
- 1 medium onion, chopped
- 3 garlic cloves, minced
- 1 Tbsp. Creole seasoning
- 3 cups uncooked long-grain rice
  Sliced green onions, for garnish

1. Place beans in a Dutch oven; add water to cover beans by 2 inches. Bring to a boil. Boil 1 minute; cover, remove from heat, and soak 1 hour. Drain.
2. Sauté sausage, celery, bell pepper, and onion in a Dutch oven over medium-high until sausage is browned, about 10 minutes. Add garlic; sauté 1 minute. Add beans, Creole seasoning, and 7 cups water. Bring to a boil; reduce heat to low, and simmer until beans are tender, 1 to 1½ hours.

3. Meanwhile, cook rice according to package directions. Serve with red beans. Garnish servings with green onion.

Quick Chicken and Barley Stew

ACTIVE 15 MIN. - TOTAL 30 MIN.
SERVES 4

- 3 bacon slices
- 1 Tbsp. olive oil
- 1 medium yellow onion, chopped
- 2 medium carrots, cut diagonally into ¼-inch-thick slices
- 3 stalks celery, cut diagonally into ¼-inch-thick slices
- 3 large garlic cloves, minced
- 1 tsp. kosher salt
- ½ tsp. black pepper
- 4 (6-oz.) boneless, skinless chicken breasts
- 4 cups lower-sodium chicken broth
- 1 cup uncooked quick-cooking barley
- 1 (8-oz.) pkg. baby spinach
- 2 Tbsp. chopped fresh flat-leaf parsley

1. Cook bacon in a large Dutch oven over medium heat until crisp, about 6 minutes, turning once. Transfer bacon to a plate lined with paper towels, reserving drippings in Dutch oven. Crumble bacon, and set aside.
2. Add olive oil to drippings in Dutch oven; increase heat to medium-high. Add onion, carrots, and celery; cook, stirring occasionally, until tender, 3 to 4 minutes. Stir in garlic, salt, and pepper, and cook until fragrant, about 1 minute.
3. Add chicken and broth to pot. Cook on medium-high until broth begins to boil, 2 to 3 minutes. Reduce heat to medium-low. Stir in barley, and cook until chicken is cooked through and a thermometer inserted in the thickest portion reads 165°F, 8 to 10 minutes more. Remove chicken, shred into large pieces, and return to pot. Add spinach, and stir until wilted, about 1 minute. Stir in parsley; top servings with crumbled bacon.

Peanut Chicken Stew

ACTIVE 15 MIN. - TOTAL 1 HOUR, 45 MIN., INCLUDING BROTH

SERVES 6

- 3 cups chopped cooked chicken
- 1½ cups creamy peanut butter
- 1 (28-oz.) can diced tomatoes, drained
- 1 Tbsp. curry powder
- 1 tsp. cayenne pepper
- 4 to 6 cups Sweet Potato Broth (recipe follows)
- Kosher salt
- ½ cup chopped unsalted roasted peanuts
- Chopped fresh cilantro, for garnish

Stir together chicken, peanut butter, tomatoes, curry powder, cayenne, and 4 cups Sweet Potato Broth in a medium stockpot. Bring to a simmer over medium, stirring occasionally, until thickened, about 20 minutes. Stir in up to 2 cups additional broth, ½ cup at a time, until desired consistency is reached. Add salt to taste. Top servings with peanuts and cilantro.

Sweet Potato Broth

ACTIVE 25 MIN. - TOTAL 1 HOUR, 10 MIN.

MAKES 6 CUPS

Heat 2 Tbsp. **olive oil** in a large stockpot over medium. Add 1 medium **onion**, sliced; 3 **celery** ribs, chopped; and 1 **carrot**, chopped. Cook, stirring often, until vegetables are tender, 8 to 10 minutes. Add 1 peeled and quartered large **sweet potato**, 5 **whole cloves**, desired amount of **kosher salt** and **black pepper**, and 6 cups water. Increase heat to high, and bring to a boil. Reduce heat to medium-low, and simmer 30 to 35 minutes or until sweet potato is tender. Discard cloves. Let mixture stand 15 minutes. Process, in batches, in a food processor or blender until smooth. Season with salt and pepper. Use immediately, or cool completely, and refrigerate in an airtight container up to 5 days. You can freeze cooked and cooled mixture up to 2 months.

Chicken Stew with Pumpkin and Wild Rice

ACTIVE 30 MIN. - TOTAL 3 HOURS, 30 MIN.

SERVES 6

- 1 Tbsp. canola oil
- 6 boneless, skinless chicken thighs (about 1¾ lb.)
- 1 cup chopped celery
- 1 cup chopped yellow onion
- 5 garlic cloves, chopped
- ⅓ cup all-purpose flour
- 4 cups chicken broth
- 4 cups (about 19 oz.) cubed sugar pumpkin or butternut squash
- ½ cup uncooked wild rice
- 2 tsp. kosher salt
- 1 cup half-and-half
- ¼ cup coarsely chopped fresh flat-leaf parsley
- 2 Tbsp. chopped fresh tarragon
- 1 Tbsp. fresh thyme leaves

1. Heat oil in a large skillet over medium-high. Add chicken, and cook until well browned, about 5 minutes. Turn chicken over, and cook 2 minutes.
2. Transfer chicken to a 5- to 6-quart slow cooker. Add celery, onion, and garlic to skillet. Cook, stirring often, until starting to soften, about 4 minutes. Add flour to skillet, and cook, stirring constantly, 1 minute. Add broth; bring to a boil, and cook, stirring constantly, until thickened, about 1 minute.
3. Transfer mixture to slow cooker. Add pumpkin, rice, and salt. Cover and cook on LOW until rice, chicken, and vegetables are tender, about 3 hours.
4. Stir in half-and-half, parsley, tarragon, and thyme leaves.

Tex-Mex Chicken Chili with Lime

ACTIVE 30 MIN. - TOTAL 45 MIN.

SERVES 6 TO 8

- 1 Tbsp. butter
- 2 Tbsp. olive oil
- 1 large white onion, diced
- 1 medium red onion, diced
- 1 poblano or green bell pepper, seeded and diced
- 1 red or green jalapeño, seeded and diced
- 1 large sweet potato, peeled and chopped
- 3 garlic cloves, minced
- 2 tsp. ground cumin
- 2 tsp. chipotle powder
- 2 tsp. kosher salt
- 2 (16-oz.) cans navy beans, drained and rinsed
- 1 (12-oz.) bottle white ale
- 4 cups shredded cooked chicken
- 4 cups chicken broth
- Toppings: Lime Cream (recipe follows), chopped fresh cilantro, green onions, lime wedges
- Green Chile Cheese Toast, for serving (recipe opposite)

1. Melt butter with oil in a Dutch oven over medium heat. Add white onion, red onion, poblano pepper, jalapeño, and sweet potato, and sauté until vegetables are softened, 5 to 6 minutes. Add garlic and sauté 1 minute more. Add cumin, chipotle powder, salt, beans, and beer, and cook until liquid is reduced by half, about 5 minutes.
2. Add chicken and broth; bring to a boil over high heat. Reduce heat to medium-low, and simmer until thickened, about 30 minutes. Serve with desired toppings. and Green Chile Toast.

Lime Cream

MAKES 1 CUP

Combine 1 cup **sour cream** and zest and juice of 1 **lim**e. Season with **salt** to taste.

Green Chile Cheese Toast

Stir together 1 cup (4 oz.) each shredded **pepper Jack cheese** and **white cheddar cheese**, ¾ cup **mayonnaise**, ½ cup freshly grated **Parmesan** cheese, 1 (4½-oz.) can **diced green chiles**, and 1 Tbsp. **ranch dressing mix**. Spread on toasted **French bread** slices. Broil 5 inches from heat until bubbly.

Old-Fashioned Chicken and Dumplings

ACTIVE 30 MIN. - TOTAL 1 HOUR, 50 MIN.
SERVES 6

- 1 (2½- to 3-lb.) whole chicken
- 2 celery stalks, roughly chopped
- 2 medium carrots, roughly chopped
- 2 qt. water
- 2½ tsp. kosher salt, divided
- ½ tsp. black pepper
- 2 cups all-purpose flour, plus more for work surface
- ½ tsp. baking soda
- 3 Tbsp. vegetable shortening
- ¾ cup whole buttermilk
  Chopped fresh chives, for garnish

1. Place chicken, celery, and carrots in a Dutch oven; add water and 2 teaspoons of the salt. Bring to a boil over high; cover, reduce heat to medium-low, and simmer until tender, about 1 hour. Remove chicken from broth, and let stand until cool enough to handle, about 15 minutes. Remove and discard skin and bones from chicken, and cut meat into bite-size pieces. Bring broth to a boil over high; stir in pepper.
2. Meanwhile, combine flour, baking soda, and remaining ½ teaspoon salt in a large bowl; cut in shortening with a pastry blender (or use your fingers) until mixture resembles coarse meal. Add buttermilk, stirring with a fork until dry ingredients are moistened. Turn dough out onto a well-floured surface, and knead lightly 4 or 5 times.
3. Pat dough to ½-inch thickness. Pinch off dough in 1½-inch pieces, and drop into boiling broth. Reduce heat to medium-low, and cook, stirring occasionally, until desired consistency is reached, 8 to 10 minutes. Stir in chicken. Garnish servings with chives.

Chicken and Herbed Cornmeal Dumplings

ACTIVE 20 MIN. - TOTAL 40 MIN.
SERVES 6

- ¼ cup butter, divided
- 3 small carrots, sliced
- 2 celery stalks, sliced
- 1 medium onion, chopped
- ½ cup, plus 2 Tbsp. all-purpose flour, divided
- 3¼ cups chicken broth
- 1 bay leaf
- ¾ tsp. kosher salt, divided
- 3 cups coarsely shredded cooked chicken
- ½ cup coarse plain yellow cornmeal
- 1 tsp. baking powder
- ¼ tsp. baking soda
- ½ cup whole buttermilk
- 2 Tbsp. chopped fresh flat-leaf parsley
- 1 Tbsp. chopped fresh tarragon

1. Melt 2 tablespoons of the butter in a Dutch oven over medium-high. Add carrots, celery, and onion; cook, stirring occasionally, until onions are tender, 5 to 6 minutes. Add 2 tablespoons of the flour; cook, stirring occasionally, 1 to 2 minutes. Add broth, bay leaf, and ½ teaspoon of the salt; bring to a boil. Cook, stirring occasionally, until thickened, 4 to 5 minutes. Stir in chicken. Remove Dutch oven from heat.
2. Whisk together cornmeal, baking powder, baking soda, and remaining ½ cup flour and ¼ teaspoon salt in a medium bowl. Cut remaining 2 tablespoons butter into flour mixture with a pastry blender or fork until mixture resembles coarse meal. Add buttermilk, parsley, and tarragon, stirring just until dough is moistened.
3. Heat Dutch oven over medium. Drop dumpling dough by tablespoonfuls ½ to 1 inch apart into chicken mixture. Cover and cook until dumplings are done and dry to the touch, 15 to 20 minutes. Serve immediately.

Gulf Coast Seafood Stew

ACTIVE 55 MIN. - TOTAL 1 HOUR, 35 MIN.
SERVES 6 TO 8

- 1½ lb. medium raw shrimp, unpeeled
- 2 celery stalks
- 1 large sweet onion
- 2 qt. lower-sodium chicken broth
- 12 oz. andouille sausage, cut into ½-inch pieces
- 1 poblano pepper, seeded and chopped
- 1 green bell pepper, chopped
- 1 Tbsp. canola oil
- 3 garlic cloves, chopped
- 1 lb. small red potatoes, halved
- 1 (12-oz.) bottle beer
- 1 Tbsp. fresh thyme leaves
- 2 fresh bay leaves
- 2 tsp. Creole seasoning
- 1½ lb. fresh white fish fillets (such as snapper, grouper, or catfish), cubed
- 1 lb. cooked crawfish tails (optional)
  Kosher salt and black pepper

1. Peel shrimp; place shells in a saucepan. (Refrigerate shrimp until ready to use.) Add celery ends and onion peel to pan; chop remaining celery and onion, and reserve. (Using the leftover bits of onion and celery will result in a flavorful broth.) Add broth; bring to a boil over medium-high. Reduce heat to low; simmer 30 minutes.
2. Meanwhile, cook sausage in a large Dutch oven over medium-high, stirring often, until browned, about 7 minutes. Remove sausage; pat dry. Wipe Dutch oven clean. Sauté chopped celery, onion, and peppers in hot oil in Dutch oven over medium-high until onion is tender, about 5 minutes. Add garlic, and sauté until fragrant, about 45 seconds. Stir in potatoes, beer, thyme, bay leaves, Creole seasoning, and sausage.
3. Pour broth mixture through a fine wire-mesh strainer into Dutch oven, discarding solids. Increase heat to high; bring to a boil. Reduce heat to low, and cook, stirring occasionally, 20 minutes.
4. Add fish, and cook just until opaque, about 2 minutes. Add shrimp, and cook just until shrimp turn pink, about 2 minutes. Stir in crawfish, and cook until hot, about 2 minutes. Add salt and black pepper to taste.
5. Spoon seafood into warmed soup bowls. Top with broth mixture.

Seafood Gumbo

ACTIVE 40 MIN. - TOTAL 2 HOURS, 20 MIN.

SERVES 10

SHELLFISH STOCK

- ¼ cup canola oil
- 1 lb. shrimp shells
- 1 large yellow onion, peeled and quartered
- 2 celery stalks, coarsely chopped
- 5 bay leaves
- 5 thyme sprigs
- 8 garlic cloves, smashed
- 1 Tbsp. black peppercorns
- 3 qt. water

GUMBO

- 1½ cups canola oil
- 2⅓ cups (about 10 oz.) all-purpose flour
- 1 medium yellow onion, chopped
- 3 celery stalks, sliced
- 2 green bell peppers, chopped
- 3 cloves garlic, minced
- 2½ Tbsp. Creole seasoning
- 1 Tbsp. filé powder
- 2 tsp. hot sauce
- 3 bay leaves
- ½ tsp. kosher salt
- 1 lb. large raw shrimp, peeled and deveined, tail-on
- 1 pt. fresh shucked oysters, drained
- 1 (1-lb.) can lump crabmeat, drained and picked over

  Hot cooked long-grain white rice

  Thinly sliced scallions, for garnish

1. Prepare the Shellfish Stock: Heat oil in a large stainless-steel Dutch oven over medium-high. Add shrimp shells, and cook, stirring occasionally, until orange, about 4 minutes. Stir in onion, celery, bay leaves, thyme, garlic, peppercorns, and water. Bring to a boil over high. Reduce heat to medium, and simmer until stock has a light shrimp flavor, about 1 hour. Pour through a fine wire-mesh strainer or a colander lined with cheesecloth into a large bowl. Discard solids. Set Shellfish Stock aside.

2. Prepare the Gumbo: Heat oil in a large Dutch oven over medium-high until shimmering. Whisk in flour; reduce heat to medium, and cook, stirring often with a wooden spoon, until roux is the color of peanut butter, 9 to 10 minutes. Reduce heat to medium-low; cook, stirring constantly, until roux is the color of melted milk chocolate (dark brown), about 12 minutes.

3. Carefully stir in onion, celery, bell peppers, garlic, Creole seasoning, filé powder, and hot sauce until coated. (Roux may splatter.) Slowly whisk in prepared Shellfish Stock. Add bay leaves. Bring to a boil over high. Reduce heat to medium, and simmer, stirring and scraping bottom of Dutch oven occasionally with a wooden spoon, until gumbo has thickened and you can no longer taste the flour, about 1 hour, skimming and discarding fat from surface as needed. Stir in salt.

4. Stir in shrimp, oysters, and crabmeat, and cook, stirring occasionally, until shrimp is cooked through, 3 to 4 minutes. Serve gumbo over hot cooked rice, and garnish with scallions.

Mediterranean Kale and Cannellini Stew with Farro

ACTIVE 20 MIN. - TOTAL 3 HOURS, 20 MIN.

SERVES 6

- 4 cups lower-sodium vegetable broth
- 1 (14½-oz.) can no-salt-added fire-roasted diced tomatoes, undrained
- 1 cup farro or Kamut
- 1 cup coarsely chopped onion
- 2 medium carrots, halved lengthwise and thinly sliced
- 1 cup coarsely chopped celery
- 4 garlic cloves, crushed
- ½ tsp. crushed red pepper
- ¼ tsp. kosher salt
- 4 cups coarsely chopped green kale or Swiss chard
- 1 (15-oz.) can no-salt-added cannellini beans, rinsed and drained
- 3 Tbsp. lemon juice

  Crumbled feta cheese and chopped fresh parsley, for garnish

1. In a 3½- or 4-quart slow cooker combine broth, tomatoes, farro, onion, carrots, celery, garlic, crushed red pepper, and salt. Cover and cook on HIGH 2 hours or until farro is tender but still chewy.

2. Stir in kale, beans, and lemon juice. Cover and cook 1 hour more. Top servings with feta and parsley.

Baking at High Altitudes

Liquids boil at lower temperatures (below 212°F) and moisture evaporates more quickly at high altitudes. Both of these factors significantly impact the quality of baked goods. Also, leavening gases (air, carbon dioxide, water vapor) expand faster. If you live at 3,000 feet or below, first try a recipe as is. Sometimes few, if any, changes are needed. But the higher you go, the more you'll have to adjust your ingredients and cooking times.

A Few Overall Tips

- Use shiny new baking pans. This seems to help mixtures rise, especially cake batters.
- Use butter, flour, and parchment paper to prep your baking pans for nonstick cooking. At high altitudes, baked goods tend to stick more to pans.
- Be exact in your measurements (once you've figured out what they should be). This is always important in baking, but especially so when you're up so high. Tiny variations in ingredients make a bigger difference at high altitudes than at sea level.
- Boost flavor. Seasonings and extracts tend to be more muted at higher altitudes, so increase them slightly.
- Have patience. You may have to bake your favorite sea-level recipe a few times, making slight adjustments each time, until it's worked out to suit your particular altitude.

Ingredient/Temperature Adjustments

CHANGE	AT 3,000 FEET	AT 5,000 FEET	AT 7,000 FEET
Baking powder or baking soda	Reduce each tsp. called for by up to ⅛ tsp.	Reduce each tsp. called for by ⅛ to ¼ tsp.	Reduce each tsp. called for by ¼ to ½ tsp.
Sugar	Reduce each cup called for by up to 1 Tbsp.	Reduce each cup called for by up to 2 Tbsp.	Reduce each cup called for by 2 to 3 Tbsp.
Liquid	Increase each cup called for by up to 2 Tbsp.	Increase each cup called for by 2 to 4 Tbsp.	Increase each cup called for by to 3 to 4 Tbsp.
Oven temperature	Increase 3°F to 5°F	Increase 15°F	Increase 21°F to 25°F

Metric Equivalents

The recipes that appear in this cookbook use the standard United States method for measuring liquid and dry or solid ingredients (teaspoons, tablespoons, and cups). The information on this chart is provided to help cooks outside the U.S. successfully use these recipes. All equivalents are approximate.

METRIC EQUIVALENTS FOR DIFFERENT TYPES OF INGREDIENTS

A standard cup measure of a dry or solid ingredient will vary in weight depending on the type of ingredient. A standard cup of liquid is the same volume for any type of liquid. Use the following chart when converting standard cup measures to grams (weight) or milliliters (volume).

Standard Cup	Fine Powder (ex. flour)	Grain (ex. rice)	Granular (ex. sugar)	Liquid Solids (ex. butter)	Liquid (ex. milk)
1	140 g	150 g	190 g	200 g	240 ml
¾	105 g	113 g	143 g	150 g	180 ml
⅔	93 g	100 g	125 g	133 g	160 ml
½	70 g	75 g	95 g	100 g	120 ml
⅓	47 g	50 g	63 g	67 g	80 ml
¼	35 g	38 g	48 g	50 g	60 ml
⅛	18 g	19 g	24 g	25 g	30 ml

USEFUL EQUIVALENTS FOR LIQUID INGREDIENTS BY VOLUME

¼ tsp.						=	1 ml		
½ tsp.						=	2 ml		
1 tsp.						=	5 ml		
3 tsp.	=	1 Tbsp.			=	½ fl oz.	=	15 ml	
		2 Tbsp.	=	⅛ cup	=	1 fl oz.	=	30 ml	
		4 Tbsp.	=	¼ cup	=	2 fl oz.	=	60 ml	
		5⅓ Tbsp.	=	⅓ cup	=	3 fl oz.	=	80 ml	
		8 Tbsp.	=	½ cup	=	4 fl oz.	=	120 ml	
		10⅔ Tbsp.	=	⅔ cup	=	5 fl oz.	=	160 ml	
		12 Tbsp.	=	¾ cup	=	6 fl oz.	=	180 ml	
		16 Tbsp.	=	1 cup	=	8 fl oz.	=	240 ml	
		1 pt.	=	2 cups	=	16 fl oz.	=	480 ml	
		1 qt.	=	4 cups	=	32 fl oz.	=	960 ml	
						33 fl oz.	=	1000 ml	= 1 l

USEFUL EQUIVALENTS FOR DRY INGREDIENTS BY WEIGHT

(To convert ounces to grams, multiply the number of ounces by 30.)

1 oz.	=	¹⁄₁₆ lb.	=	30 g
4 oz.	=	¼ lb.	=	120 g
8 oz.	=	½ lb.	=	240 g
12 oz.	=	¾ lb.	=	360 g
16 oz.	=	1 lb.	=	480 g

USEFUL EQUIVALENTS FOR LENGTH

(To convert inches to centimeters, multiply the number of inches by 2.5.)

1 in.					=	2.5 cm
6 in.	=	½ ft.			=	15 cm
12 in.	=	1 ft.			=	30 cm
36 in.	=	3 ft.	=	1 yd.	=	90 cm

USEFUL EQUIVALENTS FOR COOKING/OVEN TEMPERATURES

	Fahrenheit	Celsius	Gas Mark
Freeze Water	32°F	0°C	
Room Temperature	68°F	20°C	
Boil Water	212°F	100°C	
Bake	325°F	160°C	3
	350°F	180°C	4
	375°F	190°C	5
	400°F	200°C	6
	425°F	220°C	7
	450°F	230°C	8
Broil			Grill

Recipe Title Index

This index alphabetically lists every recipe by exact title

A

All Roads Lead To Oaxaca, 219
Apple Cider Butter, 300
Apple Cider-Doughnut Bundt Cake, 270
Apple Cinnamon Rolls, 255
Apple Jam Baby Back Ribs, 240
Apples Foster with Easy Granola, 228
Arabic Salad, 133
Aunt Brenda's Sour Cream Banana
　　Pudding, 98
Avgolemono Soup, 91
Avocado Dipping Sauce, 149
Avocado Toasts with Watermelon Radishes
　　and Herbs, 70

B

Baby Bourbon-Chocolate Bombes, 81
Back Forty Beer Mustard, 241
Bacon-Egg-and-Cheese Croissant
　　Sandwiches, 253
Bacon Pimiento Cheese, 204
Basil Smash, 124
Beef-and-Butternut Squash Chili, 350
Berry Basket Upside-Down Cake, 121
Big-Batch BLTs, 210
Blackberry-Brownie Ice-Cream
　　Sundaes, 138
Black Bean Soup, 346
Black Walnut Banana Bread, 194
Bless My Heart, 36
Blood Orange Upside-Down Cake, 313
BLT Seven-Layer Salad, 163
Bourbon-Braised Short Ribs, 299
Bourbon Cherries, 302
Bourbon-Glazed Ham Steaks, 63
Bourbon-Glazed Salmon, 93
Bourbon Mule, 124
Bourbon-Pineapple Slush, 124
Bourbon Salt, 122
Bourbon Sparkler, 286
Bourbon Sunset Tea, 215
Braised Sweet Potatoes with Piri Piri
　　Pecans, 281
Brambleberry Smoothie, 171
Brisket Chili, 350
Broccoli-Potato Soup, 347
Brothy Clams with Potlikker, 20
Brown Butter Cake, 309
Butternut Squash-and-Fennel Gratin, 283
Butternut Squash Salad with Collards and
　　Radicchio, 283

C

Cajun-Rubbed Pork Chop Bites, 180
Cajun Shrimp Stir-Fry, 92
Candied Citrus, 319

Cantaloupe Salad with Chile-Lime
　　Dressing, 128
Caramel-Apple Galette, 200
Carrot-Apple Soup, 349
Carter Family Pimiento Cheese, 338
Cast-Iron Roast Chicken, 223
Cat-Head Biscuit Sandwiches, 204
Cauliflower Personal "Pizzas", 259
Charoset, 75
Charred Zucchini-and-Halloumi Kebabs
　　with Lemon-Tahini Sauce, 134
Checkerboard Cookies, 325
Cheese-Bacon Crispies, 297
Cheese Dreams Breakfast Casserole, 287
Cheese-Toast Palmiers, 57
Cheesy Black Bean Tostadas, 31
Cheesy Caramel Corn, 332
Cheesy Dressing Muffins, 264
Cheesy Garlic French Bread, 342
Cheesy Turnip Gratin, 252
Cherry Bomb Cocktail, 302
Cherry-Cheesecake Brownies, 97
Cherry Icebox Cookies, 328
Cherry Syrup, 36
Chicken and Herbed Cornmeal
　　Dumplings, 353
Chicken-Andouille Gumbo with Roasted
　　Potatoes, 350
Chicken-and-Prosciutto Tortelloni
　　Soup, 342
Chicken-Fried Mushrooms with Creamy
　　Mushroom Gravy, 186
Chicken Parm Sandwiches, 203
Chicken Sausage-and-White Bean Stew, 351
Chicken Stew with Pumpkin and Wild
　　Rice, 352
Chicken, Sweet Potato, and Corn
　　Chowder, 345
Chicken Taco Pasta Salad, 163
Chicken Wings Three Ways, 208
Chipotle-Barbecue Sauce, 208
Chocolate Bundt Cake with Pecans, 270
Chocolate Chess Pie, 263
Chocolate Chip Pudding Cookies, 339
Chocolate Kiss Cookies, 330
Chocolate-Orange Chess Pie, 263
Chocolate-Peanut Butter Scotcheroos, 218
Chocolate Velvets, 297
Christmas Eve Lasagna, 336
Christmas Relish Tree, 295
Chunky Onion Dip, 297
Cider-Glazed Rainbow Carrots, 252
Cider Shandies, 235
Cinnamon-Toast Palmiers, 57
City Grocery Bloody Marys, 180
Classic Caramel Corn, 332

Classic Gravy, 272
Conecuh Sausage Corn Dogs with Back
　　Forty Beer Mustard, 241
Cookies-and-Cream
　　Cheesecake Brownies, 97
Corn Salad with Sumac and Feta, 134
Crab Puffs, 297
Cranberry Chutney, 278
Cranberry-Orange Filling, 310
Cranberry-Pistachio Biscotti, 327
Cranberry-Spice Spritz, 302
Cream Cheese Biscuits, 59
Creamed Corn Mac and Cheese, 143
Creamed String Beans, 281
Creamy Chicken-and-Rice Soup, 245
Creamy Chicken-and-Rice Soup with
　　Collard Greens, 342
Creamy Chicken Noodle Soup, 343
Creamy Garlic Scape Soup, 87
Creamy Kale Soup, 15
Creamy Pumpkin Soup, 348
Creamy Root Vegetable Soup with Brown
　　Butter Pecans, 246
Crispy-Ham Carbonara with Peas, 61
Crispy Ranch Chicken Cutlets, 203
Crispy Ranch Shrimp, 116
Crispy Roasted Mushrooms with Creamy
　　Grits, 190
Cucumber Cooler, 150
Curried Chicken Chowder, 345

D

Double Beet Salad with Honey-Dijon
　　Vinaigrette, 252
Double-Dill Deviled Eggs, 102
Double Potlikker Greens, 17
Dulce de Leche Brownies, 97

E

Easiest Fudge Ever, 339
Easy Buttermilk Cornbread, 245
Easy Chicken Cordon Bleu, 64
Easy Chocolate Glaze, 227
Easy Freezer Tomato Sauce, 150
Easy Granola, 228
Easy Latkes, 300
Easy Peas and Greens, 140
Easy Ranch, 173
Easy Southern-Style Beans, 40
Easy Zucchini-Basil Pasta, 155
Eggnog Snickerdoodles, 324
Elvie's Rémoulade, 236
Extra-Crispy Chicken Nuggets, 173

2024 RECIPE TITLE INDEX **357**

F

Fall Salad with Candied Black Walnuts, 198
Fancy Ranch, 300
Fava-and-Whipped Feta Bruschetta, 89
Fiddlehead-and-Bacon Tart, 86
Five-Minute Fried Chicken Salads, 203
Flourless Chocolate-Orange Cake with Grand Marnier Whipped Cream, 313
French Onion Soup, 346
French Onion Turkey, 276
French Toast Dreams, 207
Frenched Green Bean Salad, 143
Fresh Dill Dip, 102
Fried-Okra Cornbread, 140
Fried-Pickle Chicken Tenders, 143
Frozen Lemonade Pie, 137

G

Game-Day Chili, 213
Garlic Bread Pizzas, 216
Garlicky Black Walnut-Breadcrumb Pasta, 199
Ginger-Citrus Mixer, 302
Ginger-Citrus Pork Roast, 30
Ginger-Citrus Sparkler, 302
Grand Mimosas, 204
Greek Diner Meatballs, 144
Greek Pasta Salad, 208
Green Chile Cheese Toast, 353
Green Chile-Chicken Soup, 343
"Green" Peach Salad, 160
Gulf Coast Seafood Stew, 353

H

Ham-and-Cabbage Gratin, 62
Harvest Popcorn, 297
Harvest Sunrise Pie, 261
Hearty Tomato Soup, 347
Heavenly Angel Biscuits, 304
Herby Dijonnaise, 64
Hibiscus Nectar, 36
Hilda's Portuguese Stewed Chicken, 183
Hoisin Barbecue Wings, 236
Homemade Chicken Stock, 230
Homemade Tortilla Chips, 33
Honey-Bacon Topping, 208
Honey-Glazed Ham, 60
Hot Cocoa Cookies, 324
Hot Fudge, 169
Hot-Honey Grilled Chicken, 117
Hot-Honey Mustard, 173
Hot Potlikker Cornbread, 22

I

"I Can't Believe It's Not Smoked" Turkey, 276
Iced Oatmeal Cookies, 327
Italian Sloppy Joes, 31
Italian White Beans with Cauliflower, 346
Itty-Bitty Lemon Cakes with Lavender Glaze, 81

J

Jam Pinwheels, 328

K

Kale Rigatoni with Crispy Sausage, 15
Key Lime Pie Sundae, 169
King Ranch Chicken Soup, 342
Knock-Ya-Naked Brownies, 215

L

Leafy Green Salad with Sunflower Seed Dressing, 72
Lemon Chicken Soup, 344
Lemony Chicken Soup with Sweet Potatoes, 343
Lemon-Pepper Crunch, 208
Lemon-Poppy Seed Muffins, 65
Lemon-Ricotta Silver Dollar Pancakes, 123
Lemon-Tahini Sauce, 134
Lemon-Thyme Shortbread, 49
Lime Cream, 352
Lime Curd, 169
Little Carrot Layer Cakes with Coconut Buttercream, 78
Loaded Cauliflower Soup, 348
Loaded Queso, 216
Louisiana Gumbo, 350
Love Letter From Puebla, 219
Low-and-Slow Beef Pot Roast, 27

M

Macaroni and Cheese with Caramelized Onions, 66
Mango-Kiwi Green Smoothie, 171
Maple-Glazed Pumpkin Bundt Cake, 270
Maude Crawford Barton's Potato Salad, 104
Mayo-Roasted Turkey, 272
Mayo + Basil + Tomato Pizza, 216
Mediterranean Kale and Cannellini Stew with Farro, 354
Mexican-Hot Chocolate Caramel Corn, 332
Miso-Honey Roasted Root Vegetable Medley, 246
Miss River's Louisiana Crawfish Rolls, 95
Mixed Pickle Salad, 144
Molasses Cornbread for Zora Neale Hurston, 221
Molasses-Spice Kiss Cookies, 330
Ms. Ruby Mae, 36
Muffuletta Panzanella, 167
Muhammara, 134
Muscadine Dumplings, 184
Mushroom Bisque, 347
Mushroom Stock, 193
Mustard-Glazed Pretzel Bites, 235
Mustardy Glazed Barbecue Ribs, 115

N

Nana's Marinated Pea Salad, 277
Nashville Hot Fried Cauliflower Sandwiches, 258
Nick's Apple Jam, 240
No-Churn Black Walnut Ice Cream, 198
No-Churn Cantaloupe-White Balsamic Sorbet, 128

O

Old-Fashioned Chicken and Dumplings, 353
One-Pan Broccoli-Rice Casserole, 90
One-Pan Sumac Chicken Thighs, 176
One-Pot Chicken Pasta, 225
One-Pot Chicken Thighs and Potlikker Rice, 22
Orange-and-White Chocolate Crème Brûlée, 319
Orange-Bourbon Bundt Cake, 318
Orange Pavlova Wreath, 318
Orange-Roll Coffee Cake, 38
Our Best Stuffed Peppers, 223

P

Pan-Seared Rib-Eye with Mushroom-Hunter's Sauce, 190
Papaw's Peanut Butter Fudge, 292
Parmesan Crunch, 57
Pasta with Morel-and-Pea Cream Sauce, 82
Party Cheese Ball, 297
Party Quesadillas, 149
Peach-and-Tomato Salad with Buttermilk-Herb Dressing, 158
Peach-Mango Salad with Avocados, 158
Peach Melba Sundae, 169
Peach + Sausage + Red Onion Pizza, 216
Peanut Butter-Banana Upside-Down Cake, 121
Peanut Butter Molten Chocolate Cake, 35
Peanut Chicken Stew, 352
Pear, Bacon, and Gorgonzola Flatbread, 233
Pepper Jelly-Glazed Chicken Wings, 16
Pepper Jelly-Glazed Pork Chops, 140
Peppered Melon Salad, 143
Peppermint Kiss Cookies, 330
Peppermint Meringues, 321
Peppery Beef Stew with Root Vegetables, 349
Persimmon-and-Arugula Salad, 290
Pesto Deviled Eggs, 67
Pesto Meatball Stew, 349
Pimiento Cheese Cornbread, 215
Pineapple Blush Smoothie, 171
Pistachio-Honey Donut Tower, 303
Pistachio Shortbread, 49
Poached Shrimp, 236
Poblano Chile-Chicken Soup, 343
Po'Boys with Debris, 31
Pomegranate French 75, 293
Pomegranate Molasses-Glazed Eggplant with Toum-Yogurt Sauce, 133
Portobello Bolognese, 193
Portuguese Custard Tartlets, 183
Potato Kugel with Schmaltzy Onions, 75
Potlikker Bloody Marys, 20
Potlikker Boiled Peanuts, 20
Potlikker Pappardelle, 23

Q

Quick Chicken and Barley Stew, 351
Quick Chicken Noodle Bowls, 344
Quick-Pickled Jalapeños, 150
Quick Strawberry-Ginger Jam, 59

R

Radishes with Miso-Sesame Butter, 89
Rajas Poblanas with Potatoes, 281
Ramp-and-Rye Focaccia, 87
Raspberry Molten Chocolate Cake, 35
Raspberry Sauce, 169
Red Snapper in Creole Court Bouillon, 335
Refreshing Champagne Punch, 297
Reid Family Barbecue Shrimp, 180
Rice-and-Poblano-Stuffed Butternut
        Squash, 284
Riesling-Gruyère Fondue, 235
Roasted Lemon-Pepper Chicken, 26
Roasted Potatoes, 351
Roasted Whole Cauliflower with Smoky
        Mayo, 259
Roast Pork with Crackling, 254
Rugelach, 324
Rum Punch, 218

S

Sage-Honey Syrup, 36
Salted-Caramel Glaze, 227
Satsuma Margarita, 293
Sausage Minestrone, 341
Savory Veggie Fajitas, 114
Seafood Gumbo, 354
Secret Sauce Smashburgers, 118
Sharp Cheddar Butter, 59
Shaved Spring Vegetable Salad with
        Parmesan Crunch, 56
Sheet Pan Meatloaf, 225
Sheet Pan Pork Chops, 223
Sheet Pan Squash Casserole, 148
Shepherd's Pie Soup, 342
Shortcut Brisket Burnt Ends, 240
Shrimp-and-Feta Pasta Salad, 167
Shrimp-and-New Potato Chowder, 346
Simple Strawberry Strudels, 32
Skillet Pasta Primavera, 94
Skillet Pork Chops with Caramelized
        Pears, 233
Slow Cooker Bourbon-Braised Short
        Ribs, 299
Smashed Oven-Fried Okra, 119
Smoked Chicken Tortilla Soup, 345
Smoked Gouda Grits, 299
Smoked Paprika Potato Chips, 235
Smoky Bacon Snack Mix, 210
Smoky Black Bean Soup, 29
Smoky Grilled Corn Ribs, 144
Smoky Lentil Soup, 346
Smoky Pork-and-Greens Stew, 245
Smoky Tomato Butter, 300
Soulful Chicken Soup, 344
Soupe au Pistou, 44
Sourdough Bread Dressing, 264
Southern Italian Chicken Soup, 344
Southern Niçoise Salad, 163
Southern Wedding Soup, 341
Speedy Creole Comeback Sauce, 119
Speedy Grain Salad with Sugar Snap
        Peas, 43

Spiced Cranberry Compote, 261
Spiced Cranberry Mixer, 302
Spiced Cream Cheese Bundt Cake, 271
Spiced Persimmon Quick Bread, 290
Spiced Plum Upside-Down Cake, 121
Spicy Kale Chips, 15
Spicy Pear-and-Cheddar Bites, 286
Spicy Pork Lettuce Wraps, 31
Spicy Pumpkin Soup with Avocado
        Cream, 349
Spring Vegetable Sauté, 63
Stained Glass Snowflakes, 321
Stone Fruit Cobbler , 170
Stovetop Red Beans and Rice, 351
Strawberry-Ginger Poke Cake with Toasted
        Vanilla Meringue, 106
Strawberry Ladyfinger Cake, 112
Strawberry Shortcake Biscuit "Pudding", 112
Strawberry Shortcake Ice-Cream Cake, 109
Strawberry-Orange Fools, 59
Strawberry-Rhubarb Spritzes, 56
Strawberry Shortbread, 49
Strawberry Trifle with Coconut-Lime
        Whipped Cream, 112
Streusel-Topped Apple-Walnut Pie, 198
Sugar Snap Salad with Lemon-Parmesan
        Breadcrumbs, 43
Sumac 75, 177
Sumac Simple Syrup, 177
Sumac Snacking Cake, 177
Summer Garden Tart, 144
Summer Squash Skillet, 155
Sun-Dried Tomato Pasta with Chicken, 31
Sweet-and-Sour Braised Beef Brisket, 75
Sweet-and-Spicy Sausage Bites, 207
Sweet Potato Broth, 352
Sweet Potato Bundt Cake, 227
Sweet Potato Queso, 33
Swiss Chard-and-Bacon Grits Quiche, 56

T

Tailgate Margaritas, 210
Team Spirit Sugar Cookies, 210
Tex-Mex Chicken Chili with Lime, 352
The Southern Sling, 36
Three-Ingredient Pie Dough, 200
Three Sisters Succotash, 157
Tiny Caramel Cakes, 77
Tomato-and-Red Pepper Soup, 347
Toum, 133
Trinidad and Tobago Macaroni Pie, 278
Turkey Posole Verde, 345
Turtle Chess Pie, 263
Turtle Sundae, 169

V

Vanilla-Buttermilk Glaze, 227
Vegetable-Beef Soup, 245
Veggie-Packed Sourdough Dressing, 264
Vidalia Onion + Pepperoni Pizza, 216

W

Waffle Iron Hash Browns with Fried Eggs, 71
Walking Tacos Bar, 213
Watermelon, Mint, Feta, and Fried-Peanut
        Salad, 122
Watermelon Radish Salad with Brown
        Butter Vinaigrette, 70
Weeknight Pasta Bolognese, 28
Whipped Butternut Squash with Bacon
        Crumble, 284
Whipped Cream Frosting, 310
White Bean, Sausage, and Turnip Green
        Stew, 351
White Chicken Chili, 245
White Chocolate Candy Leaves, 310
White Cranberry Cosmo, 293
White Poinsettia Cupcakes with Cranberry-
        Orange Filling, 310
White Poinsettia Layer Cake with
        Cranberry-Orange Filling, 309
White Poinsettia Sheet Cake with
        Cranberry-Orange Filling, 311
Wild Mushroom Soup, 348
Winter Salad with Fennel and Oranges, 299

Z

Zesty Ketchup, 173

General Recipe Index

This index lists every recipe by food category and/or major ingredient.

A

Almonds
Lemon–Poppy Seed Muffins, 65
Parmesan Crunch, 57
Peach Melba Sundae, 169
Smoky Bacon Snack Mix, 210
Whipped Butternut Squash with Bacon Crumble, 284
Winter Salad with Fennel and Oranges, 299

Appetizers and snacks. *See also* **Dips and spreads**
Cajun Rubbed Pork Chop Bites, 180
Cheese–Bacon Crispies, 297
Cheese–Toast Palmiers, 57
Chicken Wings Three Ways, 208
Christmas Relish Tree, 295
Crab Puffs, 297
Double–Dill Deviled Eggs, 102
Fava–and–Whipped Feta Bruschetta, 89
Harvest Popcorn, 297
Hoisin Barbecue Wings, 236
Homemade Tortilla Chips, 33
Mustard–Glazed Pretzel Bites, 235
Party Quesadillas, 149
Pepper Jelly–Glazed Wings, 16
Pesto Deviled Eggs, 67
Poached Shrimp, 236
Potlikker Boiled Peanuts, 20
Radishes with Miso–Sesame Butter, 89
Riesling–Gruyère Fondue, 235
Smashed Oven–Fried Okra, 119
Smoked Paprika Potato Chips, 235
Smoky Bacon Snack Mix, 210
Spicy Pear–and–Cheddar Bites, 286
Sweet–and–Spicy Sausage Bites, 207

Apples
Apple Cinnamon Rolls, 255
Apples Foster with Easy Granola, 228
Caramel–Apple Galette, 200
Carrot–Apple Soup, 349
Charoset, 75
Creamy Pumpkin Soup, 348
Nick's Apple Jam, 240
Sheet Pan Pork Chops, 223
Streusel–Topped Apple–Walnut Pie, 198

Arugula
Bacon–Egg–and–Cheese Croissant Sandwiches, 253
Italian Sloppy Joes, 31
Muffuletta Panzanella, 167
Peach–and–Tomato Salad with Buttermilk–Herb Dressing, 158
Pear, Bacon, and Gorgonzola Flatbread, 233
Persimmon–and–Arugula Salad, 290
Sugar Snap Salad with Lemon–Parmesan Breadcrumbs, 43

Avocados
Avocado Dipping Sauce, 149
Avocado Toasts with Watermelon Radishes and Herbs, 70
BLT Seven–Layer Salad, 163
Cheesy Black Bean Tostadas, 31
Peach–Mango Salad with Avocados, 158
Spicy Pumpkin Soup with Avocado Cream, 349

B

Bacon
Bacon–Egg–and–Cheese Croissant Sandwiches, 253
Bacon Pimiento Cheese, 204
Big–Batch BLTs, 210
BLT Seven–Layer Salad, 163
Cat–Head Biscuit Sandwiches, 204
Cheese–Bacon Crispies, 297
Cheese Dreams Breakfast Casserole, 287
Double Potlikker Greens, 17
Fiddlehead–and–Bacon Tart, 86
Honey–Bacon Topping, 208
Loaded Cauliflower Soup, 348
Macaroni and Cheese with Caramelized Onions, 66
Peach–and–Tomato Salad with Buttermilk–Herb Dressing, 158
Pear, Bacon, and Gorgonzola Flatbread, 233
Pimiento Cheese Cornbread, 215
Smoky Bacon Snack Mix, 210
Smoky Lentil Soup, 346
Sweet Potato Queso, 33
Swiss Chard–and–Bacon Grits Quiche, 56
Three Sisters Succotash, 157
Whipped Butternut Squash with Bacon Crumble, 284

Bananas
Aunt Brenda's Sour Cream Banana Pudding, 98
Black Walnut Banana Bread, 194
Mango–Kiwi Green Smoothie, 171
Peanut Butter–Banana Upside–Down Cake, 121

Beans. *See also* **Green beans**
Beef–and–Butternut Squash Chili, 350
Black Bean Soup, 346
Brisket Chili, 350
Cheesy Black Bean Tostadas, 31
Chicken Sausage–and–White Bean Stew, 351
Easy Southern–Style Beans, 49
Fava–and–Whipped Feta Bruschetta, 89
Game–Day Chili, 213
Green Chile–Chicken Soup, 343
Italian White Beans with Cauliflower, 346
Loaded Queso, 216
Mediterranean Kale and Cannellini Stew with Farro, 354

Our Best Stuffed Peppers, 223
Pesto Meatball Stew, 349
Queso To Go, 216
Sausage Minestrone, 341
Smoked Chicken Tortilla Soup, 345
Smoky Black Bean Soup, 29
Soupe au Pistou, 44
Spicy Pumpkin Soup with Avocado Cream, 349
Stovetop Red Beans and Rice, 351
Tex–Mex Chicken Chili with Lime, 352
Walking Tacos Bar, 213
White Bean, Sausage, and Turnip Green Stew, 351
White Chicken Chili, 245

Beef
Beef–and–Butternut Squash Chili, 350
Bourbon–Braised Short Ribs, 299
Brisket Chili, 350
Christmas Eve Lasagna, 336
Game–Day Chili, 213
Greek Diner Meatballs, 144
Italian Sloppy Joes, 31
Low–and–Slow Beef Pot Roast, 27
Our Best Stuffed Peppers, 223
Pan–Seared Rib–Eye with Mushroom–Hunter's Sauce, 190
Peppery Beef Stew with Root Vegetables, 349
Pesto Meatball Stew, 349
Po'Boys with Debris, 30
Secret Sauce Smash Burgers, 118
Sheet Pan Meatloaf, 225
Shortcut Brisket Burnt Ends, 240
Slow Cooker Bourbon–Braised Short Ribs, 299
Sweet–and–Sour Braised Beef Brisket, 75
Vegetable–Beef Soup, 245
Walking Tacos Bar, 213
Weeknight Pasta Bolognese, 28

Beets
Double Beet Salad with Honey–Dijon Vinaigrette, 252
Miso–Roasted Root Vegetable Medley, 246
Shaved Spring Vegetable Salad with Parmesan Crunch, 56

Beverages. *See also* **Smoothies**
All Roads Lead to Oaxaca, 219
Basil Smash, 124
Bless My Heart, 36
Bourbon Mule, 124
Bourbon–Pineapple Slush, 124
Bourbon Sparkler, 286
Bourbon Sunset Tea, 215
Cherry Bomb Cocktail, 302
Cider Shandies, 235
City Grocery Bloody Marys, 180
Cranberry–Spice Spritz, 302
Cucumber Cooler, 150

360 2024 GENERAL RECIPE INDEX

Ginger-Citrus Sparkler, 302
Grand Mimosas, 204
Hibiscus Nectar, 36
Love Letter from Puebla, 219
Ms. Ruby Mae, 36
Pomegranate French 75, 293
Potlikker Bloody Marys, 20
Refreshing Champagne Punch, 297
Rum Punch, 218
Satsuma Margarita, 293
The Southern Sling, 36
Strawberry-Rhubarb Spritzes, 56
Sumac 75, 177
Tailgate Margaritas, 210
White Cranberry Cosmo, 293

Blackberries
Berry Basket Upside-Down Cake, 121
Blackberry-Brownie Ice-Cream
    Sundaes, 138
Brambleberry Smoothie, 171

Blueberries
Berry Basket Upside-Down Cake, 121
Brambleberry Smoothie, 171

Breads. *See also* **Pastries**
Apple Cinnamon Rolls, 255
Black Walnut Banana Bread, 194
Cat-Head Biscuit Sandwiches, 204
Cheesy Garlic French Bread, 342
Cream Cheese Biscuits, 59
Easy Buttermilk Cornbread, 245
French Toast Dreams, 207
Fried-Okra Cornbread, 140
Green Chile Toast, 353
Heavenly Angel Biscuits, 304
Hot Potlikker Cornbread, 22
Lemon-Poppy Seed Muffins, 65
Lemon-Ricotta Silver Dollar Pancakes, 123
Molasses Cornbread for Zora Neale
    Hurston, 221
Pimiento Cheese Cornbread, 215
Pistachio-Honey Donut Tower, 303
Ramp-and-Rye Focaccia, 87
Spiced Persimmon Quick Bread, 290

Broccoli
Broccoli-Potato Soup, 347
One-Pan Broccoli-Rice Casserole, 90

Brownies and bars
Blackberry-Brownie Ice-Cream
    Sundaes, 138
Cherry-Cheesecake Brownies, 97
Chocolate-Peanut Butter Scotcheroos, 218
Cookies-and-Cream Cheesecake
    Brownies, 97
Dulce de Leche Brownies, 97
Knock-Ya-Naked Brownies, 215

Butters
Apple Cider Butter, 300
Radishes with Miso-Sesame Butter, 89
Sharp Cheddar Butter, 59
Smoky Tomato Butter, 300

C

Cakes
Apple Cider-Doughnut Bundt Cake, 270
Baby Bourbon-Chocolate Bombes, 81
Berry Basket Upside-Down Cake, 121
Blood Orange Upside-Down Cake, 313

Brown Butter Cake, 309
Chocolate Bundt Cake with Pecans, 270
Flourless Chocolate-Orange Cake with
    Grand Marnier Whipped Cream, 313
Itty-Bitty Lemon Cakes with Lavender
    Glaze, 81
Little Carrot Layer Cakes with Coconut
    Buttercream, 78
Maple-Glazed Pumpkin Bundt Cake, 270
Orange-Bourbon Bundt Cake, 318
Orange-Roll Coffee Cake, 38
Peanut Butter-Banana Upside-Down
    Cake, 121
Spiced Cream Cheese Bundt Cake, 271
Spiced Plum Upside-Down Cake, 121
Strawberry-Ginger Poke Cake with
    Toasted Vanilla Meringue, 106
Sumac Snacking Cake, 177
Sweet Potato Bundt Cake, 227
Tiny Caramel Cakes, 77
White Poinsettia Cupcakes with
    Cranberry-Orange Filling, 310
White Poinsettia Layer Cake with
    Cranberry-Orange Filling, 309
White Poinsettia Sheet Cake with
    Cranberry-Orange Filling, 311

Candy
Cheesy Caramel Corn, 332
Chocolate Velvets, 297
Classic Caramel Corn, 332
Easiest Fudge Ever, 339
Mexican-Hot Chocolate Caramel Corn, 332
Papaw's Peanut Butter Fudge, 292

Carrots
Avgolemono Soup, 91
Carrot-Apple Soup, 349
Christmas Relish Tree, 295
Cider-Glazed Rainbow Carrots, 252
Creamy Chicken-and-Rice Soup, 245
Little Carrot Layer Cakes with Coconut
    Buttercream, 78
Low-and-Slow Beef Pot Roast, 27
Miso-Roasted Root Vegetable Medley, 246
Shaved Spring Vegetable Salad with
    Parmesan Crunch, 56
Spring Vegetable Sauté, 63
Sweet-and-Sour Braised Beef Brisket, 75
Waffle Iron Hash Browns with Fried Eggs, 71

Cauliflower
Cauliflower Personal "Pizzas," 259
Christmas Relish Tree, 295
Italian White Beans with Cauliflower, 346
Loaded Cauliflower Soup, 348
Nashville Hot Fried Cauliflower
    Sandwiches, 258
Roasted Whole Cauliflower with Smoky
    Mayo, 259

Cherries
Bourbon Cherries, 302
Cherry Bomb Cocktail, 302
Cherry-Cheesecake Brownies, 97
Cherry Icebox Cookies, 328
Cherry Syrup, 36
Stone Fruit Cobbler, 170
Winter Salad with Fennel and
    Oranges, 299

Chicken
Avgolemono Soup, 91
Cast-Iron Roast Chicken, 223
Cat-Head Biscuit Sandwiches, 204
Chicken and Herbed Cornmeal
    Dumplings, 353
Chicken-Andouille Gumbo with Roasted
    Potatoes, 350
Chicken Parm Sandwiches, 203
Chicken Stew with Pumpkin and Wild
    Rice, 352
Chicken, Sweet Potato, and Corn
    Chowder, 345
Chicken Taco Pasta Salad, 163
Chicken Wings Three Ways, 208
Creamy Chicken-and-Rice Soup, 245
Creamy Chicken-and-Rice Soup with
    Collard Greens, 342
Creamy Chicken Noodle Soup, 343
Crispy Ranch Chicken Cutlets, 203
Easy Chicken Cordon Bleu, 64
Extra-Crispy Chicken Nuggets, 173
Five-Minute Fried Chicken Salads, 203
French Onion Soup, 346
Fried-Pickle Chicken Tenders, 143
Green Chile-Chicken Soup, 343
Hilda's Portuguese Stewed Chicken, 183
Hoisin Barbecue Wings, 236
Homemade Chicken Broth, 230
Hot-Honey Grilled Chicken, 117
King Ranch Chicken Soup, 342
Lemon Chicken Soup, 344
Lemony Chicken Soup with Sweet
    Potatoes, 343
Louisiana Gumbo, 350
Old-Fashioned Chicken and Dumplings, 353
One-Pan Sumac Chicken Thighs, 176
One-Pot Chicken Pasta, 225
One-Pot Chicken Thighs and Potlikker
    Rice, 22
Party Quesadillas, 149
Peanut Chicken Stew, 352
Pepper Jelly-Glazed Wings, 16
Poblano Chile-Chicken Soup, 343
Quick Chicken and Barley Stew, 351
Quick Chicken Noodle Bowls, 344
Roasted Lemon-Pepper Chicken, 26
Smoked Chicken Tortilla Soup, 345
Soulful Chicken Soup, 344
Southern Italian Chicken Soup, 344
Speedy Grain Salad with Sugar Snap Peas, 43
Sun-Dried Tomato Pasta with Chicken, 31
Tex-Mex Chicken Chili with Lime, 352
White Chicken Chili, 245

Chili
Beef-and-Butternut Squash Chili, 350
Brisket Chili, 350
Game-Day Chili, 213
Tex-Mex Chicken Chili with Lime, 352
Walking Tacos Bar, 213
White Chicken Chili, 245

Chocolate. *See also* **White chocolate**
Baby Bourbon-Chocolate Bombes, 81
Blackberry-Brownie Ice-Cream
    Sundaes, 138
Checkerboard Cookies, 325

Cherry–Cheesecake Brownies, 97
Chocolate Bundt Cake with Pecans, 270
Chocolate Chess Pie, 263
Chocolate Chip Pudding Cookies, 339
Chocolate Kiss Cookies, 330
Chocolate–Orange Chess Pie, 263
Chocolate–Peanut Butter Scotcheroos, 218
Chocolate Velvets, 297
Cookies-and-Cream Cheesecake
  Brownies, 97
Dulce de Leche Brownies, 97
Easiest Fudge Ever, 339
Easy Chocolate Glaze, 227
Flourless Chocolate–Orange Cake with
  Grand Marnier Whipped Cream, 313
Hot Cocoa Cookies, 324
Hot Fudge, 169
Knock-Ya-Naked Brownies, 215
Mexican-Hot Chocolate Caramel Corn, 332
Molasses–Spice Kiss Cookies, 330
Papaw's Peanut Butter Fudge, 292
Peanut Butter Molten Chocolate Cake, 35
Peppermint Kiss Cookies, 330
Raspberry Molten Chocolate Cake, 35
Rugelach, 324
Turtle Chess Pie, 263
Turtle Sundae, 169

Collard greens
Butternut Squash Salad with Collards and
  Radicchio, 283
Creamy Chicken-and-Rice Soup, 245
Creamy Chicken-and-Rice Soup with
  Collard Greens, 342
Double Potlikker Greens, 17
Fall Salad with Candied Black Walnuts, 198
Hot Potlikker Cornbread, 22
One-Pot Chicken Thighs and Potlikker
  Rice, 22
Potlikker Boiled Peanuts, 20
Potlikker Pappardelle, 23
Sausage Minestrone, 341
Southern Wedding Soup, 341
Winter Salad with Fennel and Oranges, 299

Condiments
Back Forty Beer Mustard, 241
Bourbon Salt, 122
Easy Ranch, 173
Hot–Honey Mustard, 173
Quick–Pickled Jalapeños, 150
Zesty Ketchup, 173

Cookies. See also Brownies and bars
Checkerboard Cookies, 325
Cherry Icebox Cookies, 328
Chocolate Chip Pudding Cookies, 339
Chocolate Kiss Cookies, 330
Cranberry–Pistachio Biscotti, 327
Eggnog Snickerdoodles, 324
Hot Cocoa Cookies, 324
Iced Oatmeal Cookies, 327
Jam Pinwheels, 328
Lemon–Thyme Shortbread, 49
Molasses–Spice Kiss Cookies, 330
Peppermint Kiss Cookies, 330
Peppermint Meringues, 321
Pistachio Shortbread, 49
Rugelach, 324

Stained Glass Snowflakes, 321
Strawberry Shortbread, 49
Team Spirit Sugar Cookies, 210

Corn
Black Bean Soup, 346
Chicken, Sweet Potato, and Corn
  Chowder, 345
Chicken Taco Pasta Salad, 163
Corn Salad with Sumac and Feta, 134
Creamed Corn Mac and Cheese, 143
Nana's Marinated Pea Salad, 277
Our Best Stuffed Peppers, 223
Sausage Minestrone, 341
Smoked Chicken Tortilla Soup, 345
Smoky Grilled Corn Ribs, 144
Summer Garden Tart, 144
Three Sisters Succotash, 157

Cornmeal
Chicken and Herbed Cornmeal
  Dumplings, 353
Conecuh Sausage Corn Dogs with Back
  Forty Beer Mustard, 241
Crispy Ranch Shrimp, 116
Easy Buttermilk Cornbread, 245
Fried–Okra Cornbread, 140
Hot Potlikker Cornbread, 22
Molasses Cornbread for Zora Neale
  Hurston, 221
Pimiento Cheese Cornbread, 215
Smashed Oven-Fried Okra, 119
Strawberry Shortcake Ice-Cream Cake, 109

Cranberries
Cranberry Chutney, 278
Cranberry–Orange Filling, 310
Cranberry–Pistachio Biscotti, 327
Cranberry–Spice Spritz, 302
Harvest Sunrise Pie, 261
Rice-and Poblano–Stuffed Butternut
  Squash, 284
Spiced Cranberry Compote, 261
Spiced Cranberry Mixer, 302
White Cranberry Cosmo, 293

Cucumbers
Arabic Salad, 133
Cantaloupe Salad with Chile–Lime
  Dressing, 128
Cucumber Cooler, 150
Greek Pasta Salad, 208
Shrimp–and–Feta Pasta Salad, 167

D

**Desserts. See also Brownies and bars; Cakes;
  Candy; Cookies; Pies and tarts**
Apples Foster with Easy Granola, 228
Aunt Brenda's Sour Cream Banana
  Pudding, 98
Blackberry–Brownie Ice–Cream
  Sundaes, 138
Key Lime Pie Sundae, 169
Muscadine Dumplings, 184
No-Churn Black Walnut Ice Cream, 198
No-Churn Cantaloupe–White Balsamic
  Sorbet, 128
Orange-and-White Chocolate Crème
  Brûlée, 319
Orange Pavlova Wreath, 318

Peach Melba Sundae, 169
Peanut Butter Molten Chocolate Cake, 35
Raspberry Molten Chocolate Cake, 35
Stone Fruit Cobbler, 170
Strawberry Ladyfinger Cake, 112
Strawberry–Orange Fools, 59
Strawberry Shortcake Bread "Pudding," 112
Strawberry Shortcake Ice-Cream Cake, 109
Strawberry Trifle with Coconut–Lime
  Whipped Cream, 112
Turtle Sundae, 169

Dips and spreads
Bacon Pimiento Cheese, 204
Carter Family Pimiento Cheese, 338
Chunky Onion Dip, 297
Fresh Dill Dip, 102
Loaded Queso, 216
Muhammara, 134
Party Cheese Ball, 297
Queso To Go, 216
Riesling–Gruyère Fondue, 235
Sweet Potato Queso, 33

Dressing and stuffing
Cheesy Dressing Muffins, 264
Sourdough Bread Dressing, 264
Veggie–Packed Sourdough Dressing, 264

E

Eggplant
Pomegranate Molasses–Glazed Eggplant
  with Toum–Yogurt Sauce, 133

Eggs
Bacon–Egg-and-Cheese Croissant
  Sandwiches, 253
Cheese Dreams Breakfast Casserole, 287
Double–Dill Deviled Eggs, 102
Maude Crawford Barton's Potato Salad, 104
Pesto Deviled Eggs, 67
Southern Niçoise Salad, 163
Waffle Iron Hash Browns with Fried Eggs, 71

F

Fennel bulb
Brothy Clams with Potlikker, 20
Butternut Squash-and-Fennel Gratin, 283
Cast-Iron Roast Chicken, 223
Kale Rigatoni with Crispy Sausage, 15
Shaved Spring Vegetable Salad with
  Parmesan Crunch, 56
Winter Salad with Fennel and Oranges, 299

Fish. See also Shellfish; Shrimp
Bourbon–Glazed Salmon, 93
Gulf Coast Seafood Stew, 353
Red Snapper in Creole Court Bouillon, 335
Southern Niçoise Salad, 163

Frostings and icings
Easy Chocolate Glaze, 227
Salted–Caramel Glaze, 227
Vanilla–Buttermilk Glaze, 227
Whipped Cream Frosting, 310

G

Grains. See also Cornmeal; Grits; Oats; Rice
Mediterranean Kale and Cannellini Stew
  with Farro, 354
Quick Chicken and Barley Stew, 351
Speedy Grain Salad with Sugar Snap Peas, 43

Green beans
Creamed String Beans, 281
Frenched Green Bean Salad, 143
Southern Niçoise Salad, 163
Three Sisters Succotash, 157
Greens. *See also* **Arugula; Collard greens;**
Kale; Spinach
Butternut Squash Salad with Collards and
Radicchio, 283
Easy Peas and Greens, 140
Ham-and-Cabbage Gratin, 62
Smoky Pork-and-Greens Stew, 245
Swiss Chard-and-Bacon Grits Quiche, 56
White Bean, Sausage, and Turnip Green
Stew, 351
Winter Salad with Fennel and Oranges, 299
Grilled recipes
Apple Jam Baby Back Ribs, 240
Cajun Rubbed Pork Chop Bites, 180
Charred Zucchini-and-Halloumi Kebabs
with Lemon-Tahini Sauce, 134
Corn Salad with Sumac and Feta, 134
Hoisin Barbecue Wings, 236
Hot-Honey Grilled Chicken, 117
Muhammara, 134
Pepper Jelly-Glazed Pork Chops, 140
Pomegranate Molasses-Glazed Eggplant
with Toum-Yogurt Sauce, 133
Smoky Grilled Corn Ribs, 144
Grits
Crispy Roasted Mushrooms with Creamy
Grits, 190
Smoked Gouda Grits, 299
Swiss Chard-and-Bacon Grits Quiche, 56

H

Ham
Bourbon-Glazed Ham Steaks, 63
Brothy Clams with Potlikker, 20
Crispy-Ham Carbonara with Peas, 61
Double Potlikker Greens, 17
Easy Chicken Cordon Bleu, 64
Easy Peas and Greens, 140
Easy Southern-Style Beans, 49
Ham-and-Cabbage Gratin, 62
Honey-Glazed Ham, 60
"I Can't Believe It's Not Smoked" Turkey, 176
Party Cheese Ball, 297
Potlikker Pappardelle, 23
Hominy
Poblano Chile-Chicken Soup, 343
Smoky Pork-and-Greens Stew, 245
Turkey Posole Verde, 345

J

Jams
Nick's Apple Jam, 240
Quick Strawberry-Ginger Jam, 59

K

Kale
Christmas Relish Tree, 295
Creamy Kale Soup, 15
Kale Rigatoni with Crispy Sausage, 15
Mediterranean Kale and Cannellini Stew
with Farro, 354
One-Pot Chicken Pasta, 225

Smoky Lentil Soup, 346
Soupe au Pistou, 44
Spicy Kale Chips, 15

L

Lamb
Shepherd's Pie Soup, 342
Lemon(s)
Avgolemono Soup, 91
Bourbon Sparkler, 286
Braised Sweet Potatoes with Piri Piri
Pecans, 281
Frozen Lemonade Pie, 137
Garlicky Black Walnut-Breadcrumb
Pasta, 199
Itty-Bitty Lemon Cakes with Lavender
Glaze, 81
Lemon Chicken Soup, 344
Lemon-Pepper Crunch, 208
Lemon-Poppy Seed Muffins, 65
Lemon-Ricotta Silver Dollar Pancakes, 123
Lemon-Tahini Sauce, 134
Lemon-Thyme Shortbread, 49
Lemony Chicken Soup with Sweet
Potatoes, 343
Muscadine Dumplings, 184
Refreshing Champagne Punch, 297
Rum Punch, 218
Sugar Snap Salad with Lemon-Parmesan
Breadcrumbs, 43
Sumac Snacking Cake, 177
Sumac 75, 177
Lime(s)
Cantaloupe Salad with Chile-Lime
Dressing, 128
City Grocery Bloody Marys, 180
Key Lime Pie Sundae, 169
Lime Cream, 352
Lime Curd, 169
Love Letter from Puebla, 219
Refreshing Champagne Punch, 297
Rum Punch, 218
Strawberry Trifle with Coconut-Lime
Whipped Cream, 112
Tailgate Margaritas, 210

M

Mangoes
Mango-Kiwi Green Smoothie, 171
Peach-Mango Salad with Avocados, 158
Melon
Cantaloupe Salad with Chile-Lime
Dressing, 128
No-Churn Cantaloupe-White Balsamic
Sorbet, 128
Peppered Melon Salad, 143
Watermelon, Mint, Feta and Fried-Peanut
Salad, 122
Mushrooms
Chicken-Fried Mushrooms with Creamy
Mushroom Gravy, 186
Crispy Roasted Mushrooms with Creamy
Grits, 190
Mushroom Bisque, 347
Mushroom Stock, 193
One-Pan Broccoli-Rice Casserole, 90

Pan-Seared Rib-Eye with Mushroom-
Hunter's Sauce, 190
Pasta with Morel-and-Pea Cream Sauce, 82
Portobello Bolognese, 193
Potlikker Pappardelle, 23
Rice-and Poblano-Stuffed Butternut
Squash, 284
Savory Veggie Fajitas, 114
Vegetable-Beef Soup, 245
Veggie-Packed Sourdough Dressing, 264
Wild Mushroom Soup, 348

N

Noodles
Creamy Chicken Noodle Soup, 343
Quick Chicken Noodle Bowls, 344
Soulful Chicken Soup, 344

O

Oats
Easy Granola, 228
Harvest Sunrise Pie, 261
Iced Oatmeal Cookies, 327
Parmesan Crunch, 57
Streusel-Topped Apple-Walnut Pie, 198
Okra
City Grocery Bloody Marys, 180
Fried-Okra Cornbread, 140
Mixed Pickle Salad, 144
Smashed Oven-Fried Okra, 119
Southern Italian Chicken Soup, 344
Onions
Chunky Onion Dip, 297
French Onion Soup, 346
French Onion Turkey, 276
Macaroni and Cheese with Caramelized
Onions, 66
Peach + Sausage + Red Onion Pizza, 216
Potato Kugel with Schmaltzy Onions, 75
Vidalia Onion + Pepperoni Pizza, 216
Orange(s)
All Roads Lead to Oaxaca, 219
Blood Orange Upside-Down Cake, 313
Bourbon-Glazed Salmon, 93
Braised Sweet Potatoes with Piri Piri
Pecans, 281
Brown Butter Cake, 309
Candied Citrus, 319
Chocolate-Orange Chess Pie, 263
Cranberry-Orange Filling, 310
Flourless Chocolate-Orange Cake with
Grand Marnier Whipped Cream, 313
Ginger-Citrus Mixer, 302
Ginger-Citrus Pork Roast, 30
Ginger-Citrus Sparkler, 302
Grand Mimosas, 204
Honey-Glazed Ham, 60
Orange-and-White Chocolate Crème
Brûlée, 319
Orange-Bourbon Bundt Cake, 318
Orange Pavlova Wreath, 318
Orange-Roll Coffee Cake, 38
Portuguese Custard Tartlets, 183
Rum Punch, 218
Satsuma Margarita, 293
Strawberry-Orange Fools, 59
Winter Salad with Fennel and Oranges, 299

P

Parsnips
Creamy Root Vegetable Soup with Brown Butter Pecans, 246
Miso-Roasted Root Vegetable Medley, 246

Pasta. *See also* **Noodles**
Chicken-and-Prosciutto Soup, 342
Chicken Taco Pasta Salad, 163
Christmas Eve Lasagna, 336
Creamed Corn Mac and Cheese, 143
Crispy-Ham Carbonara with Peas, 61
Crispy Ranch Chicken Cutlets, 203
Easy Zucchini-Basil Pasta, 155
Garlicky Black Walnut-Breadcrumb Pasta, 199
Greek Pasta Salad, 208
Kale Rigatoni with Crispy Sausage, 15
Lemon Chicken Soup, 344
Lemony Chicken Soup with Sweet Potatoes, 343
Macaroni and Cheese with Caramelized Onions, 66
One-Pot Chicken Pasta, 225
Pasta with Morel-and-Pea Cream Sauce, 82
Portobello Bolognese, 193
Potlikker Pappardelle, 23
Sausage Minestrone, 341
Shrimp-and-Feta Pasta Salad, 167
Skillet Pasta Primavera, 94
Soupe au Pistou, 44
Southern Italian Chicken Soup, 344
Southern Wedding Soup, 341
Sun-Dried Tomato Pasta with Chicken, 31
Trinidad and Tobago Macaroni Pie, 278
Weeknight Pasta Bolognese, 28

Pastries
Cheese-Toast Palmiers, 57
Cinnamon-Toast Palmiers, 57
Simple Strawberry Strudels, 32

Peaches
"Green" Peach Salad, 160
Mixed Pickle Salad, 144
Peach-and-Tomato Salad with Buttermilk-Herb Dressing, 158
Peach-Mango Salad with Avocados, 158
Peach Melba Sundae, 169
Peach + Sausage + Red Onion Pizza, 216
Stone Fruit Cobbler, 170

Peanut butter
Chocolate-Peanut Butter Scotcheroos, 218
Papaw's Peanut Butter Fudge, 292
Peanut Butter-Banana Upside-Down Cake, 121
Peanut Butter Molten Chocolate Cake, 35
Peanut Chicken Stew, 352

Peanuts
Cajun Shrimp Stir-Fry, 92
Peanut Butter-Banana Upside-Down Cake, 121
Potlikker Boiled Peanuts, 20
Watermelon, Mint, Feta and Fried-Peanut Salad, 122

Pears
Pear, Bacon, and Gorgonzola Flatbread, 233
Skillet Pork Chops with Caramelized Pears, 233
Spicy Pear-and-Cheddar Bites, 286

Peas
Cajun Shrimp Stir-Fry, 92
Crispy-Ham Carbonara with Peas, 61
Easy Peas and Greens, 140
Lemon Chicken Soup, 344
Louisiana Gumbo, 350
Nana's Marinated Pea Salad, 277
Pasta with Morel-and-Pea Cream Sauce, 82
Skillet Pasta Primavera, 94
Southern Italian Chicken Soup, 344
Southern Wedding Soup, 341
Speedy Grain Salad with Sugar Snap Peas, 43
Spring Vegetable Sauté, 63
Sugar Snap Salad with Lemon-Parmesan Breadcrumbs, 43

Pecans
Braised Sweet Potatoes with Piri Piri Pecans, 281
Charoset, 75
Chocolate Bundt Cake with Pecans, 270
Creamy Root Vegetable Soup with Brown Butter Pecans, 246
Knock-Ya-Naked Brownies, 215
Party Cheese Ball, 297
Pesto Deviled Eggs, 67
Sweet Potato Bundt Cake, 227
Turtle Chess Pie, 263
Turtle Sundae, 169
Watermelon Radish Salad with Brown Butter Vinaigrette, 70

Peppers, bell
Hilda's Portuguese Stewed Chicken, 183
Muffuletta Panzanella, 167
Muhammara, 134
Our Best Stuffed Peppers, 223
Savory Veggie Fajitas, 114
Sheet Pan Squash Casserole, 148
Tomato-and-Red Pepper Soup, 347

Peppers, chile
Arabic Salad, 133
Avocado Dipping Sauce, 149
Chicken Taco Pasta Salad, 163
Chipotle-Barbecue Sauce, 208
Corn Salad with Sumac and Feta, 134
Greek Diner Meatballs, 144
Greek Pasta Salad, 208
Green Chile-Chicken Soup, 343
Green Chile Toast, 353
"I Can't Believe It's Not Smoked" Turkey, 176
Peach-Mango Salad with Avocados, 158
Poblano Chile-Chicken Soup, 343
Quick-Pickled Jalapeños, 150
Rajas Poblanas with Potatoes, 281
Red Snapper in Creole Court Bouillon, 335
Rice-and Poblano-Stuffed Butternut Squash, 284
Smoked Chicken Tortilla Soup, 345
Smoky Black Bean Soup, 29
Smoky Pork-and-Greens Stew, 245
Spicy Pumpkin Soup with Avocado Cream, 349
Sweet Potato Queso, 33
Tex-Mex Chicken Chili with Lime, 352

Three Sisters Succotash, 157
Trinidad and Tobago Macaroni Pie, 278
Turkey Posole Verde, 345
Walking Tacos Bar, 213
White Chicken Chili, 245

Persimmons
Persimmon-and-Arugula Salad, 290
Persimmon Puree, 290
Spiced Persimmon Quick Bread, 290

Pies and tarts
Caramel-Apple Galette, 200
Chocolate Chess Pie, 263
Chocolate-Orange Chess Pie, 263
Fiddlehead-and-Bacon Tart, 86
Frozen Lemonade Pie, 137
Harvest Sunrise Pie, 261
Portuguese Custard Tartlets, 183
Streusel-Topped Apple-Walnut Pie, 198
Summer Garden Tart, 144
Three-Ingredient Pie Dough, 200
Turtle Chess Pie, 263

Pineapple
Bourbon-Pineapple Slush, 124
Pineapple Blush Smoothie, 171

Pistachios
Corn Salad with Sumac and Feta, 134
Cranberry-Pistachio Biscotti, 327
Orange-Bourbon Bundt Cake, 318
Persimmon-and-Arugula Salad, 290
Pistachio-Honey Donut Tower, 303
Pistachio Shortbread, 49
Speedy Grain Salad with Sugar Snap Peas, 43

Pizza
Cauliflower Personal "Pizzas," 259
Garlic Bread Pizzas, 216
Mayo + Tomato + Basil Pizza, 216
Peach + Sausage + Red Onion Pizza, 216
Vidalia Onion + Pepperoni Pizza, 216

Plums
Spiced Plum Upside-Down Cake, 121
Stone Fruit Cobbler, 170

Pomegranate
Brambleberry Smoothie, 171
Persimmon-and-Arugula Salad, 290
Pomegranate French 75, 293
Pomegranate Molasses-Glazed Eggplant with Toum-Yogurt Sauce, 133

Pork. *See also* **Bacon; Ham; Sausages**
Apple Jam Baby Back Ribs, 240
Cajun Rubbed Pork Chop Bites, 180
Ginger-Citrus Pork Roast, 30
Muffuletta Panzanella, 167
Mustardy Glazed Barbecue Ribs, 115
Pepper Jelly-Glazed Pork Chops, 140
Roast Pork with Crackling, 254
Sheet Pan Pork Chops, 223
Skillet Pork Chops with Caramelized Pears, 233
Smoky Pork-and-Greens Stew, 245
Southern Wedding Soup, 341
Spicy Pork Lettuce Wraps, 31

Potatoes. *See also* **Sweet potatoes**
Broccoli-Potato Soup, 347
Chicken-Andouille Gumbo with Roasted Potatoes, 350
Easy Latkes, 300
Gulf Coast Seafood Stew, 353

364 2024 GENERAL RECIPE INDEX

Ham-and-Cabbage Gratin, 62
Hilda's Portuguese Stewed Chicken, 183
Low-and-Slow Beef Pot Roast, 27
Maude Crawford Barton's Potato Salad, 104
Potato Kugel with Schmaltzy Onions, 75
Rajas Poblanas with Potatoes, 281
Roasted Potatoes, 350
Shepherd's Pie Soup, 342
Shrimp-and-New Potato Chowder, 346
Soupe au Pistou, 44
Southern Niçoise Salad, 163
Vegetable-Beef Soup, 245
Waffle Iron Hash Browns with Fried Eggs, 71

Pumpkin
Chicken Stew with Pumpkin and Wild Rice, 352
Creamy Pumpkin Soup, 348
Harvest Sunrise Pie, 261
Maple-Glazed Pumpkin Bundt Cake, 270
Spicy Pumpkin Soup with Avocado Cream, 349

R

Radishes
Avocado Toasts with Watermelon Radishes and Herbs, 70
Cheesy Black Bean Tostadas, 31
Christmas Relish Tree, 295
Leafy Green Salad with Sunflower Seed Dressing, 72
Radishes with Miso-Sesame Butter, 89
Shaved Spring Vegetable Salad with Parmesan Crunch, 56
Spring Vegetable Sauté, 63
Watermelon Radish Salad with Brown Butter Vinaigrette, 70

Raspberries
Berry Basket Upside-Down Cake, 121
Brambleberry Smoothie, 171
Peach Melba Sundae, 169
Raspberry Molten Chocolate Cake, 35
Raspberry Sauce, 169

Rice
Avgolemono Soup, 91
Chicken Stew with Pumpkin and Wild Rice, 352
Creamed String Beans, 281
Creamy Chicken-and-Rice Soup, 245
Creamy Chicken-and-Rice Soup with Collard Greens, 342
Hilda's Portuguese Stewed Chicken, 183
One-Pan Broccoli-Rice Casserole, 90
One-Pot Chicken Thighs and Potlikker Rice, 22
Our Best Stuffed Peppers, 223
Reid Family Barbecue Shrimp, 180
Rice-and Poblano-Stuffed Butternut Squash, 284
Stovetop Red Beans and Rice, 351

S

Salads and salad dressings
Arabic Salad, 133
BLT Seven-Layer Salad, 163
Butternut Squash Salad with Collards and Radicchio, 283
Cantaloupe Salad with Chile-Lime Dressing, 128
Chicken Taco Pasta Salad, 163
Corn Salad with Sumac and Feta, 134
Double Beet Salad with Honey-Dijon Vinaigrette, 252
Fall Salad with Candied Black Walnuts, 198
Fancy Ranch, 300
Five-Minute Fried Chicken Salads, 203
Frenched Green Bean Salad, 143
Greek Pasta Salad, 208
"Green" Peach Salad, 160
Leafy Green Salad with Sunflower Seed Dressing, 72
Maude Crawford Barton's Potato Salad, 104
Mixed Pickle Salad, 144
Muffuletta Panzanella, 167
Nana's Marinated Pea Salad, 277
Peach-and-Tomato Salad with Buttermilk-Herb Dressing, 158
Peach-Mango Salad with Avocados, 158
Peppered Melon Salad, 143
Persimmon-and-Arugula Salad, 290
Shaved Spring Vegetable Salad with Parmesan Crunch, 56
Shrimp-and-Feta Pasta Salad, 167
Southern Niçoise Salad, 163
Speedy Grain Salad with Sugar Snap Peas, 43
Sugar Snap Salad with Lemon-Parmesan Breadcrumbs, 43
Watermelon, Mint, Feta and Fried-Peanut Salad, 122
Watermelon Radish Salad with Brown Butter Vinaigrette, 70
Winter Salad with Fennel and Oranges, 299

Sandwiches
Avocado Toasts with Watermelon Radishes and Herbs, 70
Bacon-Egg-and-Cheese Croissant Sandwiches, 253
Big-Batch BLTs, 210
Cat-Head Biscuit Sandwiches, 204
Chicken Parm Sandwiches, 203
Italian Sloppy Joes, 31
Miss River's Louisiana Crawfish Rolls, 95
Nashville Hot Fried Cauliflower Sandwiches, 258
Po'Boys with Debris, 30
Secret Sauce Smash Burgers, 118

Sauces
Avocado Dipping Sauce, 149
Chipotle-Barbecue Sauce, 208
Classic Gravy, 272
Cranberry Chutney, 278
Easy Freezer Tomato Sauce, 150
Elvie's Rémoulade, 236
Herby Dijonnaise, 64
Honey-Bacon Topping, 208
Hot Fudge, 169
Lemon-Pepper Crunch, 208
Lemon-Tahini Sauce, 134
Lime Cream, 352
Nick's Apple Jam, 240
Raspberry Sauce, 169
Speedy Creole Comeback Sauce, 119
Spiced Cranberry Compote, 261
Toum, 133

Sausages
Cauliflower Personal "Pizzas," 259
Chicken-Andouille Gumbo with Roasted Potatoes, 350
Chicken Sausage-and-White Bean Stew, 351
Christmas Eve Lasagna, 336
Conecuh Sausage Corn Dogs with Back Forty Beer Mustard, 241
Greek Diner Meatballs, 144
Gulf Coast Seafood Stew, 353
Hilda's Portuguese Stewed Chicken, 183
Italian Sloppy Joes, 31
Kale Rigatoni with Crispy Sausage, 15
Loaded Queso, 216
Louisiana Gumbo, 350
Peach + Sausage + Red Onion Pizza, 216
Queso To Go, 216
Sausage Minestrone, 341
Sourdough Bread Dressing, 264
Southern Wedding Soup, 341
Spicy Pumpkin Soup with Avocado Cream, 349
Stovetop Red Beans and Rice, 351
Sweet-and-Spicy Sausage Bites, 207
Vidalia Onion + Pepperoni Pizza, 216
Weeknight Pasta Bolognese, 28
White Bean, Sausage, and Turnip Green Stew, 351

Shellfish. *See also* Shrimp
Brothy Clams with Potlikker, 20
Crab Puffs, 297
Gulf Coast Seafood Stew, 353
Miss River's Louisiana Crawfish Rolls, 95
Seafood Gumbo, 354

Shrimp
Cajun Shrimp Stir-Fry, 92
Christmas Relish Tree, 295
Crispy Ranch Shrimp, 116
Gulf Coast Seafood Stew, 353
Louisiana Gumbo, 350
Poached Shrimp, 236
Reid Family Barbecue Shrimp, 180
Seafood Gumbo, 354
Shrimp-and-Feta Pasta Salad, 167
Shrimp-and-New Potato Chowder, 346

Smoothies
Brambleberry Smoothie, 171
Mango-Kiwi Green Smoothie, 171
Pineapple Blush Smoothie, 171

Soups. *See also* Chili; Stews; Stocks and broths
Avgolemono Soup, 91
Black Bean Soup, 346
Broccoli-Potato Soup, 347
Carrot-Apple Soup, 349
Chicken-and-Prosciutto Soup, 342
Chicken, Sweet Potato, and Corn Chowder, 345
Creamy Chicken-and-Rice Soup, 245
Creamy Chicken-and-Rice Soup with Collard Greens, 342
Creamy Chicken Noodle Soup, 343
Creamy Garlic Scape Soup, 87
Creamy Kale Soup, 15

2024 GENERAL RECIPE INDEX **365**

Creamy Pumpkin Soup, 348
Creamy Root Vegetable Soup with Brown
    Butter Pecans, 246
French Onion Soup, 346
Green Chile–Chicken Soup, 343
Hearty Tomato Soup, 347
Italian White Beans with Cauliflower, 346
King Ranch Chicken Soup, 342
Lemon Chicken Soup, 344
Lemony Chicken Soup with Sweet
    Potatoes, 343
Loaded Cauliflower Soup, 348
Mushroom Bisque, 347
Poblano Chile–Chicken Soup, 343
Quick Chicken Noodle Bowls, 344
Sausage Minestrone, 341
Shepherd's Pie Soup, 342
Shrimp-and–New Potato Chowder, 346
Smoked Chicken Tortilla Soup, 345
Smoky Black Bean Soup, 29
Smoky Lentil Soup, 346
Soulful Chicken Soup, 344
Soupe au Pistou, 44
Southern Italian Chicken Soup, 344
Southern Wedding Soup, 341
Spicy Pumpkin Soup with Avocado
    Cream, 349
Tomato-and–Red Pepper Soup, 347
Turkey Posole Verde, 345
Vegetable–Beef Soup, 245
Wild Mushroom Soup, 348

Spinach
Chicken-and–Prosciutto Soup, 342
Creamy Garlic Scape Soup, 87
Mango–Kiwi Green Smoothie, 171
Quick Chicken and Barley Stew, 351
Sun-Dried Tomato Pasta with Chicken, 31
Veggie–Packed Sourdough Dressing, 264

Squash. *See also* **Pumpkin; Zucchini**
Beef-and–Butternut Squash Chili, 350
Butternut Squash-and–Fennel Gratin, 283
Butternut Squash Salad with Collards and
    Radicchio, 283
Cast-Iron Roast Chicken, 223
Charred Zucchini-and–Halloumi Kebabs
    with Lemon-Tahini Sauce, 134
Fall Salad with Candied Black
    Walnuts, 198
One-Pot Chicken Pasta, 225
Rice-and–Poblano-Stuffed Butternut
    Squash, 284
Sheet Pan Squash Casserole, 148
Summer Garden Tart, 144
Summer Squash Skillet, 155
Three Sisters Succotash, 157
Veggie–Packed Sourdough Dressing, 264
Whipped Butternut Squash with Bacon
    Crumble, 284

Stews. *See also* **Chili**
Chicken and Herbed Cornmeal
    Dumplings, 353
Chicken–Andouille Gumbo with Roasted
    Potatoes, 350
Chicken Sausage-and–White Bean Stew, 351
Chicken Stew with Pumpkin and Wild
    Rice, 352

Gulf Coast Seafood Stew, 353
Louisiana Gumbo, 350
Mediterranean Kale and Cannellini Stew
    with Farro, 354
Old-Fashioned Chicken and Dumplings, 353
Peanut Chicken Stew, 352
Peppery Beef Stew with Root Vegetables, 349
Pesto Meatball Stew, 349
Quick Chicken and Barley Stew, 351
Seafood Gumbo, 354
Smoky Pork-and–Greens Stew, 245
Stovetop Red Beans and Rice, 351
White Bean, Sausage, and Turnip Green
    Stew, 351

Stocks and broths
Homemade Chicken Broth, 230
Mushroom Stock, 193
Sweet Potato Broth, 352

Strawberries
Pineapple Blush Smoothie, 171
Quick Strawberry–Ginger Jam, 59
Simple Strawberry Strudels, 32
Strawberry–Ginger Poke Cake with
    Toasted Vanilla Meringue, 106
Strawberry Ladyfinger Cake, 112
Strawberry–Orange Fools, 59
Strawberry–Rhubarb Spritzes, 56
Strawberry Shortbread, 49
Strawberry Shortcake Bread "Pudding," 112
Strawberry Shortcake Ice-Cream Cake, 109
Strawberry Trifle with Coconut–Lime
    Whipped Cream, 112

Sweet potatoes
Braised Sweet Potatoes with Piri Piri
    Pecans, 281
Chicken, Sweet Potato, and Corn
    Chowder, 345
Creamy Root Vegetable Soup with Brown
    Butter Pecans, 246
Lemony Chicken Soup with Sweet
    Potatoes, 343
Miso-Roasted Root Vegetable Medley, 246
Sweet Potato Broth, 352
Sweet Potato Bundt Cake, 227
Sweet Potato Queso, 33
Tex-Mex Chicken Chili with Lime, 352

Syrups
Cherry Syrup, 36
Sage–Honey Syrup, 36
Sumac Simple Syrup, 177

T

Tomatoes
Arabic Salad, 133
Big-Batch BLTs, 210
BLT Seven-Layer Salad, 163
Chicken Taco Pasta Salad, 163
Christmas Relish Tree, 295
Easy Freezer Tomato Sauce, 150
Five-Minute Fried Chicken Salads, 203
Frenched Green Bean Salad, 143
Game-Day Chili, 213
Greek Pasta Salad, 208
Hearty Tomato Soup, 347
Hilda's Portuguese Stewed Chicken, 183
Loaded Queso, 216

Mayo + Tomato + Basil Pizza, 216
Muffuletta Panzanella, 167
Peach-and–Tomato Salad with Buttermilk-
    Herb Dressing, 158
Portobello Bolognese, 193
Queso To Go, 216
Red Snapper in Creole Court Bouillon, 335
Shrimp-and–Feta Pasta Salad, 167
Skillet Pasta Primavera, 94
Smoky Black Bean Soup, 29
Smoky Tomato Butter, 300
Soupe au Pistou, 44
Southern Niçoise Salad, 163
Sun-Dried Tomato Pasta with Chicken, 31
Sweet-and–Sour Braised Beef Brisket, 75
Three Sisters Succotash, 157
Tomato-and–Red Pepper Soup, 347
Vegetable–Beef Soup, 245
Weeknight Pasta Bolognese, 28

Turkey
Classic Gravy, 272
French Onion Turkey, 276
"I Can't Believe It's Not Smoked" Turkey, 176
Mayo-Roasted Turkey, 272
Turkey Posole Verde, 345

Turnips
Cheesy Turnip Gratin, 252
Miso-Roasted Root Vegetable Medley, 246
Peppery Beef Stew with Root
    Vegetables, 349
White Bean, Sausage, and Turnip Green
    Stew, 351

W

Walnuts
Black Walnut Banana Bread, 194
Double Beet Salad with Honey–Dijon
    Vinaigrette, 252
Fall Salad with Candied Black Walnuts, 198
Garlicky Black Walnut–Breadcrumb
    Pasta, 199
Little Carrot Layer Cakes with Coconut
    Buttercream, 78
Muhammara, 134
No-Churn Black Walnut Ice Cream, 198
Streusel-Topped Apple–Walnut Pie, 198

White chocolate
Cranberry–Pistachio Biscotti, 327
Eggnog Snickerdoodles, 324
Orange-and–White Chocolate Crème
    Brûlée, 319
Whipped Cream Frosting, 310
White Chocolate Candy Leaves, 310

Z

Zucchini
Charred Zucchini-and–Halloumi Kebabs
    with Lemon-Tahini Sauce, 134
Christmas Relish Tree, 295
Easy Zucchini–Basil Pasta, 155
Soupe au Pistou, 44
Summer Garden Tart, 144
Summer Squash Skillet, 155

©2024 Southern Living Books, a division of Meredith Operations Corporation
225 Liberty Street, New York, NY 10281

Southern Living is a trademark of TI Inc. Lifestyle Group, a subsidiary of Meredith Operations Corporation, registered in the U.S. and other countries. All rights reserved. No part of this book may be reproduced in any form or by any means without the prior written permission of the publisher, excepting brief quotations in connection with reviews written specifically for inclusion in magazines or newspapers, or limited excerpts strictly for personal use.

DOTDASH MEREDITH CONSUMER MARKETING
Director, Direct Marketing-Books: Daniel Fagan
Marketing Operations Manager: Max Daily
Marketing Manager: Kylie Dazzo
Senior Marketing Coordinator: Elizabeth Moore
Content Manager: Julie Doll
Senior Production Manager: Liza Ward

WATERBURY PUBLICATIONS, INC.
Editorial Director: Lisa Kingsley
Creative Director: Ken Carlson
Associate Design Director: Doug Samuelson
Contributing Copy Editor: Russell Santana, E4 Editorial Services
Contributing Proofreader: Carrie Truesdell
Contributing Indexer: Mary Williams

Recipe Developers and Testers: Dotdash Meredith Food Studios

Library of Congress Control Number: 2024933922

ISBN: 978-1-4197-7936-7

First Edition 2024
Printed in the United States of America
10 9 8 7 6 5 4 3 2 1
Call 1-800-826-4707 for more information.

Distributed in 2024 by Abrams, an imprint of ABRAMS.
Abrams® is a registered trademark of Harry N. Abrams, Inc.

ABRAMS The Art of Books
195 Broadway, New York, NY 10007
abramsbooks.com

Pictured on front cover:
White Poinsettia Layer Cake with Cranberry-Orange Filling, page 309

More books from Southern Living®

Southern Living® Desserts

Enjoy more than 200 of our sweetest recipes of all time. Whether the occasion is quick and casual or formal and fancy, *Southern Living Desserts* has the perfect ending to any meal—cakes, cupcakes, pies, tarts, pastries, and everything in between. It's a must-have collection you'll turn to again and again.

Southern Living® Quick & Easy Cookbook

Discover more than 250 of our favorite recipes for fast, fresh, hearty, and delicious meals for even the busiest days of the week. With simple ingredients and quick prep and cook times, you'll never have to dread answering the question "What's for dinner?" again.

Southern Living® Slow Cooker Cookbook

This is our ultimate collection of recipes for a favorite kitchen appliance—more than 200 recipes for hearty main dishes, soups and stews, appetizers and side dishes—even desserts. From tried-and-true classics to fresh new favorites, you'll find everything you need to make memorable, easy-on-the-cook meals in this must-have volume.

TO ORDER, CALL 800-826-4707 OR VISIT **MAGAZINES.COM/SLBOOKS**